D0929785

HANDBOOK OF
CONSULTATION SERVICES
FOR CHILDREN

Joseph E. Zins
Thomas R. Kratochwill
Stephen N. Elliott

EDITORS

Foreword by John R. Bergan

HANDBOOK OF CONSULTATION SERVICES FOR CHILDREN

Applications in Educational and Clinical Settings

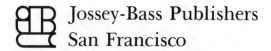

Jossey-Bass Publishers
San Francisco

Substantial discounts on bulk quantities of Jossey-Bass books are available to corporations, professional associations, and other organizations. For details and discount information, contact the special sales department at Jossey-Bass Inc., Publishers. (415) 433-1740; Fax (415) 433-0499.

For sales outside the United States, contact Maxwell Macmillan International Publishing Group, 866 Third Avenue, New York, New York 10022.

Manufactured in the United States of America

 The paper used in this book is acid-free and meets the State of California requirements for recycled paper (50 percent recycled waste, including 10 percent postconsumer waste), which are the strictest guidelines for recycled paper currently in use in the United States.

The ink in this book is either soy- or vegetable-based and during the printing process emits fewer than half the volatile organic compounds (VOCs) emitted by petroleum-based ink.

Library of Congress Cataloging-in-Publication Data

Handbook of consultation services for children : applications in educational and clinical settings / Joseph E. Zins, Thomas R. Kratochwill, Stephen N. Elliott, editors ; foreword by John R. Bergan — 1st ed.
    p.   cm. — (The Jossey-Bass social and behavioral science series)
  Includes bibliographical references and index.
  ISBN 1-55542-548-8 (alk. paper)
  1. Consultation in psychology. 2. Children—Counseling of. I. Zins, Joseph E. II. Kratochwill, Thomas R. III. Elliott, Stephen N. IV. Series.
BF637.C56H26 1993
158'.3'083—dc20   93-15407
                                     CIP

FIRST EDITION
HB Printing   10 9 8 7 6 5 4 3 2 1   *Code 9351*

THE JOSSEY-BASS
SOCIAL AND BEHAVIORAL SCIENCE SERIES

Contents _____

ix

Part Five: Training Issues

chapter 11, 12

Foreword _____

The *Handbook of Consultation Services for Children* is filled with information documenting that consultation is a unique and powerful form of service that can promote the development of children and their families. Consultation has come of age. There is a large and impressive body of scientific evidence documenting the effectiveness of consultation. The number of journals that publish the results of consultation research has grown, and professions increasingly incorporate consultation as a tool for service delivery.

The growth in consultation research and practice is part of the movement away from a society that has exploited its human resources and toward a society committed to the development of human potential in all children and families. Support for psychological and educational services that focus on labeling children and contribute to the warehousing of children in special programs has waned. We are no longer content to select those classified as most able for favored treatment and to consign those categorized as less able to programs lacking the kinds of opportunities necessary to stimulate maximum growth. We are beginning to recognize that we cannot afford to waste a single child—services provided for children with learning and adjustment problems must be held accountable for solving problems, not simply describing them.

Consultation is well suited to the task of promoting the development of children and families in a society committed to the development of human potential. As this handbook illustrates, consultation is a tool that commits psychologists, educators, and children and their families to problem solving. It encourages human service professionals, children, and families to set goals, formulate and implement plans to realize their goals, and evaluate the success of their endeavors. Ultimately, consultation should empower children and families in ways that will enable them to chart their own course toward a better life.

The *Handbook of Consultation Services for Children* contains a rich and extensive body of information, collected and organized in a single publication, that presents the most recent developments in the field and details the pressing issues calling for research to guide policy and practice in the years ahead. Those concerned with improving the quality of psychological and educational services and with increasing the impact of services on the development of children and families will regard this book as essential reading.

June 1993   John R. Bergan
                                               Professor of
                                                   Educational Psychology
                                               University of Arizona

Preface _____

There has been a proliferation of literature describing human service consultation theory, research, and practice in the past two decades. Indeed, there are some 100 books and several journals devoted exclusively to this topic. However, prior to the publication of this book no single comprehensive resource on consultation existed that met the growing informational needs of applied researchers, practitioners, students, and trainers.

Until recently, the field of consultation did not have sufficiently developed theoretical and empirical bases to justify publication of a comprehensive handbook, even though practice in this area has been expanding rapidly. Today, however, the field has attained a more sophisticated level of development, both conceptually and empirically, and consultation has become an integral component of the professional functioning of many helping disciplines. School and community psychologists, special educators, counselors, speech and language therapists, educators of gifted and talented students, and school media specialists are among those working with children who advocate and use this method of service delivery. It is clear that consultation is not another passing fad. Consequently, there is a clear need to integrate the voluminous literature on this topic and to provide the best possible summaries and interpretations of the major theoretical and research components of the field. We hope that the publication of the *Handbook of Consultation Services for Children* will stimulate the further inquiry needed to promote advances in research, training, and practice.

Purpose and Audience

Our goal is to provide a comprehensive but concise interdisciplinary resource book that offers authoritative information, state-of-the-art descriptions of practice, and critical interpretation of the research. Our intended audiences include applied researchers, practitioners, trainers, and advanced students in school psychology, special education, counselor education, speech and language therapy, educational administration, child clinical and pediatric psychology, applied developmental psychology, education for the gifted and talented, child psychiatry, community and counseling psychology, social work, nursing, and health education—helping professionals in the human service field who share an interest in providing effective indirect services to children and the organizations serving them.

Overview of the Contents

The book contains twenty chapters written by thirty national leaders in consultation. Collectively, the authors represent a number of disciplines. Each is an experienced researcher and practitioner who clearly and authoritatively provides direction for practice as well as research. The foundation of each chapter is a critical analysis of existing research and current theory.

In this book, *human service consultation* refers to interpersonal interactions in which participants engage in a joint, systematic problem-solving process to benefit clients. Consultants and consultees both contribute their expertise and experience to the process, but consultants do not directly implement interventions, and consultees retain professional responsibility for clients. There is an emphasis on intervening early so that problems do not become more serious or so that potentially negative outcomes are minimized. As participants proceed to solve problems, they recognize that there is an interdependence among various environmental factors and that contextual variables influence the development and resolution of problems. Further, they work toward preparing consultees to more skillfully address similar problems in the future. Readers will note, however, that there continue to be significant differences in how the term *consultation* is used throughout the book, as well as in the field. Although many similarities are emerging, consensus on one definition of consultation remains elusive.

Following the Foreword by John R. Bergan and this Preface, the book begins with an introduction by the editors (Chapter One) that presents a brief historical overview of consultation and a description of the current status of the field. Much of the material presented therein serves as the basis for the following chapters. The remainder of the book is divided into five major parts.

Part One, "Conceptual Foundations and Orientations," begins with Chapter Two, by Mary Henning-Stout, in which she summarizes the goals and general characteristics of consultation and reviews three major approaches: the mental health, the behavioral, and the organizational. Next, in Chapter Three, Duane Brown develops a broad definition of human service consultation and points out some of the issues related to achieving consensus on a definition. A detailed description of the behavioral approach to consultation, including a review of its major steps, is presented by Brian K. Martens in Chapter Four. In Chapter Five, Robert J. Illback and Joseph E. Zins discuss the importance of taking an organizational perspective in consultation, particularly with respect to identifying problems and developing interventions. In recognition of the fact that consultants in child-related settings usually spend extensive time working with parents, Susan M. Sheridan (Chapter Six) reviews three common methods of assisting this group: parent education, parent training, and parent consultation, with a focus on the last.

In Part Two, "The Process of Consultation," DeWayne J. Kurpius and Thaddeus G. Rozecki (Chapter Seven) discuss interpersonal communication, an essential component of effective consultation. Despite efforts to establish good interpersonal relationships, it is inevitable that conflicts and resistances will arise. In Chapter Eight, Katherine F. Wickstrom and Joseph C. Witt discuss many sources of resistance and suggest ways to overcome this barrier to effective consultation. Stephen N. Elliott and R. T. Busse (Chapter Nine) review the wide range of treatment strategies that are available to consultants and provide guidance for selecting specific interventions. The part concludes with Chapter Ten, in which Joseph E. Zins and Robert J. Illback discuss procedures for the effective and efficient implementation of consultation within child service systems.

Part Three, "Evaluation of Process and Outcome," contains two chapters that address an area in need of far more attention. In Chapter Eleven, Terry B. Gutkin reviews new and innovative as well as proven, well-established methods of conducting consultation research. In Chapter Twelve, Frank M. Gresham and George H. Noell suggest ways for practitioners to conceptualize effective consultation and document its outcomes.

Part Four, "Effective Practice," includes five chapters illustrating applications of consultation in a variety of settings. In Chapter Thirteen, Charlene R. Ponti and Janette Cahill Flower describe their experiences consulting in elementary and secondary schools; in Chapter Fourteen, Keith J. Slifer, Marilyn Cataldo, Roberta L. Babbitt, and Michael F. Cataldo review issues involved in the provision of consultation services in pediatric hospital settings. Olga Reyes and Leonard A. Jason (Chapter Fifteen) discuss school consultation from the perspective of an external consultant in community psychology. Chapter Sixteen, by Charles A. Maher, addresses an emerging and promising area of practice: working within the business sector to assist employees' children. The part concludes with Chapter Seventeen, in which Walter B. Pryzwansky offers a thoughtful presentation of ethical consultation practice and relevant professional practice guidelines.

In Part Five, "Training Issues," Lorna Idol (Chapter Eighteen) discusses preservice education and staff development, emphasizing the types of learning opportunities needed and identifying relevant skills and knowledge. In Chapter Nineteen, Sylvia Rosenfield and Todd A. Gravois also delineate skills and competencies necessary for educating skillful consultants, recognizing that the empirical base for developing training models is limited. Many professionals currently engaged in consultation did not receive training in this area during their professional preparation programs; in Chapter Twenty, Daniel J. Reschly offers suggestions for providing in-service training to meet these professionals' needs through a review of published programs.

Acknowledgments

We must express our appreciation to all of the contributors, who so willingly and graciously shared their knowledge and experience. We hope that readers will learn as much from them as we have; they have truly stimulated, challenged, and enhanced our thinking about consultation. It has also been a pleasure to work with the talented staff at Jossey-Bass Publishers, particularly Lesley Iura, Christie Hakim, and Frank Welsch. In addition, we recognize Lawrence J. Johnson, head of early childhood and special education at the University of Cincinnati, who provided a supportive environment and expanded our thinking about consultation, and Howard Margolis of Queens College of the City University of New York, who has little idea of what an inspiration he is. We also thank Karen Kramer for her editorial assistance through all phases of the project.

June 1993   Joseph E. Zins
                                                           Cincinnati, Ohio

                                                           Thomas R. Kratochwill
                                                           Stephen N. Elliott
                                                           Madison, Wisconsin

The Editors ————————————————

Joseph E. Zins is professor in the Department of Early Childhood and Special Education at the University of Cincinnati and has honorary joint appointments with the Department of Psychology and in genetic counseling in the College of Medicine. He received his Ed.D. degree (1977) in school psychology from the University of Cincinnati and completed a postdoctoral fellowship in pediatric psychology at the Johns Hopkins University School of Medicine. Zins also serves as consulting psychologist to the Beechwood, Kentucky, Independent Schools and to the Urban Appalachian Council in Cincinnati, and has consulted with educational organizations in many sections of the country.

Zins has published over ninety works, including eight books on consultation, prevention, and the delivery of psychological services in educational settings. He is consulting editor for the book series *Psychoeducational Interventions: Guidebooks for School Practitioners* (Jossey-Bass Publishers). He has served on the editorial boards of the *Journal of Educational and Psychological Consultation, Journal of School Psychology, School Psychology Quarterly, School Psychology Review,* and *Special Services in the Schools,* and as a reviewer for many other journals. He is a Fellow of the American Psychological Association, a member of the Consortium for the School-Based Promotion of Social Competence, and former secretary of the National Association of School Psychologists.

Thomas R. Kratochwill is professor of educational psychology and affiliate professor in the Department of Psychiatry as well as faculty director of research projects in the Wisconsin Center for Education Research, both at the University of Wisconsin, Madison. He received his Ph.D. degree (1973) in school psychology from the University of Wisconsin.

He is author and editor of several books including *Single-Subject Re-*

search: Strategies for Evaluating Change (1978), *Selective Mutism: Implications for Research and Treatment* (1981), *Treating Children's Fears and Phobias: A Behavioral Approach* (1983, with R. J. Morris), *The Practice of Child Therapy* (1984, 1992, with R. J. Morris), and *Single-Case Research Design and Analysis* (1992, with J. R. Levin). Kratochwill has published numerous journal articles and book chapters on behavior therapy, assessment, and research methodology. In 1977 he received the Lightner Witmer Award from Division 16 of the American Psychological Association. He has served as associate editor for *Behavior Therapy,* the *Journal of Applied Behavior Analysis,* and *School Psychology Review.* In addition to being on numerous editorial boards, he has edited the American Psychological Association Division 16 journal *Professional School Psychology,* now *School Psychology Quarterly.* He has been a practitioner in several applied settings and a consultant to numerous schools and other applied clinical treatment settings.

Stephen N. Elliott is professor of educational psychology and director of the School Psychology Program at the University of Wisconsin, Madison. He has been on the faculty of the Buros Institute of Mental Measurements, University of Nebraska, and Louisiana State University. He earned his Ph.D. degree (1980) in educational psychology at Arizona State University.

Elliott is author of numerous books, including *School Psychology: Essentials of Theory and Practice* (1984), *The Delivery of Psychological Services in Schools* (1986), and *Assessment of Special Children* (1988). He is currently senior editor of the *Guilford School Practitioners Series* and coeditor of *Advances in School Psychology.* He was editor of *School Psychology Review* (1985–1990) and coauthor of *The Social Skills Rating System* (1990, with F. Gresham) and *Strategies for Social Skills Training* (1991, with F. Gresham). He received the Lightner Witmer Award from the American Psychological Association (APA) in 1984 and was awarded Fellow status in APA in 1985. His areas of research and practice include the implementation of acceptable classroom-based interventions, the assessment and treatment of children's social behavior problems, and the development of prereferral interventions in the regular classroom.

The Contributors _____

Roberta L. Babbitt is assistant professor of psychiatry and behavioral sciences at the Johns Hopkins University School of Medicine. She is director of the Pediatric Feeding Disorders Program and Outpatient Behavioral Pediatrics Clinic in the Department of Behavioral Psychology at the Kennedy Krieger Institute. She received her B.A. degree (1981) in psychology and music from the University of Rochester and Eastman School of Music; her M.A. degree (1983) in music therapy, her M.Ed. degree (1984) in special education, and her M.Phil. degree (1985) in applied behavior analysis from Teachers College, Columbia University; and her Ph.D. degree (1986) in applied behavior analysis and research from Columbia University.

Duane Brown is professor of education at the University of North Carolina, Chapel Hill, where he is also coordinator of the School Counseling Program. He is the author or coauthor of eighteen books, five of which deal with consultation. He has also authored or coauthored seventy-four book chapters and articles. He has consulted extensively in public schools, institutions of higher education, community agencies, and businesses. He received his B.S. degree (1959) in education, his M.S. degree (1962) in education, and his Ph.D. degree (1965) in counseling from Purdue University.

R. T. Busse is a doctoral candidate in the School Psychology Program at the University of Wisconsin, Madison. He has worked for three years on a U.S. Office of Education grant to train behavioral consultants. His research has focused on the efficacy of consultation training and the outcomes of consultation. He earned his B.S. degree in psychology and his M.S. degree in educational psychology at the University of Wisconsin.

Marilyn Cataldo is the coordinator for consultation services in the Department of Behavioral Psychology at the Kennedy Krieger Institute and serves as a consultant to a variety of specialty services at the Johns Hopkins University School of Medicine. She received her B.A. degree (1974) from Jersey City State College in speech correction and special education and her M.A. degree (1980) from Johnson State College in special education. She completed postgraduate study at the University of Kansas in developmental and child psychology.

Michael F. Cataldo is professor of behavioral biology at the Johns Hopkins University School of Medicine. He holds a joint appointment in the Department of Pediatrics. He is the director of the Department of Behavioral Psychology at the Kennedy Krieger Institute. He received his B.A. degree (1968) from the University of Rochester in psychology and his M.A. and Ph.D. degrees (1971, 1974) from the University of Kansas in child development and psychology.

Janette Cahill Flower is a school psychologist with the Kenton County Schools (Kentucky). She currently is involved with preschool programs and maintains an active interest in brief strategic interventions. She received her B.A. degree (1976) from Thomas More College in psychology and German, her M.A. degree (1978) from the University of Nebraska, Lincoln, in school psychology, and her Ph.D. degree (1986) from the University of Cincinnati in school psychology.

Todd A. Gravois is a school psychologist with Howard County Public Schools in Maryland and has also worked as a school psychologist in Louisiana and Pennsylvania. He has facilitated and researched the implementation of school-based instructional consultation teams as an alternative service delivery system for children and teachers. He received his B.A. degree (1985) in psychology and specialist degree (1988) in school psychology from Nicholls State University and is a doctoral candidate in school psychology at the University of Maryland, College Park.

Frank M. Gresham is professor and director of the School Psychology Training Program at the University of California, Riverside. He has published extensively in the areas of behavioral consultation, social skills assessment and training, and classification of children's behavior disorders. Gresham is a Fellow of the American Psychological Association and the American Psychological Society. He serves on numerous editorial boards of journals in school psychology and special education such as *Journal of Emotional and Behavioral Disorders, Journal of Learning Disabilities, Journal of School Psychology, Learning Disability Quarterly, School Psychology Quarterly,* and *School Psychology Re-*

view. He received the Lightner Witmer Award from Division 16 of the American Psychological Association for his research contributions. Gresham earned his B.A. degree (1973) in psychology, his M.Ed. degree (1975) in rehabilitation counseling, and his Ph.D. degree (1979) in psychology.

Terry B. Gutkin is a professor of educational psychology at the University of Nebraska, Lincoln. Gutkin's primary research interests have been in school-based consultation. He is a Fellow of the American Psychological Association, coeditor of *The Handbook of School Psychology* (1982, 1990, with C. R. Reynolds), coauthor of *School Psychology: Essentials of Theory and Practice* (1984, with C. R. Reynolds, S. N. Elliott, and J. C. Witt), and serves on the editorial boards of numerous scholarly journals. He received his B.S. degree (1968) from Brooklyn College in psychology and his Ph.D. degree (1975) in educational psychology from the University of Texas, Austin.

Mary Henning-Stout is associate professor in the Counseling Psychology Program at Lewis and Clark College, where she also coordinates the training program in school psychology. She has published in the areas of consultation, academic intervention, and gender issues in education. She earned her B.A. degree (1978) in psychology and English and her M.A. degree (1980) in education, both from Austin College. Her Ph.D. degree (1986) in psychological and cultural foundations, with an emphasis on school psychology, was earned at the University of Nebraska, Lincoln.

Lorna Idol is codirector of the Institute for Learning and Development in Austin, Texas. She is also editor in chief of the journal *Remedial and Special Education* and executive director and founder of the Association for Educational and Psychological Consultants. Idol's research and writing activities have been in school consultation, collaboration in the schools, and reading/learning disabilities with particular emphasis on mainstreamed instruction for students in special education or at risk for school failure. She serves as consultant to school agencies, state departments of education, and university teacher preparation programs throughout the United States, as well as in Canada and Australia. Her work has appeared in several education journals, and she is the author of several books. She received her B.S. dual degree (1969) in elementary education and special education and her M.Ed. degree (1974) in special education/learning disabilities from the University of Nevada, Reno. She was awarded the Ph.D. degree (1979) at the University of New Mexico in special education/learning disabilities.

Robert J. Illback is executive director of R.E.A.C.H. of Louisville, Inc., a community agency serving children and adolescents with severe behavioral and emotional problems in Louisville, Kentucky. He is also professor of psychology in the clinical psychology training program at Spalding University, where he teaches courses in measurement, behavior therapy, program evaluation, and organizational change. His private practice work is in the area of child and family behavior therapy. He is licensed as a psychologist in Kentucky and Indiana, nationally certified as a school psychologist, and listed in the National Register of Health Service Providers in Psychology. He is a Fellow of both the American Psychological Association and the American Psychological Society. His areas of professional and research interest include program planning and evaluation, planned organizational change in child service organizations, community-based programming for children with mental retardation and behavioral disabilities (and their families), child and family behavior therapy, and professional practice issues. Illback holds a Psy.D. degree (1980) from Rutgers University in professional psychology.

Leonard A. Jason is professor of clinical-community psychology at De-Paul University. He has published extensively on issues related to prevention and community psychology. His research interests include preventive school-based interventions, psychoneuroimmunology, and community building for disenfranchised populations. He received his B.A. degree (1971) from Brandeis University in psychology and his Ph.D. degree (1975) from the University of Rochester in clinical-community psychology.

DeWayne J. Kurpius is professor of counseling psychology at Indiana University. He has been active as a consultant and a trainer of consultants for many years. He is currently the chair of the Training and Education Committee for Division 13 of the American Psychological Association (APA). He received the 1991 Perry L. Rohrer Award for Excellence in recognition of his outstanding career achievement in the field of consulting psychology. He is also a Fellow in APA's Divisions 13 and 17. His empirical research is in cognitive psychology with particular interest in how thinking and cognitive self-talk influence performance behavior. He received his Ed.D. degree from the University of North Dakota.

Charles A. Maher is professor of psychology at Rutgers University, where he previously served as chair of the Department of Applied Psychology. He has published over sixteen books and 300 articles in professional journals, is editor of the international journal *Special Services in the Schools,* and is an editorial board member of numerous journals and book series. In addition, he serves as a consultant to private businesses, governmental agencies, and educational systems worldwide in areas of program planning and evaluation, organizational development and change, management development, and self-management. Relatedly, he serves as a sport psychology consultant to professional baseball organizations and players. He is a licensed psychologist with expertise in aspects of school psychology, organizational psychology, performance enhancement, sport psychology, and consulting psychology. Maher holds master's degrees in counseling and in business administration and a Psy.D. degree in professional psychology with specializations in school psychology and organizational psychology.

Brian K. Martens is associate professor of psychology at Syracuse University and associate editor of *School Psychology Quarterly*. He received his B.S. degree (1981) in psychology and his M.S. degree (1983) in school psychology from Colorado State University and his Ph.D. degree (1985) in school psychology from the University of Nebraska, Lincoln. His research interests include applied behavior analysis and behavioral consultation. In 1990, Martens received the Lightner Witmer Award for outstanding contributions to research from Division 16 of the American Psychological Association.

George H. Noell is a doctoral student in the School Psychology Training Program at the University of California, Riverside. His research interests include cost-benefit functional outcomes analysis in consultation, behavioral consultation, and prereferral interventions. He has published several book chapters and journal articles on these topics. He is a student member of the American Psychological Association, Association for Advancement of Behavior Therapy, Association for Behavior Analysis, and National Association of School Psychologists. He received both his B.A. degree (1987) and his M.A. degree (1991) in psychology.

Charlene R. Ponti is a school psychologist with the Hamilton County Office of Education (Ohio) and has been an adjunct assistant professor at the University of Cincinnati and a visiting assistant professor at Miami University. Ponti is coauthor of *Helping Students Succeed in the Regular Classroom: A Guide for Developing Intervention Assistance Programs* (1988, with J. E. Zins, M. J. Curtis, and J. L. Graden) and has published a number of articles and chapters on consultation and the delivery of psychological services in schools. She has served on the editorial board of the *School Psychology Review* and as a contributing editor for *Special Services Digest*. She received her B.A. degree (1973) from Upsala College in psychology and her M.Ed. (1981) and Ph.D. (1985) degrees from the University of Cincinnati in school psychology. She also completed a postdoctoral fellowship in pediatric psychology at the Johns Hopkins University School of Medicine.

Walter B. Pryzwansky is professor of education in the School of Education at the University of North Carolina, Chapel Hill, where he also serves as associate dean for academic programs. His research activities have been concentrated in two areas: consultation, in which recently he has investigated the problem-solving approach of novices and experts, and professional issues. Pryzwansky's books include *Psychological Consultation* (1991, with D. Brown and A. C. Schulte) and *Professional Psychology* (1987, with R. Wendt). He received his B.S. degree (1961) from Pennsylvania State University in psychology and his M.A. (1962) and Ed.D. (1969) degrees from Teachers College, Columbia University, in school psychology.

Daniel J. Reschly is distinguished professor of psychology and director of the School Psychology Program at Iowa State University. He has served as a school psychologist in Iowa, Oregon, and Arizona, and was an assistant professor for four years at the University of Arizona. Reschly has published widely on the topics of school psychology professional practices, adaptive behavior, behavioral consultation, mild mental retardation, and legal issues. He has been active in state and national leadership roles, including president of the National Association of School Psychologists (NASP), editor of the *School Psychology Review,* and chair of NASP Graduate Program Approval. He has received three NASP Distinguished Service Awards, the Stroud Award, and appointment as a Fellow of the American Psychological Association. He received his B.S. degree (1966) from Iowa State University in history and psychology, his M.A. degree (1968) from the University of Iowa in school psychology, and his Ph.D. degree (1971) from the University of Oregon in school psychology.

Olga Reyes is assistant professor of psychology at the University of Illinois, Chicago. Her research interests are in adolescent risk factors, particularly as they relate to academic success and high school completion. Currently, her focus in this context is on transitions between school levels and how they relate to children's vulnerability to school failure. She obtained her B.A. degree (1983) with distinction from the University of Illinois, Chicago, in psychology. She received her M.A. (1986) and Ph.D. (1989) degrees from DePaul University in clinical-community psychology.

Sylvia Rosenfield is professor of school psychology and chair of the Department of Counseling and Personnel Services at the University of Maryland, College Park. She teaches consultation, has worked with schools to develop consultation-based services, and is author of the text *Instructional Consultation* (1987). She received her B.A. degree (1960) from Cornell University in speech and theater, her M.A. degree (1961) from the University of Illinois, Urbana, in speech and hearing, and her Ph.D. degree (1967) from the University of Wisconsin, Madison in educational psychology.

Thaddeus G. Rozecki is a doctoral candidate in counseling psychology at Indiana University. He was recipient of the Paul Munger Award for the outstanding doctoral student in counseling psychology at Indiana University in 1990. Formerly he was the clinical director of the Nova House Association in Dayton, Ohio, which is one of the largest not-for-profit agencies in Ohio serving those with chemical dependency concerns. His research interests are in the areas of training and supervision. He is currently investigating the cognitive processes of clinical supervisors as they review counseling tapes. He received his B.A. degree (1976) from Kent State University in English and his M.S. degree (1985) from Wright State University in counseling.

Susan M. Sheridan is assistant professor in the school psychology program at the University of Utah. Her primary research interests are in the areas of parent-teacher consultation, home-school partnerships, behavioral consultation training, and social skills interventions. She has written several journal articles and book chapters on these and related topics. She received both her B.S. degree (1982) and her M.S. degree (1984) from Western Illinois University and her Ph.D. degree (1989) from the University of Wisconsin, Madison.

Keith J. Slifer is assistant professor of psychiatry and pediatrics at the Johns Hopkins University School of Medicine. He is director of hospital consultation services for the Department of Behavioral Psychology at the Kennedy Krieger Institute. He received his B.A. degree (1979) from Western Maryland College in psychology, his M.A. degree (1981) from the University of Maryland in clinical psychology, and his Ph.D. degree (1987) from Florida State University in psychology.

Katherine F. Wickstrom is a doctoral candidate in the School Psychology Program in the Department of Psychology at Louisiana State University. Her primary research interest includes resistance and the influence process in school-based consultation. She received her B.S. degree (1988) in psychology and sociology and her M.A. degree (1990) in psychology, both from Louisiana State University.

Joseph C. Witt is professor of psychology and director of the School Psychology Program at Louisiana State University. His current research interests include resistance and treatment integrity in school-based consultation. He received his B.S. (1973) and M.S. (1978) degrees from Fort Hays State University in psychology and his Ph.D. degree (1978) from Arizona State University in school psychology.

HANDBOOK OF
CONSULTATION SERVICES
FOR CHILDREN

1

Current Status of the Field

Joseph E. Zins, Thomas R. Kratochwill, Stephen N. Elliott

Consultation is a fundamental form of interaction between a professional and an individual who wants to help a third party or a system to change. As such, it has been a basic yet underutilized component in the delivery of psychoeducational services for children for years. As we approach the beginning of the twenty-first century, it is clear that children and their families will continue to face a substantial number of significant psychosocial stressors. For example, many mothers still do not receive adequate prenatal care, violence affects increasing numbers in our society, and a large percentage of children grow up in poverty. In addition, demand for high-quality, affordable day care still outstrips its availability, high rates of mobility and divorce prevent bonding with the extended family, and children are regularly exposed to potentially health-damaging influences from the media (London, 1987). Substance abuse, AIDS, unwanted teen pregnancy, school dropouts, interpersonal violence, and suicide most likely will remain problems. And discrepancies between rich and poor school districts may intensify achievement differences, particularly between majority and minority students. Consequently, as the social fabric of our society changes, helping professionals will be expected to remedy and prevent the social, emotional, educational, and health problems that large numbers of children experience (Office of Technology Assessment, 1986).

Note: The helpful comments of William P. Erchul and Lorna Idol on an earlier draft of this chapter are greatly appreciated. Completion of the chapter was supported in part through research grants to Joseph E. Zins from the U.S. Department of Education (#HO23A20042) and from the University Research Council of the University of Cincinnati. The opinions expressed are solely those of the authors and may not represent the views of the U.S. Department of Education or the University of Cincinnati.

The need for consultation-based service delivery systems will continue for the foreseeable future, for these services provide an effective and efficient means of addressing psychoeducational and social problems. Although there will always be a need for direct treatment methods, such as counseling and psychotherapy, a wide variety of professional specialties are expected to adopt a consultative approach to help meet children's needs. In this chapter, we briefly review reasons for the development of consultation, examine definitions and models, and present an overview of the current status of the field.

Emergence of Consultation as a Method of Service Delivery

Development of the consultation field has been influenced by a number of disciplines, such as psychiatry, psychology, social work, and education, and its practice has emerged from many different settings, including schools, hospitals, and clinics. Its roots date to the late nineteenth century with the work of Lightner Witmer at the psychological clinic at the University of Pennsylvania, which offered assistance to teachers working with children who were experiencing problems. Though this service was not called consultation at that time, it was in many ways similar to the modern practice (Baker, 1988; Mannino & Shore, 1986). Despite this early beginning, however, the field did not attract widespread interest until after World War II. During the 1950s and 1960s, people such as Gerald Caplan, Seymour B. Sarason, and Irving N. Berlin developed and published useful frameworks for practice that resulted in increased training and practice in this area. (For a comprehensive discussion of the historical development of consultation, see Caplan, 1970; Gallessich, 1982; Gutkin & Curtis, 1982; Mannino & Shorer, 1986.)

Interest in consultation resulted primarily from general dissatisfaction with traditional approaches to providing mental health services. The medical and clinical models, which dominated the field until the 1960s, emphasized psychodynamic conceptions of behavior and treatment. Children's socioemotional problems were attributed to internal causes and were generally thought to be symptoms of underlying psychic conflicts. Treatment consisted of direct intervention with the child, usually long-term. Many professionals, however, believed that there were a number of practical and conceptual problems associated with these approaches.

Those involved in working with children found that traditional psychotherapeutic methods were not easily adaptable to the culture of schools or other institutions serving children. Moreover, they observed that parents and other caregivers were usually not involved in intervention implementation, despite the critical roles that they play in children's lives.

Many theorists and practitioners have also noted that children's educational and behavioral problems are often associated with environmental factors over which the child has little control (for example, living in a single-parent, economically impoverished home in an inner-city ghetto). Alternative conceptual models, based on learning theory and with strong ecological orientations (Bandura, 1969; Lewin, 1951; Skinner, 1953; Tharp & Wetzel, 1969; Ullman & Krasner, 1965), emerged and shifted the focus from intrapsychic conflicts to environmental factors. As Gutkin and Conoley (1990, pp. 208–209) pointed out, "adults rather than children control the environments within which children function [and] it makes little sense to 'cure' children of intrapersonal and intrapsychic problems only to return them to the environment that created [or at least facilitated the creation of] their problems in the first place." Further, behavioral intervention methods were more readily applicable to the treatment of large numbers of children in natural settings.

Overall, the behavioral model offers four major contributions to consultation: (1) a theory to help explain the behavior of individuals, groups, and organizations; (2) techniques to change behaviors of consultees and/or their clients; (3) a model of intervention with a built-in paradigm for evaluating change; and (4) adaptability to a wide range of settings (Gallessich, 1982). In addition, the fusion of an ecological viewpoint with the behavioral may expand our understanding of the complex system interdependencies within the consultation process (Gutkin, in press).

In the late 1960s, there was also increasing recognition of the inadequacies of the traditional service system and of the emerging shortages of mental health personnel (Albee, 1968). It was predicted that the use of individual psychotherapy to treat those with behavioral and emotional problems would result in vast numbers of unserved children and families. This concern may be even more valid today. Recently, for instance, Tuma (1989) estimated that approximately 15 to 19 percent of children in the United States are affected by problems that warrant mental health intervention. Moreover, it has been estimated that approximately one-fourth of all ten- to seventeen-year-olds in the United States are in danger of developing high-risk behaviors such as substance abuse, academic failure, early unprotected intercourse, and delinquency (Office of Technology Assessment, 1986). Tuma also noted that children are among the most neglected groups in terms of mental health needs.

Miller (1969) suggested that methods were needed to "give psychology away" to nonpsychologists because there most likely will never be enough professionals to meet these needs. His idea is highly consistent with consultation. An impressive empirical base in support of behavioral approaches also rapidly developed, in contrast to the paucity of such information about medical and clinical models. Finally, consultation expands the focus of intervention efforts by promoting changes in the behavior of consultees, the people who primarily control the environments in which children live, rather than focusing exclusively on children's behaviors. For all these reasons, consultation gained widespread support, and "the behavioral and ecological models of human behavior became the theoretical foundation on which school-based consultation was to be built" (Gutkin & Curtis, 1982, p. 798).

Significant support for consultation was also provided through passage of the Community Mental Health Act of 1963, which listed "consultation and education" as among the five essential services that community mental health centers must provide to be eligible for federal funding. Thus, members of a wide range of professional disciplines began engaging in consultation at centers throughout the country. In addition, training and practice were facilitated through a number of publications, particularly Tharp and Wetzel's classic work *Behavior Modification in the Natural Environment* (1969), in which the triadic model is described, and Caplan's seminal book *The Theory and Practice of Mental Health Consultation* (1970), which contains an in-depth discussion of the process.

Interest in consultation among school practitioners, who, in addition to providing educational assistance, are among the primary providers of mental health services to children, was motivated largely by the same factors, as well as by several additional ones. Many educators have become overwhelmed by the number of students in need of assistance and dismayed by the categorical service delivery model that continues to dominate our nation's schools. Since the passage in 1975 of Public Law 94-142 (now the Individuals with Disabilities Education Act), most schools have adopted a "refer, test, place" model of providing assistance to students. That is, students who experience difficulty in regular education classrooms are referred for psychoeducational assessments that involve many hours of work by a multidisciplinary team, and most of these students are ultimately placed in special education programs. Under this system, referral almost invariably leads to categorical classification and placement (Galagan, 1985; Ysseldyke et al., 1983). Yet we know that there is no reliable method of differentiating students by categorical label, nor are there educational prescriptions that result directly from these labels (Reynolds & Larkin, 1987).

The "refer, test, place" process appears to be an appropriate one for providing assistance, particularly since, in the past, many students with special needs did not receive help or were even excluded from school. However, there is evidence that a large percentage of them, especially those with mild handicaps, could be successful in regular education classes if given supportive assistance. As a result of these concerns, interest in alternative methods of assisting students has grown, with consultation being promoted as a means of providing these services (see Graden, Zins, & Curtis, 1988, for additional discussion).

Although we have identified many problems associated with traditional means of providing assistance to children and their families, we do not view consultation as a panacea for resolving all these difficulties, or as a method to supplant other approaches. As noted earlier, there will always be a need for direct treatment services. There is evidence, however, that consultation enables practitioners to lend assistance to larger numbers of children in a more timely manner than approaches used in the past, (Gutkin, Henning-Stout, & Piersel, 1988; Zins, Curtis, Graden, & Ponti, 1988), since one of its major characteristics is that it is directed toward providing more immediate assistance to greater numbers of people.

Essential Elements of Consultation

As scores of authors of articles, chapters, and books on consultation have noted, there is no commonly accepted definition of consultation (see, for example, Gallessich, 1982; Gutkin & Curtis, 1990). In fact, the term *consultation* sometimes connotes so many different ideas that it seems almost meaningless. As Barry (1970, p. 363) observes, "Today almost everyone is a consultant. Every program has consultants. Sometimes it seems as if there are more consultants than consultees!" To further complicate matters, various "models" of consultation have been proposed, including the mental health, behavioral, organizational, collaborative, ecological, advocacy, social learning, and triadic models (Idol & West, 1987; West & Idol, 1987). However, most of these have not been fully developed and evaluated and therefore can only loosely be considered models. Despite these issues, it is essential to have a clear conceptual framework for the process, as consultation practices that are not based on and controlled by clear conceptualizations are likely to be ineffective and may, in fact, be harmful to clients (Fullan, Miles, & Taylor, 1980; Gallessich, 1982, 1985).

We should note, nevertheless, that some models of consultation (for example, behavioral, social learning, and triadic) appear to be far more similar to than different from one another. We may, in fact, be moving toward widespread consensus about a definition, at least within the human service field. There appear to be characteristics of the consultation process common to each model, although constructs within these models in general are not well defined in the literature (Kratochwill, 1991; Witt, 1990). Readers may observe these aspects as they review succeeding chapters of this book.

First, consultation is an *indirect method of service delivery*. Generally, the consultant does not work directly with the client who is the focus of the consultative interactions but instead assists that person indirectly through the consultee. Thus, it is a triadic relationship (Tharp, 1984). Second, the consultant and consultee engage in a *joint, systematic problem-solving process* that is data-based. To resolve the presenting problem, they proceed together through a problem-solving sequence, such as problem identification, problem analysis, treatment implementation, and treatment evaluation (Bergan & Kratochwill, 1990). The interpersonal relationship between consultant and consultee, which is critical in this process, has been characterized as being *cooperative, mutually respectful, collegial, voluntary,* and *confidential.* Consultees are viewed as having the *right to accept or reject consultant suggestions* as they retain responsibility for clients. The focus is on *resolution of work-related concerns for the benefit of a client* (who may be an individual or an entire organization). Thus, it may be necessary to address consultee skills and behaviors, environmental variables, or client behaviors.

Consultation also usually has a *preventive orientation* in that consultants try to make assistance available early on, before more serious problems arise, as well as on an ongoing basis. It also has a goal of making the service available to more students and teachers than is typical with a direct service model. Therefore, consultation can be both proactive and reactive. Finally, because consultation is influenced significantly by the organizational context in which it occurs, a *systems, ecological perspective* is often assumed. Consultants recognize the complex interdependence between children and their environment and between themselves and the environment, as well as the role that these interactive systems play in the development of problem behaviors. Thus, an analysis of environmental factors that may be maintaining the problem behaviors is an essential aspect of the problem-solving process, and it may be desirable to directly train consultees in problem-solving, communication, and behavioral change skills to enhance the process (Zins, in press). Further, an organization's goals and procedures, as well as the behaviors of individuals, often must be altered if durable, long-lasting change is to be achieved.

An Overview of the Field

The current status of consultation in the human service field can be gauged by a number of means. Number of and types of *publications* is one measure. Since 1967, there have been nearly 100 books written on the topic (see Appendix A), the majority of them by people primarily associated with school, counseling, and community psychology and special education. Several have recently gone into second editions and one into a third. Two journals that have been published for many years, although they are devoted primarily to consultation in business and private practice settings, often include articles relevant to human services consultation. *Consultation: An International Journal* was begun by T. E. Backer and E. M. Glaser of the Human Interaction Research Institute's consultation program and is now published by Human Sciences Press; the *Consulting Psychology Journal* is sponsored by the Division of Consulting Psychology of the American Psychological Association (APA). In addition, special issues of a number of journals have been devoted to consultation (see Appendix B), and many regularly include articles on this topic. In 1990, the field received a major boost through the launching of the *Journal of Educational and Psychological Consultation,* sponsored by the Association for Educational and Psychological Consultants, which is devoted solely to consultation.

Several comprehensive reference guides published in recent years provide an indication of the viability of the field. Mannino (1969) published a guide to the consultation literature that included 646 references. In an update to that guide, Mannino and Robinson (1975) reviewed the literature from 1968 to 1973 and listed a total of 1,136 publications. Grady, Gibson, and Trickett (1981) identified 884 additional journal articles, dissertations, and books published from 1973 to July 1978. Another addendum was published in 1986, covering the years 1978 to 1984, which included 683 references (Kidder, Tinker, Mannino, & Trickett, 1986). The growth in the number of publications suggests that interest in the area is expanding and reflects the increased emphasis on empirical examination of the consultation process.

Not only has there been a tremendous growth in the number of publications on consultation, but the amount and quality of *research* published in refereed journals, another very important indication of the field's status, are expanding. In the past three decades, psychology journals published by far more data-based articles on consultation effectiveness than on special education, counseling, and related areas, with two-thirds of the investigations reviewed in one study using group and one-third single-case designs (Fuchs, Fuchs, Dulan, Roberts, & Fernstrom, 1992). Duncan and Pryzwansky (1988) observed that the sophistication of dissertation research in this area has also increased.

A number of extensive research reviews and meta-analyses (for example, Alpert & Yammer, 1983; Gutkin & Curtis, 1990; Mannino & Shore, 1975; Medway, 1979, 1982; Medway & Updyke, 1985) have concluded that consultation is an effective method of service delivery. However, some authors who have commented on these reviews suggest that considerable caution should be used in interpreting their findings, especially given the methodological and conceptual criteria that they apply to the research in the field (see Kratochwill, Sheridan, & VanSomeren, 1988).

Another means of examining the field is through an analysis of *practice.*

There are a growing number of disciplines engaging in the practice of consultation, but as Gallessich (1985) notes, it is not a primary activity or major responsibility of any profession. Indeed, a perusal of the membership directory of the Division of Consulting Psychology of the APA indicates diverse backgrounds of its members. In addition, many of the distinctions among various professions become quite blurred in consultation. School psychologists, for example, report that they are increasingly engaging in this practice (Smith & Lyon, 1985). West and Brown (1987) surveyed state departments of education regarding consultation practice; twenty-six of thirty-five states responding expected special educators to engage in consultation as part of their professional roles, although there was considerable variation in how consultation was conducted. Brown (1985) notes that job-vacancy announcements for counseling psychologists list consultation as part of the job description with increasing frequency and suggests that such job demands have increased in recent years. Speech and language therapists also have begun to view consultation as an important aspect of their roles (Secord, 1990).

Perhaps one of the more notable motivations for increasing consultation services for children in recent years is the "prereferral intervention" movement that seems to be sweeping the education field. Carter and Sugai (1989) found that, as of late 1987, nearly 70 percent of the states required or recommended prereferral intervention programs as a means of providing consultation-based supportive assistance. Even though educational change usually proceeds slowly, state and local education agencies are jumping on this bandwagon so rapidly that there is concern that many of these programs are being implemented too hastily. When they are "poorly conceived, their goals are unclear, minimal resources are allocated, participant training is neglected, and sparse attention is given to procedural issues . . . there is a high risk that they will not be successful" (Zins & Ponti, 1990, pp. 206–207).

Training efforts in consultation also provide an indication of the current status of the field. A survey by Gallessich and Watterson (1984) indicated that 30 percent of the APA-approved counseling psychology programs required training in consultation, while two-thirds offered courses in this area. Respondents to a survey of school psychology training programs indicated that 55 percent of the doctoral programs and 32 percent of the nondoctoral programs offered at least one course in consultation (Meyers, Wurtz, & Flanagan, 1981). These percentages most likely have increased in both areas in recent years, and it is our experience that consultation training is being required more often by other disciplines, such as special education, speech and language pathology, and counselor education.

Later chapters in this book describe current theoretical, research, training, and practice issues mentioned here in greater detail and provide examples that more fully illustrate these points.

Conclusion

This chapter has presented an overview of the historical development and current status of consultation as a method of service delivery. Consultation has emerged for a number of conceptual and practical reasons as an alternative to more traditional service approaches for a variety of professionals. The field has borrowed conceptual and pragmatic ideas from the many disciplines that use it as a means of providing services, but it has also developed some of its own theory and is becoming increasingly more data-based as many widely held assumptions are challenged and subsequently validated or modified (Gresham & Kendell, 1987; Kratochwill et al., 1988; Witt, 1990). We hope that this volume will lead to continued developments in interdisciplinary theory, research, practice, and training in consultation.

References

Albee, G. W. (1968). Conceptual models and manpower requirements in psychology. *American Psychologist, 23,* 317–320.

Alpert, J. L., & Yammer, M. D. (1983). Research in school consultation: A content analysis of selected journals. *Professional Psychology: Research and Practice, 14,* 604–612.

Baker, D. (1988). The psychology of Lightner Witmer. *Professional School Psychology, 3,* 109–122.

Bandura, A. (1969). *Principles of behavior modification.* New York: Holt, Rinehart & Winston.

Barry, J. R. (1970). Criteria in the evaluation of consultation. *Professional Psychology, 1,* 363–366.

Bergan, J. R., & Kratochwill, T. R. (1990). *Behavioral consultation and therapy.* New York: Plenum Press.

Brown, D. (1985). The preservice training and supervision of consultants. *The Counseling Psychologist, 13,* 410–425.

Caplan, G. (1970). *The theory and practice of mental health consultation.* New York: Basic Books.

Carter, J., & Sugai, G. (1989). Survey of prereferral practices: Responses from state departments of education. *Exceptional Children, 55,* 298–302.

Duncan, C. F., & Pryzwansky, W. B. (1988). Consultation research: Trends in doctoral dissertations 1978–1985. *Journal of School Psychology, 26,* 107–119.

Fuchs, D., Fuchs, L. S., Dulan, J., Roberts, H., & Fernstrom, P. (1992). Where is the research on consultation effectiveness? *Journal of Educational and Psychological Consultation, 3,* 151–174.

Fullan, M., Miles, M. B., & Taylor, G. (1980). Organization development in schools: The state of the art. *Review of Educational Research, 50,* 121–183.

Galagan, J. (1985). Psychoeducational testing: Turn out the lights, the party's over. *Exceptional Children, 52,* 288–299.

Gallessich, J. (1982). *The profession and practice of consultation: A handbook for consultants, trainers of consultants, and consumers of consultation services.* San Francisco: Jossey-Bass.

Gallessich, J. (1985). Toward a meta-theory of consultation. *The Counseling Psychologist, 13,* 336–354.

Gallessich, J., & Watterson, J. (1984, August). *Consultation education and training in APA-accredited settings: An overview.* Paper presented at the annual meeting of the American Psychological Association, Toronto.

Graden, J. L., Zins, J. E., & Curtis, M. J. (Eds.). (1988). *Alternative educational delivery systems: Enhancing instructional options for all students.* Silver Spring, MD: National Association of School Psychologists.

Grady, M. A., Gibson, M., & Trickett, E. J. (Eds.). (1981). *Mental health consultation theory, practice, and research—1973–1978: An annotated reference guide.* Washington, DC: U.S. Government Printing Office.

Gresham, F. M., & Kendell, G. K. (1987). School consultation research: Methodological critique and future research directions. *School Psychology Review, 16,* 306–316.

Gutkin, T. B. (1993). Moving from behavioral to ecobehavioral consultation: What's in a name? *Journal of Educational and Psychological Consultation, 4,* 95–99.

Gutkin, T. B., and Conoley, J. C. (1990). Reconceptualizing school psychology from a service delivery perspective: Implications for practice, training, and research. *Journal of School Psychology, 28,* 203–223.

Gutkin, T. B., & Curtis, M. J. (1982). School-based consultation: Theory and techniques. In C. R. Reynolds & T. B. Gutkin (Eds.), *The handbook of school psychology* (pp. 796–828). New York: Wiley.

Gutkin, T. B., & Curtis, M. J. (1990). School-based consultation: Theory, techniques, and research. In T. B. Gutkin & C. R. Reynolds (Eds.), *The handbook of school psychology* (2nd ed., pp. 577–611). New York: Wiley.

Gutkin, T. B., Henning-Stout, M., & Piersel, W. C. (1988). Impact of a district-wide behavioral consultation prereferral intervention service on patterns of school psychological service delivery. *Professional School Psychology, 3,* 301–308.

✔ Idol, L., & West, J. F. (1987). Consultation in special education (part II): Training and practice. *Journal of Learning Disabilities, 20,* 474–494.

Kidder, M., Tinker, M., Mannino, F. V., & Trickett, E. J. (1986). An annotated reference guide to the consultation literature: 1978–1984. In F. V. Mannino, E. J. Trickett, M. F. Shore, M. G. Kidder, & G. Levin (Eds.), *Handbook of mental health consultation* (DHHS Publication No. ADM 86-1446, pp. 523–796). Washington, DC: U.S. Government Printing Office.

Kratochwill, T. R. (1991). Defining constructs in consultation research: An important agenda in the 1990s. *Journal of Educational and Psychological Consultation, 2,* 291–294.

Kratochwill, T. R., Sheridan, S. M., & VanSomeren, K. R. (1988). Research in behavioral consultation: Current status and future directions. In J. F. West (Ed.), *School consultation: Interdisciplinary perspectives on theory, research, training, and practice* (pp. 77–102). Austin, TX: Association of Educational and Psychological Consultants.

Lewin, K. (1951). *Field theory in social science.* New York: HarperCollins.

London, P. (1987). Character education and clinical intervention: A paradigm shift for U.S. schools. *Phi Delta Kappan, 68,* 667–673.

Mannino, F. V. (1969). *Consultation in mental health and related fields: A reference guide.* Washington, DC: U.S. Government Printing Office.

Mannino, F. V., & Robinson, S. (1975). A reference guide to the consultation literature. In F. V. Mannino, B. W. MacLennan, & M. F. Shore (Eds.), *The practice of mental health consultation* (pp. 157–241). Washington, DC: U.S. Government Printing Office.

Mannino, F. V., & Shore, M. F. (1975). The effects of consultation: A review of empirical studies of the literature. *American Journal of Community Psychology, 3,* 1–21.

Mannino, F. V., & Shore, M. F. (1986). History and development of mental health consultation. In F. V. Mannino, E. J. Trickett, M. F. Shore, M. G. Kidder, & G. Levin (Eds.), *Handbook of mental health consultation* (DHHS Publication No. ADM 86-1446, pp. 3–28). Washington, DC: U.S. Government Printing Office.

Medway, F. J. (1979). How effective is school consultation? A review of recent research. *Journal of School Psychology, 17,* 275–282.

Medway, F. J. (1982). School consultation research: Past trends and future directions. *Professional Psychology, 13,* 422–430.

Medway, F. J., & Updyke, J. F. (1985). Meta-analysis of consultation outcome studies. *American Journal of Community Psychology, 13,* 489–505.

Meyers, J., Wurtz, R., & Flanagan, D. (1981). A national survey investigating consultation training occurring in school psychology programs. *Psychology in the Schools, 18,* 297–302.

Miller, G. A. (1969). Psychology as a means of promoting human welfare. *American Psychologist, 24,* 1063–1075.

Office of Technology Assessment. (1986). *Children's mental health: Problems and services.* Washington, DC: U.S. Government Printing Office.

Reynolds, M., & Larkin, K. (1987). Noncategorical special education for mildly handicapped students: A system for the future. In M. Wang, M. Reynolds, & H. Walberg (Eds.), *The handbook of special education* (Vol. 3, pp. 331–356). Oxford, England: Pergamon Press.

Secord, W. A. (Ed.). (1990). *Best practices in school speech-language pathology—collaborative programs in the schools: Concepts, models, and procedures.* San Antonio, TX: Psychological Corporation.

Skinner, B. F. (1953). *Science and human behavior.* New York: Macmillan.

Smith, D. K., & Lyon, M. A. (1985). Consultation in school psychology: Changes from 1981 to 1984. *Psychology in the Schools, 22,* 404–409.

Tharp, R. G. (1984). The triadic model. In J. A. Tucker (Module Developer), *School psychology in the classroom: A case study tutorial* (pp. 52–71). Minneapolis, MN: National School Psychology Inservice Training Network.

Tharp, R. G., & Wetzel, R. J. (1969). *Behavior modification in the natural environment.* San Diego, CA: Academic Press.

Tuma, J. M. (1989). Mental health services for children: The state of the art. *American Psychologist, 44,* 188–199.

Ullman, L. P., & Krasner, L. (1965). *Case studies in behavior modification.* New York: Holt, Rinehart & Winston.

West, J. F., & Brown, P. (1987). State departments' of education policies on consultation in special education: The state of the states. *Remedial and Special Education, 8,* 45–51.

West, J. F., & Idol, L. (1987). School consultation (part I): An interdisciplinary perspective on theory, models, and research. *Journal of Learning Disabilities, 20,* 388–408.

Witt, J. C. (1990). Collaboration in school-based consultation: Myth in need of data. *Journal of Educational and Psychological Consultation, 1,* 367–370.

Ysseldyke, J., Thurlow, M., Graden, J., Wesson, C., Algozzine, B., & Deno, S. (1983). Generalizations from five years of research on assessment and decision-making: Findings of the Minnesota Institute. *Exceptional Education Quarterly, 4,* 75–93.

Zins, J. E. (in press). Enhancing consultee problem-solving skills in consultative interactions. *Journal of Counseling and Development.*

Zins, J. E., Curtis, M. J., Graden, J. L., & Ponti, C. R. (1988). *Helping students succeed in the regular classroom: A guide for developing intervention assistance programs.* San Francisco: Jossey-Bass.

Zins, J. E., & Ponti, C. R. (1990). Strategies to facilitate the implementation, organization, and operation of system-wide consultation programs. *Journal of Educational and Psychological Consultation, 1,* 205–218.

Part One

CONCEPTUAL FOUNDATIONS AND ORIENTATIONS

2

Theoretical and Empirical Bases of Consultation

Mary Henning-Stout

Early each spring, the town of Gladewater would come alive with flowers—flowers of every color and kind. But folks were proudest of their irises. Antique irises, they said; some of them grown from bulbs that their grandparents had planted more than a hundred years earlier. Year after year, the flowers bloomed, and year after year, debate persisted on how best to tend them. Late one winter, Kay Fitzsimmons did a piece for the newspaper featuring the competing wisdom on iris growth. She counted twenty-seven distinct methods. The follow-up article in the summer showed pictures and told how every one of those methods had led to beautiful blooms.

What does a story about the horticulture of iris plants have to do with consultation? The answer: both flower tending and consultation are central activities in their respective contexts, and just as there are many ways to grow irises, there are many ways to approach consultation. As Ludwig von Bertalanffy (1968) revealed in his discussion of biological systems, many and varied circumstances bring different systems to the same evolutional point. Von Bertalanffy termed this phenomenon *equifinality*: there are many routes to the same (equifinal) destination.

In the following pages, consultation and its outcomes will be taken as the "destination" and the theoretical and empirical bases of knowledge and practice as the various routes to consultation. Good practice is not only responsive but thoughtful and reflective. We must be able to describe to ourselves what it is that we do. We need to know why we believe in what we are doing, and we need to know whether it works. The ambitious goal of this chapter, therefore, is to begin clarifying what we mean when we talk about consultation.

To accomplish this purpose, the chapter first summarizes the broad goals and general characteristics of consultation as articulated in the literature. Next detailed consideration is given to three major approaches to the practice of consultation: mental health, behavioral-ecological, and organizational. The final section of the chapter focuses on the empirical evidence that has come from efforts to explore, expand, and justify consultation.

The goals of consultation are the outcomes that we seek. While specific outcome expectations vary from case to case, there are three general goals for consultation: (1) to help make responsive educational and psychological services available to all children, (2) to engage the adults who interact with children in the service delivery process, and (3) to facilitate effective problem solving among the adults and children involved in child-related problems.

With regard to the first of these goals, it is likely that all children are at some time affected by extraordinary life stressors. The availability of support from adults at those times can turn threatening situations into opportunities for learning and growth. This is a powerful form of prevention. It is devotion to the well-being of all children that underlies service delivery in educational and child-clinical settings (National Association of School Psychologists, 1985). However, "all children" represents a population far exceeding the availability of special service providers. In fact, the number of immediately needy children is on the rise and clearly outpacing the number of adults trained to respond to their needs (Gartner & Lipsky, 1987; Connolly & Reschly, 1990).

Where can the resources be found to respond to these needs? This question invokes the second goal. There is substantial evidence to support the delivery of many psychological services by paraprofessionals (for a review, see Conoley & Gutkin, 1986). Unlike workers in professions where information is controlled for any number of good or bad reasons (for example, the military, medical practice, weight-loss programs), mental health professionals provide their most responsive services when they "give psychology away" (Miller, 1969, p. 1067)—when they empower their clients instead of creating dependencies. In the case of consultation, empowerment of the adults with whom the child has contact is intended to have the primary effect of enhancing the power of the child.

One of the most generalizable (and empowering) skills that can come from consultation is problem solving. Consultation exists to solve problems (Witt, 1990a). At the same time, a primary goal of the activity of consultation is the enhancement of problem-solving skills. Gutkin and Curtis (1990) discuss the role of problem solving in consultation in terms of remediation and prevention. Consultation should serve the immediate function of remediating an identified problem. The process of determining the best path to remediation should allow the consultee (teacher, counselor, caseworker, parent) to acquire *preventive*

skills for responding to similar problems in the future. In addition, consultation should increase the likelihood that problems will be prevented. Understanding current problems allows for anticipation and interruption of behaviors that could lead to future problems.

The three goals of consultation described here are interdependent. Responsive education occurs when children and adults are engaged in and learning from the educational process that they create. Consultation is a broadly applicable service delivery approach designed to help educators identify and remove the barriers to this educational process.

The characteristics that set consultation apart from the other service delivery approaches include indirect service to the client; joint problem solving with the consultee; a cooperative relationship based on mutual respect, collegiality, voluntary consultee participation, and confidentiality; a preventive orientation; and a systemic or ecological perspective. Elaboration on the characteristics drawing most controversy among scholars, researchers, and practitioners of consultation seems warranted.

The relational features of consultation, or what Idol (1990) refers to as "the art of consultation," have drawn significant attention of late. One question centers on whether consultation is correctly described as a collaborative relationship between the consultee and the consultant.

Historically, the foundation of the consultation relationship has been located in the characteristic of coordinate power status (Conoley & Conoley, 1991; Erchul, 1987; Tyler, Pargament, & Gatz, 1983). In this kind of relationship, the consultant is not the expert sent in to apply remediation, with the people participating in the problem passively responding to the consultant's directives. Rather, the consultant brings his or her expertise to bear on the subject while engaging the expertise of other participants in order to solve a child-related problem. The input of the other participants carries power equal to that of the consultant.

Recent behavioral research has led to the suggestion that verbal behaviors of consultants and consultees fail to support the coordinate status of the relationship (for example, Erchul, 1987; Erchul & Chewning, 1990, cited in Witt, 1990b). The data reported in these studies are interpreted by their authors as indicating that consultation works when the consultants dominate the verbal interchange. Henning-Stout and Conoley (1987) reported finding that consultants do in fact employ more directive verbalizations than do counselors in psychotherapy sessions. Such verbalization patterns seem to characterize consultation—to set it apart from other approaches to service delivery.

However, it seems a matter of interpretation rather than fact to assume that such verbalization undercuts the central characteristic of coordinate power status. The literature from social psychology reminds us that emergence of leaders and guides does not necessarily imply rigid hierarchical distribution of social power (Allen & Levine, 1968). In fact, such distributions have been found to be antagonistic to achieving real and positive change (Guba & Lincoln, 1989; Sarason, 1982).

Seemingly contingent on the atmosphere accompanying coequal power status and collaboration is the consultee's voluntary participation in the consultation relationship. It is possible that a consultee would voluntarily assume a position lower in status than that of an expert consultant. However, that kind of relationship bodes ill for the consultee's taking individual initiative with skills imparted via expert consultation. There is also ample evidence that consultees resist being told what to do (for example, Bergan & Neumann, 1980; Gutkin, 1986; Kinsala, 1984; Martin, 1978). If a consultation relationship is to be truly voluntary, consultees must be aware of and willing to act on their right to exit the relationship at any time. A hierarchical relationship decreases the likelihood of this awareness or action. The voluntary participation of the consultee is necessary to maximize the likelihood that any problem solution generated through consultation is "owned" and implemented by the consultee. Mandatory participation in the consultation process would severely reduce the likelihood that the goals of consultation could be achieved (Gutkin & Curtis, 1981).

The voluntary nature of consultation presents the challenge of keeping the consultee engaged in the process. When consultation relationships include problem descriptions, intervention plans, and discernible outcomes that have "meaning" for the consultees, ongoing engagement is more likely, and benefit to the children is enhanced. Gutkin and Curtis (1990, p. 578) identify "meaningful collaboration" as the source of this engagement and as a primary feature of successful consultation.

The question of the relational underpinnings of consultation will be addressed again in the discussion of the empirical bases of consultation. Attending directly in this chapter to issues of current debate helps to place the theoretical and empirical foundations of consultation in the enlivened context of contemporary discourse. The centrality of collaboration to most conceptualizations of consultation will be evident in the review of specific theoretical and empirical foundations.

Theoretical Foundations

A familiar story from ancient Arabia tells of three wise but blind people happening upon an elephant. Each of them explored the area of the elephant with which he or she had come into contact, and each developed quite distinct theoretical descriptions of the thing that they were all touching. Arguments ensued. Commoners were recruited to the various positions. Thought, discussion, and ego were invested, and proponents of each perspective held firmly to its exclusive truth.

The experience of the ancient Arabians is played out in the side taking of professionals pressed to identify the theoretical foundation of their practice. Theories are developed to explain experienced phenomena. Because they are necessarily human constructions, theories cannot be considered without acknowledgment of their mediation through what are variously referred to as world views, existential understandings, mythologies, or learning histories. Three perspectives mediating our understanding of consultation are considered below. Because theory is often grounded in the interpretation of practice (for example, "theoretically, consultation is voluntary"), the terms *theory* and *approach* will be used interchangeably throughout this discussion.

Mental Health Consultation

Mental health consultation has served as the cornerstone for the development of consultation as a service delivery approach. Its use dates back to 1886 and Lightner Witmer's child psychology clinic at the University of Pennsylvania (Mannino & Shore, 1986). The visiting teachers and other professionals in this and subsequent clinics had the goal of "alter[ing] various environments (home, school, etc.) to make them easier or more pleasant places for the child to live" (p. 5). This was accomplished through joint planning and implementation of change initiatives by representatives of the clinics and professionals directly serving children in various agencies.

These indirect methods were later used by Gerald Caplan (1970), who formalized the model of consultation reviewed in this section. In its contemporary rendition, the mental health consultation model is an indirect service delivery system founded on a collaborative relationship between the consultant and person directly involved with the child. The relationship is one in which both the consultant and the consultee assume responsibility for the outcome of the plans formed in consultation (Meyers, 1973, 1981).

Within its framework, mental health consultation can take any one of four tacks (Caplan, 1970). Client-centered consultation focuses on the difficulties demonstrated by the child and ways in which the consultee might intervene to remedy those difficulties. Consultee-centered consultation provides support to the adults in children's environments and is aimed at removing intrapsychic barriers to the consultee's ability to work with the child. The third and fourth approaches to mental health consultation focus on administrative concerns (Meyers, Gaughan, & Pitt, 1990). In the program-centered administrative consultation, ways of improving service delivery procedures are considered by the consultant and consultee. In consultee-centered administrative consultation, issues specific to the administrator's practices are the focus of the relationship.

As is evident in later sections of this chapter, Caplan's work has served to inspire other consultation models. For instance, client-centered consultation has influenced behavioral-ecological approaches to consultation, and administrative consultation methods have much in common with organizational approaches to consultation. The consultee-centered approach has remained unique to mental health consultation and will be the focus of the remainder of this theory's discussion.

Caplan's (1970) approach to consultation is grounded in an intrapsychic model of behavior change. From this perspective, verbalizations and behavior are taken to reflect emotional reactions. In consultation, the consultant attempts to uncover patterns in the transference of emotional responses to seemingly unrelated situations. For example, a kindergarten teacher whose nephew was irritable as a young child because of the discomfort caused by undiagnosed ear infections might refer all irritable boys to the school nurse for ear exams. In this case, the teacher's fear of overlooking another child's medical needs generalizes to all irritable boys.

From the perspective of mental health consultation, patterns of generalized emotional responses arise when there are deficits in the professional functioning of consultees. Caplan (1970) suggests four areas in which deficits might be observed: information and knowledge; skill; self-confidence; and professional objectivity. Approaches to problem solution would be developed according to the deficit discerned by the consultant.

In all cases of deficits interfering with a consultee's professional functioning, consultation is limited to work-related issues. Because of consultation's collegial nature, the consultation relationship would be severely impaired if the consultant were to assume the dual roles of colleague and therapist. Thus, in mental health consultation, the focus is, by definition, on work-related problems. This maxim of mental health consultation has generalized across all approaches to consultation. When the consultee's needs or concerns go beyond work issues, referral to an outside mental health professional should occur. With such referral, the consultee's needs can be met, and the consultant can maintain a clear collegial status. This status is central to the service provider's credibility and accessibility as a consultant within the consultee's system.

When deficits are identified and the work-related nature of the difficulty is clear, problem solution begins. In cases of information or skill deficits, the consultant and consultee might determine how training could be acquired to fill the gaps. Where the deficit is in self-confidence, professional support and encouragement would come into play. The consultant and consultee would plan ways to enhance the consultee's perception of his or her professional functioning.

Where the consultee's professional objectivity is diminished, mental health consultants employ more subtle approaches to alter the emotional theme underlying that loss of objectivity. Caplan (1970) attributes loss of professional objectivity to a number of sources that could be described as involving the consultee's overidentification with the client. One source stressed by Caplan and generally less familiar to service providers is what he terms *theme interference*. The goal of consultation in cases of theme interference is theme interference reduction.

The process of theme interference reduction (Caplan, 1970; Conoley & Conoley, 1982) requires substantial skill with psychotherapeutic techniques as well as clear understanding of the boundary between consultation and psychotherapy. Essentially, this technique involves the interruption and reorganization of a patterned response to a general set of child behaviors. In the case of the kindergarten teacher who worried about boys' ears, consultation would focus on revealing exceptions to the teacher's applied theme: "all irritable boys are experiencing dangerous ear infections." By showing convincing exception to a theme, the extent to which that theme is activated to interfere with responsive service to children is reduced. Generally, situations involving theme interference are far more complicated and elusive than in this simplified example, and the techniques of theme interference reduction are intricate (Conoley & Conoley, 1982).

Several problems have been highlighted in the research literature relative to Caplan's identification of loss of professional objectivity as a source of consultees' difficulties in working with children. For example, Gutkin (1981) surveyed teachers and found that the loss of objectivity attributed to theme interference was less common than were problems of limited knowledge, skill, or self-confidence. This study has received considerable attention in the literature of consultation in schools and seems to represent the only empirical research into the prevalence of these deficits. In adjusting the model of mental health consultation for use in child-centered settings, Meyers, Parsons, and Martin (1979) have emphasized the importance of defining loss of objectivity in objective and behavioral terms. They suggest that "consultation techniques should be related directly to the problem definitions, and they should be more straightforward, and more readily understood by both consultant and consultee. It needs to be made clear that the teacher's lack of objectivity can be helped, not only through intrapersonal clinical techniques and insight, but also through modifying the teacher's school environment" (p. 135).

The notion of lack of objectivity lends itself to the imposition of the expert model described earlier, in which the consultant has the insight into the consultee's intrapsychic barriers and is therefore the agent for inducing the psychological change necessary to enlighten the consultee. The suggestion of Meyers and his colleagues provides a foundation for developing techniques for addressing problems that might have their bases in consultee loss of objectivity but that are more consistent with the voluntary and collaborative nature of the consultation relationship. That is, directly addressing problems in the consultee's interaction with a child and encouraging collaboration for finding ways to improve that interaction will be more effective than searching for the problem's intrapsychic sources (Meyers, 1981; Meyers, Friedman, & Gaughan, 1975).

This position, however, echoes Caplan's original suggestion that loss of professional objectivity and the possibility of theme interference should be assumed only in the last resort. It remains to be shown through additional research and practice whether the more parsimonious explanations of lack of knowledge, skill, or self-confidence can account for most of the consultee-centered problems among individuals who work with children. What Caplan described as the uncommon instance of loss of objectivity may in some cases remain a salient problem—a problem that does not respond to more conventional behavioral and environmental interpretations. A clear and standard position has yet to be articulated on the appropriate responses of consultants to situations that ultimately are attributable to consultee loss of objectivity. These rare situations may best be responded to with referral to other mental health professionals so that the integrity of the work-related consultation relationship can be maintained. If consultation as a separate professional practice (Gallessich, 1982; Mannino & Shore, 1986) is moving toward a more behavioral and ecological definition, consultants will increasingly lack experience and training in responding to a consultee's loss of professional objectivity and must refer such cases to more appropriately skilled colleagues.

Behavioral Consultation

A second theoretical perspective on consultation shifts the focus away from intrapsychic themes and onto the behaviors of children and adults in their social contexts. In this section, the term *behavioral consultation* is used to afford consistency across the body of this volume (see Chapter One). There are some differences of opinion among scholars in consultation as to whether the most appropriate term for this approach is *behavioral* or *ecological*. Some scholars maintain that *ecological* better describes the necessary mediation of behavioral technology through the environmental context in which it is employed (Gutkin & Curtis, 1990; Reynolds, Gutkin, Elliott, & Witt, 1984). The

term *ecological* also modifies any implication that "the users of this consultative methodology [are] rigidly limited to a behaviorist paradigm when assessing
client problems and designing treatment programs" (Gutkin & Curtis, 1990,
p. 589). Other scholars suggest that *behavioral* is the term of preference because it highlights the data base underlying the behavioral approach to consultation (Bergan & Kratochwill, 1990; Goodwin & Coates, 1976). Because this
data base rests on the measurement of behavioral interventions, these scholars
see behavioral practices as primary in this approach to consultation, although
they concede that ecological psychology and social learning theory have become part of behavioral consultation (J. E. Zins, personal communication,
October 10, 1991).

This might seem a petty issue of turf rather than substance. However,
the name given an approach can simultaneously direct attention to vital components of that approach and mask equally important considerations. Both behavioral and ecological considerations are included in the approach reviewed
here, and neither takes precedence over the other.

The behavioral roots of this approach to consultation support its orientation toward uncovering the reinforcement contingencies maintaining behavior
(Skinner, 1953). The behaviors of the child or any of the adults in that child's
environment might be analyzed by imposing this paradigm. For the purposes
of consultation, this exclusive focus on the environmental determinants of
behavior was expanded to include features of Bandura's (1977) social learning
theory (Brown & Schulte, 1987). According to Gutkin and Curtis (1990,
p. 589), consultation practices based in "Skinnerian approaches to behavioral
psychology . . . are encompassed by and entirely consistent with Bandura's
(1978) ecologically oriented theory of reciprocal determinism."

Bandura's notion of reciprocal determinism revived Tolman's (1932)
contention that the organism should not be left out of the stimulus-response
formulation (that S-R is more appropriately S-O-R). The proponents of behavioral consultation agree that the appropriate focus of consultation is "on the
interaction between persons, environments, and behaviors" (Gutkin & Curtis,
1990, p. 589). In short, this approach to consultation recognizes the ecological
complexity of behavioral intervention and acknowledges the active roles that
the consultee and the child play in mediating their own and one another's
behaviors.

Behavioral consultation emerges directly from the behavioral paradigm
that is grounded securely in positivism. Positivism holds that making sense of
the world is best accomplished by reducing phenomena to their discrete parts
for identification and measurement. Such a process of reduction and measurement has been applied to describing and developing behavioral consultation.
The positivist underpinnings of behavioral consultation are evident in its struc-

ture and practice and can be illustrated by the sequence of events composing the behavioral consultation process.

Four fundamental steps in solving a behavioral problem through consultation have been identified (Bergan, 1977; Bergan & Kratochwill, 1990; see also Chapter Four). The first step is problem identification. In this stage, the consultant interviews the consultee to elicit a clear description of the problem that the child is experiencing. For example, if a child-care provider were to say, "I just can't control Ashley—she's either hyper or she's depressed," the consultant might ask, "What sorts of things does she do that seem 'hyper' to you?" "Well, she runs around a lot and jumps on the tables when people arrive in the morning, especially when I'm greeting the other children or talking to a parent."

In this exchange, the consultant needs to clarify the nature of the behaviors denoted as "hyper" and "depressed." Bergan and Kratochwill (1990) suggest that the problem be operationally defined (which tables? how high? for how long?) so that it can be observed and its contingencies can be more easily discerned. The validity and centrality of this first stage have been supported by Bergan and Tombari's research (1976) on verbal behavior during consultation. Their study revealed clear problem identification as a powerful predictor of successful problem resolution.

The process of identifying the problem can enhance the consultee's understanding of it and provide both the consultant and the consultee with a point of reference for monitoring behavior change. At the close of this stage, both participants should be in agreement about what the problem behavior is and what changes in the behavior will indicate improvement.

Once the problem is clearly identified, problem analysis begins. Problem analysis involves direct observation of the behavior to determine its characteristics. This observation includes collecting baseline data on the behavior's frequency, intensity, and/or duration. Following the suggestions of Goodwin and Coates (1976) for behavior analysis, one can determine the antecedents and consequences of the behavior. What triggers the behavior, and what maintains it? Why is the behavior functional? What is the child getting by using this behavior? What is the payoff?

Gutkin and Curtis (1982) expand the problem-analysis stage to provide explicit prompts for intervention planning. As the problem is analyzed, plans can be generated for its solution. In the process of brainstorming alternative solutions, the consultant and consultee can define acceptable and desired behaviors that are incompatible with the behavior of concern (Goodwin & Coates, 1976). Through a comparison of the contingencies maintaining a desired behavior with those maintaining the problem behavior, antecedents and consequences can be organized to increase one behavior while extinguishing the other. This is only one approach to planning behavioral intervention. More complete descriptions of behavioral approaches to analysis and intervention planning can be found in texts devoted to elaborating those procedures (for example; Gelfand & Hartmann, 1984; Martin & Pear, 1988; Masters, Burish, Hollon, & Rimm, 1987; Wielkiewicz, 1986).

Throughout the analysis and intervention processes, consultants using the behavioral model remain aware of the relationship between the consultant and the consultee. As alternative strategies are considered, the consultant simultaneously invites the consultee's initiative in selecting a strategy and encourages the consultee's careful consideration of all options. When a plan is ultimately developed, the consultant engages the consultee in deciding who will take responsibly for what portions of the plan's implementation.

With those responsibilities clarified, the plan is implemented and progress is monitored. The monitoring process is both formative, involving ongoing collection of data that can be applied to minor adjustments in the plan, and summative, assessing the effectiveness of the intervention after an agreed-upon period of time. Evaluation of the program allows for its refinement or, if success is lacking, a return to earlier stages of the consultation process for redirecting or reconceptualizing intervention.

These stages in the consultation process guide behavioral consultation. Because of its acknowledgment of reciprocal determinism, behavioral consultation has also drawn on systems theory for theoretical grounding (Keller, 1981). Recent modifications in behavioral consultation have encouraged expanding the purview of consultation to take into account the availability of consultee skills for problem solving and to recognize the influence of the consultee's social environment (supportive or unsupportive) on the extent to which he or she feels empowered to demonstrate skill and competency (Martens & Witt, 1988; Witt & Martens, 1988).

Careful consideration of the features of the behavioral consultation approach reveals a list of tenets that seem to underlie both its theory and its practice:

1. All behaviors are learned.
2. The establishment, maintenance, and change of social behavior can be explained through observation of functional interactions of the individual, his or her behavior, and the environment.
3. Assessment, intervention, and evaluation of the intervention's effectiveness are directly linked.
4. Behaviors of focus must be observable, measurable, and quantifiable.
5. Environmental antecedents provide powerful points for initiating change.
6. Because learning histories vary, intervention is necessarily idiosyncratic.

7. Understanding and intervening with any behavior are guided and modi-
    fied according to systematically collected data reflecting the frequency,
    intensity, or duration of that behavior.
8. For one person's behavior to be changed, behaviors in other individuals
    interacting within the environment of focus must also be modified.

Any professional adopting the behavioral approach to consultation would embrace these tenets and use them to guide consultation activity. In spirit, the
list above is quite consistent with the emphasis in mental health consultation
on recognizing an adult's role in improving the experience of a child. The
difference is clearly in the approach taken to bringing about change in the
adult's behavior so that positive change will be possible for the child.

Organizational Consultation

While the behavioral and ecological orientations described above allow for
consideration of the interaction between any person and the environment in
which he or she functions, the primary focus remains the behavior. Organizational consultation, in contrast, places greater emphasis on the point of interaction between the person and the social environment. In this sense, the process consultation approach is more directly anchored in social psychology
(Goodstein, 1978). The consultant employing this approach considers events
in the environment as they affect the socioemotional atmosphere of the system
and as they are reflected in both system effectiveness and individual behavior.

    For professionals working with children, this orientation would indicate
consultation with administrators of child service organizations (see Chapter
Five). Recent increases in the psychological and educational needs of children
(Gartner & Lipsky, 1987; Will, 1986)—increases that show no sign of abat-
ing—underscore the importance of organizational consultation. Working with
administrators of child-centered programs has taken on renewed urgency, and
the organizational consultant can be an important resource for increasing the
effectiveness of these programs.

    Organizational consultation has its historical and theoretical grounding
in industrial and organizational psychology (Schein, 1969, 1990). Organization
development is the action that a formal system takes to improve its functioning
and process consultation. A component is the service that a professional can
provide to facilitate the system's accomplishment of those improvements. According to Schmuck (1990, p. 889), "Organization development is a planned
and sustained effort at [organizational] self-study and improvement, focusing
explicitly on change in both formal and informal norms, structures, and procedures, using behavioral science concepts and experiential learning. It involves

the [members of the organization] in the active assessment, diagnosis, and transformation of their own organization."

Process consultation, then, is the facilitation of this developmental process by a consultant who understands both structural and interpersonal issues that contribute to effective organizational functioning. Goodstein (1978) suggests that typical organizational consultants come from business backgrounds and have substantial understanding of structural issues such as channels of reporting, rules of conduct, and requirements of production. He underscores the importance of adding to that understanding the awareness of interpersonal and intrapersonal dynamics as they influence organizational functioning. Further articulating this combination of structural and interpersonal factors, Conoley and Conoley (1982, 1992) suggest that consultants to organizations are most helpful when they attend to the *way* things happen rather than what happens.

Three assumptions underlie organizational consultation. First, it is assumed that the consultant must understand the culture of the organization that he or she is entering and must help the consultee understand that structure before change can occur (Beer, 1980; Blake & Mouton, 1976; Henning-Stout & Conoley, 1988; Maher, Illback, & Zins, 1984; Rosenfield, 1992; Shein, 1969; see also Chapter Five). Hoy, Tarter, and Kottkamp (1991, p. 5) define organizational culture as "a system of shared orientations that hold the unit together and give it distinctive identity." The consultant and the consultee organization must be able to identify those orientations. What are the organization's needs? What are the norms and taboos of the organization? How do these social rules support or inhibit organizational functioning?

Answering questions such as these makes the subtle social structure of an organization overt and understandable to the consultant and, more importantly, to the individuals within the organization. On the basis of this understanding, organization development interventions can be tailored. The success of organizational consultation is dependent on each intervention's match with the system for which it is intended. Canned programs for change are rarely effective because they fail to take into account the idiosyncrasies of individual systems.

A second assumption of organizational consultation is that change occurs when all affected members of the system are involved in planning, implementing, and evaluating that change (Guba & Lincoln, 1989; Henning-Stout & Conoley, 1988; Lippitt, Langseth, & Mossop, 1985; Rosenfield, 1992; Schmuck, 1990). This involvement may be direct or indirect (for example, through elected representatives). The importance of involvement matches closely with the first assumption: organizational change must be responsive to the needs of the members of the organization. At the same time, the members of the system must be actively involved for change to occur. They must be willing to find answers to questions such as: "What are we doing? Why are we here? What do we want to be doing? How do we get from where we are to where we want to be?"

Referring specifically to school organizations, Schmuck (1990) emphasizes three keys to change: clarity and authenticity in communication; collaboration founded on respect, mutual freedom, and shared control; and commitment to the organizational improvement process. These conditions defy direct measurement. They arise from a sense of group identity and positive morale. They rely on clear, authoritative leadership that balances direction with collective thought and action. The thread running throughout is engagement—engaging the adults in the system in positive change that ultimately benefits the children whom they serve.

Finally, organizational consultation assumes the goal of moving beyond understanding to planning and implementing healthy change in the organization's culture (Goodstein, 1978; Hoy et al., 1991; Rosenfield, 1992; Sarason, 1982). When members of an organization become engaged in change, the rules of their interaction are called into question along with the rules or routines underlying their service delivery practices. Perhaps more threatening than considering changes in practice is directly facing changes in relationship patterns.

Consultants employing organizational consultation to respond to child-related issues find themselves focusing on the formalized interaction patterns of adults in child-service organizations. An often overlooked subset of these patterns is the formal and informal interaction patterns between professionals and the children and families they serve. These patterns and the values sustaining them are important subjects of organizational consultation and organization development. Identification and positive alteration of these patterns tend to occur within six identifiable areas of organizational functioning (Schmuck & Runkel, 1988): (1) clarifying communication, (2) establishing clear goals, (3) uncovering and resolving conflict (see also Brett, Goldberg, & Ury, 1990), (4) improving formal procedures in the day-to-day interactions of the adults managing children's environments, (5) enhancing problem-solving, and (6) connecting decision making to action.

Process consultation is the component of organizational consultation used for attending to these interactional patterns. Sensitivity to organizational nuance, to competing but hidden agendas, and to restrictive but unquestioned procedures is the hallmark of effective process consultation. This sensitivity does not imply an evaluative or punitive posture but rather is used to gather descriptions of prevailing practice that are communicated to the organization's membership so that decisions can be made as to whether those practices will be continued or changed. The organizational consultant's agenda is clear—to facilitate the effective functioning of the organization on its own terms. This agenda reflects the notion of equifinality introduced early in this chapter and inheres in the respect that consultants maintain for the capacity of organizations to recognize their best course of operation.

Consultation's Empirical Ground

"Actualities seem to float in a wider sea of possibilities from out of which they were chosen; and *somewhere*, indeterminism says, such possibilities exist, and form part of the truth" (William James, quoted in Hofstadter & Dennett, 1981, p. 42). The "doing" of psychology has included the activity of seeking to ground its theory and practice in actuality—in the best of possible truths.

The purpose of quoting William James at this point in the discussion is to set a tone of tentativeness before considering the empirical foundations of consultation. As scientist-practitioners, we who consult want to know that our practice is legitimate. The most popularly accepted vehicle for legitimizing psychology in practice is scientific inquiry. Within scientific inquiry, the most commonly (in some cases, exclusively) accepted technique is the experimental method.

This method is a well-practiced and esteemed way of collecting and interpreting data, or, in James's words, "actualities" afloat in a "sea of possibilities." What follows is a brief (and certainly not exhaustive) consideration of the experimental empirical data available on child-centered consultation. Resources providing more thorough descriptions of the empirical bases of consultation practice are available in literature reviews of consultation research (for example, Mannino & Shore, 1979; Medway, 1979; West & Idol, 1987) and meta-analyses that have indicated general support for consultation's effectiveness across models (Medway & Updyke, 1985; Sibley, 1986).

The focus chosen for this section is the relevance of research in consultation. In particular, the seeming idiomatic bias of published consultation research will be considered in relation to the appropriate goal of such research—improvement in children's socioemotional environments. As this research evidence is presented, it seems important to heed the wisdom offered by researchers in the physics of quantum mechanisms. These scientists have found that the theory a researcher brings to the act of experimentation is an unavoidable and primary mediator of all efforts initiated to prove or disprove that theory (Heisenberg, 1971; Schroedinger, 1961/1983). The scientist's beliefs determine, to some extent, what he or she sees. Because theory is most popularly elaborated through the exercise of gathering empirical data, the inherent subjectivity of that data must be acknowledged.

Gresham and Kendell (1987, p. 306) speak to this issue as it is related to research in consultation: "The particular theoretical model within which consultation research is conducted will influence the nature of the independent and dependent variables considered in consultation and the subsequent interpretation of research results." This, of course, throws all consultation research into question. Add to that the considerable concern about the quality of this research (Duncan & Pryzwansky, 1988; Gutkin & Curtis, 1990; Gresham & Kendell, 1987; Pryzwansky, 1986; Witt, 1990b), and the picture of consultation's empirical grounding seems grim. However, texts such as this one and the ongoing effort among researchers to improve the quality and availability of empirical knowledge give reason for hope.

The empirical work considered here represents the best efforts to date at justifying and directing what we are doing in consultation. First, research focusing on consultation's processes and outcomes will be surveyed. On the basis of this survey, the gaps in our knowledge and suggestions for research will be presented. Finally, current controversies in the literature of consultation and the dangers and realities of narrowly focused research activity will be explored.

Process and Outcome Research

Service delivery practices are retained as long as they are effective. The effectiveness of practice is gauged by evaluating outcomes. Although considerable research in consultation has reflected what consultants and consultees do (for example; Alpert & Ludwig, 1979; Bergan & Tombari, 1975; Henning-Stout & Conoley, 1987; Kratochwill, 1985; Martin, 1983; Piersel & Gutkin, 1983; Witt, Moe, Gutkin, & Andrews, 1984) or has focused on whether consultees felt that consultation was successful (for example, Bergan, Byrnes, & Kratochwill, 1979; Gutkin & Hickman, 1988; Gutkin, Singer, & Brown, 1980; Weisenberger, Fine, & Poggio, 1982), few studies have made direct links between consultation practices and changes in children's socioemotional environments and behaviors (Gresham & Kendell, 1987; Gutkin & Curtis, 1990; Pryzwansky, 1986; Witt, 1990a; see also Chapter Eleven).

Research has indicated circumstances that enhance the likelihood that consultees will use consultation services. Hinkle, Silverstein, and Walton (1977) found that consultees tend to sabotage intervention plans when they are expected by an administrator to participate in consultation. This finding underscores the importance of the relationship's voluntary nature. Data collected by Reinking, Livesay, and Kohl (1978) indicate that consultees are most likely to carry out intervention plans when they have been directly involved in plan development—when they have experienced collaboration. Later research (for example, Lind & Tyler, 1988; Pruitt, 1981) supports these findings.

Related evidence indicates that consultees like to be asked rather than told what to do (Bergan & Neumann, 1980) and prefer consultants who are interpersonally accessible (Kinsala, 1984)—who have what Martin (1978) refers to as referent power. Gutkin (1986) surveyed teacher-consultees and found that they give great importance to their involvement in the development of interventions for their students. Curtis and Van Wagener (1988; as cited in Gutkin & Curtis, 1990) found that consultation fails when collaborative problem solving does not occur—even when the teacher's evaluation of the consultation interaction is favorable. Witt and Elliott (1985) present evidence that consultees are most accepting of consultation when it takes little time and results in effective interventions.

These findings can be summarized as indicating that consultees prefer brief, effective, and voluntary interaction with consultants who are personable and collaborative. Joint problem solving, cooperative and voluntary relationships, and an ecological perspective are the core characteristics of consultation reflected in these studies. Empirical studies of the processes involved in consultation help to establish consultation's character. Other research has focused on determining whether consultation works—whether it has empirically demonstrable validity.

Some evidence of consultation's validity is available in outcome studies that show various benefits to consultees. For example, a number of studies have found improvement in consultees' coping and problem-solving skills following consultation (Anderson, Kratochwill, & Bergan, 1986; Cleven & Gutkin, 1988; Curtis & Metz, 1986; Curtis & Watson, 1980; Ritter, 1978). Related to this is the finding of Gutkin et al. (1980) that teachers in schools where consultation was available perceived problems as less serious than did teachers in matched schools without consultation.

In a series of studies into the relationship between verbal interaction patterns and consultation effectiveness, Bergan and his colleagues considered both process and outcome (Bergan & Neumann, 1980; Bergan & Tombari, 1975, 1976; Tombari & Bergan, 1978). These researchers monitored consultation outcomes relative to the amount and quality of information elicited from consultees. Bergan and Tombari's early research (1975, 1976) illustrates the importance of verbal interactions between consultants and consultees for successful problem identification and analysis. Later, Tombari and Bergan (1978) determined that verbal cues used by consultants strongly influence problem descriptions provided by consultees. Bergan and Neumann (1980) found that certain verbalizations by consultants elicit more resourceful problem-solving plans from consultees. These analyses have provided important documentation of the verbal processes most predictive of consultee engagement and successful consultation outcome.

In efforts to monitor systemwide outcomes, several studies have demonstrated the effects of implementing consultation with classroom teachers before referring children for formal testing (Graden, Casey, & Bronstrom, 1985; Gutkin, Henning-Stout, & Piersel, 1988; Ponti, Zins, & Graden, 1988). Each of these studies shows increases in the use of consultation and decreases in the frequency of referral. Allowing for interference, these data can be interpreted to indicate improvements in direct service (that is, happier, more skilled teachers who are seeking help in solving classroom problems instead of referring children for placement in special education). But, stripped of inferential best wishes, we can only see changes in consultee referral practices and cannot be certain that these reflect better instructional practice.

Two recent studies provide examples of introducing consultation services into school systems (Fuchs et al., 1990; Rosenfield, 1992). Fuchs and his colleagues described a model for introducing consultation that focused on teachers' discomfort with what the researchers termed "difficult-to-teach" children (Fuchs et al., 1990, p. 263). In this model, consultants supported prereferral intervention with these children by leading teachers through a sequence of structured meetings, each one aimed at specific objectives for the child's behavior. Consultation centered on the multidisciplinary team and the child.

In another study, Rosenfield (1992) focused on the range of organizational levels that affect and are affected by the introduction of instructional consultation services to a school system. Her study was based on five years of qualitative and quantitative data that revealed three stages of a system's adoption of consultation: initiation, implementation, and institutionalization. A primary finding of this study was the importance of ongoing and systematic evaluation of the consultation program across the three stages.

The programs described by Fuchs et al. (1990) and by Rosenfield (1992) illustrate the use of consultation in larger systems. Rosenfield added detailed attention to issues of organizational development and change. Such organizational issues are the focus of a recent and extensive study conducted by Hoy et al. (1991), which has immediate application for consultants to organizations serving children. These researchers developed and tested a set of diagnostic instruments designed to assess the health and climate of a school system from an organizational perspective. Their findings provide strong support for the psychometric integrity of these instruments. The research on consultation as a part of organization development is immediately relevant to child service organizations and is given more extensive review in Chapter Five of this volume.

The research into the use of organizational consultation in child-centered agencies is indeed valuable. Rosenfield quotes Slavin, Madden, and Karweit (1990, p. 356), who write, "To make a marked difference in the chance that at-risk students will succeed in school and in life, fundamental changes are needed in the basic organization of the elementary school."

Gaps in the Empirical Foundation

In their cross-disciplinary review of consultation literature, West and Idol (1987) emphasized the logical progression from theory to model to research to application. As with most psychology in practice, consultation was in use for some time before general empirical investigation began. The fact that consultation, with and without empirical foundation, has been one of the central activities of many service providers for some time (Gallessich, 1982) demonstrates some level of validity. Practices that have "far outdistanced any theoretical or empirical base" (West & Idol, 1987, p. 404) make social scientists nervous. When practice precedes research, scientific grounding must come from applied empirical investigation—a messy step away from the laboratory construction of "basic" research. However, consultation occurs in the "applied" world and is best understood in that context.

While basic research supports refinements in practice, the more common path to expanding our knowledge base may be a circular one that most often begins with the practice itself. This notion places a different frame on the sequence suggested by West and Idol (1987). Practice outside the control of the laboratory (that is, most practice) emerges from the collected knowledge of the time. Its immediate roots may be unclear. Existing and original theories are brought to bear in attempts to understand practice and why it works. Models are built. Research occurs throughout the cycle for elaborating theory, testing models, and refining practice. So it is with the theory, research, and practice of consultation.

Consultation research seems historically to have been conducted as if existing practices were short-term substitutes for the practice that would be built from research finding and given to service providers, who would, of course, be relieved that the *real* version had finally arrived. This is the problem of linking research and application. Little attention is given by researchers to the widely available wisdom in existing practice. One of the largest gaps in consultation research lies in the narrowness of perspective applied to understanding the process. What is needed is an expansion of the empirical approaches applied for understanding the range and complexity of consultation practice. More will be offered on this issue in the final section of this chapter.

Gaps in our understanding of consultation are caused by the unavailability of research reflecting the complex, multivariate nature of the consultation relationship (Dustin & Blocher, 1984). There are gaps in our understanding of the larger systemic variables influencing the consultation relationship—variables such as school funding, policy changes, administrative support, and community values (Rosenfield, 1992). Our knowledge base is missing application and extension of research in social psychology to our understanding of the ways people interact to solve problems (Conoley & Gutkin, 1986). Evidence of the long-term and/or delayed outcomes of consultation is needed (West & Idol, 1987), as is evidence of the generalization of immediate consultation outcomes.

Across consultation research, investigators must clearly define what consultation means for each study so that research results are accurately assigned to particular approaches rather than erroneously generalized across models (Pryzwansky, 1986). At the same time, the commonalities across models should be sought and articulated. For example, there seems at present to be no unifying theory of communication in consultation (Gutkin & Curtis, 1990; West & Idol, 1987). Research is needed to discern patterns of social and verbal interactions that define consultation as a distinct clinical technique regardless of model. If each model has its own distinct communication patterns, the service delivery approach known as consultation must rest in more amorphous characteristics. At the same time, the utility of an amorphously defined approach as opposed to a tightly scripted one is also an empirical question.

As we move to fill these gaps in the empirical foundation of consultation, we must recognize that what we see is determined by the questions we ask. We need to know more about consultation, *and* we need to value and encourage diverse ways of expanding our knowledge base. Rosenfield (1992) urges the encouragement and publication of more qualitative research in consultation to get at the features of consultation that have historically been overlooked—the features that Idol (1990) describes as consultation's art (see also Chapter Eighteen).

Regardless of the approach taken to understanding what we do when we consult, the task seems clear. We need to know whether consultation is meeting the identified needs of children and the systems serving them. Using a broad range of empirical methods, we can evaluate and modify new and existing practice. If consultation is found to be effective in serving children's needs, then we will want to know what it is that successful consultants do in order to train others to construct consultation relationships in similar ways (Benes, Gutkin, & Kramer, 1990).

Consensus and Controversy in Consultation

Research intended to give empirical foundation to consultation has been accruing for more than twenty years. The past ten years have seen a marked increase in the attention of behaviorally oriented researchers to the consultation process. This activity has brought with it some valuable new insights and stimulated important controversy. Two of the controversial areas of consultation research are described below to demonstrate both the contribution and the potential ideological bias of these recent contributions.

The first illustration comes from the collection of empirical and positional probes that have been made into the mental health consultation approach (for example, Gutkin, 1981; Gresham & Kendell, 1987; Meyers et al., 1979). The general conclusion is that mental health consultation lacks empirical support. The data available in the few studies of this approach were found insufficient to support lack of objectivity as the primary impediment to effective consultee performance. In addition, no empirical support was found for theme interference reduction as a consultation technique.

These findings do not bode well for the mental health orientation. However, the relatively small number of studies available for review or meta-analysis indicates that lack of supportive evidence may not necessarily prove the insufficiency of clinical procedures but rather may demonstrate the complexity of reducing these procedures to discrete variables that can be subjected to experimental manipulation. The existing data can be taken to demonstrate weak empirical support to date but cannot be construed as conclusive evidence of insufficiency in the mental health approach to consultation.

The sharpest critics of the mental health approach tend to align themselves with the behavioral theory of consultation (for example, Gresham & Kendell, 1987). Most of the research published on consultation in the past five years has been based in this perspective. For example, sixteen of twenty-seven research studies from this period cited by Gutkin and Curtis (1990) and, according to Martens (Chapter Four), 75 percent of all research studies on consultation, were grounded in the behavioral paradigm.

Behavioral technology provides empirical support for behaviorally based data collection and intervention planning approaches. This technology lends itself well to work with young children (Achenbach, 1982; Medway, 1979; Medway & Updyke, 1985)—the population of concern in the bulk of consultation research (Alpert & Yammer, 1983). It also provides effective means for collecting outcome data (Kratochwill, Schnapps, & Bissell, 1985; see also Chapter Twelve). This is all good. It means that we have useful information for ways behavioral techniques can be applied in a consultative format. It also means that much of the information we have about consultation is filtered through the theoretical lens of behaviorism.

It is this lens that has more recently been focused on the role of collaboration in the practice of consultation. Over the course of consultation's development, proponents of each of the theoretical perspectives have emphasized collaboration and/or coordinate power status as central to its practice (Caplan,

1970; Reynolds et al., 1984; Schmuck & Runkel, 1988). Research considering this feature of consultation has repeatedly indicated that consultees prefer involvement in relationships that they consider collaborative and coequal (for example; Babcock & Pryzwansky, 1983; Brett, Goldberg, & Ury, 1990; Pryzwansky & White, 1983; Reinking et al., 1978). This evidence has been interpreted as validating collaboration as a central feature of the consultation process. Of late, however, there has been evidence interpreted to the contrary (Fuchs & Fuchs, 1989; Witt, 1990b). As mentioned earlier, the more frequent use of controlling verbalizations (including question asking) by consultants (Erchul, 1987) has been taken to indicate that consultation involves neither collaboration nor coordinate power status.

This seems a matter of definition. According to *Webster's New Ideal Dictionary* (G. C. Merriam Co., 1973), collaboration is, by definition, working together. Coordinate power implies two or more people being of equal rank, position, or class. Given these definitions, none of the findings related to consultant verbalizations (Witt, 1990b) necessarily challenges consultation's collaborative nature or the coordinate power status of its participants. In the consultation studies referred to by Witt, the consultation interactions involved the consultant and consultee working together, and there is no indication that these participants understood themselves to be of unequal rank.

However, in the tradition of operationally describing human behavior, Witt (1990b, p. 208) has defined collaboration as involving "approximately equal control of the topics selected for discussion in consultation." To make the construct measurable, this definition is accepted. However, interpreting the data accruing to Witt's definition of collaboration as evidence that consultation is in fact not collaborative seems to involve a premature inferential leap. There are two problems with this conclusion. One is a general problem in the philosophy and practice of science. The other is the more immediate and practical problem of the license that research conclusions can give for inappropriate practice.

True to the findings of the quantum physicists, all research is ideologically based and, therefore, necessarily imprecise. Ideology becomes restrictive when it ignores this fact. The work of scholars such as Witt (1990a, 1990b) and Erchul (1987) provides us with helpful insights and directions for consultation research and practice so long as we recognize those interpretations as possibilities and not ultimate truth. This caution applies to all consultation research—indeed, to all psychological research. The message for those of us interested in child-centered consultation is that we have much work ahead of us in refining our perception and practice. The gathering of empirical data to aid this work is a dynamic and ongoing process, and the interpretations of these data always represent the best understanding of the possibilities from the perspective of the researcher.

A more immediate problem lies in the suggestion that successful consultation may more accurately be described as involving domination rather than collaboration (Erchul, 1987; Witt, 1990a, 1990b). This suggestion may foster the assumption that consultants are better suited than consultees to determining how to work in a consultee's setting—that consultees just want to be told what to do. If we embrace this assumption, we are undercutting any empowerment that might occur with consultation. We are running the risk of regressing to "consultation" that contrives dependency instead of encouraging agency.

This is certainly not the agenda of any researcher from any perspective. We cannot afford to contrive dependency when the needs of children so far exceed the availability of mental health professionals to respond to them (Conoley & Gutkin, 1986; Miller, 1969). Focusing behavioral research on molecular levels such as the discrete linguistic behaviors in consultation helps us know some things about what we are doing. At the same time, we must not overlook the more complex relational features of consultation. Applying exclusively positivist research techniques to understanding a human behavior that cannot be reduced to discrete parts provides only partial understanding of that behavior. Perhaps at the level of verbalization, consultants dominate conversation. However, without the consultee, there would be no conversation. The consultee remains the direct agent of change and has the most immediate expertise on the setting in which the child functions. That expertise represents power whether the consultee is aware of it or not. As consultees recognize their power, they become more effective at determining when and how to seek assistance as they respond to children's needs.

If our goal in consultation is to improve the socioemotional experiences of children, we must be alert to the effects of our practice on molecular and social levels. We must recognize the resources of other adults in the children's environments. And we must be open to the universe of alternative solutions (Sarason, 1982).

Conclusion

Controversy is the hallmark of a vibrant profession. The controversy within consultation gives us the opportunity to look carefully at our theory and practice and to move forward into increasingly more effective service delivery. The controversies described above make room for the introduction of less familiar ways of making sense of what we do. Most of the questions asked and most of the research published about the practice of consultation have been based in positivist philosophy. These questions conform to the scientific method and, most recently, reflect behavioral notions of human experience and activity. The questions asked determine the answers perceived, and, while behaviorally based research provides useful insights and possible tools for consultation, it can give only a partial view of the activity of consultation.

Consultation may be characterized by consultants taking more directive roles in the dialogue toward problem solving (Erchul, 1987; Henning-Stout & Conoley, 1987), although this role may vary as the consultation process evolves (West & Idol, 1987). Regardless of the dialectical balance, consultation cannot lead to responsive interventions with children if the relationship between the consultant and the consultee fails. Just as the elephant cannot be described on the basis of the perceptions of one blind sage, the consultation relationship cannot be fully understood from a single research perspective. The controversies emerging as different perspectives are shared contribute to dialogue. Formal dialogue about consultation occurs in professional publications and presentations. All perspectives on consultation deserve voice in this conversation. When no single ideology dominates the discussion, controversy may increase. If tolerated and engaged, however, this controversy will lead to clearer understanding and more responsive practice.

The theory and practice of consultation are rich and promising. The opportunities for quantitative *and* qualitative empirical study are vast. Whether we come to consultation with theoretical, practical, or empirical agendas, we must remain alert to the range of possibilities. We must be willing to engage the controversies—to participate in the dialogue. And as we wrestle with the theoretical and empirical issues of consultation, we must never lose sight of the children. No matter the justification, consultation that is not responsive to the best interests of children is unworthy of discussion.

References

Achenbach, T. M. (1982). *Developmental psychopathology* (2nd ed.). New York: Wiley.

Allen, V. L., & Levine, J. M. (1968). Social support, dissent and conformity. *Sociometry, 31,* 138–149.

Alpert, J. L., & Ludwig, L. M. (1979). Selection of consultees in school mental health consultation. *Journal of School Psychology, 17,* 59–66.

Alpert, J. L., & Yammer, M. D. (1983). Research in school consultation: A content analysis of selected journals. *Professional Psychology: Research and Practice, 14,* 604–612.

Anderson, T. K., Kratochwill, T. R., & Bergan, J. R. (1986). Training teachers in behavioral consultation and therapy: An analysis of verbal behaviors. *Journal of School Psychology, 24,* 229–241.

Babcock, N. L., & Pryzwansky, W. B. (1983). Models of consultation: Preference of educational professionals at five stages of service. *Journal of School Psychology, 21,* 359–366.

Bandura, A. (1977). *Social learning theory.* Englewood Cliffs, NJ: Prentice-Hall.

Bandura, A. (1978). The self-system in reciprocal determinism. *American Psychologist, 33,* 344–358.

Beer, M. (1980). *Organizational change and development: A systems view.* Santa Monica, CA: Goodyear.

Benes, K. M., Gutkin, T. B. & Kramer, J. J. (1990, August). *A functional analysis of communication behaviors in a consultation environment.* Paper presented at the annual meeting of the American Psychological Association, Boston.

Bergan, J. R. (1977). *Behavioral consultation.* Columbus, OH: Merrill.

Bergan, J. R., Byrnes, I. M., & Kratochwill, T. R. (1979). Effects of behavioral and medical models of consultation on teacher expectancies and instruction of a hypothetical child. *Journal of School Psychology, 17,* 306–316.

Bergan, J. R., & Kratochwill, T. R. (1990). *Behavioral consultation and therapy.* New York: Plenum Press.

Bergan, J. R., & Neumann, A. J., III. (1980). The identification of resources and constraints influencing plan design in consultation. *Journal of School Psychology, 18,* 317–323.

Bergan, J. R., & Tombari, M. L. (1975). The analysis of verbal interactions occuring during consultation. *Journal of School Psychology, 13,* 209–226.

Bergan, J. R., & Tombari, M. L. (1976). Consultant skill and efficiency and the implementation and outcomes of consultation. *Journal of School Psychology, 14,* 3–14.

Blake, R. R., & Mouton, J. S. (1976). *Consultation.* Reading, MA: Addison-Wesley.

Brett, J. M., Goldberg, S. B., & Ury, W. L. (1990). Designing systems for resolving disputes in organizations. *American Psychologist, 45,* 162–170.

Brown, D., & Schulte, A. C. (1987). A social learning model of consultation. *Professional Psychology: Research and Practice, 18,* 283–287.

Caplan, G. (1970). *The theory and practice of mental health consultation.* New York: Basic Books.

Cleven, C. A., & Gutkin, T. B. (1988). Cognitive modeling of consultation processes: A means for improving consultees' problem definition skills. *Journal of School Psychology, 26,* 379–389.

Connolly, L. M., & Reschly, D. (1990, November). The school psychology crisis of the 1990s. *Communique,* pp. 1, 12.

Conoley, J. C., & Conoley, C. W. (1982). *School consultation: A guide to practice and training.* Elmsford, NY: Pergamon Press.

Conoley, J. C., & Conoley, C. W. (1992). *School consultation: A guide to practice and training* (2nd ed.). New York: Macmillan.

Conoley, J. C., & Gutkin, T. B. (1986). School psychology: A reconceptualization of service delivery realities. In S. N. Elliott & J. C. Witt (Eds.), *The delivery of psychological services in schools: Concepts, processes, and issues* (pp. 393–423). Hillsdale, NJ: Erlbaum.

Curtis, M. J., & Metz, L. W. (1986). System level intervention in a school for handicapped children. *School Psychology Review, 15,* 510–518.

Curtis, M. J., & Van Wagener, E. (1988). *An analysis of failed consultation.* Paper presented at the annual meeting of the National Association of School Psychologists. Chicago.

Curtis, M. J., & Watson, K. (1980). Changes in consultee problem clarification skills following consultation. *Journal of School Psychology, 26,* 185–190.

Duncan, C. F., & Pryzwansky, W. B. (1988). Consultation research: Trends in doctoral dissertations 1978–1985. *Journal of School Psychology, 26,* 107–119.

Dustin, D., & Blocher, D. H. (1984). Theories and models of consultation. In S. D. Brown & R. W. Lent (Eds.), *Handbook of counseling psychology* (pp. 751–781). New York: Wiley.

Erchul, W. P. (1987). A relational communication analysis of control in school consultation. *Professional School Psychology, 2,* 113–124.

Erchul, W. P., & Chewning, T. G. (1990). Behavioral consultation from a request-centered relational communication perspective. *School Psychology Quarterly, 5,* 1–20.

Fuchs, D., & Fuchs, L. S. (1989). Exploring effective and efficient prereferral interventions: A component analysis of behavioral consultation. *School Psychology Review, 18,* 260–283.

Fuchs, D., Fuchs, L., Gilman, S., Reeder, P., Bahr, M., Fernstrom, P., & Roberts, H. (1990). Prereferral intervention through teacher consultation: Mainstream asssistance teams. *Academic Therapy, 25,* 263–276.

G. & C. Merriam Company. (1973). *Webster's new ideal dictionary.* Springfield, MA: Author.

Gallessich, J. (1982). *The profession and practice of consultation: A handbook for consultants, trainers of consultants, and consumers of consultation services.* San Francisco: Jossey-Bass.

Gartner, A., & Lipsky, D. K. (1987). Beyond special education: Toward a quality system for all students. *Harvard Educational Review, 57,* 315–323.

Gelfand, D. M., & Hartmann, D. P. (1984). *Child behavior analysis and therapy.* Elmsford, NY: Pregamon Press.

Goodstein, L. D. (1978). *Consulting with human service systems.* Reading, MA: Addison-Wesley.

Goodwin, D. L., & Coates, T. J. (1976). *Helping students help themselves.* Engle-wood Cliffs, NJ: Prentice-Hall.

Graden, J. L., Casey, A., & Bronstrom, O. (1985). Implementing a prereferral intervention system: Part II. The data. *Exceptional Children, 51,* 487–496.

Gresham, F. M., & Kendell, G. K. (1987). School consultation research: Method-ological critique and future research directions. *School Psychology Review, 16,* 306–316.

Guba, E. G., & Lincoln, Y. S. (1989). *Fourth generation evaluation.* Newbury Park, CA: Sage.

Gutkin, T. B. (1981). Relative frequency of consultee lack of knowledge, skill, confidence, and objectivity in school settings. *Journal of School Psychology, 19,* 637–642.

Gutkin, T. B. (1986). Consultees' perceptions of variables relating to the out-comes of school-based consultation interactions. *School Psychology Review, 15,* 375–382.

Gutkin, T. B., & Curtis, M. J. (1981). School-based consultation: The indirect service delivery concept. In M. J. Curtis & J. E. Zins (Eds.), *The theory and practice of school consultation* (pp. 219–226). Springfield, IL: Thomas.

Gutkin, T. B., & Curtis, M. J. (1982). School-based consultation: Theory and techniques. In C. R. Reynolds & T. B. Gutkin (Eds.), *The handbook of school psychology* (pp. 796–828). New York: Wiley.

Gutkin, T. B., & Curtis, M. J. (1990). School-based consultation: Theory, tech-niques, and research. In T. B. Gutkin & C. R. Reynolds (Eds.), *The handbook of school psychology* (2nd ed., pp. 577–611). New York: Wiley.

Gutkin, T. B., Henning-Stout, M., & Piersel, W. C. (1988). Impact of a district-wide behavioral consultation prereferral intervention service on patterns of school psychological service delivery. *Professional School Psychology, 3,* 301–308.

Gutkin, T. B., & Hickman, J. A. (1988). Teachers' perceptions of control over presenting problems and resulting preferences for consultation versus re-ferral services. *Journal of School Psychology, 26,* 395–398.

Gutkin, T. B., Singer, J. H., & Brown, R. (1980). Teacher reactions to school-based consultation services: A multivariate analysis. *Journal of School Psy-chology, 18,* 126–134.

Heisenberg, W. (1971). *Physics and beyond: Encounters and conversations* (A. J. Pomerans, Trans.). New York: HarperCollins.

Henning-Stout, M., & Conoley, J. C. (1987). Consultation and counseling as procedurally divergent: Analysis of verbal behavior. *Professional Psychol-ogy: Research and Practice, 18,* 124–127.

Henning-Stout, M., & Conoley, J. C. (1988). Influencing program change at the district level. In J. L. Graden, J. E. Zins, & M. J. Curtis (Eds.), *Alternative educational delivery systems: Enhancing instructional options for all students* (pp. 471–490). Silver Spring, MD: National Association of School Psychologists.

Hinkle, A., Silverstein, B., & Walton, D. M. (1977). A method for evaluation of mental health consultation to the public schools. *Journal of Community Psychology, 5,* 262–265.

Hofstadter, D. R., & Dennett, D. C. (1981). *The mind's I: Fantasies and reflections on self and soul.* New York: Bantam Books.

Hoy, W. K., Tarter, C. J., & Kottkamp, R. B. (1991). *Open schools/healthy schools: Measuring organizational climate.* Newbury Park, CA: Sage.

Idol, L. (1990). The scientific art of classroom consultation. *Journal of Educational and Psychological Consultation, 1,* 3–22.

Keller, H. R. (1981). Behavioral consultation. In J. C. Conoley (Ed.), *Consultation in schools: Theory, research, procedures* (pp. 59–99). San Diego, CA: Academic Press.

Kinsala, M. G. (1984). *A utilization of expert and referent power framework.* Unpublished doctoral dissertation, Texas Woman's University, Denton.

Kratochwill, T. R. (1985). Selection of target behaviors in behavioral consultation. *Behavioral Assessment, 7,* 49–61.

Kratochwill, T. R., Schnapps, A., & Bissell, M. S. (1985). Research design in school psychology. In J. R. Bergan (Ed.), *School psychology in contemporary society: An introduction.* Columbus, OH: Merrill.

Lind, E. A., & Tyler, T. R. (1988). *The social psychology of procedural justice.* New York: Plenum Press.

Lippitt, G. L., Langseth, P., & Mossop, J. (1985). *Implementing organizational change: A practical guide to managing change efforts.* San Franscisco: Jossey-Bass.

Maher, C. A., Illback, R. J., & Zins, J. E. (1984). Applying organizational psychology in the schools: Perspectives and framework. In C. A. Maher, R. J. Illback, & J. E. Zins (Eds.), *Organizational psychology in the schools: A handbook for professionals* (pp. 5–20). Springfield, IL: Thomas.

Mannino, F. V., & Shore, M. F. (1979). Evaluation of consultation: Problems and prospects. In A. A. Rogawski (Ed.), *Mental health consultation in community settings* (pp. 99–114). San Francisco: Jossey-Bass.

Mannino, F. V., & Shore, M. F. (1986). History and development of mental health consultation. In F. V. Mannino, E. J. Trickett, M. F. Shore, M. G. Kidder, & G. Levin (Eds.), *Handbook of mental health consultation* (DHHS Publication No. ADM86-1446, pp. 3–28). Washington, DC: U.S. Goverment Printing Office.

Martens, B. K., & Witt, J. C. (1988). Expanding the scope of behavioral consultation: A systems approach to classroom behavior change. *Professional School Psychology, 3,* 271–281.

Martin, G., & Pear, J. (1988). *Behavior modification: What it is and how to do it* (3rd ed.). Englewood Cliffs, NJ: Prentice-Hall.

Martin, R. P. (1978). Expert and referent power: A framework for understanding and maximizing consultation effectiveness. *Journal of School Psychology, 16,* 49–55.

Martin, R. P. (1983). Consultant, consultee, and client expectations of each other's behavior in consultation. *Psychology in the Schools, 12,* 670–676.

Masters, J. C., Burish, T. G., Hollon, S. D., & Rimm, D. C. (1987). *Behavior therapy: Techniques and empirical findings* (3rd ed.). Orlando, FL: Harcourt Brace Jovanovich.

Medway, F. J. (1979). How effective is school-based consultation? A review of recent research. *Journal of School Psychology, 17,* 275–282.

Medway, F. J., & Updyke, J. F. (1985). Meta-analysis of consultation outcome studies. *American Journal of Community Psychology, 13,* 489–505.

Meyers, J. (1973). A consultation model for school psychological services. *Journal of School Psychology, 11,* 5–15.

Meyers, J. (1981). Mental health consultation. In J. C. Conoley (Ed.), *Consultation in schools: Theory, research, procedures* (pp. 35–58). San Diego, CA: Academic Press.

Meyers, J., Friedman, M. P., & Gaughan, E. J., Jr. (1975). The effects of consultee-centered consultation on teacher behavior. *Psychology in the Schools, 12,* 288–295.

Meyers, J., Gaughan, E., & Pitt, N. (1990). Contributions of community psychology to school psychology. In T. B. Gutkin & C. R. Reynolds (Eds.), *Handbook of school psychology* (2nd ed., pp. 198–217). New York: Wiley.

Meyers, J., Parsons, R. D., & Martin, R. P. (1979). *Mental health consultation in schools: A comprehensive guide for psychologists, social workers, psychiatrists, counselors, educators, and other human service professionals.* San Francisco: Jossey-Bass.

Miller, G. A. (1969). Psychology as a means of promoting human welfare. *American Psychologist, 24,* 1063–1075.

National Association of School Psychologists. (1985). *Advocacy for appropriate education services for all children.* Silver Spring, MD: Author.

Piersel, W. C., & Gutkin, T. B. (1983). Resistance to school-based consultation: A behavioral analysis of the problem. *Psychology in the Schools, 20,* 311–320.

Ponti, C. R., Zins, J. E., & Graden, J. L. (1988). Implementing a consultation-based service delivery system to decrease referrals for special education: A case study of organizational considerations. *School Psychology Review, 17,* 89–100.

Pruitt, D. G. (1981). *Negotiation behavior.* San Diego, CA: Academic Press.

Pryzwansky, W. B. (1986). Indirect service delivery: Considerations for future research in consultation. *School Psychology Review, 15,* 479–488.

Pryzwansky, W. B., & White, G. W. (1983). The influence of consultee characteristics on preferences for consultation approaches. *Professional Psychology: Research and Practice, 14,* 457–461.

Reinking, R. J., Livesay, G., & Kohl, M. (1978). The effects of consultation style on consultee productivity. *American Journal of Community Psychology, 6,* 283–290.

Reynolds, C. R., Gutkin, T. B., Elliott, S. N., & Witt, J. C. (1984). *School psychology: Essentials of theory and practice.* New York: Wiley.

Ritter, D. R. (1978). Effects of a school consultation program upon referral patterns of teachers. *Psychology in the Schools, 15,* 239–243.

Rosenfield, S. (1992). Developing school-based consultation teams: A design for change. *School Psychology Quarterly, 7,* 27–46.

Sarason, S. B. (1982). *The culture of the school and the problem of change* (2nd ed.). Needham Heights, MA: Allyn & Bacon.

Schein, E. H. (1969). *Process consultation: Its role in organization development.* Reading, MA: Addison-Wesley.

Schein, E. H. (1990). Organizational culture. *American Psychologist, 45,* 109–119.

Schmuck, R. A. (1990). Organization development in schools: Contemporary concepts and practices. In T. B. Gutkin and C. R. Reynolds (Eds.), *Handbook of school psychology* (2nd ed., pp. 899–919). New York: Wiley.

Schmuck, R. A., & Runkel, P. J. (1988). *The handbook of organization development in schools* (3rd ed.). Prospect Heights, IL: Waveland Press.

Schrödinger, E. (1983). *My view of the world* (C. Hastings, Trans.). Woodbridge, CT: Ox Bow Press. (Original work published 1961)

Sibley, S. (1986). *A meta-analysis of school consultation research.* Unpublished doctoral dissertation, Texas Women's University, Denton.

Skinner, B. F. (1953). *Science and human behavior.* New York: Macmillan.

Slavin, R. E., Madden, N. A., & Karweit, N. L. (1990). Effective programs for students at risk: Conclusions for practice and policy. In R. E. Slavin, N. L. Karweit, & N. A. Madden (Eds.), *Effective programs for students at risk* (pp. 355–372). Needham Heights, MA: Allyn & Bacon.

Tolman, E. C. (1932). *Purposive behavior in animals and men.* East Norwalk, CT: Appleton & Lange.

Tombari, M. L., & Bergan, J. R. (1978). Consultant cues and teacher verbalization, judgments, and expectancies concerning children's adjustment problems. *Journal of School Psychology, 16,* 212–219.

Tyler, F. B., Pargament, K. I., & Gatz, M. (1983). The resource collaborator role:

A model for interactions involving psychologists. *American Psychologist, 38,* 388–398.

von Bertalanffy, L. (1968). *General systems theory.* New York: Braziller.

Weissenberger, J. W., Fine, J. J., & Poggio, J. P. (1982). The relationship of selected consultant/teacher characteristics to consultation outcomes. *Journal of School Psychology, 20,* 263–270.

West, J. F., & Idol, L. (1987). School consultation (part I): An interdisciplinary perspective on theory, models, and research. *Journal of Learning Disabilities, 20,* 388–408.

Wielkiewicz, R. M. (1986). *Behavior management in the schools.* New York: Pergamon Press.

Will, M. C. (1986). Educating children with learning problems: A shared responsibility. *Exceptional Children, 52,* 411–416.

Witt, J. C. (1990a). Complaining, precopernican thought, and the univariate linear mind: Questions for school-based behavioral consultation research. *School Psychology Review, 19,* 367–377.

Witt, J. C. (1990b). Face-to-face verbal interaction in school-based consultation: A review of the literature. *School Psychology Quarterly, 5,* 199–210.

Witt, J. C., & Elliott, S. N. (1985). Acceptability of classroom intervention strategies. In T. R. Kratochwill (Ed.), *Advances in school psychology* (Vol. 4, pp. 251–288). Hillsdale, NJ: Erlbaum.

Witt, J. C., & Martens, B. K. (1988). Problems with problem-solving consultation: A re-analysis of assumptions, methods and goals. *School Psychology Review, 17,* 211–226.

Witt, J. C., Moe, G., Gutkin, T. B., & Andrews, L. (1984). The effect of saying the same thing in different ways: The problem of language and jargon in school-based consultation. *Journal of School Psychology, 22,* 361–367.

3

Defining
Human Service Consultation

Duane Brown

The purpose of this chapter is to examine some of the issues involved in defining consultation and ultimately to propose a broad definition of what will be termed human service consultation. I begin by examining the colloquial definition of consultation. I then illustrate some of the issues that have developed regarding the definition of consultation and show some of the sources of these issues. A tentative definition of human service consultation is then presented. Finally, I identify some of the unresolved questions about defining consultation and suggest directions for future research.

As has often been observed, there is considerable confusion about the "true' definition of consultation (Gallessich, 1982; Mannino & Shore, 1986b; see also Chapter One). For the most part, these definitional problems are related to questions such as, What should be the focus of consultation? What should be the nature of the consulting relationship? What is the process of consultation? What is the relationship of roles filled by the consultant to the contractual agreements between the consultant and the consultee? Should consultation have an individual or a systemic perspective? These and other questions are addressed in this discussion. However, I do offer one caveat before I begin: there is no true definition of consultation. Definitions of consultation grow out of theoretical perspectives of human functioning that have varying degrees of explanatory power. They are also influenced (or should be) by empirical findings. Since we do not have a perfect theory of human functioning from which we can draw a definition of consultation, and we have yet to devise a perfect study from which we can derive specific conclusions, definitions will be to a great degree subjective.

One of the problems inherent in defining consultation is that it has been defined for common usage as "a conference at which advice is given or views are exchanged" (*American Heritage Dictionary,* 1987, p. 378). This definition reflects some of the confusion surrounding consultation: there may be a considerable difference between a conference where views are exchanged and one where advice is given. Of course, consultation might involve both an exchange of ideas and giving of advice. The point here is that while colloquial definitions of consultation provide some general guidelines to understanding what consultation is, they are not definitive enough to allow us to use them as a guide to action in our work as human service consultants.

Unfortunately, the word *consultation* has been used by a variety of professionals to mean everything from training to providing technical advice, which has also perpetrated confusion about the meaning of the process. Recently, a colleague said to me, "I'm consulting with X school district today." When asked what he intended to do during the consultation, he replied, "Train teachers to use a learning styles inventory to individualize instruction." Further conversation with him revealed that he had been hired as a trainer and had not been involved at any point in the decision-making process that led to the conclusion that a trainer was needed. Although training can be used as an intervention by consultants to help them learn new skills, training and consultation are not synonymous, as I have repeatedly observed (for example, Brown, Pryzwansky, & Schulte, 1991). In fact, just as our dictionary definition suggests, most people are focusing on the process of getting or giving technical advice when they use the term *consultation.* This common usage connotes that consultation is a hierarchical process in which one person (the consultant) clearly possesses expertise needed by a less knowledgeable person (the consultee). People regularly engage in dyadic consultations with their accountants, lawyers, physicians, and a whole host of other experts. Human service consultation typically departs from this dyadic definition.

Human Service Consultation: Some of the Questions

Consultation had its beginning at the turn of the century, when Lightner Witmer practiced what Mannino and Shore (1986a, p. 3) term "diagnostic teaching and diagnostic education" with teachers who followed up by providing mental health services to children. Some form of "consultation" was probably practiced by many mental health professionals from that point on. However, in the 1940s, psychodynamically trained psychiatrists began to realize that consultation could increase their efficiency, and they began to see patients of other physicians to evaluate their mental health status. As Kurpius and Robinson (1978) point out, this client-centered consultation was essentially a direct service even though one physician acted as the consultee, because the consultant made direct contact with the patient (client) and developed a prescription for treatment that the consultee implemented. Consultee-centered consultation that incorporated the consultee into the problem-solving process also began in the 1940s (James, Kidder, Osberg, & Hunter, 1986) when J. V. Coleman (1946) assisted caseworkers in developing strategies to help their most troubled clients. Caplan's seminal work (1970) *The Theory and Practice of Mental Health Consultation* combined the doctor-patient, client-centered case approach with the consultee-centered case approach. To these individually oriented approaches, Caplan added program-centered administrative consultation, which, like its counterpart client-centered case consultation, is an expert model of consultation, and consultee-centered administrative consultation, in which the administrator is included in the problem-solving process.

   Caplan (1970, p. 19) defined consultation as "a process of interaction between two professionals—the consultant, who is a specialist, and the consultee, who invokes the consultant's help in regard to a current work problem with which he is having some difficulty and which he has decided is within the other's area of specialized competence. The work problem involves the management or treatment of one or more clients of the consultee, or the planning or implementation of a program to cater to such clients." Caplan went on to suggest that the relationship between the consultee and the consultant should be nonhierarchical, since the consultee and the consultant are assumed to be experts in their own right. However, expertise was not Caplan's only reason for suggesting a nonhierarchical relationship with the consultee.

   Caplan's rationale for positing that the consultation relationship should be nonhierarchical grew out of his psychodynamic perspective (James et al., 1986). He believes that most problems encountered by consultees are caused by the projection and/or displacement of their psychological problems onto the client, which results in stereotyping the client and increasing anxiety for the consultee. As a result of the dynamics resulting from the disequilibrium caused by the client's problem, the consultee gets "stuck" and seeks help from the consultant. The consultant's job is to support the consultee while avoiding direct discussion of the unresolved conflict. The consultant does focus on the result of the disequilibrium—the consultee's misperceptions of the client. One assumption of the mental health consultant is that both the client's mental health and the consultee's ability to deal with mental health problems will be improved. The client's mental health will be enhanced as a result of improved interaction with the consultee, and the consultee's mental health will improve because of the "vicarious benefits from the client's success" (James et al., 1986). Caplan (1970) sets forth four techniques aimed at reducing theme interference. These techniques are designed to manipulate the consulting relationship in

a manner that will be nonthreatening to the consultee but will produce consultee insight into the nature of his or her problem with the consultant.

Gallessich (1982) correctly notes that the majority of mental health
workers have rejected Caplan's notion that theme interference is the basis of
most problems encountered by consultees. For example, Parsons and Meyers
(1984) derived a model of consultation from Caplan's work that focuses on
the importance of coordinate relations between the consultant and consultee,
but for the purpose of empowering the consultee rather than dealing with
his or her unresolved conflicts. This is not to suggest that everyone has rejected
Caplan's ideas: they are still widely practiced, although the trend is toward
integrating mental health consultation with other perspectives (James et al.,
1986).

Caplan and other psychodynamically trained mental health consultants
advanced our thinking about consultation by suggesting that it is primarily
triadic and that it should involve a relationship that is egalitarian. Caplan also
imposed two conditions on this process: that consultation takes place between
professionals and that it involves work-related concerns. By imposing these
conditions, Caplan specified to some degree who consultants and consultees
are and the content of consultation. In the early 1970s, Dinkmeyer and Carlson
(1973) set forth an approach to consulting with parents that indirectly took
issue with Caplan's conditions. In 1978, Lippitt and Lippitt also suggested that
consultation might occur with people other than professionals, a position that
is widely embraced today (Brown et al., 1991).

Lippitt and Lippitt (1978, 1986) contributed to an expansion of the definition of the term *consultation.* They also added to the current confusion about
the "true" meaning of consultation to some degree. They did this by setting
forth a variety of roles that consultants might fill but failing to discuss the
relationship of these roles to the process of consultation, the consulting
contract, or the consultant's relationship to the consultee. Lippitt and Lippitt
(1986) identify the following consultant roles: objective observer, process
counselor, fact finder, alternative resource identifier and linker, joint problem
solver, trainer-educator, information specialist, and advocate. Unfortunately,
some naive consultants have taken the Lippitts' roles literally and assumed that
the roles themselves are synonymous with consultation. For example, it is
possible for a mental health worker to be an advocate for handicapped children or an assessment information specialist and still not be functioning as a
consultant. Similarly, a professional can be hired to train mental health workers
to perform various tasks (for example, assessing learning disabilities) and still
not be a consultant. Training and consultation are not synonymous (Brown et
al., 1991), and while a consultant may engage in a certain amount of advocacy,
advocates are not necessarily consultants either. As Caplan (1970) indicated,

and as has been reiterated many times, one becomes a consultant as a result of an agreement between the consultant and a consultee. The roles to be filled are specified implicitly or explicitly in that agreement and not determined independently by the consultant. Caplan's early definition of consultation (1970) also specified that the consultant must be from outside the organization, a position that has all but been rejected at this point (Dougherty, 1990; Lippitt & Lippitt, 1986), although there is general agreement that being internal to the organization and being external to it both have advantages and disadvantages (Brown et al., 1991).

The matter of power as a dimension of the consulting relationship is implicit in much of the foregoing discussion. Caplan's suggestion (1970) that the consulting relationship be nonhierarchical implies that the power should be equalized. However, some of the roles identified by Lippitt and Lippitt (1986) indicate that the consultant may actually assume a number of power positions (for example, advocate). Bergan and Kratochwill (1990) clearly suggest that the consultant should dominate the consulting relationship through the manipulation of the consultation conversation. Parsons and Meyers (1984), in agreement with Caplan, emphasize the necessity of maintaining an egalitarian relationship and identify techniques by which power can be equalized. Perhaps more importantly, Parsons and Meyers recognize that there are varying dimensions of power operating within the consulting relationship, including reward power, coercive power, legitimate power, expert power, referent power, and informational power. Three of the sources of power—expert, referent, and informational—are viewed as appropriate for the collaborative relationship that Parsons and Meyers believe is essential to the consulting enterprise.

Another aspect of the definition of consultation, to some degree related to the power issues, that has received varying amounts of attention is the relationship between the consultant and the consultee. For example, neither Bergan (1977) nor Kratochwill and Bergan (1990) directly discuss the nature of the consultant-consultee relationship per se but obviously place the consultee in a one-down relationship. Kratochwill and VanSomeren (1985) do discuss the relationship variable in consultation but draw no conclusions about its importance to process or outcome. Randolph (1985), who espouses a cooperative, nonhierarchical approach to consultation, sets forth a series of consultation interview strategies that will establish and maintain this type of relationship. Brown et al. (1991), who advocate a collaborative approach to consultation, also set forth a set of conversational procedures to establish this type of relationship. Few consultants would deny the importance of a relationship based on trust and open communication, and, in fact, this type of relationship seems necessary for the success of consultation (Horton & Brown, 1990).

Should a definition of consultation ignore the relationship variables as Bergan (1977) does? Should consultation be designed to control the consulting conversation, and, if so, should that be embedded in the definition? Gallessich (1982) believes that it is inappropriate to manipulate the verbal interchange with the consultee and thus is at odds with Bergan (1977).

The process of consultation has also been a point of some disagreement. Caplan (1970) believes that the consultant's chore is complete once the problem has been identified and interventions designed. Others (for example, Dougherty, 1990; Parsons & Meyers, 1984) clearly disagree and suggest that the consultant should assist in the implementation of the intervention and the evaluation of its impact. Many current definitions identify a number of stages in the consulting process, ranging from making an initial contact (Lippitt & Lippitt, 1986) to evaluation (Brown et al., 1991). Some focus on establishing a helping relationship (Randolph, 1985), while others ignore this process (Bergan, 1977). Most consultants agree that consultation is a problem-solving process, although Schein (1987) puts more emphasis on establishing conditions that enable consultees to identify their own problems than do others (for example, Bergan, 1977), who have the consultant actively involved in the problem-identification process. A few (for example, Lippitt & Lippitt, 1986) suggest that the consulting process is probably characterized by a great deal of variety and thus are less concerned with this issue.

Consultation and Systems Variables

As noted at the outset, definitions of consultation are derived from theoretical beliefs. Most definitions of human service consultation are not derived from an open systems perspective. Rather, they are typically drawn from distinct psychological perspectives, such as operant psychology (Bergan, 1977) or Adlerian psychology (Dinkmeyer & Carlson, 1973). However, Brown, Kurpius, and Morris (1988, p. 6), assert that "consultation occurs within a system context and that [this context] must be considered at each step in the process." This position reflects that of Kurpius (1985), Beer (1980), Illback and Zins (Chapter Five of this volume), and others. Kurpius comments on the importance of consultees recognizing the interrelationships between the problems encountered and systemic variables. "It is important for the consultant to help consultees recognize the level of interdependence that exists between the problem definition and proposed interventions. However, it is even more important to help consultees recognize that the problem intervention scenario exists in an even larger, and sometimes more powerful system of influence" (Kurpius, 1985, p. 369).

The question that must be posed here is "Can consultants (and consultees) continue to ignore the interrelationships in classrooms, schools, school districts, and communities?" Or, more specifically, "Should consultants ignore the obvious relationships among faculty norms, administors' expectations, and students' functioning in the classroom?" A few consultants have addressed this area. Lippitt and Lippitt (1986) identify eleven different client systems, such as religious systems and health systems, but do not carefully follow systems principles in their recommendations for consulting. Parsons and Meyers (1984) take a more systemic approach in that they recognize the need to assess the relationship of the individual to the organization and to plan interventions with the interaction in mind. It is also the case that organizational consultants such as Morasky (1982) and Beer (1980) have been more aware of the need to consider the interdependence of groups and how organizations relate to their environment and to identify person-environment interactions than have behavioral consultants such as Bergan (1977), who have focused more on individuals than on the systems in which they operate. However, Bergan has identified what he terms a background-environment category of data that may be influencing the current functioning of the client, which seems to indicate that he recognizes the importance of systems variables. Brown and Schulte (1987, p. 283), have posited that "consultant, consultee, and client functioning are the result of the interaction of behavior, internal personal variables (intra-psychic variables) and environmental variables," and it is probably this position that most closely approximates that held by most consultants. Its implication is that consultants must attend to systems variables in the assessment of the consultee as well as of the client.

While several issues regarding a definition of consultation are unresolved, a few have been settled. Most consultants accept the idea that consultants can be from either within or outside the organization. Similarly, there is little disagreement about the concepts that consulting can take place between professionals as well as nonprofessionals and that it does not have to focus on work-related issues unless *work* is interpreted in the broadest possible way. For example, the consultant to families deals with the "work" of the family. There is also general agreement that human service consultation is typically a triadic process. And most authorities seem to agree that consultation should be defined in various ways depending on the circumstances under which it occurs, although only Caplan (1970), Bergan (1977), and Kratochwill and Bergan (1990) have discussed this matter. Finally, there is an often unspoken agreement that consultation is a process governed by the ethics of the consultant (Brown et al., 1991, have discussed this matter in some detail). The next section of this chapter discusses the dimensions of consultation and implications for generating a definition of consultation.

Consulting Processes

Consultation is a problem-solving process (Pryzwansky, 1989) characterized by a series of complex human interactions. The nature of these interactions is still a matter of conjecture, but presumably, if they are to solve the consultee's problem, the consultant and the consultee must communicate, agree on the nature of the problem, and arrive at a strategy for its resolution. As has been suggested, at least some, if not all, consultants expect that a secondary benefit of consultation will be an improvement in the consultee's ability to deal with similar problems in the future. In this section, some of the subprocesses that occur in consultation are discussed, because how one characterizes these processes should be reflected in the definition adopted.

Communication

Consultation, like other helping processes, relies on accurate communication. We are aware that a variety of circumstances, including consultee motivation, psychological problems, language deficiencies, and a host of other variables, will influence the communication in consultation. However, as has already been noted, much of the discussion about communication in consultation has centered around the issue of controlling the communication of the consultee (for example, Bergan, 1977, versus Gallessich, 1982). This and other key issues regarding communication are taken up in this section.

   Controlling Communication. No one denies that open communication is essential to consultation. However, the nature of the communication process and particularly who should control it are at issue. One side of this debate suggests that the consultant should control the communication flow by asking strategic questions and responding in prescribed ways and that, if this is done, the consultee will cooperate by responding appropriately. The other side suggests that when the consultant provides the requested information and the consultee accepts assigned tasks, the flow of communication is determined more collaboratively and thus is under mutual control of the consultant and consultee. Clearly, Bergan (1977) and Kratochwill and Bergan (1990) favor the consultant controlling the flow of communication, while Pryzwansky (1974), Parsons and Meyers (1984), and Brown and Schulte (1987) favor the more collaborative approach to communication. To a certain extent, this issue is a philosophical one and cannot be resolved empirically. However, the research on the matter of control is interesting in this respect because it does address this issue.

   In two studies of the control issue in behavioral consultation, Erchul (1987) and Erchul and Chewning (1990) looked at whether the consultant or the consultee dominated the consulting relationship and at the relationship between control and consultee satisfaction with consultation. Erchul concluded that consultant dominance was positively related to consultee satisfaction, but, interestingly, this conclusion could be reached only when he revised what appears to be his original alpha level of .05 to .08, which I consider inappropriate research strategy. He also failed to find a significant relationship between domineeringness scores and consultees' ratings of satisfaction.

The Erchul and Chewning (1990) investigation was a follow-up of Erchul's study aimed at determining the link between consultee satisfaction and consultant domination in the consulting process. The authors concluded that "the first hypothesis that consultees who engaged in behavioral consultation would be characterized as passive, accepting, and cooperative" (p. 14) was supported because consultant-initiated bids were accepted six times more often than those initiated by consultees. What was not explained was why consultees made significantly more evasive responses than did consultants, which could reasonably be interpreted as resistance to the consultant. Erchul and Chewning also suggest that consultee requests in the first interview have a negative impact on the outcome of consultation as measured by consultee satisfaction. This conclusion is puzzling when one considers that it is based on a set of correlational analyses that are extremely weak to start with and of which only two were statistically significant. It is an unfortunate fact that because of the nature of the dependent variable (satisfaction versus compliance or successful intervention), some of the analyses (correlational), and the interpretation of the results (changing alpha levels, ignoring certain key results, such as significantly higher numbers of avoidance responses, and interpreting nonsignificant correlations as suggesting a trend), none of the conclusions reached by the researchers is warranted. It is also worth noting that the rather simplistic coding strategies used in the Erchul (1987) and Erchul and Chewning (1990) studies cannot do justice to the consulting relationship. It may well be that we can better understand the nature of the consultation process by conducting qualitative studies (Pryzwansky & Noblit, 1990). It may also be that whether the consultant should control the consulting interview is more a function of the characteristics of the consultee than of any other variable.

It is naive of theorists and researchers to assume that all consultees will respond uniformly and that there is no need to vary approaches to consultation according to individual differences such as personality or ethnicity. Babcock and Pryzwansky (1983) and White and Pryzwansky (1983) report that teachers prefer collaborative consultations to behavioral, expert, or mental health approaches. However, not all teachers prefer collaborative approaches. The more interesting question is not which type of consultation is preferred by the most consultees but what types of consultation are preferred by various types of consultees. This question has been explored to some degree (see Brown et al., 1991), but not to the extent or with the degree of sophistication needed to answer it.

Culture and Communication. Cross-cultural issues in consultation have not been addressed in any detail by any of the various advocates of consultation (Brown et al., 1991). This is curious when one considers the growing numbers of Hispanic and Asian Pacific Americans and the already large numbers of Native Americans and African Americans. For the consultee who has recently arrived in the United States, the technical language of the consultant may pose a major barrier to the consulting process. The consultant who is of a different race than the consultee may encounter distrust because of the historical record of discrimination in our society. Cultural values may also impinge on the communication process. For example, the Hispanic mother who has been raised to accept "hembrismo," or female subservience, may be reluctant to voice opinions to a male consultant. It would be culturally insensitive to presume that a single approach to the consultation conversation will suffice. However, we will have to wait for researchers to develop precise approaches to cross-cultural consultations. In the meantime, we are ethically bound to tailor our approaches to our consultees.

Summary. It should be concluded that communication at all stages of consultation must be characterized by accuracy. However, most consultants recognize that distortions in communication occur because of resistance and incomplete information. To minimize defensiveness, some consultants have suggested the use of communications models developed primarily to facilitate counseling and/or therapy. Given the apparent importance of the relationship to perceptions of the consultant, and perhaps to outcomes, this seems to be acceptable at this point with the caveat that consultees are not clients and are not to receive therapy. Randolph's (1985) supportive refocus technique, in which he recognizes the psychological problem ("I can tell this is very painful to you") and thus returns to what Caplan (1970) saw as the safe ground of the client ("and I'm wondering how this is affecting the client"), seems advisable.

Problem Solving

Much of the discussion about communication is also applicable here. It is certainly the case that accurate data collection about the nature of the client is essential to the consultation process and that if the potential of consultees to develop and generate an intervention is to be assessed, they must be willing to disclose information about their behavior and attitudes. However, different consultants conceptualize the problem-solving process differently, and these differences will be the focus of this section.

Nature of Problem Solving. The nature of the problem-solving process depends on the theoretical orientation of the consultant and the willingness of the consultee to accept that orientation. Caplan (1970) assumes that most problems encountered by consultees are the result of their own unresolved psychological problems and structures consultation to accommodate that assumption: the consultant engages in specific techniques designed to resolve the theme interference that has developed. Similarly, Bergan (1977) developed an approach to consultation that includes a set of interview strategies to elicit information that can be used in the design of behavior modification strategies, and the techniques he suggests for preparing the consultee to implement and evaluate the implementation are taken from operant conditioning. Brown and Schulte (1987) drew on Bandura's social learning model (Bandura, 1977, 1982) for their approach to consultation and posited the need to give careful attention to the person-environment interaction when designing interventions. Perhaps the key issue here is the willingness of the consultee to accept the consultant's perspective.

Short and Ringer (1987) asked fifty-six school psychologists to identify their most and least successful consultation experiences and the reasons for those successions and failures. Overwhelmingly, consultants attributed their successes and failures to the teachers' actions rather than their own consulting behavior. A question that needs to be explored is what occurs when consultees are unwilling to accept or perhaps have some minor disagreements with the perspective of the consultant. It may be that the consultee will appear to be compliant and then not follow through in the implementation phase. If may also be that the consultees will exert less effort if they have misgivings about the process. It does seem clear that consultees want to have assurances that they can influence the client's behavior. Cleven and Gutkin (1988) found in their analogue study of teachers' preferences for type of service that teachers preferred consultation over referral when they felt that they could make an impact on the client's functioning.

The role of the consultee in the actual process of analyzing the client's problem and arriving at a solution to that problem is further compounded when we revisit an issue raised earlier: cross-cultural consultation. Pinto (1981) has warned against selecting strategies that are not in accord with cultural values, a warning that seems appropriate when one considers the diversity in human values. I once set up a behavior modification program based on individual rewards for a group of Native American children only to find that the children were more interested in the approval of their peers than in the rewards we had so carefully selected. When the program was altered to incorporate rewards based on group performance, the importance of cultural values became quite clear to me. Pinto concludes that consultants must be flexible enough to design interventions that are in accord with cultural expectations. This suggestion, if taken literally, probably means that no single approach to consultation will be sufficient.

Medway (1989) suggests that some consultees—namely, teachers—probably enter consultation with certain "scripts" or expectations about the manner in which the client's problem may be resolved and that the best consultants may be those who can ascertain what those scripts are and generate ways of altering them. If Medway is correct, and only research will be able to determine the answer to this question, consultants who adhere to a single approach to problem solving will be severely disadvantaged in their efforts to assist consultees.

Focus of Problem Solving. As Lippitt and Lippitt (1986), Schein (1987), and others have suggested, consultation can focus on processes (communication, problem solving), the tasks of the consultee (for example, production), or on a combination of the two. Schein (1969, 1987) has emphasized the importance of a process orientation by which the consultant becomes an unobtrusive observer and then raises questions that will enable the consultee to identify his or her own problems. For example, after some initial contract setting, school psychologists might observe a classroom and raise questions about communication and problem solving in the classroom to promote insight into the nature of the teaching process. Once the teacher and psychologists have decided on the teaching strategies that need remediation, the psychologists might become resource linkers to help the teacher identify strategies to overcome the deficiencies that have been identified. Other task-oriented consultants might directly diagnose areas in the instructional process that require attention, including the use of audiovisual aids, the need for more time on task, and different cuing mechanisms to let students know what is important. These consultations would then pass their diagnoses on to the teacher and might actually model new instructional strategies. It may be the case, as the Lippitts suggest it is in organizational consultation, that process and content can be unlinked. However, most consultations in the human service areas often find themselves working simultaneously on tasks and processes. In the case of school psychologists working with a teacher, it seems reasonable that while communication and classroom problem solving are being observed, pacing, approaches to discipline, level of content, individualization of instruction, and so forth would also be considered.

It is probably a truism that the task and process dimensions of consultation should not be unlinked, but there may be times when they are. For example, it is unlikely that school-based consultants will be unable to judge the adequacy of the content of an American history unit or a prealgebra course. However, they may become experts in the areas of disciplining students, promoting the acquisition of specific skills (for example, solving algebra problems), or even the overall teaching process. For example, one could conceive of a consultant being hired as a technical expert to examine the mechanics of the communication system of an organization—look at the use of telephones, facsimile machines, voice mail, and so on and recommend needed changes—while another consultant might be hired to improve the "human" dimensions of the organization.

Defining Consultation

The discussion above leads to the following assumptions about the nature of consultation:

1. The consultant is a trained mental health professional.
2. Authentic, honest communication is essential for successful consultation.
3. The nature of the client's problem will influence the roles of the consultant and consultee and thus the process in which they engage.
4. While consultation can be initiated by either the consultant or the consultee, the client and the consultee must ultimately both subscribe to the process if consultation is to occur. Thus, the real *power* in the consultation process rests with the consultee and perhaps ultimately with the client.
5. Task-content variables and the process of consultation interact and must be considered simultaneously.
6. Systemic variables impinge on consultant, consultee, and client and must be considered as an integral part of the process.
7. Consultation is governed by certain ethical guidelines that influence consultant roles as well as the process of consultation.
8. The goal of most consultations is to improve the functioning of the client while simultaneously enhancing the functioning of the consultee.
9. The conditions that lead to the initiation of consultation will influence both the process and the content.

Consultation is an enabling process. It is aimed at solving the educational and/or psychological problems of a client who is typically not involved directly with the consultant. The primary mechanisms that allow consultation to be effective are the transfer of skills and knowledge from the consultant to the consultee, the marshaling of the consultee's own resources, and secondary educational processes, such as bibliotherapy or the linking of the consultee to another source of knowledge or skills. A by-product of consultation is that the consultee develops new knowledge and skill and has improved self-efficacy and self-confidence.

The nature of the client problem that precipitates consultation may temporarily influence the roles that the consultant and consultee take initially (Kratochwill & Bergan, 1990). For example, if a teacher who believes that a student is suicidal goes to the school counselor for assistance, the counselor may help the teacher to deal effectively (and immediately) with the problem by giving direct advice, with little concern for skills or knowledge acquisition. The counselor might also see the client and assist in the assessment of the likelihood of suicide. This is, of course, client-centered consultation in the Caplanian sense. However, consultation should always be concerned with the empowerment of the consultee so that the consultee can deal with educational and psychological problems in the future and thus reduce the load on the consultant.

The unique expertise of the consultant is understanding the consultation process and knowing how to develop expertise in the consultee. The consultant and the consultee typically share expertise regarding the client's problem. For example, a parent knows what has been tried, how effective the interventions have been, the norms of the neighborhood in which the student functions, and a great deal about the temperament and abilities of the student. The consultant should have some knowledge of parenting skills, which, when melded with the parent's knowledge, can serve as the basis for a solution to the problem. It becomes the consultant's responsibility to *teach* the consultee strategies for implementing the solution that has been generated.

As noted earlier in this chapter, the matter of the consultee "controlling" the consultation conversation has come under considerable discussion. Realistically, consultants must elicit information that will allow them to adequately understand the client's problem; the consultee's attitudes, skills, and motivation; what approaches the consultee has used to resolve the problem; and how effective these approaches have been. Since consultation typically operates under rather severe times limitations (Brown et al., 1991), this information usually must be elicited quickly, and thus it is necessary for the consultant to engage the consultee in a consultation conversation that is acceptable to both. However, because it is necessary for the information elicited to be authentic, the consultation conversation must be characterized by qualities such as respect, warmth, genuiness, and caring (Horton & Brown, 1990). It is therefore incumbent on consultants to develop strategies that will allow them to communicate caring while eliciting information about the client-consultee interaction.

It is clear that the nature of the communication must be tempered to account for the cultural background of the parents. Asian-Pacific American parents are likely to be ashamed if one of their children is having difficulties and thus may be reluctant to engage in discussions about the family. Mexican American parents may value education less than other parents because education has not been rewarded in Mexico as it has in the United States, and they may be less enthusiastic about interventions that would enhance educational performance. Of course, all these factors are influenced by acculturation, the community in which the parents live, their socioeconomic level, and a variety of other factors (Sue & Sue, 1991). The point is that consultation communication must be altered to meet the cultural expectations of the consultee.

The actual information to be elicited will depend on the theoretical perspective of the consultant. For example, an Adlerian consultant who engages in consultation with a parent will want to elicit information about birth order, childhood illnesses, disciplinary strategies, and the use of democratic principles in the family, while most of this information would be of little concern to a traditional behavioral consultant. In the area of generating educational or psychological change, no one school of thought has a monopoly on effectiveness.

The nature of the power relationship between consultant and consultee seems to be the area that is least understood. Because consultees are often responsible for implementing solutions that are generated, they have the ultimate power. The consultant has the power of expertise, may have the ability to develop referent power, and so on, and these factors play an important role in consultations, but when the consultee leaves the consultant's office (or vice versa), the power of action is totally in the consultee's hands. I believe that compliance with the plan that has been established between the consultee and the consultant will be greatly enhanced if the power relationship between the two is viewed as egalitarian, but there is no empirical support for this.

Systemic variables impinge on consultants, consultees, and clients and *must* be considered in consultation. Early in my career, one of my students was working with a teacher to reduce aggressive behavior in one of her pupils by helping him develop negotiation skills. The interventions that the two of them had devised seemed to be working until the client came to school one day and reported that his parents had learned that he had not "stood up for himself" when he was hit by another child and had spanked him. Most parents have learned that an intervention with one child precipitates changes in the rest of the family. Indeed, this is the most basic principle of systems-oriented approaches to family therapy. Consultants must also consider the systems influences on the consultees, particularly teachers and parents, as well as those that influence their own functioning. I have long advocated that counselors and school psychologist be released from their schedule one morning a week to consult with parents who are unavailable in the evenings. Certainly, there are more subtle "rules" that influence consultee functioning, and these must be understood by the consultant.

In sum, consultation is a collaborative problem-solving process (Pryzwansky, 1989) consisting of several, often nondistinct stages that requires an open, trusting relationship between the consultant and the consultee (Horton & Brown, 1990). The consultant's involvement in each stage of consultation is open to negotiation. To be effective, consultants must elicit accurate information about the client's problem and the consultee's attempts to resolve the problem. To resolve the client's problems, consultants must be able to develop the knowledge base and skills required to intervene (Kratochwill & Bergan, 1990). The power relationship between the consultant and consultee will vary at various points in the consulting relationships but probably should be perceived as egalitarian by the consultee if the consulting process is to have its maximum impact (Parsons & Meyers, 1984). A number of factors will impinge on the consulting process and require variations in it, including the culture of the consultee (Pinto, 1981), systemic variables that bear directly or indirectly on the consultant, consultee, and client (Kurpius, 1985), and the circumstances (for example, crisis) surrounding the initiation of the consultation (Kratochwill & Bergan, 1990; Lippitt & Lippitt, 1986).

Conclusion

Definitions of consultation grow out of a variety of perspectives, the primary one being the theoretical orientation of the consultant. In this chapter, I have tried to examine some of the disparate perspectives and fold them into a single definition of consultation. The definition that I have forged will undoubtedly be unsatisfactory to some, because I have left out certain of their key beliefs. I must admit that I am not totally satisfied with the definition rendered, because it is necessarily built on supposition, but so, of course, are all approaches to intervention in human functioning.

It is standard procedure to recommend that more research be conducted on key variables, and I will follow that track. The line of research initiated by Erchul (1987) and followed up by Erchul and Chewning (1990) needs to be further followed up with studies that compare different approaches to dealing with the consultation conversation. There is a long history of support for the idea that some consultees prefer collaborative approaches to the expert model addressed in these initial studies (see, for example, Wenger, 1979). It is not sufficient to conclude that consultees seem to be more satisfied with consultation when the consultant dominates the process or when the process is more collaborative. The question to be answered is what types of consultation are most effective with which consultees and clients. Researchers need to turn to the task of defining which approaches to consultation are most effective with different types of consultees under varying conditions.

References

American Heritage Dictionary. (1987). *American heritage illustrated encyclopedic dictionary.* Boston: Houghton Mifflin.

Babcock, N. L., & Pryzwansky, W. B. (1983). Consultation outcome as a result of in-service resource teacher training. *Psychology in the Schools. 19,* 495–502.

Bandura, A. (1977). *Social learning theory.* Englewood Cliffs, NJ: Prentice-Hall.

Bandura, A. (1982). Self-efficacy mechanism in human agency. *American Psychologist, 37,* 122–147.

Beer, M. (1980). *Organization change and development: A systems view.* Santa Monica, CA: Goodyear.

Bergan, J. R. (1977). *Behavioral consultation.* Columbus, OH: Merrill.

Bergan, J. R., & Kratochwill, T. R. (1990). *Behavioral consultation and therapy.* New York: Plenum Press.

Brown, D., Kurpius, D. J., & Morris, J. R. (1988). *Handbook of consultation with individuals and small groups.* Alexandria, VA: Association for Counselor Education and Supervision.

Brown, D., & Schulte, A. C. (1987). A social learning model of consultation. *Professional Psychology: Research and Practice, 18,* 283–287.

Brown, D., Pryzwansky, W. P., & Schulte, A. (1981). *Beyond Consultation: Introduction to Theory and Practice* (2nd ed.). Needham Heights, MA: Allyn & Bacon.

Caplan, G. (1970). *The theory and practice of mental health consultation.* New York: Basic Books.

Cleven, C. A., & Gutkin, T. B. (1988). Cognitive modeling of consultation processes: A means for improving consultees' problem definition skills. *Journal of School Psychology. 26,* 379–389.

Coleman, J. V. (1947). Psychiatric consultation in casework agencies. *Journal of Orthopsychiatry, 18,* 533–539.

Dinkmeyer, D., & Carlson, J. (1973). *Consulting: Facilitating human potential and change processes.* Columbus, OH: Merrill.

Dougherty, A. M. (1990). *Consultation: Practice and perspectives.* Pacific Grove, CA: Brooks/Cole.

Erchul, W. P. (1987). A relational communication analysis of control in school consultation. *Professional School Psychology, 2,* 113–124.

Erchul, W. P., & Chewning, T. G. (1990). Behavioral consultation from a request-centered relational communication perspective. *School Psychology Quarterly, 5,* 1–20.

Gallessich, J. (1982). *The profession and practice of consultation: A handbook for consultants, trainers of consultants, and consumers of consultation services.* San Francisco: Jossey-Bass.

Horton, E., & Brown, D. (1990). The importance of interpersonal skills in consultee-centered consultation: A review. *Journal of Counseling and Development, 68,* 423–426.

James, B. E., Kidder, M. G., Osberg, J. W., & Hunter, W. B. (1986). Traditional mental health consultation: the psychodynamic perspective. In F. V. Mannino, E. J. Trickett, M. F. Shore, M. G. Kidder, & G. Levin (Eds.), *Handbook of mental health consultation* (DHHS Publication No. ADM 86-1446, pp. 31–48). Washington, DC: U.S. Government Printing Office.

Kratochwill, T. R., & Bergan, J. R. (1990). *Behavioral consultation in applied settings: An individual guide.* New York: Plenum Press.

Kratochwill, T. R., & VanSomeren, K. R. (1985). Barriers to treatment success in behavioral consultation: Current limitations and future directions. *Journal of School Psychology, 23,* 225–239.

Kurpius, D. J. (1985). Consultation interventions: Successes, failures and proposals. *The Counseling Psychologist, 13,* 368–389.

Kurpius, D. J., & Robinson, S. (1978). An overview of consultation. *Personnel and Guidance Journal, 56,* 321–323.

Lippitt, G., & Lippitt, R. (1978). *The consulting process in action.* San Diego, CA: University Associates.

Lippitt, G. & Lippitt, R. (1986). *The consulting process in action* (2nd. ed). San Diego, CA: University Associates.

Mannino, F. V., & Shore M. F. (1986a). History and development of mental health consultation. In F. V. Mannino, E. J. Trickett, M. F. Shore, M. G. Kidder, & G. Levin (Eds.), *Handbook of mental health consultation* (pp. 3–28). Washington, DC: U.S. Government Printing Office.

Mannino, F. V., & Shore, M. F. (1986b). Introduction. In F. V. Mannino, E. J. Trickett, M. F. Shore, M. F. Kidder, & G. Levin (Eds.), *Handbook of mental health consultation* (DHHS Publication No. ADM 86-1446, pp. xi–xvii). Washington, DC: U.S. Government Printing Office.

Medway, F. J. (1989). Further considerations of a cognitive problem-solving perspective on school consultation. *Professional School Psychology, 4,* 21–28.

Morasky, R. L. (1982). *Behavioral systems.* New York: Praeger.

Parsons, R. D., & Meyers, J. (1984). *Developing consultation skills: A guide to training, development, and assessment for human services professionals.* San Francisco: Jossey-Bass.

Pinto, R. F. (1981). Consultant orientations and client systems perception: Styles of cross-cultural consultation. In R. Lippitt & G. Lippitt (Eds.), *Systems think-*

ing: A resource for organizational diagnosis and interventions (pp. 57–74). Washington, DC: International Consultants Foundation.

Pryzwansky, W. B. (1974). A reconsideration of the consultation model for delivery of school-based psychological sources. *American Journal of Ortho-psychiatry, 44,* 579–583.

Pryzwansky, W. B. (1989). School consultation: Some considerations from a cognitive psychology perspective. *Professional School Psychology, 4,* 1–14.

Pryzwansky, W. B., & Noblit, G. W. (1990). Understanding and improving consultation practice: The qualitative case study approach. *Journal of Educational and Psychological Consultation, 1,* 293–308.

Randolph, D. L. (1985). *Micro consulting: Basic psychological consultation skills for helping professionals.* Johnson City, TN: Institute of Social Sciences and Arts.

Schein, E. H. (1969). *Process consultation: Its role in organization development.* Reading, MA: Addison-Wesley.

Schein, E. H. (1987). *Process consultation: Lessons for managers and consultants* (Vol. 2). Reading, MA: Addison-Wesley.

Short, R. J., & Ringer, M. M. (1987). Consultant experience and attributions in school consultation. *Professional School Psychology, 2,* 273–280.

Sue, D. W., & Sue, D. (1991). *Counseling the culturally different* (2nd ed.). New York: Wiley.

Wenger, R. D. (1979). Teachers' response to collaborative consultation. *Psychology in the Schools, 16,* 127–131.

White, G., & Pryzwansky, W. B. (1983). Models of consultation: Preferences of educational professionals at five stages of services. *Journal of School Psychology, 21,* 359–366.

4

A Behavioral Approach to Consultation

Brian K. Martens

As noted in Chapter One, reports of consultation research have increased dramatically over the past decade. One might conclude from such activity that a substantial empirical base now exists for each of the major consultation models represented in the literature—mental health, organizational, and behavioral. This, however, is not the case. Rather, an overwhelming majority (approximately 75 percent) of the consultation research studies conducted to date have concerned the processes and outcomes of behavioral consultation (Alpert & Yammer, 1983; Gresham & Kendell, 1987). Recent trends in psychoeducational service delivery toward prereferral intervention and the use of teachers as consultants predict an even greater focus on behavioral consultation in the near future (Fuchs & Fuchs, 1989; Reschly, 1988).

Why is it that behavioral consultation enjoys such widespread empirical support in the literature? Why do consultation researchers continue to focus so extensively on the behavioral consultation model? Although a variety of factors (both historically and recently) have tended to support a behavioral-ecological approach to the delivery of children's mental health services (Albee, 1968; Gutkin & Curtis, 1982; Hobbs, 1964; Reynolds, Gutkin, Elliott, & Witt, 1984; Tharp & Wetzel, 1969), two aspects of the behavioral consultation model itself have contributed to its popularity. First, the processes and outcomes of behavioral consultation enjoy a high degree of specificity (Kratochwill, Van-Someren, & Sheridan, 1989). That is, behavioral consultation has been sufficiently operationalized to support the development of standard interviewing

Note: The author wishes to thank William P. Erchul and Joseph C. Witt for their consultative reviews of an earlier draft of the chapter and Blair T. Johnson for preparing the figure.

protocols, competency-based training programs, and consultant effectiveness indices (Bergan & Tombari, 1975, 1976; Fuchs & Fuchs, 1989; Kratochwill et al., 1989; McDougall, Reschly, & Corkery, 1988). Second, the problem-solving objectives of behavioral consultation are based on the strategies and tactics of behavior analysis (for example, collecting time-series data, identifying behavioral antecedents and consequences, specifying treatment procedures). Over the past twenty years, a great deal of research has accumulated demonstrating the effectiveness of behavior-analytical techniques in responding to children's learning and adjustment problems (Martens & Meller, 1990). The goals of this chapter are to describe the behavioral consultation model (Bergan & Kratochwill, 1990) and to examine issues surrounding its effectiveness through a review of available research.

Overview of the Behavioral Consultation Process

The historical roots of behavioral consultation derive from efforts in the 1960s and early 1970s to apply the principles of behavior modification in human service settings (for example, Repucci & Saunders, 1974). A critical feature of these early efforts was the involvement of direct care providers, such as parents and teachers, as principal change agents in the therapeutic process. As early as 1969, Tharp and Wetzel described a consultative model for implementing contingency management techniques that required at least three participants: the behavioral consultant—someone with knowledge of behavior analysis and intervention; the target client—someone who exhibits problem behavior; and the mediator—someone who is in direct contact with the client and therefore controls available reinforcers. During the 1970s, researchers attempted to formalize behavioral consultation methods by articulating specific training procedures, problem-solving objectives, and interviewing techniques (Bergan, 1970; Bergan & Tombari, 1975; D'Zurilla & Goldfried, 1971; Goodwin, Garvey, & Barclay, 1971). Many of the concepts and strategies currently associated with behavioral consultation were first summarized in Bergan's volume *Behavioral Consultation* (1977), which has recently undergone revision (Bergan & Kratochwill, 1990).

Over the years, behavioral consultation has continued to evolve as a method of psychoeducational service delivery. For example, researchers in behavioral consultation have become increasingly concerned with such variables as interpersonal influence processes (for example, relational control), consultee perceptions and behavior (for example, judgments of treatment acceptability), and the organizational context in which consultation occurs (for example, principal leadership style) (Bossard & Butkin, 1983; Elliott, 1988; Erchul, 1987; Gutkin & Conoley, 1990). Although separate from behavioral

Figure 4.1. The Behavioral Consultation Process.

Participant characteristics	The consultative interview	Participant responsibilities
Consultee	**I. Core characteristics**	**Consultee**
1. Educational content expertise 2. Attributions and perceptions 3. Problem history	**II. Interviewing objectives**	1. Data collection 2. Plan implementation 3. Generalization of problem-solving objectives
Consultant		**Consultant**
1. Psychological content expertise 2. Knowledge of problem solving 3. Communication and relationship–building skills	**III. Interviewing tactics**	1. Assessment of treatment integrity 2. Plan evaluation 3. Consultee support

consultation as a problem-solving activity, findings in these areas have added to the model's viability as a means of delivering comprehensive services to children. Figure 4.1 is a schematic overview of the behavioral consultation process that incorporates these recent advances in consultation research.

Participant Characteristics

As indicated in the left-hand portion of Figure 4.1, the consultant and consultee both bring unique skills and understanding to the consultative relationship. Because of the emphasis placed on behavioral consultation as a problem-solving process, research has tended to focus on the skills and characteristics of effective *consultants* (for example, Conoley & Conoley, 1991). Within the past several years, however, arguments have been made for examining the influence of consultee characteristics on behavioral consultation outcomes (Brown, Pryzwansky, & Schulte, 1991; Pryzwansky, 1986).

A principal feature of behavioral consultation is the active involvement of consultees in the problem-solving process. Consultee participation is important because the teacher is viewed as "an expert in the area of education and the workings of his/her classroom" (Gutkin & Curtis, 1982, p. 801). By bringing this expertise in educational content to the relationship, the consultee contributes important information to problem analysis and plan implementation. Beyond contributing their knowledge and skill, consultees also make attributions for children's classroom behavior problems and hold subjective perceptions of how best to respond to these problems. Research has demonstrated that teachers distinguish among suggested intervention alternatives on the basis of acceptability and that perceptions of treatment acceptability are influenced by characteristics of the teacher, the child, and the consultative relationship (Elliott, 1988; Elliott, Turco, & Gresham, 1987; Martens & Meller, 1989; Witt & Martens, 1983; Witt, Moe, Gutkin, & Andrews, 1984). Finally, several authors have observed that entering into a consultative relationship requires implicit recognition of one's inability to deal effectively with the presenting problem (Piersel & Gutkin, 1983; Witt & Martens, 1988). Before meeting with a consultant, however, teachers typically engage in their own problem-solving efforts involving informal discussions with colleagues and two or three attempts to modify the child's educational program (Ysseldyke, Pianta, Christenson, Wang, & Algozzine, 1983). The point here is that consultees bring to the consultative relationship a history of dealing with the problem, the success of which is likely to influence their willingness to attempt additional intervention strategies.

Just as the consultee is expected to contribute expertise in educational content, the consultant is expected to have expertise in psychological principles (that is, psychological content). To apply the principles of behavior to children's learning and adjustment problems through consultation, individuals must be skilled in behavior analysis and intervention, the problem-solving objectives of behavioral consultation, and communication and relationship building (Gutkin & Curtis, 1990; Kratochwill & Bergan, 1990). The latter two skill areas constitute core aspects of the consultative interview and are discussed in detail in subsequent sections.

The Consultative Interview

Behavioral consultation is an indirect service model wherein one professional (for example, a school psychologist) works directly with another professional (for example, a teacher) as a means of producing change in the client (for example, a child). Typically, the consultant has little contact with the client and must rely on direct care providers to carry out recommendations and implement treatment. Because of this alignment, achieving the remedial and preventive goals of behavioral consultation depends to a large extent on the consultant's ability to influence the actions of other adults (Gutkin & Conoley, 1990). The primary mechanism through which this process of interpersonal influence occurs is the consultative interview. As shown in the middle portion of Figure 4.1, the consultative interview can be separated into three levels of interaction defined by (1) the parameters of consultation as an indirect service model (core characteristics), (2) the problem-solving objectives of behavior analysis (interviewing objectives), and (3) the tactics of effective communication and relationship building (interviewing tactics). Each level of interaction within the consultative interview subsumes the levels below it. Thus, the success of behavioral consultation as an indirect service (level I) is dependent on achieving the various interviewing objectives (level II), which can occur only through face-to-face verbal interaction (level III).

As described in Chapter One, all school-based consultation models, including behavioral consultation, are defined by a common set of core characteristics (level I). These characteristics derive from the historical antecedents of consultation as a method of service delivery and serve to establish boundaries for the consultative interaction. For example, consultation is defined in the conceptual literature as a collaborative relationship between coequal professionals that is work-related in focus (Conoley & Conoley, 1991; Gutkin & Curtis, 1982). By focusing on professional issues in the school setting, the consultative dialogue is constrained to topics that are relevant to the client.

Within the parameters of the consultative relationship, behavioral consultation can be distinguished from other models by its emphasis on behavioral technology in the development of intervention plans and its use of behavioral-analytical strategies in the evaluation of treatment outcomes (Bergan & Kratochwill, 1990). Perhaps most central to the behavior consultation model, however, is reliance on a systematic problem-solving process that occurs in four stages: problem identification, problem analysis, plan implementation, and problem evaluation (level II). The interviewing objectives at each stage are based on the strategies and tactics of behavior analysis and are designed to maximize the likelihood of successful problem resolution (D'Zurilla & Goldfried, 1971; Witt & Elliott, 1983). Failure to accomplish these interviewing objectives not only reduces the likelihood of success but is inconsistent with a behavioral approach to intervention (Reschly, 1988).

To accomplish the problem-solving objectives of behavioral consultation, the consultant must engage in face-to-face verbal interaction with the consultee (level III; Witt, 1990). As Gutkin & Curtis (1982, p. 822) observe, "At its most basic level, consultation is an interpersonal exchange. As such, the consultant's success is going to hinge largely on his or her communication and relationship skills." Both direct and indirect measures of consultant interviewing effectiveness (for example, number of questions asked, ratings by the consultee) have been related to the occurrence of initial consultative interviews as well as consultee satisfaction (Bergan & Tombari, 1976; Gutkin, 1986; Martens, Lewandowski, & Houk, 1989a). In addition, several methodologies now exist for quantifying interpersonal communications that occur during the consultative interview (Martens, Erchul, & Witt, 1992). Application of these coding schemes shows promise in revealing consultant communications that can direct consultee behavior (Erchul & Chewning, 1990; Witt, Erchul, McKee, Pardue, & Wickstrom, 1991).

Participant Responsibilities

The goals of behavioral consultation are twofold: to solve the presenting problem and to increase the consultees' ability to deal effectively with similar problems in the future (Gutkin & Curtis, 1990). To achieve these goals, the consultant and consultee must engage in separate yet complementary activities following each meeting. These activities constitute outcomes of the consultative interaction and are depicted in the right-hand portion of Figure 4.1.

Following completion of the problem-identification interview (PII) and problem-analysis interview (PAI), the consultee is expected to collect baseline data and then implement the agreed-upon intervention plan. Although most behaviorally based treatments involve either stimulus retraining (for example, systematic desensitization) or environmental manipulation (for example, contingency management), interventions in the latter group are more consistent with the logic of indirect service delivery (Gutkin & Curtis, 1990). In fact, Tharp and Wetzel (1969) suggested that any consultee can be an effective behavior change agent if that individual (1) controls the reinforcers in a given setting and (2) is able to deliver those reinforcers contingently.

Whereas the consultee maintains primary responsibility for plan implementation, Gresham (1989) suggests that the consultant be responsible for monitoring treatment integrity, or the extent to which treatment is implemented in the manner intended. A variety of behavioral assessment methods can be used to monitor treatment integrity, including systematic observation, self-monitoring, and teacher rating scales and checklists. By assessing treatment integrity, consultants can recommend changes in treatment procedures that help consultees incorporate suggested interventions into their professional repertoires.

In addition to monitoring treatment integrity, the consultant also plays a principal role in the evaluation of treatment outcomes. This role involves helping the consultee determine whether the goals established for behavioral change were achieved, partially achieved, or not achieved and whether the changes observed in client behavior were a function of the treatment procedure or resulted merely from chance (Gresham & Davis, 1988). According to these determinations, the decision can be made to continue implementing treatment or recycle through aspects of the consultation process as necessary. In either event, the consultant is responsible for providing ongoing support to the consultee until a mutual decision is reached to terminate the relationship (Gutkin & Curtis, 1990).

The preventive functions of consultation are served when the consultee's professional skills are enhanced as a result of implementing treatment and when level II problem-solving objectives are applied successfully in other situations. Although a major goal of consultation has always been to increase the independent functioning of the consultee, relatively little research has been conducted documenting the preventive effects of the behavioral consultation process. The evidence that is available indicates that teachers perceive their professional skills to have improved following receipt of consultation services (Gutkin, 1980, 1986; Ponti, Zins, & Graden, 1988) and that more children referred for special education services are maintained in regular classrooms following the implementation of prereferral intervention and instructional consultation programs (Gutkin, Henning-Stout, & Piersel, 1988; Rosenfield, 1992). Clearly, more research is needed that directly evaluates the impact of consultation services on consultees' professional skills, problem-solving abilities, and success in future problem situations.

Interviewing Objectives

Broadly conceived, all psychoeducational services can be viewed as attempts to solve problems or reduce the discrepancy between observed and desired behavior (Reynolds et al., 1984; Shinn, 1989). In accordance with this view, the essence of behavioral consultation as a method of service delivery lies in achievement of the level II problem-solving objectives. The objectives associated with each behavioral consultation interview are listed in the following outline (adapted from Kratochwill & Bergan, 1990; Gresham & Davis, 1988; and Gutkin & Curtis, 1982). The following paragraphs describe these objectives in further detail and present research demonstrating their importance to successful problem resolution.

Problem-identification interview (PII)
1. Assess the scope of consultee concerns
2. Prioritize problem components or identify a target problem area
3. Define the target problem in overtly observable behavioral terms
4. Estimate the frequency, intensity, or duration of the problem behavior
5. Identify tentative goals for change
6. Tentatively identify conditions surrounding the problem behavior as antecedents, sequences, and consequences
7. Establish data-collection procedures and responsibilities
8. Schedule the next interview

Problem-analysis interview (PAI)
1. Determine the adequacy of baseline data
2. Establish goals for change
3. Analyze conditions surrounding the problem behavior as antecedents, sequences, and consequences

4. Design and implement an intervention plan
5. Reaffirm data-collection procedures
6. Schedule the next interview

Problem-evaluation interview (PEI)
1. Determine whether intervention goals were met
2. Evaluate plan effectiveness
3. Discuss continuation, modification, or termination of the plan
4. Terminate consultation or schedule additional meetings to recycle through the problem-solving process

The Problem-Identification Interview (PII)

The primary goals of the PII are threefold: (1) to identify a target behavior and define it in overtly observable terms; (2) to obtain tentative estimates of how often and under what conditions the behavior occurs; and (3) to initiate ongoing collection of data for use in evaluating treatment effectiveness.

The importance of successful problem identification in line with the objectives stated above cannot be overestimated. Lambert (1976) found that although teachers were sensitive to a variety of classroom problems, they tended to state those problems in vague or general terms (for example, "the child is poorly motivated"). She concluded from these data that "teachers will need considerable support for gathering more precise information about the nature of children's problems before interventions can be considered" (p. 515). McDougall et al. (1988) evaluated the effectiveness of a one-day training workshop on consultant interviewing skills. Participants in the workshops were asked to submit audiotaped referral interviews before and after training, which were subsequently scored for the number of PII objectives met. Consistent with the findings by Lambert (1976), the number of subjects meeting each PII objective at baseline ranged from only 5.9 to 47.1 percent. Finally, in the often-cited study by Bergan and Tombari (1976), approximately 60 percent of the variance in plan implementation was accounted for by merely identifying the problem. Equally as interesting, the study found that consultant variables (for example, message control) had their greatest impact on problem resolution during the initial interview.

The Problem-Analysis Interview (PAI)

During the PAI, the consultant and consultee are responsible for (1) using the baseline data to establish goals for behavioral change, (2) conducting a functional analysis of behavior using descriptive assessment methods, and (3) designing and implementing a treatment plan. Perhaps the most critical step in designing an intervention plan is the identification of events that covary with the target behavior as antecedents, sequences, and consequences. Referred to as the functional analysis of behavior, the identification of events that control responding has been the hallmark of behavior-analytical research for more than twenty years. Other disciplines as well have begun to adopt this strategy as a means of identifying potential treatment options. For example, Nelson and Hayes (1979, p. 1) acknowledged as the goal of behavioral assessment the identification of "meaningful response units and their controlling variables . . . for the purposes of understanding and altering behavior." More recently, arguments have been made for adopting a functional-analytical approach by behavior therapists (Branch, 1987), school psychologists (Reschly, 1988), and even cognitive-behavior therapists (Hawkins, 1989).

During the PAI, the consultant elicits from the consultee descriptive information identifying events that covary with the target behavior. On the basis of this information, hypotheses are generated about possible functional behavior-environment relationships (Mace, Yankanich, & West, 1989). These hypotheses are tested empirically by implementation of the treatment plan while changes in the target behavior are monitored. Linking assessment and intervention through the functional analysis of behavior enables controlling events to be identified with greater confidence, thereby maximizing treatment effectiveness. Hypothesis-testing approaches similar to that described above have proved successful in treating such recalcitrant behavior as self-injury, pica, and reluctant speech where other approaches have failed (Iwata, Dorsey, Slifer, Bauman, & Richman, 1982; Mace & Knight, 1986; Mace & West, 1986).

The Problem-Evaluation Interview (PEI)

The primary focus of the PEI is determining whether the goals established during the PAI have been met and whether the treatment plan has been sufficiently effective to warrant continuation. Assessment of goal attainment requires that the frequency, intensity, or duration of behavior under the treatment condition be compared to the goal established at baseline. Although a variety of methods are available for making this comparison, the most common strategy is to display the data in the form of a time-series graph or figure. The effects of monitoring child behavior in this fashion were examined in a meta-analysis by Fuchs and Fuchs (1986). Results indicates that measuring student academic performance twice a week and graphing the data produced an effect size of .80. That is, student achievement scores improved by nearly one standard deviation over those for control subjects simply as a function of how treatment was evaluated.

Beyond evaluating changes in client behavior, at least two other issues must be addressed to conclude that treatment was effective enough to warrant continuation. First, as mentioned previously, it must be determined that treatment was implemented in the manner intended by the consultee (that there was treatment integrity). Second, it must be determined that the treatment procedure was responsible for the changes observed (that there is internal validity). Toward this goal, several authors have described the design and implementation of treatment as a problem-solving process that closely resembles single-case experimental research (Barlow, Hayes, & Nelson, 1984; Hayes, 1981; Gresham, 1985). Given the logistical similarities between plan implementation and single-case research, incorporating experimental design elements into the treatment plan can provide a basis for inferring cause and effect (Gresham & Davis, 1988). Conversely, in the absence of experimental design elements (either deliberate or naturally occurring), the consultant and consultee run the risk of "persisting in essentially superstitious behavior—improvement caused by other factors may be attributed to treatment procedures" (Kratochwill & Piersel, 1983, p. 169).

Interviewing Tactics

To evaluate consultant effectiveness during the problem-solving process, Bergan and Tombari (1975) developed the Consultation Analysis Record (CAR). Although a variety of methods exist for quantifying verbal interactions that occur in counseling (see, for example, Tracey & Ray, 1984), the CAR is the only coding scheme designed specifically for consultation. Categories appearing on the CAR allow the topic or content of discussion to be coded as well as the type of utterance used to convey the information (that is, verbal process). Content categories include both environmental and organismic factors influencing behavior, whereas process categories address functions of speech that are relevant to a consultative dialogue (for example, *specifying* information or *summarizing* what was said previously).

The analysis of consultative interviews using the CAR is accomplished in two steps. First, consecutive independent clauses or implied independent clauses are identified from transcripts of audiotaped interviews and numbered consecutively. (An independent clause is an utterance that can be stated as a sentence and that conveys a subject-action-object relationship—for example, "Tony hits other students"; Bergan, 1977). Second, each independent clause is coded according to four categories (see Bergan & Tombari, 1975, for a complete description of these categories):

1. The *content* or topic under discussion (background environment, behavior setting, behavior, individual characteristics, observation, plan, other)

2. The *process* or function served by the statement (negative or positive evaluation, inference, specification, summarization, negative or positive validation)
3. The *source* of the statement (consultant or consultee)
4. How the statement *controls* the dialogue (as an elicitor or emitter)

Data resulting from application of the CAR include single- and combined-category percentages. Interrater agreement in assigning clauses to individual categories of above .90 has been reported (Bergan & Tombari, 1975, 1976). To date, the CAR has been used primarily to obtain indices of consultant effectiveness that are then related to measures of consultation outcome. For example, early research by Bergan and Tombari (1976) examined the relationship between consultants' interviewing skills and the number of consultation contacts made during an academic year. Results indicated that consultants who controlled the dialogue with questions (that is, elicitors), stayed on a topic of conversation that concerned child behavior, and summarized and validated consultee statements engaged in a higher number of initial consultative interviews.

In a subsequent application of the CAR, Tombari and Bergan (1978) examined the effects on consultee behavior of two types of verbal cues provided by the consultant: medical and behavioral. Sixty student teachers participated in a problem-identification interview during which they were separated from the consultant by an opaque screen. Results indicated that verbal cues by the consultant that were classified as behavioral produced significantly more consultee statements about behavior or conditions surrounding behavior, higher expectations for problem resolution, and more behavioral definitions of the child's problem. More recently, Martens, Deery, and Gherardi (1991) compared two types of consultant summarization statements for their effects on consultee verbal behavior during the PII. Using a procedure similar to that reported by Patterson and Forgatch (1985) with therapist-client dyads, consultants alternated between statements reflecting consultee affect and statements reflecting message content, using a counterbalanced ABCBC design. Consultee agreement was found to occur significantly more often during conditions of reflected content, while consultees made statements about themselves and their emotions significantly more often during conditions of reflected affect. Application of lag sequential analysis to the response sequences revealed an immediate dependency between consultee agreement and consultant summarization.

The CAR has also proved useful in evaluating behavioral consultation training programs. McDougall et al. (1988) found that after participation in a one-day training workshop, consultants made significantly more statements overall during the PII, significantly more statements about procedures for collecting baseline data, and significantly fewer statements concerning background characteristics of the child. The researchers concluded that, as well as increasing the number of PII objectives achieved, the brief training experience was effective in teaching PII interviewing tactics to consultants. In a similar study, Curtis and Zins (1988) found that participation in an eleven-week behavioral consultation training course resulted in greater use of directive questioning and more behaviorally specific statements by consultants. The behavioral specificity of consultant statements was also shown to increase as a result of instructor feedback. (Chapters Eighteen and Nineteen also review studies of consultation training.)

Although behavioral consultation involves both a problem-solving process and an interpersonal influence process (Gutkin & Conoley, 1990), there has been a paucity of research examining relational aspects of the consultative interview or the effects of consultant verbalizations on consultee perceptions (West & Idol, 1987). Using a modified version of the CAR, Matens, Lewandowski, and Houk (1989a) attempted to predict consultee satisfaction on the basis of consultant and consultee statements made during the PII. Results indicated that more than 40 percent of the variance in consultees' satisfaction ratings was accounted for by the number of consultee inference statements (for example, speculations about the causes of problem behavior), consultant statements expressing agreement with the consultee, and consultee statements describing child behavior followed by consultant agreement. In addition, the more often consultants validated consultee descriptions, the more often consultees tended to speculate about causes of behavior ($r = .70$). Since speculation about the causes of behavior is not an objective of the PII, the researchers concluded that "efforts by the consultant to validate consultees' perceptions . . . may have the additional effect of encouraging consultees to move prematurely through the problem-solving process" (p. 338).

Erchul and Chewning (1990) used the relational coding scheme developed by Folger and Puck (1976) to analyze consultant-consultee interactions in thirty problem-identification, problem-analysis, and problem-evaluation interviews. In contrast to the CAR, Folger and Puck's relational coding scheme is applied only to requests and responses to these requests. Requests are coded as dominant or submissive and affiliative or hostile, whereas responses to these requests are coded as accepted, rejected, or evaded. (Erchul and Chewning, 1990, provide a complete description of the coding categories.) Results of the study indicated that the requests made by consultants far outnumbered those made by consultees (more than six to one) and that the majority (94 percent) of consultee responses involved acceptance of these bids. It was also found that the number of consultant requests decreased during the PEI, whereas requests coded as instructions or orders occurred most frequently during the PAI. These latter findings suggest that consultees had become more equal in status with the consultant by the time the PEI occurred but that "a mixture of persuasion and negotiation" (p. 15) was used by the consultant during the PAI to ensure plan implementation.

The variables of topic following and topic initiation were applied to the consultative interview in a recent study by Witt et al. (1991). These researchers found that consultants were successful at initiating a new topic significantly more often than were consultees. Moreover, topic determination by the consultant was positively related to consultee perceptions of the interviewing process.

A Critical Appraisal of the Behavioral Consultation Approach

As a method of psychoeducational service delivery, behavioral consultation relies on a systematic problem-solving process (Bergan & Tombari, 1975). As an *indirect* service delivery model, behavioral consultation can meet its objectives only through an interpersonal influence process (Gutkin & Conoley, 1990; Witt, 1990). To date, the majority of research conducted in behavioral consultation has been concerned with advancing the model as a problem-solving process.

Beginning with Mannino and Shore (1975), reviews of consultation research generally have supported the conclusion that behavioral consultation is an effective professional practice (Alpert & Yammer, 1983; Medway, 1979; Medway & Updyke, 1985). More recent reviews (for example, West & Idol, 1987), however, have criticized both the quantity and the quality of research in consultation. Of the more than 660 articles on consultation that appeared in *Psychological Abstracts* from 1978 to 1985, only 26 percent were empirically based (Pryzwansky, 1986). This percentage suggests that principles believed to be important in the consultation process outnumber those demonstrated to be important through empirical inquiry (Martens et al., 1989b). In their 1987 review, Gresham and Kendell characterized state-of-the-art consultation research as being nonexperimental and univariate, failing to employ adequate control groups, relying on subjective outcome measures, and lacking ecological validity. In suggesting future research agendas in behavioral consultation, Gresham and Kendell (1987) argued for greater use of single-case experimental designs and the routine assessment of treatment integrity. Observations by Gutkin and Curtis (1990) would add improving our understanding of communication processes and examining the sociopsychological aspects of consultative interactions to this list of prescriptions.

At the level of interviewing tactics, Bergan and Tombari (1975) originally proposed that consultants direct the interviewing process by asking questions about children's behavior problems and the conditions surrounding these problems, paraphrasing information provided by the consultee, and soliciting confirmation of the accuracy of the summaries from the consultee. Sufficient evidence has now accumulated to support the conclusion that consultants who function as effective problem solvers do indeed follow this specification elicitor–summarization emitter–validation elicitor sequence (Bergan & Tombari, 1976; Curtis & Zins, 1988; Martens et al., in press; McDougall et al., 1988; Tombari & Bergan, 1978). Research has further suggested that employing these interviewing tactics enables a greater number of interviewing objectives to be achieved in a shorter period of time (Bergan, Feld, & Swarner, 1988; McDougall et al., 1988).

Given the power of behavioral consultation as a problem-solving technology, it seems somewhat paradoxical that consultation services are frequently underutilized in school settings. For example, Martens, Peterson, Witt, and Cirone (1986) found that consultation with a specialist was rated by teachers as being among the least effective and most difficult-to-use methods of responding to children's learning and adjustment problems. Consistent with these perceptions, Ysseldyke et al. (1983) reported that when generating ideas for prereferral intervention, teachers ranked consultation with the school psychologist fifth, behind speaking with the principal. When consultation does occur, it appears that only half the intervention plans that consultees consent to are actually completed (Happe, 1982, cited in Gresham & Kendell, 1987). Clearly, these data argue for a need to examine the accessibility of behavioral consultation services and the extent to which these services represent viable programming options. Efforts along these lines have recently appeared in the literature with promising results (Fuchs & Fuchs, 1989; Fuchs, Fuchs, & Bahr, 1990). Using teachers as consultants, Fuchs and Fuchs (1989) provided consultation services to twenty-four teachers of difficult-to-teach (DTT) students in four schools. Evaluation of consultation integrity revealed that the interviewing process occurred as planned in more than 80 percent of cases. This finding was attributed in large part to the consultants' being equipped with standard interviewing protocols. Conversely, the integrity of plan implementation was poor in the absence of attempts to standardize the treatment procedures. Outcomes of the study included positive changes in consultees' perceptions of the DTT students following receipt of services, although changes in student behavior were equivocal.

Perhaps behavioral consultation has been underutilized in the schools because of the relative inattention paid to the model as an interpersonal influence process (see Chapter Seven for a discussion of this topic). Tharp and Wetzel (1969) anticipated the difficulties in relying on third-party adults as treatment agents by suggesting that consultee behavior is controlled by numerous sources of social reinforcement in addition to the consultant (for example, spouse, colleague, employer, client). These authors went on to suggest that sociopsychological role theory might be useful in identifying treatment activities in which the consultee would be likely to engage.

In his review of research concerning relationship factors in behavior therapy, Sweet (1984) found that behavior therapists were rated superior to psychotherapists on variables such as empathy, genuineness, and warmth; that relationship factors were important determinants of clients' remaining in behavior therapy; and that relationship factors were predictive of positive outcomes for certain types of behaviorally based treatments, such as exposure. On the basis of these findings, Sweet concluded that "a positive therapeutic relationship should only facilitate further cooperation and, thus, attainment of therapeutic goals. It is equally sensible that if this relationship is poor, one might well encounter difficulties in managing treatment, or in having the client accept therapy" (p. 264). Although this conclusion was derived from research in clinical behavior therapy, it would seem equally applicable to the consultative relationship. Indeed, recent discussion of consultee resistance and empowerment suggest that the manner in which help is provided is likely to influence consultees' decisions to seek assistance and follow through with suggested interventions (Witt, 1986; Witt & Martens, 1988).

The growing realization that successful consultation also involves an interpersonal influence task would suggest that the field is finally moving away from an empirical-rational approach to consultee change (Owens, 1981). Consistent with this perspective, arguments have been made for applying the principles of social learning, involvement and persuasion, and small-group functioning to the behavioral consultation process (Gutkin & Conoley, 1990; Gutkin & Curtis, 1990; Tingstrom, Little, & Stewart, 1990). For example, Gutkin and Hickman (1988) found that increasing consultees' perceptions of self-efficacy and control over the presenting problem resulted in an increased willingness to engage in consultation. Cleven and Gutkin (1988) examined the effects of cognitive modeling on the quality of consultee problem descriptions. In their study, 195 subjects viewed a videotape of either a typical behavioral consultation interview (control condition) or an interview in which the consultant made incidental statements about the nature of the problem-solving process (cognitive-modeling condition). Subjects assigned to the cognitive-modeling condition provided more behaviorally specific problem definitions and expressed more knowledge of problem solving. Given the vast amount of literature in both social psychology and relational communication concerning interpersonal influence processes (for example, Erchul & Chewning, 1990;

Johnson & Eagly, 1989), it would appear that researchers in behavioral consultation have much to learn about effecting changes in the consultee.

Conclusion

In their review of consultation research, Gresham and Kendell (1987, p. 314), concluded that "to say there are 'experts' in consultation is an oxymoron because expertise denotes that an individual has special knowledge in a particular field. We simply do not know enough about consultation, how it works, under what conditions it works, or the most important variables in predicting successful consultation outcomes." Although there is much to recommend such a position, I would like to offer an alternative conclusion, based on the perspective taken in this chapter. Given the emphasis on behavioral consultation as a problem-solving process, it would appear that consultation experts do in fact exist. However, the expertise of these individuals appears to rest primarily in the application of behavior-analytical techniques to children's learning and adjustment problems. There is a growing body of evidence suggesting that expertise in behavior analysis and intervention with children is insufficient to promote lasting changes in consultees. Clearly, we need to become more knowledgeable about behavioral consultation as an interpersonal influence process and how to apply behavior-analytical principles to the consultant-consultee relationship. Failure to do so may indeed result in consultation "experts" becoming an endangered species because of fewer and fewer requests for them to ply their trade.

References

Albee, G. W. (1968). Conceptual models and manpower requirements in psychology. *American Psychologist, 23,* 317–320.

Alpert, J. L., & Yammer, M. D. (1983). Research in school consultation: A content analysis of selected journals. *Professional Psychology: Research and Practice, 14,* 604–612.

Barlow, D. H., Hayes, S. C., & Nelson, R. O. (1984). *The scientist practitioner: Research and accountability in clinical and educational settings.* Elmsford, NY: Pergamon Press.

Bergan, J. R. (1970). A systems approach to psychological services. *Psychology in the Schools, 8,* 315–319.

Bergan, J. R. (1977). *Behavioral consultation.* Columbus, OH: Merrill.

Bergan, J. R., Feld, J. K., & Swarner, J. C. (1988). Behavioral consultation: Macroconsultation for instructional management. In J. C. Witt, S. N. Elliott,

& F. M. Gresham (Eds.), *Handbook of behavior therapy in education* (pp. 245–273). New York: Plenum Press.

Bergan, J. R., & Kratochwill, T. R. (1990). *Behavioral consultation and therapy.* New York: Plenum Press.

Bergan, J. R., & Tombari, M. L. (1975). The analysis of verbal interactions occurring during consultation. *Journal of School Psychology, 13,* 209–226.

Bergan, J. R., & Tombari, M. L. (1976). Consultant skill and efficiency and the implementation and outcomes of consultation. *Journal of School Psychology, 14,* 3–14.

Bossard, M. D., & Gutkin, T. B. (1983). The relationship of consultant skill and school organizational characteristics with teacher use of school based consultation services. *School Psychology Review, 12,* 50–56.

Branch, M. N. (1987). Behavior analysis: A conceptual and empirical base for behavior therapy. *The Behavior Therapist, 10,* 79–84.

Brown, D., Pryzwansky, W. B., & Schulte, A. C. (1991). *Psychological consultation: Introduction to theory and practice* (2nd ed.). Needham Heights, MA: Allyn & Bacon.

Cleven, C. A., & Gutkin, T. B. (1988). Cognitive modeling of consultation processes: A means for improving consultees' problem definition skills. *Journal of School Psychology, 26,* 379–389.

Conoley, J. C., & Conoley, C. W. (1991). *School consultation: A guide to practice and training* (2nd ed.). Elmsford, NY: Pergamon Press.

Curtis, M. J., & Zins, J. E. (1988). Effects of training in consultation and instructor feedback on acquisition of consultation skills. *Journal of School Psychology, 26,* 185–190.

D'Zurilla, T. J., & Goldfried, M. R. (1971). Problem solving and behavior modification. *Journal of Abnormal and Social Psychology, 78,* 107–126.

Elliott, S. N. (1988). Acceptability of behavioral treatments: Review of variables that influence treatment selection. *Professional Psychology: Research and Practice, 19,* 68–80.

Elliott, S. N., Turco, T. C., & Gresham, F. M. (1987). Consumers' and clients' pretreatment acceptability ratings of classroom-based group contingencies. *Journal of School Psychology, 25,* 145–154.

Erchul, W. P. (1987). A relational communication analysis of control in school consultation. *Professional School Psychology, 2,* 113–124.

Erchul, W. P., & Chewning, T. G. (1990). Behavioral consultation from a request-centered relational communication perspective. *School Psychology Quarterly, 5,* 1–20.

Folger, J. P., & Puck, S. (1976, April). *Coding relational communication: A question approach.* Paper presented at the meeting of the International Communication Association, Portland, OR.

Fuchs, D., & Fuchs, L. S. (1989). Exploring effective and efficient prereferral interventions: A component analysis of behavioral consultation. *School Psychology Review, 18,* 260–283.

Fuchs, D., Fuchs, L. S., & Bahr, M. W. (1990). Mainstream assistance teams: A scientific basis for the art of consultation. *Exceptional Children, 57,* 128–129.

Fuchs, L. S., & Fuchs, D. (1986). Effects of systematic formative evaluation on student achievement: A meta-analysis. *Exceptional Children, 53,* 199–208.

Goodwin, D. L., Garvey, W. P., & Barclay, J. R. (1971). Microconsultation and behavior analysis: A method of training psychologists as behavioral consultants. *Journal of Consulting and Clinical Psychology, 37,* 355–363.

Gresham, F. M. (1985). Behavior disorder assessment: Conceptual, definitional, and practical considerations. *School Psychology Review, 14,* 495–509.

Gresham, F. M. (1989). Assessment of treatment integrity in school consultation and prereferral intervention. *School Psychology Review, 18,* 37–50.

Gresham, F. M., & Davis, C. J. (1988). Behavioral interviews with teachers and parents. In E. S. Shapiro & T. R. Kratochwill (Eds.), *Behavioral assessment in schools: Conceptual foundations and practical applications* (pp. 455–493). New York: Guilford Press.

Gresham, F. M., & Kendell, G. K. (1987). School consultation research: Methodological critique and future research directions. *School Psychology Review, 16,* 306–316.

Gutkin, T. B. (1980). Teacher perceptions of consultation services provided by school psychologists. *Professional Psychology, 11,* 637–642.

Gutkin, T. B. (1986). Consultees' perceptions of variables relating to the outcomes of school-based consultation interactions. *School Psychology Review, 15,* 375–382.

Gutkin, T. B., & Conoley, J. C. (1990). Reconceptualizing school psychology from a service delivery perspective: Implications for practice, training, and research. *Journal of School Psychology, 28,* 203–223.

Gutkin, T. B., & Curtis, M. J. (1982). School-based consultation: Theory and techniques. In C. R. Reynolds & T. B. Gutkin (Eds.), *The handbook of school psychology* (pp. 796–828). New York: Wiley.

Gutkin, T. B., & Curtis, M. J. (1990). School-based consultation: Theory, techniques, and research. In T. B. Gutkin & C. R. Reynolds (Eds.), *The handbook, of school psychology* (2nd ed., pp. 577–611). New York: Wiley.

Gutkin, T. B., Henning-Stout, M., & Piersel, W. C. (1988). Impact of a district-wide behavioral consultation prereferral intervention service on patterns of school psychological service delivery. *Professional School Psychology, 3,* 301–308.

Gutkin, T. B., & Hickman, J. A. (1988). Teachers' perceptions of control over presenting problems and resulting preferences for consultation versus referral services. *Journal of School Psychology, 26,* 395–398.

Happe, D. (1982). Behavioral intervention: It doesn't do any good in your briefcase. In J. Grimes (Ed.), *Psychological approaches to problems of children and adolescents* (pp. 15–41). Des Moines, IA: Iowa Department of Public Instruction.

Hawkins, R. P. (1989). Developing potent behavior-change technologies: An invitation to cognitive behavior therapists. *The Behavior Therapist, 12,* 126–131.

Hayes, S. C. (1981). Single case experimental design and empirical clinical practice. *Journal of Consulting and Clinical Psychology, 49,* 193–211.

Hobbs, N. (1964). Mental health's third revolution. *American Journal of Orthopsychiatry, 34,* 822–833.

Iwata, B. A., Dorsey, M. F., Slifer, K. J., Bauman, K., & Richman, G. S. (1982). Toward a functional analysis of self-injury. *Analysis and Intervention in Developmental Disabilities, 2,* 3–20.

Johnson, B. T., & Eagly, A. H. (1989). Effects of involvement on persuasion: A meta-analysis. *Psychological Bulletin, 106,* 290–314.

Kratochwill, T. R., & Bergan, J. R. (1990). *Behavioral consultation in applied settings: An individual guide.* New York: Plenum Press.

Kratochwill, T. R., & Piersel, W. C. (1983). Time-series research: Contributions to empirical clinical practice. *Behavioral Assessment, 5,* 165–176.

Kratochwill, T. R., VanSomeren, K. R., & Sheridan, S. M. (1989). Training behavioral consultants: A competency-based model to teach interview skills. *Professional School Psychology, 4,* 41–58.

Lambert, N. M. (1976). Children's problems and classroom interventions from the perspective of classroom teachers. *Professional Psychology, 1,* 507–517.

Mace, F. C., & Knight, D. (1986). Functional analysis and treatment of severe pica. *Journal of Applied Behavior Analysis, 19,* 411–416.

Mace, F. C., & West, B. J. (1986). Analysis of demand conditions associated with reluctant speech. *Journal of Behavior Therapy and Experimental Psychiatry, 17,* 285–294.

Mace, F. C., Yankanich, M. A., & West, B. J. (1989). Toward a methodology of experimental analysis and treatment of aberrant classroom behaviors. *Special Services in the Schools, 4,* 71–88.

Mannino, F. V., & Shore, M. F. (1975). The effects of consultation: A review of empirical studies of the literature. *American Journal of Community Psychology, 3,* 1–21.

Martens, B. K., Deery, K. S., & Gherardi, J. P. (1991). An experimental analysis of reflected affect versus reflected content in consultative interactions. *Journal of Educational and Psychological Consultation, 2,* 117–132.

Martens, B. K., Erchul, W. P., & Witt, J. C. (1992). Quantifying verbal interactions in school-based consultation: A comparison of four coding schemes. *School Psychology Review, 21,* 109–124.

Martens, B. K., Lewandowski, L. J., & Houk, J. L. (1989a). Correlational analysis of verbal interactions during the consultative interview and consultees' subsequent perceptions. *Professional Psychology: Research and Practice, 20,* 334–339.

Martens, B. K., Lewandowski, L. J., & Houk, J. L. (1989b). The effects of entry information on the consultation process. *School Psychology Review, 18,* 225–234.

Martens, B. K., & Meller, P. J. (1989). Influence of child and classroom characteristics on acceptability of interventions. *Journal of School Psychology, 27,* 237–245.

Martens, B. K., & Meller, P. J. (1990). The application of behavioral principles to educational settings. In T. B. Gutkin & C. R. Reynolds (Eds.), *The handbook of school psychology* (2nd ed., pp. 612–634). New York: Wiley.

Martens, B. K., Peterson, R. L., Witt, J. C., & Cirone, S. (1986). Teacher perceptions of school-based interventions. *Exceptional Children, 53,* 213–223.

McDougall, L. M., Reschly, D. J., & Corkery, J. M. (1988). Changes in referral interviews with teachers after behavioral consultation training. *Journal of School Psychology, 26,* 225–232.

Medway, F. J. (1979). How effective is school consultation? A review of recent research. *Journal of School Psychology, 17,* 275–281.

Medway, F. J., & Updyke, J. F. (1985). Meta-analysis of consultation outcome studies. *American Journal of Community Psychology, 13,* 489–505.

Nelson, R. O., & Hayes, S. C. (1979). Some current dimensions of behavioral assessment. *Behavioral Assessment, 1,* 1–16.

Owens, R. G. (1981). *Organizational behavior in education.* Englewood Cliffs, NJ: Prentice-Hall.

Patterson, G. R., & Forgatch, M. S. (1985). Therapist behavior as a determinant for client noncompliance: A paradox for the behavior modifier. *Journal of Consulting and Clinical Psychology, 53,* 846–851.

Piersel, W. C., & Gutkin, T. B. (1983). Resistance to school-based consultation: A behavioral analysis of the problem. *Psychology in the Schools, 20,* 311–320.

Ponti, C. R., Zins, J. E., & Graden, J. L. (1988). Implementing a consultation-based service delivery system to decrease referrals for special education: A case study of organizational considerations. *School Psychology Review, 17,* 89–100.

Pryzwansky, W. B. (1986). Indirect service delivery: Considerations for future research in consultation. *School Psychology Review, 15,* 479–488.

Repucci, N. D., & Saunders, J. T. (1974). Social psychology of behavior modification: Problems of implementation in natural settings. *American Psychologist, 29,* 649–660.

Reschly, D. J. (1988). Special education reform: School psychology revolution. *School Psychology Review, 17,* 459–475.

Reynolds, C. R., Gutkin, T. B., Elliott, S. N., & Witt, J. C. (1984). *School psychology: Essentials of theory and practice.* New York: Wiley.

Rosenfield, S. (1992). Developing school-based consultation teams: A design for organizational change. *School Psychology Quarterly, 7,* 27–46.

Shinn, M. R. (1989). *Curriculum-based measurement: Assessing special children.* New York: Guilford Press.

Sweet, A. A. (1984). The therapeutic relationship in behavior therapy. *Clinical Psychology Review, 4,* 253–272.

Tharp, R. G., & Wetzel, R. J. (1969). *Behavior modification in the natural environment.* San Diego, CA: Academic Press.

Tingstrom, D. H., Little, S. G., & Stewart, K. J. (1990). School consultation from a social psychological perspective: A review. *Psychology in the Schools, 27,* 41–50.

Tombari, M. L., & Bergan, J. R. (1978). Consultant cues and teacher verbalizations, judgments, and expectancies concerning children's adjustment problems. *Journal of School Psychology, 16,* 212–219.

Tracey, T. J., & Ray, P. B. (1984). Stages of successful time-limited counseling: an interactional examination. *Journal of Counseling Psychology, 31,* 13–27.

West, J. F., & Idol, L. (1987). School consultation (part I): An interdisciplinary perspective on theory, models, and research. *Journal of Learning Disabilities, 20,* 388–408.

Witt, J. C. (1986). Teachers' resistance to the use of school-based interventions. *Journal of School Psychology, 24,* 37–44.

Witt, J. C. (1990). Face-to-face verbal interaction in school-based consultation: A review of the literature. *School Psychology Quarterly, 5,* 199–210.

Witt, J. C., & Elliott, S. N. (1983). Assessment in behavioral consultation: The initial interview. *School Psychology Review, 12,* 42–49.

Witt, J. C., Erchul, W. P., McKee, W. T., Pardue, M. M., & Wickstrom, K. F. (1991). Conversational control in school-based consultation: The relationship between consultant and consultee topic determination and consultation outcome. *Journal of Educational and Psychological Consultation, 2,* 101–116.

Witt, J. C., & Martens, B. K. (1983). Assessing the acceptability of interventions used in the classroom. *Psychology in the Schools, 20,* 510–517.

Witt, J. C., & Martens, B. K. (1988). Problems with problem-solving consultation: A re-analysis of assumptions, methods, and goals. *School Psychology Review, 17,* 211–226.

Witt, J. C., Moe, G., Gutkin, T. B., & Andrews, L. (1984). The effect of saying the same thing in different ways: The problem of language and jargon in school-based consultation. *Journal of School Psychology, 22,* 361–367.

Ysseldyke, J. E., Pianta, B., Christenson, S., Wang, J., & Algozzine, B. (1983). An analysis of prereferral interventions. *Psychology in the Schools, 20,* 184–190.

5

Organizational Perspectives in Child Consultation

Robert J. Illback, Joseph E. Zins

Human service professionals consulting with child service systems (schools, social service agencies, child mental health agencies, juvenile justice systems) recognize that intervention programs are carried out within complex organizational contexts and involve the integration of a range of personal, social, and ecological variables (Maher, Illback, & Zins, 1984). Therefore, child-oriented consultants must be able to conceptualize problems and interventions from an organizational perspective and utilize information about organizational processes in their consultation activities with agencies and organizations (Illback & Maher, 1984; Maher & Illback, 1983). Organizational consultation can serve as the basis for improved child service organization effectiveness, which is a priority need for the 1990s and beyond (National Commission on Children, 1991).

Consultation occurs in the context of complex organizational processes. To understand these processes and how they affect consultation, consultants must have a language system for "thinking organizationally," a conceptual model for viewing varying and seemingly disconnected organizational events, and a perspective on the relationships between problems faced by consultees and certain organizational attributes. The following sections provide an overview of relevant principles and concepts from organizational psychology; a discussion of an integrative model for conceptualizing human service organizations; a review of organizational features of child service organizations that affect the consultation process; a discussion of the link between organizational effectiveness and important child and family outcomes; and an examination of organizational assessment and intervention strategies available to consultants who seek to facilitate planned organizational change in child service organizations.

Terminology and Concepts

Human service organizations have been described by Katz and Kahn (1966) as maintenance organizations. From the perspective of society, human service organizations are often seen as central to preserving and protecting societal institutions; in other words, maintaining the status quo and providing a mechanism for handling deviance from the norm. People within human services, however, may come to view their role in terms of facilitating change in people or society. These values can be at variance and are often the source of much conflict for those in human service agencies.

Thus, in their social, educative, and rehabilitative roles, child service organizations assume that (1) clients (children, youth, and families) have needs that emanate from developmental, familial, and societal tasks and demands, (2) meaningful helping activities, such as counseling and teaching, can be delineated and targeted to facilitate growth and development, (3) services can be comprehensive and accessible to all who are eligible (for example, children with learning and behavior problems), (4) services can be integrated in a systemic fashion (for example, K–12 curriculum scope and sequence, individual and group therapy experiences, foster care and adoptive services), and (5) service providers can be accountable to consumers and society (Baker, 1974).

Theories of organizational functioning typically derive from general systems theory (Miller, 1965; von Bertalanffy, 1968), which describes organizations as systems of interdependent components that work in harmony. Various levels of systems, from the suprasystem (molar) level of large societal institutions (health, welfare, education) to the subsystems (molecular) level of individuals and small groups, are seen as integrally related to one another. As open systems, organizations engage in a continual process of change in response to surroundings (adaptation). Therefore, changes in one system lead to changes in related systems. Organizational systems engage in self-regulation and maintenance activities, seek homeostasis and stability, and grow and develop over time (Berrien, 1976).

Organizations vary in dimensions such as size, complexity, formality, and purpose. However, all organizations share common features: identifiable boundaries, patterned behavioral regularities, systems of authority and decision making, communications systems, and mission (Hall, 1977). Any organization can be described in terms of these dimensions.

A human service organization, such as a social service agency, has **Boundaries**
boundaries delineated through its mission statement, expressed in documents
such as administrative regulations, annual reports to the community, and program descriptions; the physical environment in which it is housed (for example, administrative and program offices); its relationship to other organizations
and individuals in its environment (for example, clients or consumers, governmental regulators); and the resources such as people, money, information,
and technology that make up the organization and their relationships to one
another (for example, subunits within the organization defined by function,
such as treatment services, adoption services, and quality assurance).

In addition, people in the organization engage in behavioral routines
established by their roles and functions and interact with one another in predictable ways as they carry out responsibilities. Typically, an organizational **Lines of**
chart specifies *lines of authority* for decision making. For example, a school **authority**
system is governed by an elected board of education responsible to the community; the board delegates power to the superintendent, who works through
subordinates, such as program directors and principals, to carry out board
policy.

The careful observer will note that there are informal human influence
processes at work in the human service organization that affect decision mak- **communicat.**
ing as well. *Information is regularly transmitted* across the boundaries within
the organization (for example, departments), both in a formal, hierarchical
manner and in less formal (and sometimes unpredictable) ways. Actual communication and decision making in an organization may or may not reflect
the formal authority structure.

Finally, there is *organizational mission*—a shared set of beliefs and
attitudes regarding the overall task that the organization has been established **Mission**
to accomplish (Katz & Kahn, 1966). Most organizations promulgate mission
and goal statements. To the extent that these are explicit, operational policies
and procedures can be derived to enhance goal attainment by focusing organizational effort.

In business organizations, profit and economic viability are central to
organizational goal statements. Human service (both for-profit and not-for-
profit) organizations are more difficult to characterize in terms of mission and
goals. Goal statements may focus on ambiguous concepts such as adjustment,
adaptation, thinking processes, and values. At best, these are difficult to specify,
measure, and link together. Despite these difficulties, progressive human service organizations engage in systematic program planning and evaluation activities by specifying, measuring, and evaluating salient variables.

An Integrative Organizational Model

A model for viewing child service organizations as organizations that can lead to more effective intervention strategies is provided by Maher et al. (1984). The model posits three interactive organizational domains—structure, process, and behavior—and their related elements. These elements are often the targets of organizational change programs.

Organizational Structure

Organizational structure, the enduring and basic elements of the organization, is the foundation on which other functions rest. Child service organizations provide structure in order to focus organizational processes and behavior. Structure is provided through philosophy, policy and procedures, and service and programs.

Organizational Philosophy. The foundation of an organization's philosophy is found in its mission and goal statements. For example, the mission statement of a child and adolescent department of a community mental health center may state that the overall purposes of the department include (1) diagnostic assessment of clinic-referred children to ascertain their psychosocial needs; (2) determination of eligibility for a range of available mental health services (for example, individual counseling, family therapy, psychopharmacology); and placement of identified children in the least restrictive family-oriented environments.

Policies and Procedures. Given the focus provided by the mission statement, more specific policies and procedures are formulated to operationalize the overall perspective. Thus, in the area of child evaluation and classification, elaborate guidelines to ensure a broad data base for decision making, the use of team approaches, and a process for conflict resolution are specified. Similarly, to ensure that sound and integrated interventions are developed for each identified client, the organization promulgates policies and procedures that describe the planned and ongoing collaboration of treatment team members, features of acceptable therapeutic approaches, and methods for regular progress assessment and case review.

Policies and procedures also articulate formal authority (power) relationships within the organization. A policy handbook in a school system, for instance, states the authority and limitations of the board of education and its role in the administration and operation of the schools. Other documents delineate lines of authority throughout the organization, including the "chain of command" (subordinate-superordinate relationships), often in the form of an organizational chart.

Services and Programs. The specific services and programs provided by the organization and their relationship to one another make up the third element of organizational structure. Common child-oriented programs can be organized into five subdomains: assessment services, intervention services, supplemental (adjunctive) services, personnel development services, and administrative and support services. These subdomains represent a generic means of categorizing a range of programs and practices and are interrelated.

Specification of services and programs makes them more manageable, evaluable, and comprehensible to staff and others. Targeted structural interventions seek to improve organizational performance by enhancing these underlying elements of the child service organization.

Organizational Process

Organizational processes are ongoing actions (patterned behaviors) that are taken within the context of organizational structure. These processes allow for the implementation of policies, procedures, and programs, in addition to providing stability (homeostasis) for the organization. Organizational processes include planning and evaluating, communicating information, and making decisions.

Planning and Evaluation. These activities concern the ongoing management of resources within the setting, including monitoring and revising existing programs and developing new ones. Teachers deliver services in classrooms and are therefore responsible for the self-management of the program that they deliver (for example, ninth-grade biology). Given the overall program objectives reflected in available curriculum documents, the teacher plans and implements a sequence of lessons, assesses their impact on student learning, revises content and presentation, and then develops new materials and approaches to enhance the course.

Communication. Child service organizations transmit a vast amount of both verbal and written information. Information communicated about clients may include clinical records, diagnostic data, daily schoolwork, progress reports, attendance and service utilization data, and correspondence with parents. At the organizational level, administrators and supervisors process fiscal reports, utilization and outcome data, policy revisions, employment-related documents, and program material.

In addition to formal information transmission, there is an informal information process at work in child service organizations that does not usually correspond directly to the established authority structure. People in organizations are microcosms of the communities in which the organization is embedded, and there are untold informational connections between people who would appear to be unrelated in a structural sense. Sometimes these connections are obvious, as when a teacher is the spouse of the school superintendent. Often, however, the interpersonal connections are subtle and related to proximity (for example, being neighbors), history (for example, growing up together), or circumstance (for example, working together on a community project). These connections are especially notable in small communities. An understanding of informal information networks within a particular organization is essential to the change process.

Decision Making. People in organizations engage in daily decision making, the third element of organizational process. Child protective service workers decide whether there is sufficient evidence to suggest child abuse or neglect. Program administrators make decisions about program efficacy. Other types of decisions are longer-term, such as deciding which intervention approaches to adopt, which programs to fund or cut back, and how services can be most effectively organized.

There are certain regular features to decision processes, including clarifying the decision problem; specifying decision rules, procedures, and criteria; selecting a decision alternative; and assessing the decision outcome. Effective child service organizations tend to be systematic in their decision-making practices.

Organizational Behavior

Organizational behavior includes the activities, duties, and interactions of people in child service organizations as they provide services, communicate information, and make decisions. As we examine organizational structure and process, it should not be forgotten that organizations are most fundamentally aggregations of people interacting. The examination of organizational behavior, then, seeks to portray individual actions as they occur in the context of structure and process.

In well-functioning organizations, each individual perceives clear guidance about the role that he or she is to perform (for example, teacher, psychologist, child-care worker). Some roles may be highly circumscribed, such as that of the business office worker who processes benefits data. However, many human service roles are complex, involving responsibility for assorted program tasks and frequent crossing of boundaries between subunits of the organization. Organizational roles are prescribed by history and tradition ("we always did it this way"), needs and circumstances (for example, new regulatory requirements), and personal characteristics, such as particular employee strengths.

Responsibilities are more specific than roles, although they derive from the overall role that the person fulfills in the organization. Responsibilities are usually established through an explicit job description; at the very least, they are communicated through systematic interaction with a superordinate, such as a direct supervisor (McInerney, 1985). For example, the key responsibilities of a school psychologist may include establishing and managing a referral system, evaluating students with special needs, planning and facilitating psychoeducational interventions, and consulting with administrators and parents. Ancillary responsibilities may include program planning and evaluation, training and supervision of paraprofessionals, and grant writing.

The final, and perhaps most essential, element of organizational behavior is relationships. Organizational health and survival are highly dependent on effective interaction between people in accomplishing the mission. Harmonious group interaction involves the ability to identify problems, share responsibilities, collaborate, and manage conflict situations.

Factors Affecting the Organizational Process

Child service organizations are subject to a number of factors that can lead to organizational complexity, uncertainty, unresponsiveness, and occasionally immobilization that can interfere with the fulfilling of their mission. This section first reviews external influences that can affect the organization and then discusses some of the organizational problems that may result from them.

External Influences

As open social systems, child service organizations respond to inputs from a range of external sources, which can have a profound impact on the ability of the organizations to function effectively.

Regulatory and Bureaucratic Influences. The regulatory and bureaucratic environment is a primary determinant of how child service organizations must function. It consists of a broad array of federal and state legislative and judicial mandates in such areas as child abuse and neglect, desegregation, education for handicapped and disadvantaged students, family preservation, and child mental health services; administrative regulations such as accreditation standards, program guidelines, and organizational policies and procedures; and less formal directives and interactions with members of the bureau-cracy.

Many child service programs are explicitly designed to conform to the standards and guidelines established by the bureaucracy, resulting in a "patch-work quilt" of programs and practices. The regulatory environment can lead to rigidity in organizations, with people focusing on fulfilling regulations and providing documentation of compliance to the detriment of client service. In highly bureaucratic environments, staff members feel that they have little local control over program decisions. When applied judiciously, however, many rules and regulations are compatible with systematic intervention, conform-ance with legislative intent, and best practices.

Professional and Advocacy Groups. Another complex web of external influences on child service organizations is created by organizations of profes-sionals (psychologists, social workers, teachers) and paraprofessionals (sup-port personnel, instructional aides); parent and family groups, such as parents teacher associations; community organizations such as the Association for Re-tarded Citizens; institutions such as universities; and other people and groups that can affect how child service personnel accomplish their task. For example, local and national organizations representing psychologists, social workers, counselors, teachers, administrators, and parent and community groups are active in promoting standards and guidelines for programs. Such groups have been instrumental in a variety of areas, including the passage of legislation such as Public Laws 94-142 and 99-457 (guaranteeing preschool and elemen-tary school education for children with disabilities) and Public Law 101-336 (the Americans with Disabilities Act) and movements for educational reform and deinstitutionalization of people with mental illness.

Advocacy groups, which typically operate as nonprofit organizations, have been especially influential in dramatizing problems faced by children in society through such means as the publication of high-profile reports, testi-mony to legislators, the introduction of reform legislation, and local initiatives (see, for example, National Commission on Children, 1991). Examples of prob-lem areas that have been effectively addressed by such groups include low achievement scores, high dropout rates, functional illiteracy, child nutrition, out-of-home placement by social service agencies, and overuse of child psychi-atric hospitalization.

Another source of professional influence on child service organizations is their close links to institutions of higher education where staff members were trained or where they pursue advanced study while they work. From these institutions, program staff acquire many of the beliefs, attitudes, knowl-edge, and skills that they employ in their work.

Cultural, Political, and Social Context. Features of the community in which an organization is located can affect the characteristics of that organization. Organizations in rural, agrarian settings, for example, will differ from those in urban areas because of differences in cultural values, tax base and funding adequacy, availability of goods and services, and social, recreational, and employment opportunities. Schools in rural communities may be heavily politicized because they are often the primary employer and one of the central institutions, along with local government and religious organizations, that define the community. And agencies that draw their clientele from particular areas (for example, neighborhood school) or groups (for example, racial minorities, those with a specific handicapping condition) are likely to be confronted with agendas and issues that are essential to their client group.

The impact of local events and issues is readily seen in public meetings of an organization's governing board, the formal mechanism by which the community expresses its wishes regarding the services to be provided. Agency boards set policy, hire administrators, and are often involved in various phases of program operation (fiscal, programmatic, management). Those who make up these boards, whether elected or appointed, are generally influential members of the local community and thought to be representative of it. While board members reflect themes prevalent in the community, they may also have personal issues that they bring to the agenda of the organization, which may result in competition, conflict, and tension. It is not unusual for community issues not technically related to the child service organization to be played out in this forum.

Social and political influence processes also operate at the individual, group, departmental, and system levels through all of the interactions between community members and child service organization staff. External consultants may be insensitive to these subtle processes unless they immerse themselves in the system.

Organizational Consequences

The external influences on child service organizations make them highly susceptible to conflicting and inconsistent inputs (the problem of *overpermeable boundaries*). Child service personnel, such as teachers and social workers, are continually asked to adapt to new regulations or procedures, revised methods and materials, the latest intervention trend, dissatisfied parents, scheduling and logistical problems, increasingly specialized duties and responsibilities, special requests, and various other interruptions and discontinuities. The problem of overpermeable boundaries is associated with high job stress, overload, and dysfunction in child service organizations (Forman, 1981).

Overpermeable boundaries can cause immobilization within the organization by making personnel fearful of taking actions that may alienate one or another constituency. On the other hand, overpermeable boundaries make child service personnel vulnerable to the latest intervention "fads," which may not be theoretically or conceptually sound or may be inconsistent with current successful practices within the organization. To avoid such problems, the organization needs to establish boundaries that are sufficiently permeable to ensure responsiveness to external trends, issues, and concerns but that also allow for reflective processing of information and ideas.

Another problem facing many organizations is *goal diffuseness*—poorly specified input (for example, intervention strategies), throughput (learning processes, situational dynamics), and output (achievement, adjustment). Child service organizations often rely on mission and goal statements that are global in their orientation and that serve political but not necessarily accountability functions. For example, many organizations state their purpose as "enabling each child to attain his or her fullest human potential." While admirable, this is hardly evaluable, since it is impossible to determine what an individual's full potential may be. Some organizations may employ such ambiguity to deflect criticism about inadequacies and undesired outcomes and to reduce scrutiny and control by external sources, such as regulators.

A related problem is that it is not always possible to link child service programs and services to goal attainment with any degree of certainty. This may lead to *low accountability* for intervention-related outcomes. There are many variables operating in child service organizations that can account for changes (multiple treatment interference), and the design problems inherent in attributing change to specific intervention practices are daunting. Nonetheless, there are methods for accomplishing this task within the emergent field of program planning and evaluation (see Illback, Zins, Maher, & Greenberg, 1990). Program planning and evaluation approaches seek to improve organizational functioning through activities such as evaluability assessment, program (treatment) specification, needs assessment, implementation evaluation, and outcome determination. However, child service organizations have resisted program planning and evaluation efforts, and departments of research, planning, and evaluation are generally found only in large organizations, where their efforts focus on high-profile projects and programs (often federally funded initiatives).

A final organizational problem for child service organizations, especially those in the public sector, is that they may face a *lack of competition*. Many such organizations, such as schools and social service agencies, are legally mandated monopolies with an exclusive franchise for the services they provide to the public. When there are few competitors to motivate improved organizational performance, complacency and resistance to innovation can develop. Further, the organization may cease to see clients as consumers who are purchasing a service and therefore deserve to be treated with respect and dignity. This attitude can lead to practices in which help giving becomes usurping, disabling, and disempowering for children and their families (Dunst, Trivette, & Deal, 1989). The effects of such poor organizational functioning can include dependency on the system (Merton, Merton, & Barber, 1983), negative reactions and stress (Dunst & Leet, 1987), poor self-esteem (Fisher, Nadler, & Whitcher-Alagna, 1983), and learned helplessness (Coates, Renzaglia, & Embree, 1983).

There recently has been recognition of the need to promote competition. Some in the educational community, for example, have suggested promoting entrepreneurial private alternatives through tuition tax credits, voucher systems, and special incentive plans to increase the competitive atmosphere and thereby improve organizational performance (National Commission on Excellence in Education, 1983).

Organization Effectiveness and Services Integration

The features of child service organizations described above can result in uncoordinated, fragmented, narrow, and ineffective service delivery to children and families. A recent comprehensive examination of child service organizations and programs concluded that "the present system of services and supports is totally inadequate" (National Commission on Children, 1991, p. 312). The report further indicates that severe organizational ineffectiveness in children's services dramatically impedes the ability of professionals to provide coordinated, comprehensive, and intensive assistance to children and families in need.

A major challenge facing consultants working in child service organizations is to develop and improve the capacity of these organizations to provide integrated services to children and families (Schorr & Schorr, 1988). In this context, extensive national attention has focused on the reform and restructuring of child service organizations, with particular emphasis on service coordination and interagency collaboration (Edelman & Radin, 1991; Melaville & Blank, 1991). The reformers believe that collaboration, coordination, and integration of children's services will improve access, efficiency, quality, and effectiveness.

Recent writing about services integration assumes that there are links between service delivery system process variables and essential child and family outcomes in areas such as cognitive development, social competence, behavioral self-control, self-efficacy, placement stability and restrictiveness, family support, and satisfaction with services. Recommendations for change in this area include (1) decategorization of programs and services, (2) uniformity of eligibility standards, (3) interprofessional collaboration across levels and systems within the organization, (4) promotion of innovation and flexibility, (5) a change in focus from crisis intervention and remediation to prevention and early intervention, (6) attention to the needs of consumers of services, and (7) facilitation of professional development and effective working conditions. Figure 5.1 provides a graphic representation of how improvements in structural, process, and behavioral features of organizations can lead to more integrated and responsive service delivery patterns, thereby enhancing the ability of targeted children and families to profit from intervention programs.

Organizational Assessment and Intervention

Consultants who work in child service organizations are often called on to engage in efforts to promote organizational development and improvement, requiring the use of systematic assessment and intervention processes at the organizational level. Organizational change efforts are challenging to conceptualize and difficult to organize and implement. They meet with resistance as the child service organization struggles to maintain homeostasis, leading to failure and frustration (Derr, 1976). Organizational change may fail because of insufficient information about the problem areas and inadequate diagnosis (poor problem clarification), inattention to organizational readiness for change, simplistic intervention strategies and procedures, and lack of follow-up (Fullan, Miles, & Taylor, 1980). Change efforts will be more likely to succeed if the following principles are kept in mind (see Illback & Zins, 1984, for a more thorough discussion of these principles):

1. Child service organizations are continually changing and evolving in response to both internal and external factors, and the consultant must accurately perceive and utilize this ongoing process in the change effort.
2. Change efforts that apply multiple methods and strategies are more likely to reflect organizational complexity than are approaches that rely on narrow methods and strategies targeted toward specific aspects of the organization, resulting in more meaningful and durable change.
3. Successful change efforts involve balancing and controlling a large number of mediating variables involving people, procedures, and processes.
4. Success in change efforts in child service organizations depends on timely, accurate, and continuous assessment information about organizational functioning.
5. Some child service organizations are more ready for change than others,

Figure 5.1. Linking Organizational Effectiveness with Child and Family Outcomes.

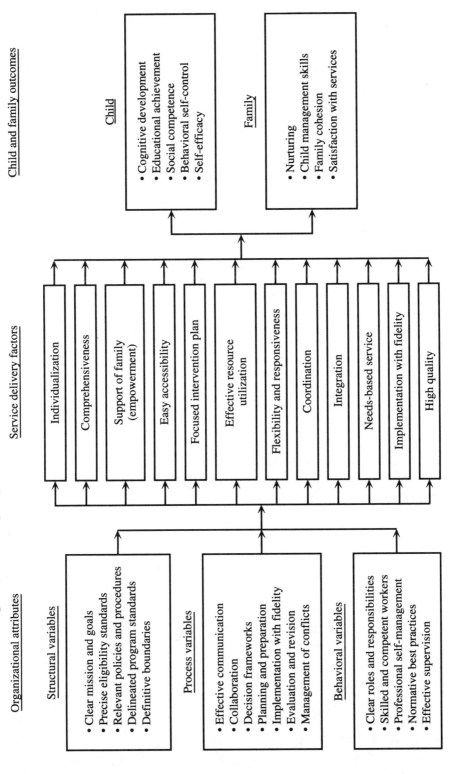

and it may be appropriate to defer the change initiative until the organization can be made more hospitable to the intervention.

6.   The interdependency of the organization's elements may cause organiza-
     tional change efforts to have unintended effects.

7.   Meaningful change is most likely to occur when people within the child
     service organization have a sense of "ownership" of the organizational
     change effort.

8.   An overriding goal of planned organizational change is the facilitation of
     self-evaluation and self-renewal processes that become a part of the rou-
     tine of a more functional organization.

Organizational Assessment

As in change efforts with individuals, organizational intervention is more likely
to be effective when there is reliable and valid information about the identified
organizational problems (needs) and the context in which they are embedded.
Organizational assessment may be the most important stage of the intervention
process in that it culminates in selection of the variables that will be targeted
for intervention and thereby focuses the change effort (Hersey & Blanchard,
1982).

Organizational assessment is typically conceived as the first stage of a
larger intervention process. The initial diagnostic process is difficult to separate
from intervention processes because it is continuous, leads to problem reframing and goal setting, and promotes a sense of collaboration and problem
ownership on the part of those involved with the assessment. These factors
argue for the inclusion of key organizational members in the process of change
from the earliest stage (Beer, 1980).

Consultants have available a range of methods for conducting organizational assessments. They can review *documents and data,* such as policy and
procedure manuals, descriptive literature about programs and practices, and
routine data such as service utilization information. Most child service organizations collect a vast array of information about programs and service recipients, although it is not often synthesized for any purpose. *Interviews and
direct observation* methods can provide important information about process
variables within the organization, such as interaction patterns and decision
making. Many organizational consultants also rely on formal diagnostic instrumentation, including *questionnaires, surveys, and ratings.* These are often
standardized and well-researched procedures that assess global variables such
as organizational climate, communication, stress, and leadership (see Hoy,
Tarter, & Kottkamp, 1991). Alternatively, organizational consultants may

choose to develop measurement instruments that focus on the particular variables under investigation but that are unvalidated. Moos (1979) provides an excellent overview of conceptual, technical, and practical issues in assessing social and organizational environments.

Critical to the process of organizational assessment is the formulation of assessment questions. When presented with a presumed problem of organizational functioning, the consultant must first conceptualize the questions that will focus the assessment. Such questions might include (1) What population and what needs are served by the program? (2) What organizational unit (department, program, system) will the consultation and organizational intervention focus on? (3) Do staff members have the problem-solving and collaborative skills necessary for an effective consultative intervention? (4) What contextual and circumstantial features of the organization are likely to affect the organizational intervention? (5) What resources are available for conducting the various stages of the consultation process and intervention? (6) How ready is this particular child service organization for change?

Maher and Illback (1982) recommend a multidimensional needs assessment framework to examine the recipients of services and their psychoeducational needs in relation to available resources within organizational units of the organization. This framework includes the following steps:

1. *Select a needs assessment committee* to represent multiple perspectives and constituencies within the organization and assume responsibility for the design and conduct of the needs assessment.
2. *Determine the unit(s) of analysis that will focus the needs assessment*—those units and aspects of the organization that need to be assessed to provide reliable and valid information for the intervention (for example, staff members and clients, programs). Specified evaluation questions provide focus to this analysis.
3. *Design and conduct the needs assessment* to gather information relevant to the evaluation questions through methods such as observation, interview, document review, and surveys and synthesize this information to form operating hypotheses about the present state of affairs within the organization in relation to the problem area.
4. *Disseminate the needs assessment information.* Report the information gleaned from the above activities to program planners in a format that lends itself to decision making, including the needs of clients and client systems; present service delivery system information; recommendations for planning and development of new services and/or alterations to present programming; and suggestions for allocation of resources.

Organization Intervention

The following paragraphs provide a detailed discussion of organization intervention approaches that target process, structural, and behavioral dimensions
of organizational functioning.

Process Interventions. Planning and evaluation, decision making, and
communication are major components of the process that an organization
uses to accomplish its mission. In dysfunctional organizations, breakdowns in
cooperation and collaboration result in inefficiency and ineffectiveness in
these areas. These problems are especially troublesome in the human service
arena, where productive interactions are central to mission attainment. Considerable attention has therefore been devoted to "organization development"
or process interventions (Schein, 1969; Schmuck & Miles, 1971).

Process interventions have typically focused on variables such as teamwork, conflict, group norms and group growth, member roles and functions,
creative problem solving, trust and cooperation, attitudes and values, leadership styles, and listening and communication (Goodstein, 1978). These interventions assume that improving the capabilities of individuals to work together
along these dimensions will enhance the overall productivity and health of
the organization. Not surprisingly, the field has drawn heavily from social
psychology and group dynamics. In fact, much of the early work grew out of
the sensitivity training and "T-group" literature (Bradford, Gibb, & Benne,
1964).

Beer (1980) has classified methods of process interventions according
to four categories: survey feedback, group development and team building,
intergroup development, and process consultation. *Survey feedback* methods
involve systematic collection of data about the variables of concern (for example, morale, job satisfaction), which are then summarized and discussed among
organizational members to clarify the nature and scope of the problems and
attempt to resolve them. Survey feedback is most effectively used as a component of a larger change process; when used in isolation, it appears to be
insufficient to promote lasting change.

Group and team development methods are based on the principles and
procedures of group dynamics. Work groups or teams are formed to address
specific issues, especially issues that cannot be addressed individually (Zander,
1985): a new problem (for example, an increase in substance abuse), a new
mandate (for example, to provide preschool handicapped services), or an
unexpected opportunity (for example, an increase in revenue). Some work
groups are mandated by federal, state, and local laws, regulations, or policies
(such as Public Law 94-142, requiring multidisciplinary teams), whereas others

appear on an ad hoc basis and are more time-limited (for example, a committee to identify priorities for a newly formed program for medically fragile children). All work groups, formal or informal, proceed through stages of development that must be facilitated if the group is to accomplish its ultimate objectives (Dimock, 1987).

Intergroup development methods focus not on the development of individual working groups but rather on the interdependency of subunits within the organization. Teacher, administrator, parent, or professional groups may engage in activities to promote improved communication, role definition, and intergroup perceptions, especially in situations of conflict and dysfunction.

An example of the use of intergroup development methods is the effort to improve service delivery systems for mildly handicapped students. Will (1986) has recommended that to decrease instructional fragmentation and rigidity, increase and improve social and academic experiences, and better utilize resources, the focus of intervention programs for such students should change from special educational environments to a "regular education initiative" (Will, 1986). This process requires various role groups, such as special and remedial education teachers, school psychologists, counselors, speech clinicians, and general education personnel, to alter their roles, responsibilities, and relationships. Considerable intergroup development is necessary to accomplish this objective (Graden, Zins, & Curtis, 1988).

A more general category of intervention is termed *process consultation*. With this type of intervention, the consultant seeks to help clients and client systems behave more effectively within the social ecology of the organization. Many of the methods associated with process interventions can be used with this approach. In essence, the process consultant is the mental health consultant and therapist to the organization, building relationships, facilitating interaction, giving process feedback, and suggesting alternative means for communicating and collaborating. Broad-based interventions focusing on organizational climate, interpersonal relationships, morale issues, and community concerns are examples of this mode of functioning.

Structural Interventions. Structural interventions are oriented toward "redesigning" fundamental aspects of policies, procedures, reward systems, service and program configurations, and other such mechanisms within the organization. Changes in organizational structure are presumed to alter organizational processes and behavior. Organizational design (and redesign) may take a variety of forms, such as reward systems, performance management and control systems, and task and organizational design (Beer, 1980).

Within all organizations, there are implicit and explicit *systems of reward and punishment*. Staff members receive salaries, benefits, and job security as compensation for the services they provide; in some organizations, they may receive bonuses for exemplary performance or organizational productivity. Praise, recognition, and approval serve as social reinforcers to develop and maintain desired behaviors. When people in the organization deviate too much from what is expected, they may receive mild reprimands, poor evaluations, suspension, or termination. There is also an informal culture in which other staff members provide reinforcement (and punishment) by recognizing special efforts and ignoring or criticizing deficient performance or unwanted actions.

Structural interventions seek to capitalize on both formal and informal reward systems in organizations. Much of the information on this area is provided in the literature on *organizational behavior management* (OBM) (Frederickson, 1978). OBM interventions include providing special incentives to attract and retain staff (for example, extra planning time, bonus pay, recognition), emphasizing positive accomplishments through intermittent but regular performance feedback, and providing clear feedback about practices that may be detrimental to the growth and development of the program (for example, worker self-isolation). Informal reward system strategies may focus on developing a sense of collegiality among team members that encourages them to reinforce one another and arranging for reinforcement to be delivered by others in the organization, such as supervisors.

Effective organizations are likely to also use *performance management and control systems* to enhance the behavior of organization members. This involves delineating and describing key goals and activities for individuals, groups, and subgroups, followed by measurement, feedback, and modification. Child service organizations use systems of this type, including management by objectives (Bell, 1974), goal attainment scaling (Kiresuk & Sherman, 1968), performance appraisal (Beer, 1980), and program analysis and review (Maher & Bennett, 1984).

Another means to structure interaction and behavior is *task and organization design* methods. Most employees have job descriptions that set parameters on their behavior; task design is more explicit, undertaking to analyze and alter physical and psychological aspects of the work task so as to enhance worker productivity, collaboration, and satisfaction. Methods used for effective task design include grouping tasks so that they relate naturally to one another and to the overall mission; establishing task identify by combining similar tasks; ensuring that staff members have direct contact with those who will ultimately receive services; allowing staff members to perceive a sense of ownership of their work environment; and opening feedback channels (Beer, 1980).

Organization design is more global and far-reaching than task design.

Child service organizations often engage in reorganization when faced with internal (often political) problems. This change may mean shifting lines of authority, moving subunits of the organization, or adding or deleting programs and services. There may be debate about the amount of centralization of authority that is necessary. Some programs, such as personnel and administrative services, function more smoothly when centrally coordinated. Others, such as direct service provision, can be more effective when decision making is centered at the program level.

Another debate centers around the amount of specialization necessary in a child service organization. For example, in a mental health center, should a multidisciplinary team concept be used, or is it more efficient for generic services to be provided through individual providers? Should a school system use "pull-out" programs in reading for students with learning disabilities, children of migrant families, and those who need remedial or basic skills education, or should it design the organization so that all reading instructions is conducted within the general education program?

Individual Interventions. This domain of intervention strategies focuses attention on individual behavior within the organization. When a problem is conceptualized as pertaining specifically to a person or subunit, it may be most efficient to develop an intervention targeted toward modifying the behavior of that person or unit. Approaches associated with this domain include personnel recruitment and selection, remedial and disciplinary actions, continuing professional development, personal counseling, and self-supervision.

When an organization determines that a staff member is required to fill a key position such as case manager or child-care worker, it specifies the training, experience, general competencies, and related characteristics required. People in organizations are not interchangeable; they cannot be "slotted" into positions without regard to their particular professional strengths and weaknesses. *Personnel recruitment and selection* methods consider the idiosyncratic nature of particular roles and responsibilities and strive for the best fit between the job candidate and the job.

When a person has been found deficient in the performance of duties, the organization has a special obligation to its clients to improve performance through *remedial actions* or, failing that, to remove the ineffective staff member from the position through *disciplinary actions.* Due process requires that administrative assistance and a remedial plan of action be developed in conjunction with the deficient staff member. If, after a reasonable period of time, the person does not improve, management must choose reassignment, suspension, or termination.

The organization is also required to provide for the ongoing professional development needs of its members to enhance and maintain skills, develop new knowledge, and foster self-renewal. This is done through a program of *continuing professional development,* or in-service training. Additionally, child service organizations are recognizing that personal problems can greatly affect workplace functioning, and some now offer *personal counseling* through employee assistance programs (EAPs) (Farkas, 1989). Ultimately, staff members should be encouraged to engage in *self-supervision,* a process of self-monitoring, self-evaluating, and personal goal setting.

Summary

Child-oriented consultants will benefit from the ability to conceptualize problems and interventions from an organizational perspective, use information about organizational processes in their consultation activities with agencies and organizations, and facilitate organization development and improvement through planned change efforts. This chapter has provided an overview of principles, terms, and concepts from organizational psychology; discussed an integrative conceptual model for human service organizations; considered organizational features of child service organizations that impinge on the consultation process; and presented a range of organizational assessment and intervention strategies consistent with the conceptual model underlying the approach.

References

Baker, F. (1974). From community mental health to human service ideology. *American Journal of Public Health, 64,* 576–581.

Beer, M. (1980). *Organization change and development: A systems view.* Santa Monica, CA: Goodyear.

Bell, T. H. (1974). *A performance accountability system for school administrators.* West Nyack, NY: Parker.

Berrien, F. K. (1976). A general systems approach to organizations. In M. D. Dunnette (Ed.), *Handbook of industrial and organizational psychology* (pp. 48–73). Skokie, IL: Rand McNally.

Bradford, L. P., Gibb, J. R., & Benne, K. D. (Eds.). (1964). *T-group theory and laboratory method.* New York: Wiley.

Coates, D., Renzaglia, G. J., & Embree, M. C. (1983). When helping backfires: Help and helplessness. In J. D. Fisher, A. Nadler, & B. M. DePaulo (Eds.), *New directions in helping: Vol. I. Recipient reactions to aid* (pp. 251–279). San Diego, CA: Academic Press.

Derr, C. B. (1976). "OD" won't work in schools. *Education and Urban Society, 8*(2), 227–241.

Dimock, H. G. (1987). *Groups: Leadership and group development.* San Diego, CA: University Associates.

Dunst, C. J., & Leet, H. E. (1987). Measuring the adequacy of resources in households with young children. *Child Care, Health, and Development, 13,* 111–125.

Dunst, C. J., Trivette, T. M., & Deal, A. (1989). *Enabling and empowering families: Principles and guidelines for practice.* Cambridge, MA: Brookline Books.

Edelman, P. B., & Radin, B. A. (1991). *Serving children and families effectively: How the past can help chart the future.* Washington, DC: Education and Human Services Consortium.

Farkas, G. M. (1989). The impact of federal rehabilitation laws on the expanding role of employee assistance programs in business and industry. *American Psychologist, 12,* 1482–1490.

Fisher, J. D., Nadler, A., & Whitcher-Alagna, S. (1983). Four theoretical approaches for conceptualizing reactions to aid. In J. D. Fisher, A. Nadler, & B. M. DePaulo (Eds.), *New directions in helping: Vol. I. Recipient reactions to aid* (pp. 51–84). San Diego, CA: Academic Press.

Forman, S. G. (1981). Stress-management training: Evaluation of effects on school psychological services. *Journal of School Psychology, 19,* 233–241.

Frederickson, L. W. (1978). Behavioral reorganization of a professional service system. *Journal of Organizational Behavior Management, 2,* 1–11.

Fullan, M., Miles, M. B., & Taylor, G. (1980). Organization development in schools: The state of the art. *Review of Educational Research, 50,* 121–183.

Goodstein, L. D. (1978). *Consulting with human service systems.* Reading, MA: Addison-Wesley.

Graden, J. L., Zins, J. E., & Curtis, M. J. (Eds.). (1988). *Alternative educational delivery systems: Enhancing instructional options for all students.* Silver Spring, MD: National Association of School Psychologists.

Hall, R. H. (1977). *Organizations: Structure and process.* Englewood Cliffs, NJ: Prentice-Hall.

Hersey, P., & Blanchard, K. H. (1982). *Management of organizational behavior: Utilizing human resources.* Englewood Cliffs, NJ: Prentice-Hall.

Hoy, W. K., Tarter, C. J., & Kottkamp, R. B. (1991). *Open schools/healthy schools: Measuring organizational climate.* Newbury Park, CA: Sage.

Illback, R. J., & Maher, C. A. (1984). The school psychologist as an organizational boundary role professional. *Journal of School Psychology, 22,* 63–72.

Illback, R. J., & Zins, J. E. (1984). Organizational interventions in educational settings. In C. A. Maher, R. J. Illback, & J. E. Zins (Eds.), *Organizational psychology in the schools: A handbook for professionals.* (pp. 21–51). Springfield, IL: Thomas.

Illback, R. J., Zins, J. E., Maher, C. A., & Greenberg, R. (1990). An overview of principles and procedures of program planning and evaluation. In T. B. Gutkin & C. R. Reynolds (Eds.), *Handbook of school psychology* (2nd ed., pp. 801–822). New York: Wiley.

Katz, D., & Kahn, R. L. (1966). *The social psychology of organizations.* New York: Wiley.

Kiresuk, T. J., & Sherman, R. E. (1968). Goal attainment scaling: A general method for evaluating comprehensive community mental health programs. *Community Mental Health Journal, 4,* 443–453.

Maher, C. A., & Bennett, R. E. (1984). *Planning and evaluating special education services.* Englewood Cliffs, NJ: Prentice-Hall.

Maher, C. A., & Illback, R. J. (1982). Planning for the delivery of special services in public schools: A multidimensional needs assessment framework. *Evaluation and Program Planning, 4,* 249–259.

Maher, C. A., & Illback, R. J. (1983). Planning for organizational change in schools: Alternative approaches and procedures. *School Psychology Review, 12,* 460–466.

Maher, C. A., Illback, R. J., & Zins, J. E. (Eds.). (1984). *Organizational psychology in the schools: A handbook for professionals.* Springfield, IL: Thomas.

McInerney, J. F. (1985). Authority management. In C. A. Maher (Ed.), *Professional self-management: Techniques for special services providers* (pp. 129–148). Baltimore, MD: Brookes.

Melaville, A. I., & Blank, M. J. (1991). *What it takes: Structuring interagency partnerships to connect children and families with comprehensive services.* Washington, DC: Education and Human Services Consortium.

Merton, V., Merton, R. K., & Barber, E. (1983). Client ambivalence in professional relationships: The problem of seeking help from strangers. In B. DePaulo, A. Nadler, & J. Fisher (Eds.), *New directions in helping: Vol. 2. Help-seeking* (pp. 13–44). San Diego, CA: Academic Press.

Miller, J. G. (1965). Living systems. *Behavioral Science, 10,* 193–237.

Moos, R. H. (1979). *Evaluating educational environments.* Palo Alto, CA: Consulting Psychologists Press.

National Commission on Children. (1991). *Beyond rhetoric: A new American agenda for children and families.* Washington, DC: U.S. Government Printing Office.

National Commission on Excellence in Education. (1983). *A nation at risk: The imperative for educational reform.* Washington, DC: U.S. Government Printing Office.

Schein, E. H. (1969). *Process consultation: Its role in organization develop-ment.* Reading, MA: Addison-Wesley.

Schmuck, R. A., & Miles, M. B. (Eds.). (1971). *Organization development in schools.* Palo Alto, CA: National Press Books.

Schorr, L. B., & Schorr, D. (1988). *Within our reach: Breaking the cycle of disadvantage.* New York: Doubleday.

von Bertalanffy, L. (1968). *General systems theory.* New York: Braziller.

Will, M. (1986). *Educating students with learning problems: A shared responsi-bility.* Washington, DC: U.S. Department of Education.

Zander, A. (1985). *The purposes of groups and organizations.* San Francisco: Jossey-Bass.

6

Models for Working with Parents

Susan M. Sheridan

Working with parents to maximize treatment outcomes for children is a valued role for mental health professionals. In a society with more and more families living in poverty, single-parent households, child abuse, and juvenile crime, the complexities and responsibilities of parenting are paramount. Yet how does one learn to parent? What supports are readily available to parents in need of assistance? This chapter briefly reviews some of the common approaches to working with parents, discusses issues in implementing parent consultation, explores new avenues in parent consultation, and reports research findings and future directions.

Several alternatives to working with parents are available. In general, three models are typically suggested: parent education, parent training, and parent consultation. Although these terms are often used interchangeably, there are some fundamental and qualitative differences among them. A number of dimensions can be identified on which they differ, including breadth of information disseminated, depth of skill development, specificity of skill and knowledge imparted, and individuality of focus. A matrix characterizing parent education, training, and consultation on each dimension is presented in Table 6.1.

Parent Education and Training

Parent education has been defined as "a systematic and conceptually based program, intended to impart information, awareness, or skills to the participants on aspects of parenting" (Fine, 1980, pp. 5–6). In general, parent educa-

Table 6.1. Characteristics of Different Models for Working with Parents.

	Dimensions			
	Breadth of information disseminated	Depth of skill development	Specificity of skill and knowledge imparted	Individuality of focus
Parent education	High	Low	Low	Low
Parent training	Medium	Medium	Medium	Medium
Parent consultation	Low	High	High	High

tion models depend on lectures and discussions to disseminate information, heighten awareness, and change attitudes (Kramer, 1990a). The goals of parent education typically include helping parents to achieve greater self-awareness, improve parent-child communication, make family life more enjoyable, and obtain useful information on child development (Fine, 1980).

Parent education is typically considered as an umbrella that subsumes more specific approaches to working with parents (including parent training and parent consultation). Basic characteristics of parent education include limited involvement with parents' personal problems, a limited scope of interpersonal communication, and predetermined number and length of sessions. The focus is typically on achieving behavioral change without intensive personality changes in parents (Dembo, Sweitzer, & Lauritzen, 1985). Readers are referred to comprehensive texts edited by Fine (1980, 1989) for a more thorough discussion of parent education.

According to Dembo et al. (1985, p. 156), "parent training, which is subsumed under parent education, is defined as a process that includes at least one component, teaching specific skills." Some parent training models are broad programs that attempt to develop general parenting skills, such as effective discipline or compliance training. Others are specific programs designed to remediate certain behavioral problems (such as bedwetting) or develop discrete skills at behavioral management (such as the use of positive reinforcement, differential attending, or time out). Detailed analyses of parent training programs are provided by Dangel and Polster (1984), Dembo et al. (1985), Fine (1980, 1989), Kramer (1990b), and Medway (1989).

Theoretical Approaches

Three general approaches to parent training have received the most attention: humanistic, Adlerian, and behavioral (Dembo et al., 1985). *Humanistic approaches,* such as Parent Effectiveness Training (PET) (Gordon, 1975), focus on learning human relations strategies that include the use of active listening, sending "I messages," and negotiation between parent and child. *Adlerian approaches,* such as Systematic Training for Effective Parenting (STEP) (Dinkmeyer and McKay, 1976), attempt to help parents understand their children, their thought processes, and what motivates their behaviors. *Behavioral approaches* are based on the assumption that behavior is learned and sustained by the positive and negative reinforcement that children receive from social agents, especially parents. Behavioral parent training programs typically review basic behavioral concepts, provide information about how child behaviors shape parent responses, and attempt to establish a shift in social contingencies. Specific training in the nature and use of reinforcers, observations and recording procedures, and techniques for weakening undesirable and strengthening desirable responses are highlighted (Dembo et al., 1985; Dumas, 1989).

Several effective behavioral parent training programs have been developed, such as those described by Barkley (1987, 1990), Forehand and McMahon (1981), Patterson, Reid, Jones, and Conger (1975), and Webster-Stratton (1989a). They all share common features that emphasize the acquisition and performance of specific behavioral management skills. Parent trainers typically use methods such as discussion, modeling, role playing, guided practice, and homework assignments (Dumas, 1989; Kramer, 1990a, 1990b).

The Parents and Children Series (Webster-Stratton, 1989a) is an innovative parent training program for parents of children three to eight years old. This ten- to twelve-week program incorporates therapist-led group discussion with videotape modeling. More than 250 videotaped vignettes are used to teach parents specific techniques, such as playing with children, praise, tangible rewards, effective limit setting, time out, ignoring, compliance training, and problem solving. The program is very comprehensive, and the videotapes are geared appropriately to parents who may demonstrate a range of skills. The program has been shown to produce positive changes in clinic and non-clinic parents and children in both laboratory and home settings. Positive treatment effects have been shown to be maintained at one-year follow-up (Webster-Stratton, Hollinsworth, and Kolpacoff, 1989). Consumer satisfaction data indicate that parents are very satisfied with the outcome of training, the techniques taught, and the specific methods used (Webster-Stratton, 1989b).

Research Findings and Limitations

Parent education and training have been found to resolve child behavior problems, alter parental attitudes, and enhance parent-child relationships (Dembo et al., 1985; Dumas, 1989). Dembo et al. (1985) conducted a detailed evaluation of representative group parent education and training research from humanistic, Adlerian, and behavioral perspectives. Given the different assumptions, goals, and objectives of the various approaches, it is difficult to conduct comparative outcome studies and draw conclusions regarding differential effectiveness. For example, humanistic and Adlerian programs typically assess parental child-rearing attitudes as the primary outcome measure. The Parent Effectiveness Training program (Gordon, 1975) has yielded mixed results in this area. Some Adlerian approaches have indicated positive changes in child-rearing attitudes (Dinkmeyer & McKay, 1976). However, additional research revealed that parents' knowledge of behavior principles of child management had not improved following involvement in an Adlerian-based program (Active Parenting: Popkin, 1983). Likewise, there is little evidence that such programs produce change in the targeted child's behavior (Dembo et al., 1985). Parental reports of child behavior and child self-concept also remained unchanged (Kramer, 1990b; Weise, 1989).

Behavioral parent training programs have received the greatest amount of research attention and generally have yielded promising results. In a meta-analysis of the parent education and training literature, Medway (1989) concluded that the behavioral model had the greatest effects on child behavior measures. Furthermore, Dembo et al. (1985) suggest that behavioral parent training studies have fewer methodological flaws and use a larger number of outcome variables than other models.

Although parent education and training programs typically report positive outcomes in relation to their stated goals, many investigations have suffered from methodological limitations. Problems have been found in such areas as outcome evaluations, reliability of observations, and clinical utility (cost-effectiveness). Few studies provide information on treatment procedures, leader characteristics, and costs to the consultant and consultee. Likewise, assessment of generalization and maintenance of treatment effects, family variables that may affect treatment outcome, and contiguous covariation in parents' and children's behavior are not typically examined (Bijou, 1984; Dembo et al., 1985; Kramer, 1990b; Medway, 1989; Moreland, Schwebel, Beck, & Wells, 1982). An additional weakness in the parent education and training literature is the dearth of information about specific operational procedures typically provided (Dembo et al., 1985). Although most studies report the general model espoused, the consistency with which procedures are applied is typically left unreported (Medway, 1989).

Parent Consultation: Models and Research

Whereas the parent education and training areas are well developed, very few structured models of parent consultation are available. Furthermore, research in the area is limited. This section describes models of parent consultation and addresses issues surrounding the lack of an empirical base for its practice.

Models of Parent Consultation

In an early review of the literature on the subject, Cobb and Medway (1978) described three models of parent consultation: reflective, behavioral, and child guidance. Reflective parent consultation emphasizes parental awareness, understanding, and acceptance of the child's feelings to influence the child's behavior and the parent-child relationship. Behavioral parent consultation emphasizes actual observable behavior and the environmental variables that maintain certain behavior patterns. The child guidance model emphasizes the clinical diagnosis and interpretation of the child's problem in analytical or psychiatric terms and typically results in referral for psychiatric treatment (Cobb & Medway, 1978).

There are several theoretical models of consultation in the psychological and educational literature. West and Idol (1987) and Chapters Three, Four, and Five in this volume offer current reviews. This chapter focuses on behavioral parent consultation, which is defined as an indirect form of service delivery that involves the problem-solving efforts of a consultant and a parent-consultee. The goals of parent consultation are similar to those of other forms of consultation: resolution of presenting problems and increased skills and knowledge to enable parents to prevent or address future problems.

The seminal work by Bergan, Kratochwill, and their associates (Bergan, 1977; Bergan & Kratochwill, 1990; Kratochwill & Bergan, 1990) provides a structure and operational format by which consultants can guide their practice with parents. The process of behavioral consultation typically includes four stages involving a series of standardized behavioral interviews. In general, *problem identification* involves specification of the problem or problems to be targeted in consultation; *problem analysis* explores the problem through evaluation of baseline data, identifies the variables that might facilitate problem solution, and suggests a plan for solving the problem; *treatment implementation* involves carrying out the plan designed during problem analysis; and *treatment evaluation* is undertaken to determine the extent of plan effectiveness. (Chapter Four provides a discussion of specific objectives of each of the stages of behavioral consultation.)

Bergan and Duley (1981) provide a conceptual overview of behavioral consultation with families. Of particular interest is their extension of the model to address the family as system. Difficulties in family functioning and the "dysfunctional member" are dealt with as a system, with each member reciprocally influencing each other member. Three types of messages—factual, inferential, and affective—that can be communicated by the consultee in family consultation are described, and methods of guiding the consultee's communication through the use of emitters and elicitors are suggested.

Brown, Pryzwansky, and Schulte (1991) present an eclectic model of family consultation, guided by general assumptions from social learning, mental health, and systems theories. Their stages of family consultation, which are similar to those of behavioral consultation, are structuring and relationship building, assessment and problem identification, goal setting, explaining psychological principles, selecting intervention strategies, and evaluation and follow-up. An important feature of this model is the inclusion of relationship variables. Specific and pragmatic recommendations are provided to help consultants strengthen interpersonal relations with parents.

Research Findings and Limitations

Previous research in parent consultation has been plagued with methodological flaws. Reviews of the parent consultation literature have concluded that many studies fail to control for the effects of individual consultants, to describe experimental procedures sufficiently to allow for cross-study comparisons, and to use broad dependent variables (both immediately and at follow-up) that could tap a range of parent and child behaviors (Cobb & Medway, 1978).

An additional weakness in the parent consultation literature is the paucity of information typically provided in regard to specific operational procedures used to implement consultation. Although several reports indicate that "parent consultation" occurred (for example, Humes & Clark, 1989; Palmo & Kuzinar, 1972; Strother & Jacobs, 1986; Wright, 1976), the specific procedures employed are usually unidentified. Furthermore, definitional inconsistencies are apparent, as much of this work involves simply a combination of parent training and direct child intervention.

A recent study by Bergan et al. (1991) examined the effects of behavioral parent consultation on kindergarten children's summer learning of math and reading skills. Consultation services were examined in relation to the effects of school socioeconomic status (SES) on learning. Volunteer families were assigned at random to consultation treatment and control conditions. Treatment parents received consultation to help them provide summer learning opportunities for their children. Structural equation modeling revealed a direct effect of school SES on learning during the school year and an indirect effect on learning over the summer. Parent consultation provided at the beginning of the summer directly influenced summer learning. Although the findings of this study suggest important benefits of consultation with parents, the integrity with which behavioral consultation was implemented is questionable. Specifically, problem identification and problem analysis interviews were conducted together, all interviews were carried out over the telephone, with no face-to-face contact with consultees, and consultants' verbal behaviors were not systematically evaluated.

Implementing Parent Consultation

Several skills have been identified as being important to effective consultation, including consultation with parents. Among these are procedural skills, to effectively guide the problem-solving process, and interpersonal skills, to maximize one's usefulness as a facilitative collaborator. General considerations and specific skills necessary for parent consultation will be addressed in this section.

Procedural and Process Considerations

Certain interpersonal and procedural considerations are important in maximizing the effectiveness of parent consultation. It is important early on to establish rapport with consultees and begin the complex process of relationship building that will likely affect all future problem-solving efforts. A consultant's interpersonal and relationship building skills greatly influence consultees' perceptions of the consultant and the consultation process (Horton & Brown, 1990). A positive interpersonal relationship is important to allow parents to discuss sensitive and personal information regarding their child, their home environment, and other family characteristics. Furthermore, trust in the consultant is important throughout all stages of consultation, especially as psychological principles are being explained and interventions explored (Brown et al., 1991).

Early on, parents should be informed of the purpose, procedures, and potential benefits and limitations of consultation. It is important to discuss confidentiality issues, establish roles and responsibilities, review procedural details, and address any parental concerns or questions. Brown et al. (1991, pp. 255–256) suggest the following techniques for initiating the consultation relationship with parents:

1. Greet parents immediately upon arrival when consulting in clinic or school settings.
2. Reassure parents that the purpose of the visit is to work together for the benefit of their child. Avoid any indication that parents are being treated.
3. Spend time with the parents alone and make sure that they are comfortable before bringing others (for example, teachers, principal) into the situation.
4. Discuss confidentiality as soon as possible.
5. Establish an informal environment by offering coffee, soft drinks, and a comfortable chair.
6. If consultation is occurring in the parents' home, be prompt, accept re-

freshments when offered, and suggest that you have your discussion in a place comfortable to the parents.

Necessary Skills

Skills necessary to maximize one's effectiveness as a parent consultant include problem-solving, interpersonal, and interviewing skills (Fine, 1990). Problem-solving skills are important to help consultants and parents remain focused and on task throughout the consultation process. Structured interview forms are available to maximize the integrity of the behavioral consultation problem-solving process (Kratochwill & Bergan, 1990). Effective interpersonal skills, such as genuineness, empathy, active listening, reflection, and paraphrasing, are important to monitor parental reactions and to ensure that parents do not feel that they are being blamed for a problem situation.

Strategic questioning and interviewing skills such as the use of clear, unambiguous questions and statements and appropriate nonverbal behaviors are important in parent consultation. Open-ended questions are generally superior to closed, linear questions. Questions such as "How do others react to Johnny's tantrums at home?" and "What is a typical morning at home before school?" broaden the scope of behaviors. They consider an ecological context and integrate various sources and settings in defining a problem and its correlates. Furthermore, when linked with accurate hypotheses, they may lead directly to an appropriate intervention.

Advances in Parent Consultation: Conjoint Behavioral Consultation

Most models of parent consultation address service delivery from narrow theoretical and contextual frameworks. For example, behavioral approaches emphasize actual observable behaviors and the environmental variables that maintain behavior patterns. Reflective programs emphasize parental awareness, understanding, and the child's feelings. Although all of these appear to be grounded in theoretical tradition, they lack a holistic appraisal of the family and the child in relation to multiple and interacting ecological systems. It may be more fruitful to consider the child and family as parts of a network of interdependent subsystems, including the family, the school, mental health agencies, and the larger community system.

There is an increasing need to work effectively with the significant adults who interact in a child's life. Coordination of parents, teachers, and other adults can be critical in the remediation of difficulties (Anderson, 1983; Conoley, 1987). Consultation has been suggested as the "single most important tool in the ecological model" (Rhodes, 1970, p. 50).

To facilitate effective, comprehensive service delivery, simultaneous

Figure 6.1. Conjoint Behavioral Consultation.

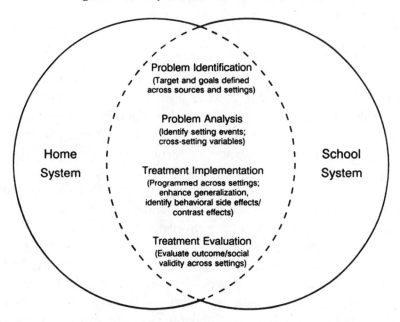

("conjoint") rather than parallel (parent-only or teacher-only) consultation may be helpful. *Conjoint behavioral consultation* (CBC) is defined as a systematic, indirect form of service delivery in which parents and teachers are joined to work together to address the academic, social, or behavioral needs of an individual for whom both parties bear some responsibility. It is designed to engage parents and teachers in a collaborative problem-solving process with the assistance of a consultant. In conjoint behavioral consultation, the interconnections between home and school systems are considered critically important. Therefore, an expanded contextual base in assessment and intervention, cross-setting influences on a child's behavior, and the reciprocity within and between systems are central (Sheridan & Kratochwill, 1992). A conceptual model of CBC, emphasizing the reciprocal, interacting systems in a child's life, is depicted in Figure 6.1.

Goals and Objectives

Conjoint behavioral consultation represents a conceptual expansion of traditional behavioral parent consultation, with a focus on the interacting systems within a child's life. In conjoint behavioral consultation, parents and teachers serve as joint consultees, and a collaborative home-school relationship is emphasized. Through the active involvement of parents and teachers in a structured collaborative problem-solving framework, comprehensive and systematic data can be collected on the child's behavior over extended temporal and contextual bases. Continuous data collection across settings may help identify various potential setting events that may be functionally related but temporally and contextually distal to the target behavior (Wahler & Fox, 1981). Likewise, consistent programming across settings may serve to enhance generalization and maintenance of consultation treatment effects (Drabman, Hammer, & Rosenbaum, 1979; Stokes & Baer, 1977). Generalization of consultee skills may also be enhanced, because more people are working collaboratively to attain a shared goal. Furthermore, engaging significant treatment agents across settings makes it easier to monitor the occurrence of behavioral contrast and behavioral side effects. Contrast effects—unplanned effects of an intervention that are contradictory to its intended effects—can be manifested in other settings or behaviors that are not under the control of specific environmental contingencies (Johnson, Bolstad, & Lobitz, 1976; Wahler, 1975). Behavioral side effects are unplanned or unexpected changes in behaviors that are not specifically targeted in treatment (Voeltz & Evans, 1982). Finally, linking parents and teachers in collaborative problem solving can result in improved relationships between home and school and increased parental supports. Sheridan and Kratochwill (1992) list the various process and outcome goals of CBC as follows:

Process Goals

1. Improve communication and relationship among the child, family, and school personnel
2. Establish home-school partnership
3. Promote shared ownership of problem definition and solution
4. Increase parent and teacher commitments to educational goals
5. Recognize the need to address problems as occurring across rather than within settings
6. Promote greater conceptualization of a problem
7. Increase the diversity of expertise and resources available

Outcome Goals

1. Obtain comprehensive and functional data over extended temporal and contextual bases
2. Establish consistent treatment programs across settings
3. Improve the skills, knowledge, or behaviors of all parties (family members, school personnel, and the child-client)
4. Monitor behavioral contrast and side effects systematically via cross-setting treatment agents

5. Enhance generalization and maintenance of treatment effects via consistent programming across sources and settings
6. Develop skills and competencies to promote further independent conjoint problem solving between the family and school personnel

Stages of Conjoint Behavioral Consultation

The stages of CBC mirror the behavioral consultation problem-solving model advanced by Bergan, Kratochwill, and their colleagues. However, specific attention is given to the manner in which the process can be utilized with parents and teachers as joint consultees. Semistructured interview forms with detailed instructions, objectives, and definitions are available to help consultants proceed through the conjoint consultation process.* Although the stages are presented as distinct and linear, they actually overlap in practice.

Problem Identification. In the first stage of CBC, problem identification, the consultant, parents, and teacher work together to clearly identify the problems to be targeted in consultation. Because ecological considerations are of central importance, the target behavior is identified in the context of situational conditions surrounding its occurrence across settings. Particular emphasis is placed on the identification of setting events (Wahler & Fox, 1981)—environmental events that are functionally related but temporally and contextually distal to the target behavior. For example, early-morning occurrences in the home may serve as antecedent events to child behaviors manifested later at school. Although temporally and contextually removed from the school setting, these setting events may be clearly related to the occurrence of the target behavior at school. Likewise, events at school may trigger certain behavioral patterns at home. Given the simultaneous involvement of people across settings, identification of ecological conditions and setting events may be particularly feasible within the context of conjoint problem solving.

Problem Analysis. During the second stage of CBC, problem analysis, the consultant helps the consultees identify environmental factors across settings that might influence the attainment of problem solution. Together, the consultant and consultees use the immediate and distal factors that have been identified to design a plan to achieve problem solution across settings. Because behavioral data are collected across settings by a number of people, several variables (such as cross-setting antecedents, consequences operating to maintain the behavior, and situations during which the behavior does not occur)

---

* Semistructured interview forms for conducting conjoint behavioral consultation can be obtained by writing to the author.

can be highlighted. Finally, because parents and teachers are working collaboratively, all resources that could be used in the development and implementation of interventions can be identified.

The parameters of the intervention should not be limited solely to behaviors of the child. Because the scope and focus of the target are broadened, interventions may occur at several levels (for example, home-school communication, manipulation of setting events, environmental restructuring). It is the role of the consultant to elicit and identify salient factors that are related to the problem and assist in developing a plan that will be consistent across settings.

Treatment Plan Implementation. The third stage of CBC involves the implementation of the treatment strategy agreed on during problem analysis. An expanded, cross-setting contextual base is desirable to promote consistency across people and settings (Kratochwill & Sheridan, 1990). Furthermore, cross-setting interventions should enhance setting generality and minimize unintended intervention side effects.

The components of effective home-school programs include an acceptable cost-return ratio, minimal intrusion in time and facilities, and ease in implementation (Nye, 1989). Treatment integrity is also important. With the added complexities of cross-setting interventions and multiple treatment agents, adherence to treatment components across home and school is critical. This can be maximized with use of treatment manuals that specify the objectives and procedures of treatment programs clearly and operationally. Parent and teacher manuals have been developed and used in previous conjoint behavioral consultation research with socially withdrawn children (Sheridan, Kratochwill, & Elliott, 1990).

Treatment Evaluation. During the treatment evaluation stage, the attainment of the goals of consultation and the efficacy of the treatment across settings are determined. The consultant and parent-teacher consultees analyze cross-setting data, determine the future of consultation (continuation, termination, or maintenance and follow-up), and set the stage for continued parent-teacher problem solving.

A critical consideration in parent-teacher consultation is planning for maintenance and generalization. This includes maintenance of both child-related behavioral change and the parent-teacher relationship. Several methods have been suggested to maximize maintenance of child behavioral change (Johnson et al., 1976; Stokes & Baer, 1977). Regarding the parent-teacher relationship, systematic methods of continued communication and collaboration should also be established. For example, when possible, parent visits to school may be arranged. Parents may help with classroom-related tasks, curricular activities, or behavioral programming. Home-school notes or structured homework plans might be developed for parents who cannot attend school regularly. These types of parent involvement programs should occur systematically and not only when problems occur. These and other activities may further enhance the maintenance of child-related behavioral changes and increase the potential of long-term parent-teacher partnerships.

Follow-Up. Extensive, systematic follow-up may increase the persistence of treatment effects. Follow-up assessment should include assessment of both child behavioral change and the parent-teacher relationship. Direct and indirect behavioral assessments (such as behavioral observations, behavioral interviews, and checklists or rating scales) may be used to assess both of these areas objectively.

Depending on several case-related factors (for example, parent and teacher variables, severity of the problem, recurrence or nonrecurrence of the target behavior), parent and teacher consultees may or may not have continued their interactions and joint problem-solving efforts. Methods to reestablish communication and parent-teacher partnerships should be implemented. This can be done informally, through discussion and encouragement, or formally, by developing specific formats with parents and teachers.

Contraindications

Although CBC may enhance services to parents, there are several conditions under which the approach may not be advisable. For example, there may be instances when intervention is necessary in one setting only (for example, with problems such as bedwetting or sleeping difficulties). Likewise, a number of factors, such as time, personal resources, acceptability, and institutional sanction, may militate against parent-teacher consultation. In these cases, alternative models of parent involvement should be investigated, such as structured school-home notes or weekly phone calls by a school representative.

Clinical case considerations may also dictate for or against the use of conjoint consultation. For example, in cases where severe family dysfunction exists, inclusion of an individual external to the family may be inefficient and may even impede the family's progress.

Research Findings

Initial investigation of the efficacy of conjoint behavioral consultation with parents and teachers of socially withdrawn children provides support for its use. Sheridan et al. (1990) investigated CBC and teacher-only consultation for socially withdrawn children and found that both forms of consultation were effective in increasing the amount of initiations that withdrawn children made toward peers in the school setting. However, changes in the home environment and maintenance of treatment effects were apparent only in the conjoint consultation condition. Variables that accounted for the findings were believed to include the conjoint home-school problem-solving consultation focus, a specific behavioral program (goal setting, self-monitoring, and positive reinforcement) instituted across home and school settings, and increased communication and follow-through on the part of parents and teachers in the conjoint condition.

A second study evaluated the effectiveness of two methods of home-school collaboration: CBC and a self-instruction manual with no consultation (Galloway & Sheridan, 1992). Six primary-grade students and their parents and teachers served as subjects. Students were selected who evidenced difficulties and inconsistencies in mathematics accuracy and completion despite adequate skills and previous intervention attempts. Findings of the study suggested that both interventions can be effective at improving task completion and accuracy. Students in the CBC condition, however, performed at a higher and more consistent level than students in the self-instruction manual condition during treatment. Furthermore, subjects in the consultation condition maintained their gains more consistently over time. In addition, parents of students in the conjoint condition tended to select more powerful reinforcers and use them more regularly than did parents with the self-instruction manual. Consumer satisfaction and treatment acceptability were also greater in the consultation condition, despite a somewhat greater time investment on the part of teachers and parents.

The empirical investigation of CBC is still in its infancy. Additional research is needed to understand its effects empirically. Future directions for research include clinical replication studies with various populations, investigation of consultee variables, effects of consultee training, and methods of overcoming consultee resistance.

Case Study in CBC

Carla was a nine-year-old third-grade student with average intellectual and language abilities. Although she appeared to be well liked, she interacted little with peers. Furthermore, her interactions were generally in response to initiations made by others. Both at home and at school, Carla initiated very few interactions with peers.

A conjoint Problem Identification Interview (PII) was conducted with Carla's mother and teacher to discuss Carla's social behaviors at home and at school. During the PII, both consultees stated that their primary concern was Carla's low level of initiating interactions with peers. At both home and school, Carla typically waited for others to approach her or to initiate an activity. Although she generally responded positively, she rarely or never spontaneously started a conversation or activity with others. As a result, she often sat or walked alone during play times, unless peers approached her and suggested an activity. During the PII, Carla's mother reported that Carla's twin brother often initiated activities or responded for Carla when approached by others at home. Carla's teacher reported similar behavior patterns at school. The behaviors of Carla's brother (established early at home) may have been a setting event for her lack of social initiations across settings.

The general behavior that was chosen for intervention was initiating interactions with peers. This was defined operationally as "approaching a peer and emitting a question or making a statement, clearly suggesting mutual participation in an activity or requesting a response from the peer." Behavioral goals established by Carla's mother and teacher during the PII were three initiations at school and one initiation at home per day. For purposes of baseline assessment, daily direct observations were conducted by Carla's mother and teacher to monitor her social initiation behaviors at home and school. Thirty-minute direct observations were conducted twice weekly by an independent observer at school throughout all stages of consultation.

A conjoint Problem Analysis Interview (PAI) was conducted to review baseline data and confirm or disconfirm existence of a problem across settings. During two weeks of direct observations, independent probes of Carla's social behaviors at school revealed zero initiations toward peers. Baseline observations conducted daily by Carla's mother and teacher revealed one initiation at home and one at school during one week of data collection. Thus, development and implementation of a treatment plan to be instituted across settings were warranted. Identical procedures were instituted at home and at school, and Carla's mother and teacher were provided with treatment manuals to maximize treatment consistency and integrity.

The treatment package was implemented in two general phases. Phase 1 consisted of three primary components: goal setting, self-report, and positive reinforcement. Phase 2 involved self-monitoring and positive reinforcement. Multiple methods were used to determine the effectiveness of treatment, including direct observations, behavioral interviews, and behavioral rating scales. Direct observational data are provided in Figure 6.2. Information obtained through all measures indicated increases in Carla's level of social initiations both at home and at school.

Two conjoint Treatment Evaluation Interviews (TEIs) were conducted with Carla's mother and teacher. At the first one, which was held approximately three and a half weeks after the beginning of treatment, treatment modifica-

Figure 6.2. Behavioral Data from Case Study in Conjoint Behavioral Consultation.

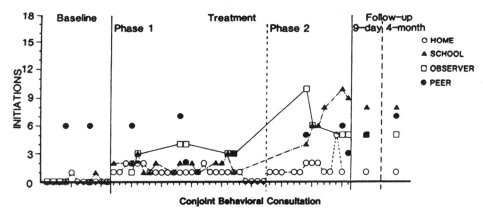

Source: Sheridan, Kratochwill, & Elliott, 1990. Copyright 1990 by the National Association of School Psychologists. Reprinted by permission of the publisher.

tions were made, and phase 2 of the intervention was initiated. At the second TEI, held two weeks later, both Carla's mother and her teacher noted great improvements in her overall social behaviors in conjunction with the treatment plan. A review of observational data collected by her mother at home revealed a range of 1 to 5 initiations, with an average of 2 per day. Initiations observed by her teacher at school revealed a range of 4 to 10, with an average of 7.17 per day. Independent observations at school revealed a range of 5 to 10 initiations toward peers, with an average of 6.5 per observation.

Because the initial goals of initiating one interaction at home and three interactions at school per day were exceeded, procedures to fade program components were discussed. Specifically, concrete reinforcers were discontinued. Carla continued to monitor her own initiations indefinitely (at her own discretion), and intermittent home-school communication to monitor maintenance of treatment effects across settings continued.

Follow-up evaluations were conducted nine days and four months following termination of treatment. These consisted of conjoint parent-teacher interviews, direct behavioral observations, and completion of behavioral rating scales. Observations by Carla's mother, her teacher, and an independent observer at both follow-up probes revealed maintenance of Carla's increased initiations toward peers. Her mother and teacher provided several examples of Carla's comfort in social interactions and outward desire to participate voluntarily in social activities.

Research Agenda in Parent Consultation

Research in parent consultation is in an unfortunate state. There are a number of important variables in need of exploration, including consultation outcomes, process issues, consultee characteristics, relationship variables, parent resistance, consultee training, and consumer satisfaction.

Process Issues

Process issues with parent and parent-teacher consultation pose some interesting research questions. Important areas of analysis include consultant and consultee verbal behaviors, communication styles, and interactional patterns. Through the empirical investigation of such variables, complex process and relationship issues may be clarified. Various methods of examining verbal exchanges between a consultant and consultee are described in Chapter Four. Review of several interview excerpts and use of relational and content coding systems may begin to demonstrate important factors that enhance or impede parent consultation outcomes.

Outcome Evaluation

Traditionally, child behavioral change has been considered the most important outcome variable that determines consultation effectiveness. However, several indirect consultation effects may be identified independent of child behavioral change. For example, increases in parent skill and changes in parent behaviors are important considerations, often prerequisite to child behavioral change. Parent consultation may also affect important home factors, such as family routines, structure, use of time, and parental attitude toward the child and child rearing. All of these present alternative ways to conceptualize parent consultation outcome and are high priorities in empirical investigation.

Broader outcome variables in parent-teacher behavioral consultation should also be investigated. For example, collaborative problem solving between parents and teachers may alter parents' and teachers' perceptions of each other and of the problem context. Likewise, more active involvement of parents at school, enhanced parent-teacher relations, mutual and shared understanding of broader problem contexts, heightened interest in collaborative home-school programs, and reciprocal education of parents and teachers by each other are possible (Conoley, 1987).

Consumer Satisfaction and Treatment Acceptability

Along with the assessment of indirect efforts, evaluation of consultees' satisfaction with consultation services may be conducted. For example, the Consultation Services Questionnaire (Zins, 1984) is a twenty-five-item rating scale that can be used to assess consultee perceptions of parent or parent-teacher consultation. Relatedly, it is important to assess the degree to which the process of consultation is accepted by parents. Acceptability research to date has focused on the acceptability of behavioral interventions, with little or no emphasis given to the acceptability of the consultation process. Issues surrounding time and cost requirements, interest and availability of parents, collection of behavioral data, and other practical and logistical considerations should be investigated. (See the related discussion in Chapter Twelve.) Methods of reducing empirically identified barriers could then be developed.

Consultee Characteristics and Relationship Variables

Consultation research has identified teacher variables that appear to contribute to consultation outcomes. Among the teacher characteristics that have been found to be especially influential in the consultation process are expectations and preferences, experience, ethnic background, perception of consultants, perceived sense of control, and emotional state (Brown et al., 1991). However, the effect of various parent characteristics on consultation process and outcome is not known.

In the parent training literature, there are several studies addressing characteristics of "difficult" parents. The majority of studies indicate that the most difficult parents are those from low-socioeconomic-status, low-income, and low-education families. Single parents also seem to be more difficult than those in two-parent families (Bernal, 1984). Parent expectations also play a role. Specifically, parents who do not expect services to be effective are more difficult clients than those with positive expectations. Finally, parents who have an aversive life situation, with frequent aversive interchanges with other adults both within and outside the family, show a good deal of difficulty learning positive parenting behaviors (Wahler & Dumas, 1984). The degree to which this literature can be generalized to parent consultation is unknown. These or other factors may contribute differentially to parental reactions to consultation. Only through careful observation and monitoring of behaviors, statements, and interactions will we begin to understand parent characteristics and their relationships to consultation.

In parent-teacher consultation, complex interaction and relationship variables are likely. Variables such as prior parent-teacher meetings and problem-solving efforts, parent and teacher perceptions of each other, and consultees' comfort in a dual problem-solving role may be critical to the outcome of conjoint consultation. These and other consultee and relationship characteristics should be investigated empirically.

Consultee Training

The systematic training of treatment agents has recently been identified as an important consideration in the behavior technology training literature (Vern-

berg & Repucci, 1986). Group training has been found to be effective in training parents of oppositional and defiant children (Patterson et al., 1975). However, parent training in the process and structure of consultative problem
solving has been unexplored. The most effective way to train parents in problem identification, behavior analysis, treatment implementation, and plan evaluation is unknown, but it may include models such as group training, cooperative small-group learning, or individualized sessions. The training of
behavioral consultation procedures using these and other parent training
methods should be investigated empirically.

Resistance to Consultation

There has been some research attention to consultee resistance to consultation
and to systemic factors impeding the practice of consultation. Sources of consultee resistance to consultation include demands on energy, incongruence
of expectations, anxiety, role confusion, and a sense of responsibility for the
problem and intervention failures (Piersel & Gutkin, 1983). However, the research has focused primarily on teachers as consultees, with little or no attention to parent resistance to consultation. While some of the same forces may
be operating with parents (such as fear of the unknown, time pressures, and
theoretical differences), others may be specific to this group of consultees.
For example, lack of knowledge regarding behavioral change principles, uncertainty regarding skills necessary to assist with child difficulties, and personal
values and beliefs concerning behavior management and discipline techniques
may be sources of parental resistance. Empirical research is needed to clarify
the unique aspects of parental resistance and to develop strategies to overcome
such barriers.

Patricia Chamberlain's seminal research on resistance in family therapy
is often cited as important in conceptualizing resistance in parent training and
parent consultation (Chamberlain & Baldwin, 1988; Chamberlain, Patterson,
Reid, Kavanagh, & Forgatch, 1984). In general, parent resistance appears to
be highest at mid-treatment; parents who are resistant during the initial stages
of training tend to remain difficult throughout all stages of treatment; and
clinic- or agency-referred parents tend to be more resistant than self-referred
parents. Chamberlain also identifies clinician behaviors that are effective in
dealing with resistance, including (a) developing a strong therapeutic alliance
with the parents and continuing to support this alliance throughout treatment,
(b) reframing suggestions made to parents to keep them consistent with the
parents' preferred parenting style, (c) confronting parents and teaching them
new skills despite objections, and (d) developing a network of support for
the therapist (Chamberlain & Baldwin, 1988). It is uncertain whether these

aspects of parental resistance and methods of dealing with them are operative in parent consultation. Again, a systematic line of research aimed specifically at understanding parental resistance to consultation is needed.

Conclusion

Gutkin and Conoley (1990) suggest that if we truly hope to bring about meaningful change in the lives of children, we will have to begin exerting meaningful influence on the adults that control children's environments. Parenting is being recognized as an important yet challenging task facing many adults today. Increasingly, the roles of mental health service providers include some form of parent education, training, or consultation.

The challenge is clear. There is a critical need to work effectively with parents. Professional interest in serving this client group is increasing, yet empirical support for parent consultation is meager. The development and validation of operational, systematic, and empirically documented models of parent consultation are more important than ever.

References

Anderson, C. (1983). An ecological developmental model for a family orientation in school psychology. *Journal of School Psychology, 21,* 179–189.

Barkley, R. A. (1987). *Defiant children: A clinician's manual for parent training.* New York: Guilford Press.

Barkley, R. A. (1990). *Attention-deficit hyperactivity disorder: A handbook for diagnosis and treatment.* New York: Guilford Press.

Bergan, J. R. (1977). *Behavioral consultation.* Columbus, OH: Merrill.

Bergan, J. R., & Duley, S. (1981). Behavioral consultation with families. In R. W. Henderson (Ed.), *Parent-child interactions: Theory, research, and prospects* (pp. 265–291). San Diego, CA: Academic Press.

Bergan, J. R., & Kratochwill, T. R. (1990). *Behavioral consultation and therapy.* New York: Plenum Press.

Bergan, J. R., Reddy, L. A., Feld, J. K., Sladeczek, I. E., & Schwarz, R. D. (1991, August). *Parent consultation, school socioeconomic status, and summer learning.* Paper presented at the annual meeting of the American Psychological Association, San Francisco.

Bernal, M. E. (1984). Consumer issues in parent training. In R. F. Dangel & R. A. Polster (Eds.), *Parent training* (pp. 477–503). New York: Guilford Press.

Bijou, S. W. (1984). Parent training: Actualizing the critical conditions of early childhood development. In R. F. Dangel & R. A. Polster (Eds.), *Parent train-*

ing: Foundations of research and practice. (pp. 15–26). New York: Guilford Press.

Brown, D., Pryzwansky, W. B., & Schulte, A. C. (1991), *Psychological consultation: Introduction to theory and practice* (2nd ed.). Needham Heights, MA: Allyn & Bacon.

Chamberlain, P., & Baldwin, D. V. (1988). Client resistance to parent training: Its therapeutic management. In T. R. Kratochwill (Ed.), *Advances in school psychology* (Vol. 6, pp. 131–171). Hillsdale, NJ: Erlbaum.

Chamberlain, P., Patterson, G., Reid, J., Kavanagh, K., & Forgatch, M. (1984). Observation of client resistance. *Behavior Therapy, 15,* 144–155.

Cobb, D. E., & Medway, F. J. (1978). Determinants of effectiveness in parent consultation. *Journal of Community Psychology, 6,* 229–240.

Conoley, J. C. (1987). Schools and families: Theoretical and practical bridges. *Professional School Psychology, 2,* 191–203.

Dangel, R. F., & Polster, R. A. (Eds.). (1984). *Parent training: Foundations of research and practice.* New York: Guilford Press.

Dembo, M. H., Sweitzer, M., & Lauritzen, P. (1985). An evaluation of group parent education: Behavioral, PET, and Adlerian programs. *Review of Educational Research, 55,* 155–200.

Dinkmeyer, D., & McKay, G. (1976). *Systematic training for effective parenting.* Circle Pines, MN: American Guidance Services.

Drabman, R. S., Hammer , D., & Rosenbaum, M. S. (1979). Assessing generalization in behavior modification with children: The generalization map. *Behavioral Assessment, 1,* 203–219.

Dumas, J. E. (1989). Treating antisocial behavior in children: Child and family approaches. *Clinical Psychology Review, 9,* 197–222.

Fine, M. J. (1980). The parent education movement: An introduction. In M. J. Fine (Ed.), *Handbook on parent education* (pp. 3–26). San Diego, CA: Academic Press.

Fine, M. J. (Ed.). (1989). *The second handbook on parent education: Contemporary perspectives.* San Diego, CA: Academic Press.

Fine, M. J. (1990). Facilitating home-school relationships: A family-oriented approach to collaborative consultation. *Journal of Educational and Psychological Consultation, 1,* 169–187.

Forehand, R., & McMahon, R. J. (1981). *Helping the noncompliant child: A clinician's guide to parent training.* New York: Guilford Press.

Galloway, J., & Sheridan, S. M. (1992, March). *Parent-teacher consultation: Forging home-school partnerships in treating academic underachievement.* Paper presented at the annual meeting of the National Association of School Psychologists, Nashville, TN.

Gordon, T. (1975). *P.E.T.: Parent effectiveness training.* New York: American Library.

Gutkin, T. B., & Conoley, J. C. (1990). Reconceptualizing school psychology from a service delivery perspective: Implications for practice, training, and research. *Journal of School Psychology, 28,* 203–223.

Horton, G. E., & Brown, D. (1990). The importance of interpersonal skills in consultee-centered consultation: A review. *Journal of Counseling and Development, 68,* 423–426.

Humes, C. W., & Clark, J. N. (1989). Group counseling and consultation with gifted high school students. *Journal for Specialists in Group Work, 14,* 219–225.

Johnson, S. M., Bolstad, O. D., & Lobitz, G. K. (1976). Generalization and contrast phenomena in behavior modification with children. In E. J. Mash, L. A. Hamerlynck, & L. C. Handy (Eds.), *Behavior modification and families.* New York: Brunner/Mazel.

Kramer, J. J. (1990a). Best practices in parent training. In A. T. Thomas & J. Grimes (Eds.), *Best practices in school psychology* (2nd ed., pp. 263–273). Silver Spring, MD: National Association of School Psychologists.

Kramer, J. J. (1990b). Training parents as behavior change agents: Successes, failures, and suggestions for school psychologists. In T. B. Gutkin & C. R. Reynolds (Eds.), *The handbook of school psychology* (2nd ed., pp. 683–702). New York: Wiley.

Kratochwill, T. R., & Bergan, J. R. (1990). *Behavioral consultation in applied settings: An individual guide.* New York: Plenum Press.

Kratochwill, T. R., & Sheridan, S. M. (1990). Advances in behavioral assessment. In C. R. Reynolds & T. B. Gutkin (Eds.), *Handbook of school psychology* (2nd ed., pp. 328–364). New York: Wiley.

Medway, F. J. (1989). Measuring the effectiveness of parent education. In M. J. Fine (Ed.), *The second handbook on parent education: Contemporary perspectives* (pp. 237–255). San Diego, CA: Academic Press.

Moreland, J. R., Schwebel, A. I., Beck, S., & Wells, R. (1982). Parents as therapists: A review of the behavior therapy parent training literature—1975 to 1981. *Behavior Modification, 6,* 250–276.

Nye, B. A. (1989). Effective parent education and involvement models and programs: Contemporary strategies for school implementation. In M. J. Fine (Ed.), *The second handbook on parent education: Contemporary perspectives* (pp. 325–345). San Diego, CA: Academic Press.

Ollendick, T. H., & Cerny, J. A. (1981). *Clinical behavior therapy with children.* New York: Plenum Press.

Palmo, A. J., & Kuzinar, J. (1972). Modification of behavior through group counseling and consultation. *Elementary School Guidance and Counseling, 6,* 258–262.

Patterson, G. R., Reid, J. G., Jones, R. R., & Conger, R. E. (1975). *A social learning approach to family intervention.* Eugene, OR: Castalia Press.

Piersel, W. C., & Gutkin, T. B. (1983). Resistance to school-based consultation: A behavioral analysis of the problem. *Psychology in the Schools, 20,* 311–320.

Popkin, M. H. (1983). *Active parenting.* Atlanta, GA: Active Parenting.

Rhodes, W. (1970). *The emotionally disturbed and deviant children: New views and approaches.* Boston: Houghton Mifflin.

Sheridan, S. M., & Kratochwill, T. R. (1992). Behavioral parent-teacher consultation: Conceptual and research considerations. *Journal of School Psychology, 30,* 117–139.

Sheridan, S. M., Kratochwill, T. R., & Elliott, S. N. (1990). Behavioral consultation with parents and teachers: Delivering treatment for socially withdrawn children at home and school. *School Psychology Review, 19,* 33–52.

Stokes, T. F., & Baer, D. M. (1977). An implicit technology of generalization. *Journal of Applied Behavior Analysis, 10,* 349–367.

Strother, J., & Jacobs, E. (1986). Parent consultation: A practical approach. *The School Counselor, 33,* 292–296.

Vernberg, E. M., & Repucci, N. D. (1986). Behavioral consultation. In F. V. Mannino, E. J. Trickett, M. F. Shore, M. G. Kidder, & G. Levin (Eds.), *Handbook of mental health consultation* (DHHS Publication No. ADM 86-1446, pp. 49–80). Washington, DC: U.S. Government Printing Office.

Voeltz, L. M., & Evans, I. M. (1982). The assessment of behavioral interrelationships in child behavior therapy. *Behavioral Assessment, 4,* 131–165.

Wahler, R. G. (1975). Some structural aspects of deviant child behavior. *Journal of Applied Behavior Analysis, 8,* 27–42.

Wahler, R. G., & Dumas, J. E. (1984). Changing the observational coding styles of insular and noninsular mothers: A step toward maintenance of parent training effects. In R. F. Dangel & R. A. Polster (Eds.), *Parent training: Foundations of research and practice* (pp. 379–416). New York: Guilford Press.

Wahler, R. G., & Fox, J. J. (1981). Setting events in applied behavior analysis: Toward a conceptual and methodological expansion. *Journal of Applied Behavior Analysis, 14,* 327–338.

Webster-Stratton, C. (1989a). *The parents and children series.* Eugene, OR: Castalia.

Webster-Stratton, C. (1989b). Systematic comparison of consumer satisfaction of three cost-effective parent training programs for conduct problem children. *Behavior Therapy, 20,* 103–115.

Webster-Stratton, C., Hollinsworth, T., & Kolpacoff, M. (1989). The long-term effectiveness and clinical significance of three cost-effective training programs for families with conduct-problem children. *Journal of Consulting and Clinical Psychology, 57,* 550–553.

Weise, M. J. (1989). *Evaluation of an Adlerian parent training program with multiple outcome measures.* Unpublished doctoral dissertation, University of Nebraska, Lincoln.

West, J. F., & Idol, L. (1987). School consultation (Part I): An interdisciplinary perspective on theory, models, and research. *Journal of Learning Disabilities, 20,* 388–408.

Wright, L. (1976). Indirect treatment of children through principle-oriented parent consultation. *Journal of Consulting and Clinical Psychology, 44,* 148.

Zins, J. E. (1984). A scientific problem-solving approach to developing accountability procedures for school psychologists. *Professional Psychology: Research and Practice, 15,* 56–66.

Part Two

THE PROCESS
OF CONSULTATION

7

Strategies for Improving Interpersonal Communication

DeWayne J. Kurpius, Thaddeus G. Rozecki

Words and the subsequent actions associated with them are often powerful interventions that can ultimately do more than simply describe an event—they can actually influence the thinking, feeling, and behavior of others. In this regard, people are not passive in their verbal interactions, often attempting to insert structure and influence so that the verbal interaction is more mutually beneficial and less threatening (Schlenker & Weigold, 1992). The verbal interactions in which we invest are often the structure by which our relationships are formed, our goals are announced, and our values emerge. It is not surprising, then, that many of us are constantly searching for ways to increase and sharpen our communicative competence. This is especially true in professions, such as consultation, that rely heavily on verbal interactions to investigate and often to evoke change in others. Interpersonal communication can be thought of as the way by which the consultation process takes shape and also the way it is eventually reviewed and evaluated. In this chapter, we provide a conceptual foundation identifying some of the underpinnings of communicative competence, as well as a complete description of the communication skills so basic to the consultation process.

In examining the effects of interpersonal communication on the process and outcomes of consultation, it is helpful to consider the concept of interpersonal competence as a contributing factor. Early investigators (Leuba, 1955; Woodworth, 1958) found that being competent in interpersonal communication is an important factor to consider, especially when the communication is intended to help others reach a particular goal. While consultation is often focused on helping the consultee to define and solve a problem, many subgoals, such as encouraging the consultee to work collaboratively, are also part of the overall process. This added dimension of working collaboratively reinforces the importance of communicative competence for the consultant.

A working definition for conceptualizing communicative competence is offered by Parks (1985). He believes that people are competent communicators if they perceive that they have achieved their intended goal without hindering their chances to work with the person at another time. A sign of competence in consultation is the ability to recognize that an interaction used to satisfy one goal might also be used to satisfy other work-related goals in the future. While most consultants hope for a collaborative interpersonal relationship with their consultees, the strength of ongoing relationships and the quality of communication are especially important for internal consultants, because they remain in the same work environment over a period of years and will likely work with many of the same consultees again and again.

Theory and Research

Effective interpersonal communication between the consultant and the con-.sultee requires both skill and theory. Even though the practice of consultation tends to be atheoretical, interpersonal competence in consultation can be grounded in theory (Gallessich, 1985; Kurpius, Fuqua, & Rozecki, 1993). Two examples of theories that strengthen the consultation process are personal construct theory, introduced by Kelly (1955), and causal attribution theory, proposed by Heider (1958). Both theoretical positions can help consultants to recognize that one's personal beliefs and perceptions, independent of one's skill, have a significant impact on how a consultant and consultee learn to communicate with each other.

More recently, while studying the Kelly influence, Delia, O'Keefe, and O'Keefe (1982) have found that the effectiveness of one's communication is directly related to the personal construct system that is being followed. That is, one can communicate more effectively if one is able to conceptualize the situation and the other person (consultee) from a variety of perspectives rather than from a single point of view. In *The Structure of Scientific Revolutions*, Kuhn (1970) introduced a personal construct that he refers to as a paradigm: that we humans are scientist-practitioners and consequently tend to adopt a theory about something and discard it only if we have a new theory to replace it with. Kurpius and Scott (1989) apply the paradigm concept to consultation, describing a paradigm as a belief that functions as a scaffold or superstructure to provide consultants and consultees with a cognitive structure for assessing, understanding, and justifying the procedure that is being followed in a particular situation. The concept of paradigm testing was researched by Hunt (1983), who found that good problem solvers are able to apply information from one situation to another and to conceptualize a problem in an open rather than an absolute manner. Consultants who follow this more open and flexible approach are more likely to help consultees to rethink, reconceptualize, and reframe the beliefs and constructs that have the greatest influence on a given problem definition and proposed solution. Consequently, more effective and long-lasting communication is likely.

The contribution of attribution theory and research is also useful to the consideration of the interpersonal transactions between consultant and consultee. According to Brinkman et al. (1982), attribution theory can be very helpful for those working in problem-solving situations to clarify who is responsible for the problem and who is responsible for the solution and at the same time to work toward understanding the errors of attribution that may be associated with the problem. Zuckerman (1979), Martin (1983), and Graham and Folkes (1990) report that one of the most consistent findings in the attribution research literature is that humans use internal attributions (view personal traits or characteristics of a person with a problem as the primary causal factor) to describe the problem of another person but use external attribution (view the situation or environment as the primary causal factor) to describe their own problems. It is very possible that this situation could occur between consultant and consultee—that is, that through errors of attribution, each would blame the other as well as the system for the problem—and it is easy to see that under these conditions, little or no effective communication would take place. And if the client of the consultee made the same errors in attribution, the client would perceive the consultee as the cause of his or her problem and thus be unable to recognize that part or all of the problem might be self-inflicted.

One additional aspect of attribution theory is noted by Weiner (in Dalal, 1988), Parks (1985), and Martin (1983), who recognize that the typical person's approach to attribution often falls short when judged against rigorous logical standards. Parks (1985, p. 181) notes that "among the biases routinely brought to the attribution process are tendencies to give more weight to information that is vivid, concrete, or readily available; to treat a very small amount of information as if it were highly representative; to search only for information that confirms our preconceptions; to distort or ignore information that violates our expectations; and to overestimate the consistency and constancy of others' behaviors."

Working from an operational definition Caplan (1970), who has probably influenced the interpersonal nature of consultation more than any other person, found that the relationship between consultee and consultant has a great impact on the effect of the subsequent intervention. The basic elements for developing a positive working relationship with the consultee include trust, respect, genuineness, competence, and objectivity. These are traditionally communicated by the consultant through a framework of attending behaviors (genuineness, empathy, and positive regard), verbal behaviors (listening, action, sharing, and teaching responses), and nonverbal behaviors (for example, proxemics and kinesics). Caplan recognized the importance of these basic elements when he conceptualized the relationship between consultant and consultee as one of "coordinate interdependence." The trust developed through the interdependent relationship allows for considerable give-and-take between consultant and consultee. The consultee must inform and educate the consultant about the problem, the context and culture surrounding the problem, and examples of what has been tried. Only with a trusting relationship can the consultant help the consultee to see the different factors that may be causing the problem and possible solutions to it. The consultee must trust the cognitive and affective influence of the consultant and feel comfortable sharing ideas and assumptions about the nature of the problem. It is the trust developed in this two-person interaction that is so important for ensuring that the problem is defined accurately. If the consultant is too influential or the consultee too deferent, it is possible for the consultant to overpower the consultee and propose an intervention that is inappropriate.

Because consultation as an interdependent and mutually beneficial helping process for solving work-related problems is still unclear to many consultees, some will expect evaluative judgments for poor performance such as might be received from an administrator. Consequently, it is important for the consultant to be aware of the consultee's undue defensiveness or dependence on the consultant. (See the related discussion in Chapter Eight.) At this early stage, it is the consultant who must shape, model, and reinforce a truly interdependent relationship. Properly done, this will enable the consultee to learn how the dynamics of this interpersonal relationship can be used not only to solve the current problem but also to positively influence related problem-solving interactions in the future.

Consultees sometimes feel that they have failed as professionals by failing to solve work related problems on their own and see themselves as inadequate and ineffective. Young professionals may be particularly vulnerable to this. While educating staff members about the nature and function of consultation is one way to address this problem, the consultant should above all continue to model interdependence by respecting the consultee's knowledge while guarding against acting as an expert with all of the right answers. Even though the consultant may have considerable experience and insight with similar situations, it may be best to work at the consultee's pace.

Caplan and Caplan (1993) state that building a consultant-consultee relationship is a "directed process"—directed by the consultant, who must take responsibility for developing an optimal working relationship. To begin with, the consultant should not doubt the objectivity or substance of the consultee's reporting but should help the consultee focus on the clients (or client system) with little or no reference to the consultee. Caplan feels that each consultant must work out his or her own method of directing the process during the early stages so that the strength and importance of an interdependent relationship is realized. The method that Caplan has developed is especially effective with case consultation. The following description of an initial interview with a consultee is (still, more than twenty years later) an appropriate statement of the importance of developing an effective interpersonal relationship between the consultant and consultee.

> I sit beside the consultee, actually or metaphorically, and I involve him by questioning the material he presents about the case. I do not allow the consultee to talk for more than a few minutes without interrupting him with a question. I avoid, under all circumstances, a situation in which I listen in relative silence while the consultee tells a long story about the client and then turns to me and says, "What do you think about it and what should I do?" First, I probably will not know what he should do. Second, since I may not yet know what the elements in the story really mean to the consultee, I risk saying something that has an inner meaning to the consultee. Third, by then my silence will have allowed the consultee to develop doubts about my attitude to him, and when he asks, "What do you think?" he may mean "about me?" I prefer him to know the answer to that question without having to ask.
>
> My constant interruptions of the consultee's story are made tactfully, so that he will not consider them a hindrance or a frustration. On the contrary, the questions I ask always give him the chance to enrich his story by bringing in additional details about the client and his human predicament. My questioning never takes the form of a cross examination of the consultee. He does not feel that I am scrutinizing or testing his knowledge, actions, or attitudes. I accept and respect his current state of knowledge about the case. The purpose of my questions is to get as full a statement of this knowledge as possible, so that the two of us may try to understand the complications of the case and jointly wonder about possible patterns of forces and inner meanings in the client's life.

My questions demonstrate my own expert knowledge by bringing into focus a wider series of issues that the consultee may previously have considered irrelevant and therefore not worthy of his attention. In this way I am also continually showing my respect for the consultee's powers of observation and for the privileged position of his profession in being able to get such significant data. I am careful to avoid questions that the consultee is likely not to be able to answer; where I am in doubt I phrase the question in such a way that he does not lose face if he has not made the necessary observations. In fact, consultees usually have a wealth of detailed information about cases they present. This information has often not been collected systematically, or with the same system as that involved in a psychiatric investigation; but since the consultee is likely to be especially concerned about this case, he will have observed a great deal more than he himself believes to be relevant.

The net result of such an interview technique is that, as the consultation discussion progresses, the consultee's thinking about the case gradually becomes richer and more complicated, and at the same time he feels supported, because the consultant is working actively with him in a joint endeavor to make sense out of the confusing material. He feels that his confusion is shared by the consultant, and he is reassured that this lack of clarity is an expectable stage in solving the mysteries of the client's predicament [Caplan, 1970, pp. 64–66].

According to Caplan, this approach of grappling with the complexities of the case and other relevant material about its context fosters the relationship and develops personal self-respect for the consultee. Both consultant and consultee offer their professional expertise toward a better understanding of the case. If the consultant continues with this shared and mutually beneficial approach, the consultee does not feel inadequate or lose self-respect. The consultant's skills and help are viewed as supplemental to the case, and this strengthens the consultee's self-confidence for dealing with this and other similar future cases. Only if the consultee is overanxious or otherwise unable to follow through on a potentially hazardous case does the consultant shift from the collaborative approach to a more directive approach. According to Caplan, this merits emergency action, which will always take precedence over the existing consulting contract. Although this may upset the consultee and the consultation relationship, it is necessary, because no other choice is known at this time. Fortunately, this situation is rare.

General Skills for Enhancing Interpersonal Communication in Consultation

Although the consultation relationship may sometimes differ from other interpersonal contacts in its purpose and scope, it is common for the consultant to use many of the same verbal and nonverbal behaviors that facilitate any interpersonal communication process (Henning-Stout & Conoley, 1987; Claiborn & Lichtenberg, 1989). If the consultant does not have a mastery of the art of communication and an understanding of the intricacies of interpersonal interaction, the consultation process will most often appear lifeless and unlikely to be of long-lasting help. Thus, the consultant must understand approaches and techniques usually associated with other helping professions. While this is not to say that consultants must somehow take on the role of personal helper, they must be able to attend to the various need levels of the consultee, effectively and actively listen, communicate their ideas in a helpful and nonthreatening manner, provide the consultee with feedback and instruction, and understand the verbal and nonverbal messages that the consultee communicates (Cormier & Cormier, 1985).

What follow are specific strategies for the enhancement of interpersonal communication, especially within the framework of the consultation relationship. These include not only guiding behaviors but also specific techniques. Many of these techniques are needed to carry out the different approaches presented earlier. Cormier and Cormier (1985) provide a topical outline that can be used to separate these strategies and techniques into specific behavior categories.

Attending Behaviors

A general approach to interpersonal communication and interaction must focus first on the values and behaviors that the consultant demonstrates, which in many cases will make a lasting impression on the consultee (Sexton & Whiston, 1991). The consultee should be given the consultant's full attention and made to feel relaxed and unthreatened. Primary here is the attitude with which the consultant approaches the consulting situation.

The consultant should be able to suspend judgment of the consultee's actions or competencies and avoid condemning or condoning the consultee's personality or performance. The consultant cannot simply assess the situation through his or her own paradigm (Kurpius & Scott, 1989) but must understand the world view of the consultee. The consultant's conceptual framework and attitude may be the two most important factors in the consultee's ability to define and structure the situation so that it is eventually clear and manageable. An attitude of hopelessness or confusion on the part of the consultant can infect what might be an already delicate situation with unproductive tension and additional stress. Consider the differences in the following situations:

Consultee: I've never really used a consultant before, but things seem a bit unmanageable right now. I don't think it's that serious yet, but I'm afraid of what is going to happen if things continue on the same course. The bottom line is I just don't know in which direction to go.

Consultant A: It seems strange that with all your management experience, you really don't have a handle on this. Perhaps you are not looking at things clearly right now. I suggest that you allow me some time to investigate the situation and get back to you. I'll call you if I can see any way out.

Consultant B: Consultation is a process that we all use from time to time to get a different perspective about situations that we are often too close to. Let's discuss what the issue is and some of the things you have tried up until now to give us both a clearer indication of where things stand. I think moving slowly for now is important. What do you think?

It is clear that the attitude of consultant A can do much to additionally burden the consultee. Consultant B, however, reserves judgment and attempts to obtain more information before discussing an intervention. The attitude of consultant B is one of openness and illustrates the attending behaviors that are generally considered to be crucial in the establishment of any positive relationship—genuineness, empathy, and positive regard. Each offers a unique benefit to the total working relationship.

   Genuineness. Genuineness is the consultant's ability to be sincere without presenting a false front. Genuine people are those who consistently exhibit, examine, discuss, and act on the thoughts and feelings in which they most strongly believe (Cormier & Cormier, 1979; Ivey, 1988). They are not role playing a scenario for the benefit of the consultee, nor are they changing their approach to living in order to make an artificial impression that will allow them some secondary gain. This echoes the point that Argyris (1991) makes about sending mixed messages. Because of the doubts and questions we all have about our daily work styles, it is sometimes difficult to remain genuine. We often act in a way of which we believe others will be most accepting. In many cases, the end result of being ungenuine is ungenuineness and rejection on the part of those we are trying so hard to impress.
   Consultants should consider modeling genuineness for the consultees with whom they wish to collaborate. This allows the consultant-consultee rela-

tionship to grow in an atmosphere of honesty and openness that will guide its progress, maturation, and eventual termination.

Empathy. A natural progression from the consultant's genuineness is his or her ability to emphathize with the consultee—to deeply understand the situation with which the consultee is dealing. Unlike sympathy, which most often indicates sadness or attitudinal distance from another, empathy focuses on the ability to think and feel as if one were oneself dealing with the consultee's problem. This is hardly an easy task; it requires that the consultant understand his or her own motivations and values as well as the values and beliefs of another (Truax & Carkhuff, 1967; Rogers, 1961).

In the example given previously, consultant B allows empathy to guide her exchange by listening closely to what the consultee is saying, providing some immediate relief from the pressure, and allowing the consultee to become an active partner in the process. Consultant A, on the other hand, is judgmental and seems to be unaware of the doubt that the consultee is expressing.

Simply stated, empathy involves putting yourself in another person's situation and attempting to fully understand the complexities of that position.

Positive Regard. Positive regard emerges from both empathy and genuineness and is a way of highlighting a proactive and encouraging consultation relationship. As with the other general attending behaviors, positive regard does not mean that the consultant proceeds and operates from only the consultee's viewpoint. On the contrary, it means that the consultant understands the situation and its complexities, is able to deal with that situation as if it were his or her own, and can identify the aspects and conditions that have the most meaning. Positive regard is another way of indicating that the consultee, as well as the situation that the consultee is presenting, is normal and shares some qualities with other people, situations, problems, or organizational structures that the consultant has encountered in the past. Positive regard on the part of the consultant adds normality to a sometimes chaotic situation. It combines a nonjudgmental attitude, respect, concreteness, authenticity, and genuineness, and it promotes success and collaboration. As an overriding principle, positive regard means that the consultant is willing to accept the consultee and his or her situation in a manner that promotes openness, honesty, and equity (Truax & Carkhuff, 1967; Rogers, 1961). Consultant B in our example uses positive regard in her opening remarks to the consultee.

Verbal Behaviors

The wide variety of verbal behaviors that the consultant employs are the most significant interpersonal skills that are used in the establishment and maintenance of the consultation relationship. Verbal behaviors can be classified as consisting of listening responses, action responses, sharing responses, and teaching responses employed throughout the consultation relationship, from entry and contracting to termination and review.

Listening Responses. Listening responses are the cornerstone for everything else that the consultant does. Although consultants usually understand the need for specific listening skills as a powerful reinforcer, a necessary foundation for later intervention, and a way to promote collaboration, they often forget to listen. Some common blocks to listening are the tendency to judge or evaluate the consultee's statements, inattention or apathy, asking too many questions prematurely, feeling the need to define and solve the problem quickly, and pursuing one's own agenda regardless of the consultee's needs. Listening responses include clarification, reflection, and summarization (Cormier & Cormier, 1985).

Clarification. In consultation, the inquiry process is used to help the consultee focus more clearly on the situation and problem. Clarification is a particular type of questioning designed to encourage elaboration on specific points that the consultee has made so that the accuracy of the consultant's interpretation of the consultee's statements can be gauged. Clarification usually begins with "what did you mean when you said" or "are you saying that" plus a rephrasing of the consultee's original statement (Cormier & Cormier, 1985). For example,

Consultee: We seem to have a lot of trouble with the chain of command in our organization. The lines of communication are tangled.

Consultant: Are you saying that the messages received by your staff are not explicit and may be confusing?

Clarification helps the consultant and consultee gather accurate data to more specifically define the problem.

Reflection. Consultants use reflective statements to examine overt or covert messages communicated by a consultee. Reflective responses may be either objective or affective statements. Reflection requires that the consultant listen intently to consultee information and quickly reframe that information so that the consultant can hear it in another form. In using reflection with cognitively oriented statements, consultants paraphrase the important points and allow the consultee to verify their accuracy:

Consultee: I am having a hard time pinpointing where the communication process is stalling. I suspect that decisions are being made without notification of the proper managerial staff members.

Consultant: You sense that many of your staff members are acting independently and not informing supervisors of their decisions.

Consultants might also choose to focus on the more affective components of a consultee's statements. This is a delicate matter that requires that the consultant move cautiously and respond nonjudgmentally and openly:

Consultee: I am having a hard time pinpointing where the communication process is stalling. I suspect that decisions are being made without notification of the proper managerial staff members.

Consultant: You are feeling frustrated with your inability to define the problem, as well as with your lack of information.

Egan's description (1986) of the role of reflection in counseling applies to consultation as well: reflection can encourage consultees to express more of their feelings about a situation, help them understand how their feelings intensify or change the way in which problems are defined, and remind them that consultation is not only a problem-solving strategy but also an examination of personal and procedural components.

❧ *Summarization.* When a variety of consultee statements or issues have been explored, it is important that the consultant verbally recount what has occurred. Summarization serves this purpose by integrating reflective statements into a unit that can measure the progress that has been made. It not only serves as a good source of feedback for the consultee but can also be used to highlight themes that have emerged during specific phases of the consultation process:

Consultant: You've stated that things are confusing right now, and you've had a difficult time defining the problem, but you suspect that communication is a big part of it. You would like to see procedures, especially communication procedures, become more orderly and better defined.

Summarization is the tool that ensures accuracy for both consultant and consultee throughout the consultation relationship.

Action Responses. As the consultation relationship progresses, the consultant continues to help establish interventions to meet goals. This may require a more active posture than does problem definition. Action responses tend to be more consultant-directed than listening responses; they consist of probes, competency statements, confrontation, and interpretation.

Probes. Although we all use questions as a form of inquiry and clarification, we sometimes overlook their effectiveness as means of gathering data, as effective relationship enhancers, and as a way of revealing our own interest in a subject. Probes are questions used by consultants for these purposes. Probes can be either closed questions or open-ended questions. Closed questions (questions that can be answered yes or no or ask for specific objective data) help consultants understand the dimensions of the situation with which they are working. Open-ended questions, which usually begin with "what" or "how," are used to help consultants understand the culture and system in which they are involved. Probes that may be useful at the beginning of the consultation relationship include "What approaches have been tried in the past?" "What do you see as the culture of the organization?" and "What would you ultimately like to see happen?"

Probes allow consultants to begin the process of connecting problem definition, evaluation, and intervention. They generate information that simply listening does not always provide. As with other types of questioning, however, consultants should remain alert to the possibility of errors of attribution (Martin, 1983).

Competency Responses. Because many consultees feel that consultation is their last chance for successful problem resolution, they often view consultants as "experts" who are finally going to "fix the problem." But the goal of many consultation efforts is for the consultee to actively engage in finding ways not only to remedy the current crisis but also to establish longer-term procedures for solving similar problems in the future. Competency responses can help consultees recognize the importance of this.

Competency responses are encouraging statements that reframe consultees' perceived weaknesses by accentuating the more positive aspects of their thoughts and behaviors. Although these responses should be used sparingly, competency responses can help the consultees to recognize that they will have more and more responsibility in the relationship. For example:

Consultee: I am having a hard time pinpointing where the communication process is stalling. I suspect that decisions are being made without notification of the proper managerial staff members.

Consultant: You seem to be able to conceptualize the situation well. You're sensitive to the complex nature of the organizational decision-making process and how it affects your job.

These responses can be used as evaluative encouragement and, when used sparingly, can prompt the consultee to think about the situation without feeling defeated.

Confrontation. The term *confrontation* has become a cliché and is sometimes incorrectly thought of as meaning a moment of high antagonism when we face our adversary (Myerson, 1983). In consultation, however, confrontation is a powerful communication tool that allows the consultant and consultee to clarify discrepancies in any number of areas, including consultee attitudes, performance, or attributions that may be hampering the consultation process; the consultant's paradigm, agenda, or willingness to help; or the system's reluctance to incorporate change. A simple example is a discrepancy between what a consultant or consultee says and what he or she does. Not all discrepancies, however, are so easily clarified. Before confrontation is used, the relationship should have developed to the point where the consultee understands his or her own involvement in the organizational problem. A common idiom in many organizations is "If you are not interested in solving the problem, you cannot be part of the solution."

Confrontation responses can be soft and should be well defined if they are to be helpful in clarifying a discrepancy. They are not generalizations of consultee weakness but must stress the importance of defining the problem accurately, even to the point of noting that the consultee may be part of the problem (Argyris, 1991):

Consultee: I am having a hard time pinpointing where the communication process is stalling. I suspect that decisions are being made without notification of the proper managerial staff members.

Consultant: You have said a lot about the ineffective communication patterns within the organization, but I've noticed that you are also concerned about how you delegate responsibilities verbally and don't follow up with written instructions.

In using confrontation, the consultant should remember to move slowly and incrementally (for example, not listing all the discrepancies at one time), to be aware of possible consultee resistance to confrontive messages, to ensure that the relationship is stable before confronting, and to realize that behavior can often be misinterpreted as discrepant even when it is not.

Interpretation. After listening intently, probing, summarizing, and synthesizing the situation, the consultant may be able to associate a number of consultee behaviors or statements and to make a general statement of what characteristics of the problem or situation seem connected. Interpretation is the conceptual analysis by the consultant of the consultee's situation after all the information has been collected. It is often viewed by the consultee as "expert advice" and must be framed in a way that allows for future consultee-directed growth and work. Interpretations are not a set of rules or instructions for the consultee to follow, but they do provide a framework or paradigm shift for later action in remediation or prevention. It is essential that consultants know that interpretations must be presented as hypotheses to be tested, should be based on the consultee's acceptance and the system he or she is operating from and not on the consultant's values, and should be well timed so that resistance is minimized. Interpretations should always confront the situation or problem rather than an individual:

Consultant: Could we be looking at a situation in which those most responsible for ensuring the effectiveness of the communication process within the organization are themselves unable to get their point across? What I'm saying is that maybe there is a culture in this organization that believes that the only way to get anything done is to bulldoze their ideas through, without checking them out with others first. If so, this could bring about some of the problems you've been describing during the past weeks.

Sharing Responses. As the personal relationship between consultant and consultee becomes stronger, the consultant may use other types of interactions than just listening and responding to the consultee. Because of the nature of consultation, consultants often become personally involved with a number of different people, even though the relationship is very different from that in counseling, which puts the primary focus on the client. While the guiding principles of genuineness and positive regard prevail, there are specific responses that can enhance personal contacts in consultation. Two important responses of this type are self-disclosure and immediacy.

Self-Disclosure. This is an important tool for the consultant to use when attempting to help the consultee understand that the problem that is the focus of the consultation may also have arisen in the consultant's past experience (Brown, Kurpius, & Morris, 1988). While self-disclosure can take many forms, it can generally be defined as sharing with the consultee thoughts or experiences of the consultant, such as strategies that the consultant has used to deal with other problems or affective information that seems to sensitively match what the consultee is experiencing. We often learn from each other by the sharing of relevant information about thoughts and feelings. Self-disclosure is a specific kind of sharing that isolates past thoughts or actions that are most relevant to the current situation. It should be noted that extensive self-disclosure by either the consultant or the consultee can interfere with the consultation relationship if it begins to resemble a counseling session, which is person-focused. Consultation should remain primarily issue-focused. Keeping the tone of consultation in the present tense as much as possible is very important. The following self-disclosing statements serve as examples:

Consultant A: An organization very similar to yours that I worked with last year seemed to be running into the same kind of communication questions that you have been expressing. We found that because of quick growth in the company, established policies and procedures were nonexistent until a problem arose that prompted their adoption. There was a lot of crisis intervention going on. How do you think that compares with your present situation?

Consultant B: In the past, I have often encountered communication problems in my work that seemed insurmountable at the time. However, I found that if I took one piece at a time, I was much less likely to feel overwhelmed and defeated. How have you been working with this problem personally?

It is evident from these examples that self-disclosure statements can be coupled with more active responses or probes to enhance their effectiveness.

Immediacy. Immediacy is conveyed by consultant statements made in direct response to present events. When the consultant has demonstrated genuineness, good listening, and action responses, consultant statements that act as a barometer of the immediate situation can be very powerful. These sharing responses help the consultee to understand that, although the focus of the consultation is often on something outside a particular consultation meeting, what goes on in that meeting need not be passive reactions to what is happening on the outside. In other words, although the focus might be on past, present, or future situations, problems, or concerns, consultation takes place in the here and now. Immediacy statements can measure how the consultation process itself is progressing, as opposed to focusing on the problem definition or solution. They can help change the focus of a consultee who is not dealing directly with the present situation:

Consultee: We should be talking about how that particular solution is going to affect the way we distribute funds in the future, as well as how the training is going to proceed. I don't think we can afford to train the entire staff.

Consultant: I think we should slow down and not move too fast in establishing procedures before the problem is completely defined. I'm sensing your need to press toward solutions that I don't think we're quite ready to deal with yet. Could you tell me some more about how you are experiencing this situation in our meeting right now?

Immediacy responses give all participants a chance to be human and discuss their own frustrations and fears. They can enhance personal communication in the consultation relationship when they are used with discretion and demonstrate empathy and positive regard.

Teaching Responses. Teaching responses are the responses with which we are all perhaps most familiar and yet have the most difficulty delivering effectively and succinctly. These responses generally revolve around the theme of information giving. The consultant and the consultee both teach each other in many ways. Consultants often use a direct approach to teaching, such as describing the potential effects of following a specific model. Such a description is most valuable if it is presented as a vignette depicting a specific situation at a specific time.

Instructions. Instructions are statements by which the consultant directs or coaches the consultee to follow a particular course of action. These are often used when the consultant is considered an expert who is prescribing strategies for the consultee or client to use to deal with a particular situation. However, the best instructions are those that are developed collaboratively by the consultant and consultee and that may serve as a guide for problem definition and resolution for the entire organization.

Instructions are usually a series of statements specifying particular actions and their purpose, usually concerning problem definition or intervention. They should be succinct and specific. It can be very helpful for the consultant to repeat and reinforce the meaning and use of actions or ways of thinking that need to be undertaken.

Instructions are most effective when they contain four basic elements: (1) what to do, (2) how to do it, (3) what not to do, and (4) how to tell when the instructions have been successfully completed:

Consultant: I want you to make an accurate record of the communication process within the organization. You can begin by reviewing all the written memos sent during the last month that have to do with policy and procedure. Do not include memos that concern personal matters, such as birthdays, parties, or donation requests. Record from each memo the policy or procedure involved and make a list of the policies and procedures that are cited most often. Your list will be complete when you have compiled all the citations for the last three months or when you see a pattern concerning which policies and procedures are most often cited.

Information Giving. In giving information, the consultant should help the consultee to identify and evaluate alternatives and dispel myths. In the early stages of consultation, information giving is used to familiarize the consultee with the consultation process. In the contracting and data-gathering stages, it is the primary verbal tool for communicating the needs and wants of both the consultant and the consultee, as well as for defining the situation and the strategies that have been used in the past. In the later stages of the consultation process, information giving serves as the foundation for the intervention steps that need to be taken and for the termination process. Throughout the consultation process, information giving can be used by both parties to check their progress within the relationship.

As Parks (1985) has suggested, information also has to do with the kind of data that the consultant and consultee are working with and on which they base a number of their decisions. In general, good data are those that are current, comprehensive, and understandable, while bad data are outdated, statistically unintelligible, and limited. The sharing of objective and reliable information can benefit both parties in the processes of problem definition, strategy planning, and termination. Information giving might be used to follow up on the instructions in our last example as follows:

Consultant: Your compilation of the data from the memos indicates that the organizational members are most concerned about compensatory time, production schedules, and sick leave. These all have to do with the amount of time spent on the job and the amount of production within that time. This could indicate that employees are experiencing trouble meeting production quotas in the time allotted, that extra time spent in production is not being compensated, or that there is some uncertainty about how to allot time effectively. This could be one of the hurdles in the communication process if employees feel that they are undervalued or not being compensated. What else do the data suggest to you?

Modeling. Much of the research on how people model behavior and learn from others' behavior can be found in the work of Bandura (1977, 1978), who has contributed a great deal to the literature with his explanation of social learning theory. His research indicates that models who are at least somewhat similar to the consultee and those who are high in status or are rewarded for their performance are generally more effective than others. For consultants, this may mean that the behavioral interventions that they use should in some way identify the characteristics of the consultee that the consultant can strengthen through individual modeling or teach through the use of examples of models that have been successful in the past. Other social learning approaches use behavioral reversals or role plays to teach specific responses, to discriminate between appropriate and inappropriate strategies and techniques, to increase self-awareness, and to develop consultee confidence in performing in difficult situations (Blocher, 1987).

Nonverbal Behavior

Nonverbal behavior plays a prominent role in our communication with others, contributing a significant portion of the meaning of our statements. Highlen and Hill (1984) suggest that nonverbal behavior serves a number of functions, including communicating emotion, regulating interactions, and repeating, contradicting, or managing the meaning of verbal behavior. Although words are powerful, tone, volume, gestures, facial expressions, and movement can induce the consultee to hear something completely different from the message that we intended to deliver verbally. Thus, consultants should examine not only what they say but also how they say it, as well as what messages may be received from just watching their movements and not listening to their words. Of course, overinterpretation of nonverbal behavior can be dangerous. Consultants should both listen to the consultees' words and watch their physical behavior and determine whether the two types of behavior are saying the same thing. Consultees who constantly examine their watch during an interview yet indicate verbally that they have "all the time in the world" might be sending a double message that indicates that a rescheduling of the meeting might be in order. The consultant should approach the subject softly and not allow the consultee to feel pressured. Confrontation of this mixed message is not recommended, especially in the initial stages of the consultation process. Dimensions of nonverbal behavior include kinesics, paralinguistics, autonomic responses, and proxemics.

Kinesics. Kinesics is the mode of communicating through body motion, such as gestures, facial expressions, eye movement, and posture. As with other nonverbal behavior, the consultant and the consultee are both participants in kinesic communication. Nonverbal signaling is crucial in establishing rapport and conveying genuineness. Consultants generally wish to reveal an "open" posture toward the client—direct eye contact without staring, arms and legs uncrossed or undefensively positioned, a relaxed yet alert posture, and facial expressions, such as smiling and head nodding, that help the consultee to feel relaxed and send the message that you are listening. Gestures such as finger pointing, turning one's shoulders away from the consultee, or hanging one's head down might send a message to consultees that things are as bad as they think they are. It should be noted again that interpretation of the consultee's kinesic behavior is culture-specific and should be used with much caution.

Paralinguistics. Paralinguistics concern how a verbal message is delivered—the volume, intonation, pitch, and fluency of the speech pattern. We all know that telling a child in a soft and singing tone that it has misbehaved and must go to its room will bring about quite a different reaction than will a harsh, loud voice, a stiff posture, direct eye contact, and clenched fists. Consultees likewise respond to the way in which words are delivered. If the subject is serious, a chuckling tone sends a mixed message. If the intention is to be forceful, a whisper can sound inappropriate. If the consultant is fluent and forceful when speaking about planning and suddenly becomes hesitant and stuttering when the subject changes to the negotiation of a fee for the consultation service, the message may be conveyed that the consultant is uncomfortable about setting a fee that is too high or too low. This can make a significant difference in the contracting process, and may change the consultee's mind about using that consultant's services.

Autonomic Responses. Autonomic responses are nonverbal cues over which we have little control—physical reactions to thoughts or feelings, such as clammy hands, sweating, pupil dilation, itching, paleness, blushing, shallow breathing, or even rashes. Like other nonverbal behaviors, these are very difficult to interpret. But they may give indications of how consultees react to certain topics of discussion. And consultants' own autonomic responses can serve as their own personal indicator of comfort level.

Proxemics. Proxemics is the study of people's interactions with their environmental space, including cultural and personal territory demands. A general understanding of proxemics can help consultants monitor consultees' comfort level. Standing close may appear as warm or open to some people but be very frightening to others. Consultants should be aware of how they physically approach consultees and how the environment affects their interaction. It may be helpful for them to ask themselves questions such as "How close can I get without making the consultee feel nervous?" "Is the furniture in the room conducive to the promotion of conversation?" "Is the consultee more comfortable in his or her own office?" "Is the consultee more comfortable sitting behind the desk?" Being aware of how others react to one's physical behavior can promote the establishment of a sensitive consultation relationship.

Conclusion

It is evident that the process of consultation is shaped very directly by the participants' understanding and use of interpersonal communication to establish priorities, define problems, analyze data, generate solutions, and evaluate the consultation relationship. The communicative competence of the consultant appears to be most tested in the areas of problem definition and analysis and interpretation of events. But it is also clear that consultees will benefit from defined and specific interpersonal communication in the areas of information giving, self-disclosure, and probing. If the consultant lacks an overall knowledge of and at least some skill in all the areas of interpersonal communication, the consultation relationship will suffer.

The success of the consultation relationship hinges on the ability of both the consultant and the consultee to define the parameters and limitations of the process in which they are both so heavily invested. They must also be able to establish a course that can be communicated to all others in the organization, community, or school with relative ease and define a vision of what they expect for the future. Perhaps the single most important aspect of consultation is the ability to competently communicate cognitive, affective, and behavioral strategies.

References

Argyris, C. (1991). Overcoming client-consultant defensive routines that erode credibility: A challenge for the 90's. *Consulting Psychology Bulletin, 43,* 30–35.

Argyris, C. (1992). Conceptual and operational strategies in consultation. In D. J. Kurpius & D. Fuqua (Eds.), *Consulting Psychology Bulletin.*

Bandura, A. (1977). *Social learning theory.* Englewood Cliffs, NJ: Prentice-Hall.

Bandura, A. (1978). The self-system in reciprocal determinism. *American Psychologist, 33,* 344–358.

Blocher, D. (1987). *The professional counselor.* New York: Macmillan.

Brickman, P., Rabinowitz, V., Karuza, J., Coates, D., Cohn, E., & Kidder, L. (1982). Models of helping and coping. *American Psychologist, 37*(4), 368–384.

Brown, D., Kurpius, D., & Morris, J. (1988). *Handbook of consultation with individuals and small groups.* Alexandria, VA: American Association for Counseling and Development.

Caplan, G. (1970). *The theory and practice of mental health consultation.* New York: Basic Books.

Caplan, G., & Caplan R. (1993). *Mental health consultation and collaboration.* San Francisco, CA: Jossey-Bass.

Claiborn, C., & Lichtenberg, J. (1989). Interactional counseling. *The Counseling Psychologist, 17*(3), 355–453.

Cormier, W., & Cormier, L. (1985). *Interviewing strategies for helpers: A guide to assessment, treatment and evaluation.* Pacific Grove, CA: Brooks/Cole.

Dalal, A. K. (1988). Interview with Weiner. In *Attribution theory and research* (pp. 183–195). New Delhi: Wiley Eastern.

Delia, B., O'Keefe, D. L., & O'Keefe, D. J. (1982). The constructivist approach to communication. In F. Dance (Ed.), *Human communication theory: Comparative essays* (pp. 147–191). New York: HarperCollins.

Eckman, P. (1964). Body position, facial expression, and verbal behavior during interview. *Journal of Abnormal and Social Psychology, 63,* 295–301.

Egan, G. (1986). *The skilled helper: A systematic approach to effective helping* (3rd ed.). Pacific Grove, CA: Brooks/Cole.

Gallessich, J. (1985). Toward a meta-theory of consultation. *The Counseling Psychologist, 13*(3), 336–354.

Graham, S., & Folkes, V. (1990). *Attribution theory: Applications to achievement, mental health and interpersonal conflict.* Hillsdale, NJ: Erlbaum.

Heider, F. (1958). *The psychology of interpersonal relations.* New York: Wiley.

Henning-Stout, M., & Conoley, J. C. (1987). Consultation and counseling as procedurally divergent: Analysis of verbal behavior. *Professional Psychology: Research and Practice, 18,* 124–127.

Highlen, P., & Hill, C. (1984). Factors affecting client change in individual counseling: Current status and theoretical speculation (pp. 20–52). In R. Brown & R. Lent (Eds.), *Handbook of counseling psychology.* New York: Wiley.

Hill, C., & Stephany, A. (1990). Relation of nonverbal behavior to client reactions. *Journal of Counseling Psychology, 37*(1), 22–26.

Horton, G., & Brown, D. (1990). The importance of interpersonal skills in consultee-centered consultation: A review. *Journal of Counseling and Development, 68,* 423–426.

Hunt, E. (1983). On the nature of intelligence. *Science, 219,* 141–146.

Ivey, A. E. (1988). *Intentional interviewing and counseling: Facilitating client development* (2nd ed.). Pacific Grove, CA: Brooks/Cole.

Kelly, G. (1955). *The psychology of personal constructs* (Vols. 1 & 2). New York: W. W. Norton.

Kuhn, T. (1970). *The structure of scientific revolutions.* (2nd ed.) Chicago: University of Chicago Press.

Kurpius, D., Fuqua, D., & Rozecki, T. (1993). The power of consultant's conceptual thinking: Paradigms, models and processes. *Consulting Psychology Bulletin, 43,* 2–12.

Kurpius, D., & Scott, M. M. (1989). Conceptualizing the future of school psychology. In M. J. Fine (Ed.), *School psychology: Cutting edges in research and practice* (pp. 7–19). Washington, D.C.: National Education Association of the United States and National Association of School Psychologists.

Leuba, C. (1955). Towards some integration of learning theories: The concept of optimal stimulation. *Psychological Reports, 1,* 27–33.

Martin, R. (1983). Consultant, consultee, and client explanations of each other's behavior in consultation. *School Psychology Review, 12,* 35–41.

Myerson, P. G. (1983). The meanings of confrontation. In G. Adler & P. Myerson, *Confrontation in psychotherapy* (pp. 21–39). New York: Jason Aronson.

Parks, M. (1985). *Handbook of interpersonal communication.* Newbury Park, CA: Sage.

Rogers, C. (1961). *On becoming a person.* Boston: Houghton Mifflin.

Schein, E. H. (1990). Organizational culture. *American Psychologist, 45*(2), 109–119.

Schlenker, B. R., & Weigold, M. F. (1992). Interpersonal processes involving impression regulation and management. *Annual Review of Psychology, 43,* 133–168.

Sexton, T., & Whiston, S. (1991). A review of the empirical basis for counseling: Implications for practice and training. *Counselor Education & Supervision, 30*(4), 330–334.

Taylor, S. E. (1979). Hospital patient behavior: Reactance, helplessness or control? *Journal of Social Issues, 35,* 156–184.

Truax, C. B., & Carkhuff, R. R. (1967). *Toward effective counseling and psychotherapy: Training and practice.* Chicago: Aldine-Atherton.

Woodworth, R. S. (1958). *Dynamics of behavior.* New York: Holt, Rinehart & Winston.

Zuckerman, M. (1979). Attribution of success and failure revisited or: The motivation bias is alive and well in attribution theory. *Journal of Personality, 47,* 245–287.

8

Resistance Within School-Based Consultation

Katherine F. Wickstrom, Joseph C. Witt

Habit is habit, and not to be flung out of the window by any man, but coaxed downstairs a step at a time.

— Mark Twain

That people resist change is both fundamental and paradoxical to the work of psychologists who have been asked to help facilitate change. At first glance, it is paradoxical that people requesting assistance might engage in maneuvers to impede or halt change processes. They may offer arguments for why change should not occur in a particular way, complain about what they are asked to do, provide excuses for uncompleted assignments, or simply drop out of the intervention process. It would be a mistake, however, to assume that resistance to change is a negative or inappropriate response to a request for change; rather, resistance can be more constructively viewed as a natural process that is both a correct and an intelligent response to proposed changes that may or may not benefit the help seeker in desired ways. Thus, resistance to change is a signal to a consultant that, if change is to occur, a better understanding of the person requesting assistance, the situation in which help is to be provided, and the type of help needed will be required. And beyond a mere understanding of resistance, there is a burden on the help giver to speak and act in ways that either decrease the probability of additional resistance or anticipate resistance and utilize it within the consultation process.

The goals of this chapter are to examine the research on resistance, summarize what has already been done, and recommend areas for future research. It provides a definition of resistance, examines the concept within a theoretical framework, reviews the pertinent research, and offers practical

159

suggestions on how a consultant might deal with resistance. The chapter concludes with suggestions for additional research.

Definition of Resistance

Any attempt to define resistance is plagued with the implications of the term itself. It conjures forth an image of a consultant encountering a teacher who is acting in a contrary manner because of pernicious motives that interfere with what the consultant knows to be in the best interest of the student. This view is unnecessarily limiting and not prescriptive. Although it is tempting to view resistance as something bad that resides within a teacher, this view is too simplistic; it is more constructive to view the problem systemically and to understand under which conditions problems are solved easily and under which ones solutions are implemented with difficulty or not at all. With this in mind, the following definition for resistance is offered:

> Within the context of the consultant-consultee relationship, resistance includes those system, consultee, consultant, family, and client (that is, child) factors that interfere with the achievement of goals established during consultative interactions. Resistance, then, is *anything* that impedes problem solving or plan implementation and ultimately problem resolution, including both passive and active components of an ecology that functionally operate to get in the way of intervention planning, implementation, or outcome.

This definition is both ecological and multidirectional. It is ecological in the sense that resistance cannot be considered independently of the context in which it occurs. For example, school system policies that force a teacher to go to extraordinary lengths to obtain help with a child can cause a teacher to enter the consultative interaction with a different attitude than that teacher would have if help were frequently and readily offered. For the consultant, it is perhaps a double-edged sword that a number of states now mandate prereferral intervention. Resistance may be more likely if teachers are required to intervene and, prior to intervention, to complete extensive paperwork than if they may meet informally with a consultant in the lounge. The attitude of the teacher may be even more negative if a consultant fails to consider system barriers to problem solving and even condescends to a teacher who has the temerity to complain.

The definition is multidirectional in that resistance cannot be considered to reside in only one part of the system. Resistance may have multiple determinants that interact reciprocally and synergistically. For example, people are more likely to attribute the cause of the problems of other people to internal factors over which those people have control but to attribute problems in their own life to forces outside their control, a phenomenon that social psychologists refer to as the fundamental attribution error (Forsyth, 1987). This phenomenon means that the two parties in a consultative interaction may have very different views about the causes of a problem and thus may both play a role in "resistance."

Theoretical Foundations of Resistance

The theoretical underpinnings of resistance within consultation can be examined through several perspectives. This section discusses five approaches to resistance in consultation: Caplan's mental health model, the organization development model, Gross's relationship model, Bergan's behavioral consultation model, and social psychology's reactance theory.

Caplan's Mental Health Model

Although when Caplan (1970) set forth his environmental and psychodynamic perspective on consultation, he never used the term *resistance,* he did address the concept in discussing his idea of "theme interference" as a cause of consultee lack of objectivity. According to this controversial aspect of Caplan's model, a consultee who, because of theme interference, views a situation as hopeless will cognitively manipulate the situation to make it congruent with his or her preconceived beliefs: "Unconsciously, his consolation is that this time the catastrophe will occur to a client and not to himself. At a deeper level, there may also be the reassurance that he stage-managed and directed the whole drama by manipulating the actors to conform to his theme and so achieve some measure of mastery by this vicarious experience" (Caplan, 1970, p. 147).

The consultee's feelings of hopelessness about the case will be confirmed by ill-conceived, hasty, and ineffective problem-solving attempts. To counter this problem, Caplan (1970) recommends theme interference reduction as the preferred intervention. This intervention involves recognizing consultees' unconscious premise that a client's difficulty is a test case for their own theme and persuading them that the outcome is not inevitable. This approach will reduce consultees' anxiety and increase their ability to resolve their problem with the client. Caplan also believes that invalidation of the theme will improve a consultee's professional functioning in the future.

Caplan's theme interference reduction involves four methods by which the consultant can loosen the perceived tie between the presenting situation and the unavoidable outcome. The first method, verbal focus on the client, stresses the objective examination of the case by the consultant and the consultee. The consultant encourages the consultee to view the immediate situation more realistically, considering how it is distinct from similar cases, so that more positive outcomes may be envisioned. With the second method, the parable, the consultant uses personal experiences to show the consultee that a particular outcome is not inevitable. For example, the consultant might describe a consultation case similar to that facing the consultee where the client made significant improvements. With the third method, nonverbal focus on the case, the consultant indirectly communicates to the consultee that concerns about the client are exaggerated, modeling a more objective and realistic attitude toward the case and discussing in detail the feared outcomes to make sure that the consultee has not misunderstood the case.

The final method of theme interference reduction proposed by Caplan is nonverbal focus on the consultation relationship. Given that the consultation process may be affected not only by the consultee's feelings and perceptions about the case but also by the consultee's feelings about the consultative relationship itself, the consultant may need to nonverbally focus on the relationship to invalidate the consultee's theme. For instance, a consultant who has never been a classroom teacher might ignore a consultee's antagonistic remarks about professionals with no teaching experience working in the school system to show the consultee that his or her expectations about nonteachers are incorrect.

Organization Development Approach

The model of organization development consultation, based on principles of systems theory, has also incorporated resistance. This model, derived primarily from the work of Kurt Lewin (1951), has been the focus of numerous approaches, including the behavioral science view (Argyris, 1970) and process consultation (Schein, 1969). The organization development approach to consultation maintains that resistance to change is a natural phenomenon, perhaps even an adaptive process (Brown, Pryzwansky, & Schulte, 1987). Yet resistance may delay adaptational processes and be counterproductive for an organization. Hence, management of resistance is one of the primary objectives of the consultant (Brown et al., 1987). From this point of view, the first step in managing resistance is recognizing its sources. Kurpius (1985) identified three categories of resistance: fear of the unknown, satisfaction with the existing situation, and conflict of interest. These sources of resistance may stem from rational as well as irrational concerns.

A primary source of resistance between individuals or within a group is poor communication. Obviously, then, communication is of vital importance to the management of resistance. To reduce conflict, people involved must know the exact reason for the change, the strategies to be used to bring about the change, and the implications of the change (Brown et al., 1987). Accurate communication may not be enough to prevent resistance when there is a lack of trust among those initiating the change or when the magnitude of the change is great. This approach assumes that resistance will be present and that conflict will be the result. Through conflict management, members involved in consultation can work together to develop mutual respect (Lippitt, 1982) and open communication (Kast & Rosenzweig, 1974).

Gross's Relationship Model

A third view of resistance in consultation, similar to the organizational perspective, considers resistance in the consultation process to be "a coping behavior having as its purpose the preservation of the organism rather than the obstruction of change" (Gross, 1980; cited in Brown et al., 1987, pp. 181–182). Resistance is seen as a natural part of the consultation process. In Gross's relationship model, the consultant focuses on resistance by examining and conceptualizing resistance so the consultant is more likely to discuss it with the consultee and less likely to ignore it (Meyers, 1981). This may be difficult to accomplish. The consultant may choose to avoid the issue of consultee resistance and not address it directly. Or the consultant may address resistance in a way that implies that the consultee is being blamed for the resistant behavior. As Gross (1978) explains, the goal of the consultant should be "to consider the resistant behavior in a nonevaluative manner to facilitate the relationship" (cited in Meyers, 1981, p. 45).

Gross conceptualizes resistance as the consultee externalizing the problem or avoiding responsibility for it and placing it on other parties, such as administrative staff, the child's parents, or the child's past teachers. He identifies the following four categories of teacher resistance:

1. *Blaming*—attributing the origin of the problem to others
2. *Labeling*—attempting to explain the problem by putting a label on it, such as "hyperactivity" or "learning disability"
3. *Solution*—Giving up the power to search for a solution and urging the consultant to take responsibility
4. *Justifying*—attempting to explain why past as well as intended actions were appropriate, implying that there is no need for change within the teacher

Unlike Caplan, Gross proposes that consultation can be affected not only by the consultee's resistance but also by the consultant's (Gross, 1978). Becoming aware of their own resistance is the primary step for consultants to take to reduce their resistant behavior, according to Gross. This awareness should make consultants better able to reduce the resistance of the consultee. To acknowledge their own resistance, consultants can ask themselves the following questions: Are they placing responsibility for the difficulty of the case on the teacher; that is, are they blaming the teacher for not changing? Do they fail to use effective consultative techniques? If so, is the ineffectiveness of the consultant contributing to the communication gap between consultant and consultee?

An attempt by the consultant to reduce resistance in consultation might create a threat to the consultee's competence. Gross (1980) recommends the involvement of both parties. He also suggests that the consultant must work through all aspects of consultation that brought about the threat. Communication is a key factor. Support for the ideas of the consultee is an important communication element in working with resistance. Gross also recommends that the consultant confront the consultee about the difficulty once the source of resistance has been identified. Thus, the consultee's perceptions of situations leading to the threat should be changed.

Bergan's Behavioral Consultation Approach

The behavioral approach to consultation advocated by John Bergan (1977, 1985) addresses resistance to consultation in terms of antecedents and consequences of the consultee's behavior. Bergan assumes that "resistance during the consultation process results from the consultee's perception or anticipation of an unpleasant situation (aversive stimulus), and/or the immediate loss of positive reinforcement (rewards)" (Bergan, 1985, p. 269). This approach to resistance is indebted to both the problem-solving literature (D'Zurilla & Goldfried, 1971) and the behavior analysis literature (Bergan, 1977; Bijou, 1976; Kratochwill, 1982). *Setting events,* a term coined by Bijou (1976), play an important role in a behavioral approach to consultation. A setting event is "one of the conditions that is taken into account in any analysis of behavior because it influences the functional properties of the stimuli and responses in the interaction" (Bijou, 1976, p. 201). Thus, a setting event takes into account all the variables that contribute to interactions in the particular behavioral situation—for example, the consultee's previous knowledge, experience, and skills; the rewards and punishment anticipated by the consultee; the principal's attitudes and behaviors; and the school system expectations regarding problem solving. For resistance to be understood from a behavioral approach, it is necessary to have a description of setting events, as well as antecedents and consequences of resistant behavior.

Control over some variables in the situation is also necessary for resistance to be reduced. To address resistance in consultation, the consultant needs to change the setting event (for example, negative attitudes) so that reinforcing properties (for example, cooperative teacher input) are achieved and needs to terminate punishment for problem solving and remove reinforcement for resistance (Bergan, 1985). Effective consultation (that is, verbal communication that elicits information necessary for assessing the problem) will increase rewards and decrease punishments for the consultee. Unfortunately, these outcomes are usually delayed and less powerful than the immediate consequences of consultation. Also, the immediate consequences (for example, beginning an intervention, recording data) are often more aversive. This is unfortunate, since the consultee's concern is the present, not the future (Bergan, 1985). In other words, during the consultation process, what matters to the consultee is what is happening during the process (for example, the consultant developing interventions for the consultee to administer, which involves additional work for the consultee), not the anticipated satisfaction from resolving a client's problem (for example, five months after the initial consultation session, the client is no longer disrupting the class). The consultee also evaluates outcomes in consultation in relation to other possible outcomes. Completing a referral may require only an hour and may result in complete removal of the annoying child, whereas consultation may require several hours and produce unwanted side effects.

Reactance Theory

The social psychological theory of reactance assumes that "people have the subjective experience of freedom to do what they want, to do it in the way they want, and to do it when they want in regard to limit and specifiable areas of behavior" (Brehm, 1966, p. 118) and that, when something interferes with that freedom, they will react in a way designed to restore it—that is, they experience psychological reactance.

When experiencing reactance, people may respond in a number of ways (Hughes & Falk, 1981). They may attempt to restore their freedom directly, by ignoring the person by whom they are threatened and engaging in the threatened behavior, or indirectly, by engaging in a similar behavior or encouraging another person to engage in that behavior. When it is not possible to engage in the behavior either directly or indirectly, the behavior may increase in attractiveness. Finally, people experiencing reactance may engage in an aggressive response. For example, if a forceful consultant recommends the use of positive reinforcers for mild misbehavior when the consultee believes that time out would be more appropriate, the consultee might attempt to restore his or her freedom by using the time-out procedure directly in his or her classroom; by using a response-cost system instead of a time-out procedure or sending the child to the office so that the staff may use time out; by increasing thoughts about and desire for time-out use; or by confronting the consultant.

Consultants may employ several approaches to dealing with consultee reactance. One of these is suppressing the reactance. Brehm's (1976) review of the research on clinical applications of techniques to suppress reactance in psychotherapy is also relevant to consultation. In both areas, verbal persuasion is used to bring about change (behavioral or attitudinal) in the targeted person. Rather than being suppressed, reactance is sometimes used to facilitate progress in psychotherapy and consultation (Hughes & Falk, 1981). "Paradoxical injunctions," a therapeutic technique developed by Haley (1963), are one way in which reactance theory might be used for beneficial effects. In psychotherapy, the use of paradoxical methods typically means that the therapist instructs the client to engage in a higher rate of the reported symptomatic behavior; reactance theory predicts that the client will disobey the therapist's instructions. This method may also be used in consultation. For example, if a consultee reports spending too much time giving attention to a "clinging" student who needs help with everything, the consultant may instruct the consultee to increase this behavior. According to reactance theory and paradoxical psychotherapy, the consultee will disobey the consultant's instructions and decrease the "helping" behaviors.

Research on Resistance

While the theoretical perspectives presented above are valuable conceptual and heuristic guides for understanding the process of resistance, data in support of the theory have not been systematically collected. This is particularly true in regard to resistance by teachers receiving consultation about actual cases in a school setting. Most of the research on resistance has been conducted in settings other than schools or has used graduate student consultants. In this section, we review research that has sought to investigate behaviors associated with resistance. While the bulk of this research comes from areas such as psychotherapy, family therapy, counseling psychology, and social psychology, studies from these fields seem relevant to school-based consultation. Their primary focus has been on the process of communication rather than on other categories of resistance. In this area, two distinct methodologies have been advanced: content coding systems and relational coding systems (Witt, 1990).

Content Coding Systems

One of the most influential empirical approaches to verbal interaction research is that adopted by Gerald Patterson and his associates at the Oregon Social Learning Center (OSLC) (Chamberlain, Patterson, Reid, Kavanagh, & Forgatch, 1984; Patterson, 1985; Patterson & Forgatch, 1985). These researchers conducted a number of studies to examine the verbal interactions between therapists serving as consultants and families referred for treatment of antisocial behaviors of one or more of their children. As weekly reviews of videotapes of the therapy sessions began to focus on resistance in the sessions, the researchers developed two coding systems to be used to understand and resolve resistance in family therapy: the Client Noncompliance Code (CNC) (Kavanagh, Gabrielson, & Chamberlain, 1982) and the Therapist Behavior Code (TBC) (Forgatch & Chamberlain, 1982). Categories and definitions of the CNC and the TBC are shown in Tables 8.1 and 8.2, respectively.

The purpose of the studies using these coding systems has been to exhibit, from a social interactional approach, the relationship between what the therapist says and how the client responds. Thus, Patterson and his colleagues assume that resistance is not "in" the client but is a result of the interactive process involving the therapist and the client (Patterson, 1985). Studies conducted at the OSLC have focused on analyzing interaction *sequences* in therapy sessions. Thus, a microsocial analysis of the functional relationships between client behavior and therapist behavior can be used to develop techniques for coping with resistance. The researchers computed conditional probabilities for

Table 8.1. Client Resistance Code Categories.

	Responses	*Definitions of responses*
Resistant responses		
1.	Interrupting or talking over	Coded *only* when the client is obviously cutting the therapist off or talking over the therapist
2.	Displaying negative attitude	Responses indicating unwillingness or inability to cooperate with therapist's suggestions (for example, blaming others, disagreements, defeats)
3.	Challenging or confronting	Responses challenging the therapist's qualifications and/or experience
4.	Pursuing own agenda	Bringing up new topics or concerns to avoid discussing the issue(s) that the therapist was on
5.	Not tracking	Inattention, not responding, answering a question directed to another
Cooperative responses		
6.	Nonresistant	All responses that are neutral, cooperative, or following the direction set by the therapist
7.	Facilitative	Short utterances indicating attention or agreement

Source: Adapted from Patterson, 1985.

Table 8.2. Therapist Behavior Code Categories.

Behavior	Definitions of behavior
1. Supporting	Positive responses toward the client (warmth, understanding)
2. Teaching	Providing information about parenting or family life; responses that structure the session
3. Questioning	Seeking information
4. Confronting	Responses that tend to challenge the client, including disagreement, disapproval, and negative comments
5. Reframing	Reconstructing what another person has said such that the result is something different from the initial statement
6. Talking	Responses not codable within another category
7. Facilitating	Responses primarily indicating that the therapist is listening to the client, such as "um-hum," "yeah," "right," and so on

Source: Adapted from Patterson, 1985.

each consultant-consultee dyad and then compared the conditional probability values of a particular consultee response with the base-rate likelihood of the same response given a particular consultant behavior as an antecedent. To determine the level of significance for each comparison, z-scores were used.

In two studies, Patterson and Forgatch (1985) examined the instant impact of therapist behavior on client noncompliance. The first study predicted that directive therapist behaviors ("teach" and "confront") would increase the likelihood of client noncompliance. Videotaped sessions of all phases of treatment between therapists and six families were coded (only mother data were analyzed) with the CNC and the TBC. Results showed that the CNC and the TBC had adequate reliability in that mean entry-by-entry percentages of agreement were .74 and .75, respectively. The conditional likelihood of client noncompliance given therapist "teach" was significantly higher than the base-rate likelihood for client noncompliance in four of the six dyads. Significant increases in noncompliance over the base-rate likelihood given therapist "confront" were also seen in three of the six comparisons. Further, therapist behaviors "support" and "facilitate" were associated with highly significant decreases in the conditional probability of noncompliance in all six dyads.

The second study by Patterson and Forgatch examined whether the causal status of the client and therapist behaviors found in the first study was related to an increase in the base rate of the client's present noncompliance. Also examined was whether some unknown variable produced client noncompliance. Seven single-subject ABAB designs were conducted with seven therapist-parent dyads. During the A phases, therapists refrained from using "teach" and "confront" behaviors, while during phase B, they increased these behaviors. Therapy sessions were videotaped and coded with the CNC and the TBC as in the first study. It was hypothesized that if therapist "teach" and "confront" behaviors determine client noncompliance, this noncompliance should be higher when these variables are increased and lower when they are decreased. The researchers tested this hypothesis by comparing experimental (B) periods and the baseline period for the likelihood of client noncompliance.

Results indicated that controlling therapist behavior was clearly related to client noncompliance. In both of the B phases, client noncompliance increased when "teach" and "confront" behaviors increased. Decreasing the level of "teach" and "confront" behaviors resulted in client behavior returning to baseline levels. Although there was an increased rate of therapist "teach" and "confront" behaviors from B_1 to B_2, there was a slight *decrease* in client noncompliance. This suggested, as Patterson and Forgatch had predicted, that unknown variables may influence client noncompliance. Thus, from these two studies, it may be assumed that "client noncompliance alters the behavior of the therapist" (Patterson & Forgatch, 1985, p. 850), which may be detrimental to the family's therapy, as well as to the therapist's future functioning.

A study by Chamberlain et al. (1984) used the Client Resistance Code to measure client resistance during three phases of treatment for twenty-seven families referred for child-management problems. Two important results were noted: client noncompliant behavior increased from .18 responses per minute during the early treatment phase to .31 responses per minute during the midtreatment phase, and client resistance at the end of treatment was moderately and positively correlated with the therapists' posttreatment ratings of the success or failure of therapy. Cases with lower levels of observed resistance at the end of treatment were rated by therapists as more successful (Pearson $r(16) = .48, p < .05$). In addition, the study found that ratings of successful outcomes by therapists were correlated with decreases in the responses per minute of resistance from mid- to late treatment ($r = .68$) and that ratings of successful outcomes were correlated with decreases in resistance from initial to termination sessions ($r = .48$).

In a recent study, Wickstrom (1990) developed a content verbal interaction coding system based on the Oregon Social Learning Center's resistance coding system and applied it to school-based consultation. Consultative interactions were examined in relation to consultee speech acts, evaluation of the consultant by the consultee, overall evaluation of the consultation by the consultee, and consultee perceptions of consultation and intervention effectiveness.

Conditional probabilities for each consultant-consultee dyad were computed to examine the influence that consultant behaviors had on consultee responses. It was found that consultant efforts to support and to teach during consultation produced significant increases in the likelihood that the consultee's immediate reaction was to cooperate in four of nine dyads. Relationships were also found between specific consultant statements and consultee outcome measures. "Information seek" statements (inquiries made by the consultant that lead the consultee to provide a response) were negatively related to consultant performance ($r = -.70$), consultant evaluation ($r = -.81$), and consultation effectiveness ($r = -.66$) as perceived by the consultee. In addition, statements coded "support" (consultant statements to the consultee that embody understanding, encouragement, reinforcement, agreement, humor, and/or warmth) were positively related to consultation evaluation ($r = .68$) and consultation effectiveness ($r = .77$).

Relational Coding Systems

Relational coding systems are used to examine the nature of the relationship between two speakers. The pioneering research in this area was conducted by Erchul (1987). Erchul studied the role of interpersonal power or control in school-based consultation by examining statements of eight consultant-consultee dyads across three behavioral consultation interviews: the problem-identification interview (PII), the problem-analysis interview (PAI), and the problem-evaluation interview (PEI). After the PAI and the PEI, the consultants rated the consultees' level of participation in the collection of baseline data on a seven-point scale. After the PEI, consultees completed a Consultant Evaluation Form (CEF) that asked them to rate twelve items on a seven-point scale to measure consultees' perceptions of the effectiveness of consultants.

Consultation statements were audiotaped and coded with a modified version of the relational communication coding scheme of Rogers and Farace (1975). This system gives each statement a three-digit message code indicating speaker (for example, consultant or consultee), grammatical form of the message (for example, assertion or question), and the specific metacommunicational function that the message serves in relation to the preceding message (for example, answer or topic change). In addition, each message is assigned one of three control codes: one-up, signifying a bid for social power or dominance and an attempt to control the relationship; one-down, signifying acceptance of the other's relational definition; and one-across, signifying a nondemanding movement made to neutralize relational control. Erchul (1987) used this coding scheme to measure two key variables: domineeringness, measured by "A's rate of bids for control regardless of whether they were accepted or rejected by B" (p. 155), and dominance, measured by "the percentage of A's bids for control that were accepted by B" (p. 115). Consultants' scores on both domineeringness and dominance variables were higher than those of consultees (that is, consultants exercised a greater degree of control over the consultation relationship) during all three interviews. In addition, consultees perceived consultants with high dominance scores as more effective than those with low scores, and consultants perceived consultees with high domineeringness scores as less willing to collect baseline data than those with low scores. Erchul concluded that "behavioral consultation is *not* typified by a coequal, nonhierarchical relationship between participants" (p. 122), as generally believed about school-based consultation.

Evaluating dominance in a different way, Erchul and Chewning (1990) examined consultant and consultee control in audiotaped behavioral consultation interviews using the Folger and Puck (1976) Request-Centered Relational Coding System (F-P). This coding scheme also analyzes "bids," or requests, and the responses to these bids between members of a dyad. Erchul and Chewning (1990) further coded bids as dominant or submissive (requests for the other to take an action or requests seeking permission to take an action) and affiliative or hostile (polite terms, endearments, use of affiliative intonations or rude language, insults, use of hostile intonations). Responses to bids were coded as accepted (for example, the other person agreed to perform the requested action), rejected (for example, the other person did not perform the requested action), or evaded (for example, the other person equivocated or promised to perform an unrelated act). Intercoder reliabilities of .87 were obtained for both bids and responses with the use of Cohen's kappa for 22.7 percent of all transactions coded.

The results of Erchul and Chewning's study (1990) indicated that consultees initiated an overall average of only 15.0 bids, while consultants initiated an overall average of 93.5 bids. Further, acceptance responses by consultees to consultants' bids outnumbered those by consultants to consultees' bids by more than six to one. Therefore, the prediction that consultees involved in behavioral consultation are likely to be passive, accepting, and cooperative was supported. Significant support was also found for the prediction that a greater number of requests made to consultees would reflect control in consultation by the consultant.

The frequency of bids and responses for consultant and consultee was also correlated with three measures of consultation outcome used as dependent measures: the Consultation Evaluation Form (CEF) (Erchul, 1987) measuring overall consultation outcome, consultee willingness to collect baseline data (rated by consultant on a seven-point Likert-type scale), and consultee willingness to implement the treatment plan (also rated by consultant on a seven-point Likert-type scale). Results demonstrated statistically significant correlations for the three dependent measures. A strong negative relationship was found between most types of consultee bids and outcome. Also exhibited was a strong positive relationship between consultee submissive bids and outcome. Therefore, outcome of consultation was evaluated more positively by consultant and consultee when the consultant was dominant and the consultee was submissive. Erchul and Chewning (1990, p. 17) concluded that school-based consultation is more accurately described as "involving a 'cooperative,' rather than a 'collaborative,' relationship wherein the consultee follows the lead of the consultant."

Another study of school-based consultation using a relational coding system was conducted by Witt, Erchul, McKee, Pardue, and Wickstrom (1991). The purpose of the research was to examine the meaning of collaboration between consultee and consultant in controlling interactions in school-based consultation and to illustrate its relationship to important consultation outcomes. Audiotaped behavioral consultation interviews were coded by the topic-following/topic-initiation method of Tracey and Ray (1984) and were rated according to three outcome measures: overall consultation evaluation, rated by the Consultation Evaluation Form (CEF) (Erchul, 1987); consultee willingness to collect baseline data, rated by the consultant on a seven-point Likert-type scale; and consultee willingness to carry out the treatment plan, also rated by the consultant on a seven-point Likert-type scale.

The results of the Witt et al. (1991) study indicated that consultants successfully executed a topic change 78 percent of the time (particularly during the PII), whereas consultees successfully executed a topic change only 58 percent of the time. Consultant topic determination was positively related to all outcome measures, while consultee topic determination was negatively related to most outcome measures. Hence, the following conclusions were made: consultants had significantly more control in consultation interviews than consultees, and there was a positive relationship between degree of control by consultant and consultation outcome and a negative relationship between degree of control by consultee and consultation outcome.

Managing Resistance

Having defined resistance and reviewed the research about it, we are confronted with the question of what we, as consultants, can do about it. How can we influence consultees to effect behavioral and/or attitudinal change? How can we promote consultee compliance with consultant requests? This section offers some practical recommendations for preventing or remedying resistance within consultation.

Behavioral Fixity

When attempting to work cooperatively with a resistant person, consultants should keep in mind that they are facing an extremely difficult problem. In general, it is very difficult for people to alter their own behavior. Vincent

(1971), for example, followed patients who were told that they must use eye drops or go blind and found that 58 percent did not follow the treatment regimen closely enough to produce positive results. The reader can probably think of individuals who fail to make changes (for example, stopping smoking, losing weight, taking medications) that are potentially life preserving. It is in this context that consultants must evaluate their efforts to promote change in a teacher who is being asked to help a child. Resistance to consultation is probably a natural extension of the normal inability to change one's behavior (Patterson & Chamberlain, in press).

Recommendations for Responding to Resistance

The following recommendations are based on what we and others *think*. Given that there are very few empirical studies to help us understand the process of resistance, there is even less research on what consultants can *do* to work with someone who is resistant. For psychology, this seems roughly equivalent to a physicist who does not understand fundamental properties such as gravity, light, or motion. That is, we lack a basic understanding of how to talk to people in ways that bring about change. Since consultation is primarily talking, and we have no empirical basis for doing it one way or another, this is an extremely serious void in the research literature.

"Join" the Consultee. In any interaction between individuals, the parties bring to the situation their own attributions of the problem, which influence their perceptions of how the problem should be solved; in turn, this influences their expectations concerning consultation. For example, a teacher might see a classroom behavior problem as an internal child problem and might focus expectations on the school psychologist "fixing" the child, whereas the school psychologist might see the problem as a function of ineffective teaching practices and have expectations of providing the teacher with classroom management skills. Therefore, it is important that an assessment of resistance include an analysis of the consultee's attributional system (Jahn & Lichstein, 1980).

When a teacher attributes the cause of a problem to an internal child variable, such as attention deficit–hyperactivity disorder (ADHD), and the consultant, who may come from a behavioral perspective, asks for changes in *teacher* behavior, the teacher sees no need to change. After all, the child has a disorder. Teachers may be more involved in treatment for what they believe to be the "correct" cause of the problem being resolved.

In their work with families at the Oregon Social Learning Center, Patterson and Chamberlain (in press) have found that patients come to therapy with "stories" about what is causing their children to be antisocial. Common stories are those that attribute the problem to low self-esteem and "bad genes" from an antisocial father. Sometimes a pediatrician who is highly respected by the family will say that the child has ADHD. Instead of arguing about the cause, Patterson and his colleagues recommend an attempt to link their behaviorally oriented treatment program to the patients' notions about cause. For example, a parent who believes that the cause of the problem is low self-esteem might be told, "The reason children have low-self-esteem is that they have not learned to interact cooperatively with others. When they learn this skill, they will get more positive feedback from people and feel better about themselves. So what we need to do is teach your child to be more cooperative." Following this linkage of parent attribution to treatment, Patterson and his colleagues describe their standard treatment program. Although their clinical experience suggests that this is effective at the OSLC, they do not have data to support this. Further, their process has yet to be tested in schools. Our hunch is that the problems there are more difficult, since many teachers attribute child problems to poor parenting, and linking a classroom-based intervention to that "story" is difficult.

Emphasize Referent Power. According to Parsons and Meyers (1984), referent power (Martin, 1978) should be emphasized during the action phases of consultation. For the consultant to become more similar to the consultee (and thus promote consultee identification with the consultant), Parsons and Meyers (1984) suggest the following techniques: using nonauthoritarian and noncoercive means of control; using cooperative modes of interaction, such as empathy, genuineness, and respect; responding to resistance with cooperative behavior; asking questions to provide support, facilitate discussion of referral problem, facilitate discussion of intervention, and confront the consultee; making suggestions tentatively; and avoiding overselling consultation—that is, being realistic and pointing out problems that may arise.

Strengthen Consultee Skill and Knowledge. Resistance to an intervention may result from the consultee's lack of necessary skills and knowledge to implement the intervention (Curtis, Zins, & Graden, 1987; Shelton & Levy, 1981). While consultants often assume that consultees already understand what, why, and how to do something, failure to check for deficits in skill and knowledge may impede successful consultation outcome. There are a number of steps that consultants can take to facilitate intervention skill and knowledge of the consultee.

When requesting implementation of an intervention plan, the consultant should provide a written transcript of the treatment plan steps (Pardue, 1989). The transcript should specify how, when, for how long, in what circumstances

(Shelton & Lefy, 1981), and by whom the intervention is to be implemented. The more specific a written plan is, the more likely compliance will be (see, for example, Rappaport, Gross, & Lepper, 1973).

When verbal or written instructions alone are inadequate, the consultant should use participant modeling and direct skill training (Shelton & Levy, 1981) to enhance learning behavior and intervention compliance (Bandura, 1969). This training may take place in the consultation session, in the actual environment in which the intervention will take place (classroom, home, hospital), or both.

Increase Consumer Satisfaction. Intervention research has until recently focused exclusively on whether an intervention is effective (Witt, 1986). Although effectiveness of treatment is an important variable, there are other factors that consultants must consider when deciding whether a consultee will be satisfied with (and will use) a proposed intervention (Witt, 1986; see also Chapter Twelve). First, in developing an intervention plan, consultants should focus on interventions that require relatively little time and few personal and material resources to implement. Second, interventions should be described in pragmatic rather than behavioral or humanistic terms. Finally, consultants need to keep in mind the possibility of intervention side effects when developing intervention techniques.

Directions for Future Research

There are several directions that future research will need to pursue. First, to determine whether the process of consultation—that is, what occurs during sessions—actually influences teacher intervention implementation outside the sessions, studies that focus on *direct* measures, as opposed to *perceptions* of intervention integrity and effectiveness, are greatly needed. Second, more studies using resistance coding are crucial to enable us to understand teacher resistance. Ultimately, recommendations for specific words and phrases to be used during consultation are needed for effective consultation. Finally, future research will need to measure resistance in different ways to determine whether there are subtle indicators of resistance that markedly influence the consultation process.

References

Argyris, C. (1970). *Integrating the individual and the organization.* New York: Wiley.

Bandura, A. (1969). *Principles of behavior modification.* New York: Holt, Rinehart & Winston.

Bergan, J. R. (1977). *Behavioral consultation.* Columbus, OH: Merrill.

Bergan, J. R. (1985). *School psychology in contemporary society: An introduction.* Columbus, OH: Merrill.

Bijou, S. W. (1976). *Child development: The basic stages of early childhood.* Englewood Cliffs, NJ: Prentice-Hall.

Brehm, J. W. (1966). *A theory of psychological reactance.* San Diego, CA: Academic Press.

Brehm, S. S. (1976). *The application of social psychology to clinical practice.* New York: Wiley.

Brown, D., Pryzwansky, W. B., & Schulte, A. C. (1987). *Psychological consultation: An introduction to theory and practice.* Needham Heights, MA: Allyn & Bacon.

Caplan, G. (1970). *The theory and practice of mental health consultation.* New York: Basic Books.

Chamberlain, P., Patterson, G. R., Reid, J. B., Kavanagh, K., & Forgatch, M. S. (1984). Observation of client resistance. *Behavior Therapy, 15,* 144–155.

Curtis, M. J., Zins, J. E., & Graden, J. L. (1987). Prereferral intervention programs: Enhancing student performance in regular education settings. In C. Maher & J. Zins (Eds.), *Psychoeducational interventions in the schools* (pp. 7–25). Elmsford, NY: Pergamon Press.

D'Zurilla, T. J., & Goldfried, M. R. (1971). Problem solving and behavior modification. *Journal of Abnormal and Social Psychology, 78,* 107–126.

 Erchul, W. P. (1987). A relational communication analysis of control in school consultation. *Professional School Psychology, 2,* 113–124.

Erchul, W. P., & Chewning, T. G. (1990). Behavioral consultation from a request-centered relational communication perspective. *School Psychology Quarterly, 5,* 1–20.

Folger, J. P., & Puck, S. (1976, April). *Coding relational communication: A question approach.* Paper presented at the meeting of the International Communication Association, Portland, OR.

Forgatch, M. S., & Chamberlain, P. (1982) *The therapist behavior code.* Unpublished instrument and technical report, Oregon Social Learning Center, Eugene.

Forsyth, D. R. (1987). *Social psychology.* Pacific Grove, CA: Brooks/Cole.

Gross, S. J. (1978). *A basis for direct methods in consultee-centered consultation.* Unpublished manuscript, Indiana State University.

Gross, S. J. (1980). *Interpersonal threat as a basis for resistance in consultation.* Paper presented at the meeting of the American Psychological Association, Montreal.

Haley, J. (1963). *Strategies of psychotherapy.* Philadelphia: Grune & Stratton.

Hughes, J. N., & Falk, R. S. (1981). Resistance, reactance, and consultation. *Journal of School Psychology, 19,* 134–142.

Jahn, D. L., & Lichstein, K. L. (1980). The resistive client: A neglected phenomenon in behavior therapy. *Behavior Modification, 4,* 303–320.

Kast, F. S., & Rosenzweig, J. E. (1974). *Organization and management: A systems approach* (2nd ed.). New York: McGraw-Hill.

Kavanagh, K., Gabrielson, P., & Chamberlain, P. (1982). *Manual for coding client resistance* (Tech. Rep. No. A.2). Eugene: Oregon Social Learning Center.

Kratochwill, T. R. (1982). Advances in behavioral assessment. In C. R. Reynolds & T. B. Gutkin (Eds.), *The handbook of school psychology.* New York: Wiley.

Kurpius, D. J. (1985). Consultation interventions: Success, failures and proposals. *The Counseling Psychologist, 13,* 368–389.

Lewin, K. (1951). *Field theory in social science.* New York: HarperCollins.

Lippitt, G. L. (1982). *Organizational renewal* (2nd ed.). Englewood Cliffs, NJ: Prentice-Hall.

Martin, R. P. (1978). Expert and referent power: A framework for understanding and maximizing consultation effectiveness. *Journal of School Psychology, 16,* 49–55.

Meyers, J. (1981). Mental health consultation. In J. C. Conoley (Ed.), *Consultation in schools: Theory, research, procedures* (pp. 35–58). San Diego, CA: Academic Press.

Pardue, M. M. (1989). *Effects of knowledge of behavioral principles, treatment acceptability, and treatment recall on treatment integrity: A model proposal.* Unpublished master's thesis, Louisiana State University, Department of Psychology, Baton Rouge.

Parsons, R. D., & Meyers, J. (1984). *Developing consultation skills: A guide to training, development, and assessment for human services professionals.* San Francisco: Jossey-Bass.

Patterson, G. R. (1985). Beyond technology: The next stage in developing an empirical base for parent training. In L. L'Abate (Ed.), *Handbook of family psychology and therapy* (Vol. 2, pp. 1344–1379). Homewood, IL: Dorsey Press.

Patterson, G. R., & Chamberlain, P. (in press). A functional analysis of resistance (A neobehavioral perspective). In H. Arkowitz (Ed.), *Why don't people change? New perspectives on resistance and noncompliance.* New York: Guilford Press.

Patterson, G. R., & Forgatch, M. S. (1985). Therapist behavior as a determinant for client noncompliance: A paradox for the behavior modifier. *Journal of Consulting and Clinical Psychology, 53,* 846–851.

Rappaport, J., Gross, T., & Lepper, C. (1973). Modeling, sensitivity training and instruction. *Journal of Consulting and Clinical Psychology, 40,* 99–107.

Rogers, L. E., & Farace, R. V. (1975). Analysis of relational communication in dyads: New measurement procedures. *Human Communication Research, 1,* 222–239.

Schein, E. H. (1969). *Process consultation: Its role in organization development.* Reading, MA: Addison-Wesley.

Shelton, J. L. & Levy, R. L. (1981). *Behavioral assignments and treatment compliance.* Champaign, IL: Research Press.

Tracey, T. J., & Ray, P. B. (1984). Stages of successful time-limited counseling: An interactional examination. *Journal of Counseling Psychology, 31,* 13–27.

Vincent, P. (1971). Factors influencing patient noncompliance: A theoretical approach. *Nursing Research, 20,* 509–516.

Wickstrom, K. F. (1990). *Consultant-consultee verbal interaction in school-based consultation: An examination of cooperative and resistant behaviors in the consultation relationship.* Unpublished master's thesis, Louisiana State University, Department of Psychology, Baton Rouge.

Witt, J. C. (1986). Teachers' resistance to the use of school-based interventions. *Journal of School Psychology, 24,* 37–44.

Witt, J. C. (1990). Face-to-face verbal interaction in school-based consultation: A review of the literature. *School Psychology Quarterly, 5,* 199–210.

Witt, J. C., Erchul, W. P., McKee, W. T., Pardue, M. M., & Wickstrom, K. F. (1991). Conversational control in school-based consultation: The relationship between consultant and consultee topic determination and consultation outcome. *Journal of Educational and Psychological Consultation, 2,* 101–116.

9

Effective Treatments with Behavioral Consultation

Stephen N. Elliott, R. T. Busse

A wide range of treatment strategies can be employed within a consultation service delivery approach. As research and practice in consultation expand, there will be greater need for clarification of qualities of effective consultation treatments. This chapter reviews the literature on effective treatments and identifies strategies that can be efficiently used in consultation. While each of the major models of consultation (mental health, organizational and behavioral) merits analysis, the chapter gives primary consideration to behavioral consultation. Since the process, focus, and outcome of consultation generally differ among the models, limiting discussion and analysis to one model may prove more fruitful than the traditional comparative approach. In addition, the preponderance of consultation outcome studies have been conducted within a behavioral consultation framework (Alpert & Yammer, 1983).

Behavioral consultation is generally characterized as a collaborative, systematic problem-solving activity by which a consultant delivers a service to a client (for example, a child) indirectly through a consultee (for example, a parent or teacher) (Kratochwill & Bergan, 1990). Behavioral consultants employ a wide variety of intervention methods derived from behavior therapy and behavior modification theories, including applied behavior analysis and

Note: Both authors shared equally in the writing of this chapter. A portion of the writing was funded by a U.S. Office of Special Education Grant entitled "Preparation of School Psychologists to Serve as Consultants to Teachers Trained in Consultation and Classroom Intervention Strategies" (Grant no. OSER H029F80013-89) and by the Wisconsin Center for Education Research, School of Education, University of Wisconsin, Madison. The opinions expressed in this chapter are those of the authors and do not necessarily reflect the views of the grantors.

social learning theory (Kratochwill, Sheridan, & VanSomeren, 1988; see also Chapter Four).

In theory, almost any treatment strategy that a consultant can employ probably can be shared with a consultee. Thus, the challenge in the practice of consultation is to select treatment strategies from a pool of potentially effective strategies that can be efficiently delivered and managed by people who have not had specific training in behavioral change methods. To begin our discussion of effective behavioral consultation treatments, we must first define what we mean by an effective treatment.

Paul (1967, p. 111) offered a question to those interested in psychotherapy outcomes that also provides an initial basis for thinking about consultation treatment effectiveness: "What treatment, by whom, is most effective for this individual with that specific problem, under which set of circumstances?" From a behavioral standpoint, an effective treatment can be defined in terms of problem resolution. Thus, if a problem is defined as the discrepancy between the present behavior or situation and the desired behavior or situation, then the ability of a treatment to eliminate that discrepancy defines the level of treatment effectiveness. Several characteristics of the treatment and the individual delivering the treatment, however, appear to play a significant role in determining a treatment's effectiveness. We examine some of the key characteristics below.

Components of Effective Treatments

Consultation treatments should be judged by the same criteria as any other treatment (for example, psychotherapy) to evaluate their likelihood of success. This section examines the most important of these criteria—treatment acceptability, integrity, and maintenance and generalization—and the methods used to evaluate them.

Treatment Acceptability

The acceptance of behavioral treatments means that consumers of those treatments validate the social significance of treatment goals, the appropriateness of treatment procedures, and the significance of treatment effects. Behavioral consultation is an indirect mode of service delivery, employing consultees as treatment agents; if the consultees do not accept a treatment as valid, it is unlikely that it will be implemented as intended.

The study of treatment acceptability is based on conceptual work on social validity (for example, Wolf, 1978). Elliott (1988) provided a review and synthesis of treatment acceptability research, which indicates that systematic research has been performed in several studies using analogue situations and objective measures of treatment acceptability, such as the Behavior Intervention Rating Scale (BIRS), the Children's Intervention Rating Profile (CIRP), and the Treatment Evaluation Inventory (TEI). The following paragraphs summarize the findings on variables related to psychologists and consultants, caregivers and consultees, and children.

Psychologists and Consultants. The major finding from research regarding consultant-related variables is that professional jargon adversely influences consultees' overall perceptions of treatment acceptability and effectiveness. Research with teachers indicates that they prefer treatments that require minimal consultant involvement and that can be used in their classrooms (Rhoades & Kratochwill, 1992). Surprisingly, few researchers have explored these latter findings.

Only one published study has included consultants' acceptability of treatments (Elliott, Turco, & Gresham, 1987). This study explored school psychologists' evaluations of the acceptability of classroom group contingencies and found that they preferred contingency treatments that based the consequences for the individual on the individual (independent group contingency) or the entire group (interdependent group contingency). Allowing a subset of the group to determine consequences (dependent group contingency) was found to be unacceptable.

Caregivers and Consultees. Research on consultees' evaluations of treatment acceptability has been conducted with teachers, parents, hospital staff, and college students. Teachers' acceptability of treatments has been vigorously studied. In general, the research findings indicate the following: (1) The severity of a child's problem is positively related to treatment acceptability, such that teachers tend to rate any given treatment as more acceptable as problem severity increases. (2) Positive treatments, such as praise, differential reinforcement, and token economy, are consistently rated as more acceptable than reductive or negative procedures, such as time out and response cost. (3) Teachers prefer treatments that are less time-consuming, although the length of time acceptable tends to increase as problem severity increases. (4) Information regarding treatment effectiveness influences acceptability ratings; that is, teachers give higher ratings to treatments described as strong and successful, even those treatments previously viewed as less acceptable, such as reductive procedures. (5) Increased teacher knowledge of behavioral intervention principles has tended to be predictive of higher acceptability ratings for behavioral treatments. (6) Teachers with more experience in the field tend to rate all treatments as less acceptable than their less experienced counterparts.

Although fairly extensive research has been conducted on teacher-related variables, little work has been done regarding the last two variables, teacher knowledge and experience. Further exploration of these variables is needed before informed conclusions may be drawn regarding the impact of each on treatment acceptability.

Although Elliott's review (1988) did not specifically focus on caregivers other than teachers, it did include the few published studies that have incorporated other caregivers' perceptions of treatment acceptability. In general, the findings from these studies have tended to mirror those of studies conducted with teachers: parents, hospital staff, and college students have generally rated positive procedures as more acceptable than reductive procedures, and given treatments are rated as more acceptable as problem severity increases.

Children. Few researchers have explored children's perceptions of treatment acceptability, and generalizations regarding children's acceptance of treatments thus remain tenuous. Because children are often the recipients of treatments, it is important to consider their perspectives regarding their acceptance of treatments; understanding what a child client perceives as an acceptable treatment may help minimize client resistance, thereby enhancing treatment outcome. The findings to date indicate that children tend to rate all the treatments under study as less acceptable than do adults. Younger children's acceptability ratings do not appear to be influenced by problem severity; they tend to be higher for positive treatment procedures and procedures modeled by adults. Older children's ratings are influenced more by problem severity, and, while they prefer positive procedures, older children rate aversive procedures as more acceptable than do younger children.

Summary. This summarization of Elliott's literature review (1988) raises several issues that are especially relevant to consultation. Researchers and practitioners must remain cognizant of the variables that influence treatment acceptability and the social validity of treatment choices. Research needs to be conducted on those variables that are less well understood, such as teacher experience and consultant involvement. As the research literature on consultation more often includes cases with parents and other caregivers as consultees, research on parent and caregiver variables that are related to treatment acceptability is warranted. Consultation studies should include treatment acceptability to afford further naturalistic information regarding the generalizability of current research and to expand the current data base. Perhaps one of the best models of a consultation treatment that was determined to be both acceptable and effective to parents and teachers alike is that of Sheridan, Kratochwill, and Elliott (1990). This treatment study is reviewed later in this chapter.

Treatment Integrity

Treatment integrity is the degree to which treatments are implemented as intended. Although treatment integrity raises the probability of successful outcomes and provides internal validity control for evaluating variables that influence treatment outcomes, the consultation literature is practically devoid of systematic assessments of treatment integrity (Gresham, 1989; Gresham & Kendell, 1987). Two forms of treatment integrity in consultation need to be addressed: the integrity of the consultation process and the integrity of the intervention program (Kratochwill et al., 1988; see also Chapter Eleven).

Assessment of the consultation process is important to ensure that consultation is actually being practiced as intended and, perhaps most importantly, to allow for replication of the consultation process. Several methods can be employed to assess process integrity, including audio and video recording, objective coding procedures, and process checklists (Kratochwill et al., 1988).

Gresham (1989) identified several factors that appear to be related to the integrity of treatment implementation: more complex treatments tend to result in lower treatment integrity; the time required to implement treatments is inversely related to integrity; interventions that require minimal extra materials and resources are more likely to result in higher integrity; multiple treatment agents may result in decreased integrity; the consultee's perception that treatment is effective may enhance integrity; and treatment integrity may be related to the motivation level of a treatment agent.

Practical methods that can be used to assess and enhance treatment integrity include direct systematic observation and indirect self-report treatment integrity ratings; clear, written treatment protocols; feedback to consultees regarding integrity; and periodic integrity checks (for example, phone calls, notes). As Gresham (1989; p. 137) stated, "Many failures in consultation and interventions probably can be attributed to the fact that intervention plans are not implemented as intended." For consultants, assessing treatment integrity may lead to a better understanding of the components of a given treatment that are responsible for behavioral change and, just as importantly, may identify intervention steps that are more likely to be adhered to by consultees.

Researchers in consultation can study the effects of treatment integrity on treatment outcomes and effectiveness. What is needed is an assessment technology to measure the integrity of treatments across treatment agents and settings, with comparisons of different treatments at various levels of integrity (Gresham, 1989). The assessment of the integrity of different treatment steps will also add to the current knowledge base regarding which aspects of treatments produce desired effects and increase the probability of treatment integrity.

Maintenance and Generalization

For treatments to be truly effective and valid, the level of change produced must be maintained and generalized to the natural environment. Maintenance and generalization, however, are two components of effective treatments that are seldom broached in the consultation literature. Although maintenance is often subsumed under the rubric of generalization, the two terms actually refer to different aspects of treatment *generality* (Cooper, Heron, & Heward, 1987). Specifically, *maintenance* refers to behavior changes that persist over time, whereas *generalization* refers to behavior changes that occur under nontraining conditions.

Although treatment generality is most often evaluated as a passive, hope-for-the-best treatment side effect, maintenance and generalization should be explicit, systematic facets of treatment programming (Stokes & Baer, 1977; Stokes & Osnes, 1989). In consultation, programming for generality should occur for both consultee and client behaviors. Stokes and Osnes (1989) provide several generality facilitation procedures that can be easily adapted into consultation treatment strategies: targeting behaviors that will be maintained by natural reinforcement contingencies; including examples for behavioral change across different settings and people; reinforcing behavioral change in novel and appropriate settings; teaching self-management techniques; and systematically withdrawing or fading intervention procedures to approximate the natural environment.

Treatment Evaluation

The final question to be asked about treatment is the deceptively simple one, "Was it effective?" Although many practitioners and researchers assess treatment effectiveness as a matter of course, methodologically sound measurement is often overlooked in treatment evaluation. Reviewers of the consultation literature have cited the relative lack of controlled studies (Alpert & Yammer, 1983; Medway, 1979) and a dearth of follow-up assessments to determine treatment maintenance (Pryzwansky, 1986). Not surprisingly, behavioral consultation studies have made extensive use of single-case designs (Kratochwill et al., 1988). Single-case designs enjoy the advantage of obviating the need for comparison groups, since subjects serve as their own controls, and are thus methodologically sound, cost-effective treatment assessments (Gresham, 1989). Further, practitioners can easily employ single-case designs in applied settings. The use of other treatment evaluation approaches depends, of course, on the evaluator's needs and conceptual framework. Case studies, for example, continue to play an important role in behavioral consultation research (Bergan & Kratochwill, 1990). For researchers using large samples, group comparisons, such as randomized experimental designs and quasi-experimental designs, may be the preferred method of evaluation.

Treatment evaluation extends beyond simply assessing behavioral change at the completion of treatment; it should also include the ongoing assessment of each of the components of effective treatments: acceptability, integrity, maintenance, and generalization. Ideally, assessment will be multifaceted, involving multiple settings, informants (for example, consultant, consultee, client), and methods (for example, direct observation, self-report, rating scales) (Kazdin, 1988).

A final aspect of treatment evaluation is related to the concepts of acceptability and social validity. Although a treatment may be quantitatively effective; it should result in effects that are socially important (Wolf, 1978) and clinically significant—that is, it should produce practical and perceptible behavioral change (Jacobson, Follette, & Revenstorf, 1984). Common sense allows that treatments may produce results that hold no meaning for the consumers. Posttreatment assessment of the acceptability of treatment procedures and treatment effects will provide researchers and practitioners with valuable documentation of client satisfaction and guidelines for establishing effective future treatments. Further, posttreatment assessment of social validity may lead to improved consumer satisfaction with treatment and consultation services; consultees may be more likely to request consultation services again or to recommend consultation to others if they are satisfied with the services.

Effective Behavioral Consultation Treatments

Few investigators have employed the various components of effective treatments reviewed above, nor have many studies of consultation provided procedural documentation of the specific consultation process used. Therefore, researchers and practitioners must remain mindful of the limitations of the current consultation research base. Because specification is lacking, the review in this section includes treatments that, although not studied through consultation, are appropriate for consultation (that is, can reasonably be delivered indirectly). The section begins with brief discussions of organization development consultation and behavioral technology training and then presents a more extensive review of behavioral case consultation.

Organization Development Consultation

Organization development consultation is aimed at producing change in the organization in which clients and consultees function (Bergan & Kratochwill, 1990; Zins, 1988; see also Chapter Five). The growing body of literature in the area of organizational consultation addresses two broad categories of consultation goals: communication and problem solving (Bergan & Kratochwill, 1990). Communication goals concern enhancing the effectiveness of communication among different organizational components, such as administrators, staff, and departments. Problem-solving goals often are closely aligned with behavioral consultation and include providing groups with skills in problem definition, problem-solving techniques, and treatment evaluation. Interventions at the organizational level generally focus on modifying certain aspects of the organizational structure, such as policies, planning procedures, and role definitions (Zins, 1988). The intervention technique chosen depends on the particular consultation model used (for example, human relations, organizational thinking, or advocacy) (Idol, 1988).

Behavioral Technology Training

Behavioral technology training—the teaching of behavioral principles and skills to consultees (Vernberg & Reppucci, 1986)—is based on the assumption that children's behavior is largely a function of environmental contingencies (Griest & Wells, 1983). Because the focus of this form of consultation is on training consultees in the use of behavioral technology to resolve a prespecified problem, it generally does not involve collaborative problem solving. The recipients of behavioral technology training, usually parents or teachers, are provided training for several reasons: consultees who apply behavioral techniques are often successful in changing problem client behaviors; understanding social learning principles may increase the probability of treatment integrity; consultees who understand behavioral techniques and principles may be more likely to generalize behavioral approaches to novel situations and problems; and, because behavioral technology training can be applied to groups of consultees, it is a cost-effective and efficient means of disseminating mental health services (Vernberg & Reppucci, 1986).

The largest number of behavioral technology training studies have been conducted with parents (see Kramer, 1990, for a comprehensive review). The major focus of parent training has been conduct problems (for example, noncompliance and aggression), since these behaviors are most often identified as problematic for parents (Kramer, 1990). Among the techniques most often provided to parents are attending to appropriate behaviors, modeling, behavioral rehearsal, effective commands, and appropriate and consistent use of rewards and punishment, such as time out.

Reviewers of the outcome literature indicate that while parent training is often an effective treatment for changing consultee and client behavior, the results often are short-term and fail to transfer to other settings (Griest & Wells, 1983; Kramer, 1990; Vernberg & Reppucci, 1986). The lack of treatment maintenance and generalization severely diminishes the effectiveness of parent training. Vernberg and Reppucci (1986) suggest that the unitary focus on parenting skills that currently characterizes parent training may diminish its potential treatment impact. Researchers of parent training need to advance beyond a model that focuses on parenting skill deficiencies and begin to incorporate a systemic, molar perspective that accounts for other variables in the family system, such as social, marital, and parent psychological variables (Griest & Wells, 1983; Kramer, 1990).

Behavioral Case Consultation

The bulk of behavioral consultation research has been case-centered. The following paragraphs review the effectiveness of the consultation process in changing consultee behavior and effective treatments for changing children's behavior.

Consultee Outcomes. One of the major goals of behavioral consultation is to effect changes in consultee behavior that will in turn promote positive changes in children. Research on the effectiveness of consultation in educational settings has shown that teachers receiving consultation services rate problem behaviors as less severe than do controls not receiving such services (Gutkin, Singer, & Brown, 1980). Research has also found that consultation results in reductions in referral rates (Ponti, Zins, & Graden, 1988; Ritter, 1978), maintenance of the benefits of attention to positive behaviors and ignoring, and generalization to nontargeted children (Jason & Ferone, 1978). Given that one of the stated goals of consultation is to prevent future problems, it seems reasonable to expect future investigators of behavioral consultation to provide more documentation of consultee behavior.

The well-established literature on proactive teaching reinforces the notion that teacher-consultee behaviors should be considered a critical set of components in any classroom-based treatment plan. A recent review of proactive teaching by Gettinger (1988) identifies a rich array of discrete behaviors that many effective teachers use in the management of their classes. Elliott and Gresham (1989) used this knowledge base on proactive teaching to develop a self-report rating form that teachers can use to identify preferred classroom management strategies (see Exhibit 9.1). This form includes thirty discrete behaviors, twenty-seven of which are empirically supported as effective methods for proactively managing students' classroom behavior and facilitating academic performance. A close examination of the form reveals that the teaching behaviors can easily be conceptualized as operant procedures stressing either antecedent control or consequences. Many practitioners are using this

Exhibit 9.1. A Section of the Teacher Self-Report of Activities and Resources.

Teachers play a critical role in facilitating students' academic and social development. Therefore, understanding a teacher's behavior and his or her classroom is often essential to developing a plan for improving a referred student's performance. Please complete the following sections on classroom management and resources accurately.

My classroom management and instructional behaviors	Frequency of performance		
	Almost never	Often	Almost always
1. I provide prompts and reminders of task procedures *before* students are expected to carry them out.	1	2	3
2. I clearly state classroom rules.	1	2	3
3. I require participation of all students.	1	2	3
4. I establish and follow a classroom routine and procedures.	1	2	3
5. I provide systematic feedback on student performances.	1	2	3
6. I clearly explain consequences of appropriate and inappropriate behavior.	1	2	3
7. I use negative or failure experiences to teach more appropriate ways of functioning.	1	2	3
8. I clearly state my expectations for student behavior or performance.	1	2	3
9. I schedule time for students to review work.	1	2	3
10. I circulate through the room and observe student work behavior.	1	2	3
11. I hold students accountable for timely completion of required work.	1	2	3
12. I follow through with stated consequences quickly and consistently.	1	2	3

self-report form as part of their consultative interviews with teachers, thus focusing attention on the importance of consultees' behaviors in regulating children's behaviors.

Effective Treatments with Children. Effective behavioral consultation treatments with children focus on four areas of children's adjustment problems that occur with high frequency: academic performance problems, externalizing problems, internalizing problems, and social skills deficits. While the research literature does not provide much strong evidence for the consultative and treatment effectiveness of the intervention techniques used to treat these problems (their use in consultation either has not been studied or has not been the primary focus of the research), these techniques have high potential for use with a behavioral consultation approach.

Academic performance. A large body of research has focused on both positive behaviors (for example, being on task, work completion) and negative behaviors (being off task, inattention) related to academic difficulties (Hoge

& Andrews, 1987). Numerous techniques have been effectively employed to remediate these academic performance problems. This discussion focuses on a few that appear most promising for consultation.

Classroom behavior management techniques are ideal interventions for use in behavioral consultation (see the example provided in Chapter Thirteen). Randolph and his colleagues (Randolph, 1979; Randolph & Hartage, 1972; Randolph & Wallin, 1973) provided early work that pointed to the efficacy of consulting with teachers on behavior management. In a study with fifth- and sixth-grade students and their teachers, Randolph and Hartage (1972) compared the effects of behavior management through consultation to the results for a no-treatment control group. The behavior management technique used focused on rule setting, verbal praise, and ignoring. Pretest and posttest comparisons of on-task behavior indicated that the treatment group evidenced increased on-task behavior over a twelve-week period, while the control group exhibited decreased on-task behavior. The mean grade point average revealed no significant group differences; however, the on-task behaviors targeted for observation were not delineated. It appears that on-task behavior was targeted as the behavior management vehicle for change, so that the effects may not have generalized to grade attainment.

Differential reinforcement of appropriate behavior through praise is an easily administered, socially valid method of intervention. In a well-delineated investigation, Cossairt, Hall, and Hopkins (1973) employed a multiple-baseline design with multiple subjects in a study that explored teacher praise for student attending behavior. The manifest purpose of the study was to examine the differential effects of consultant verbal interactions (for example, instructions, feedback, social reinforcement) on teacher praising behavior and, in turn, on student behavior. The results of the study indicated increases in students' attending behavior and work accuracy in math. Interestingly, the greatest effects were found when the teachers received social praise from the consultants for the teachers' praise of students' attending behavior.

Self-management techniques are cost-efficient, effective interventions that have inherent advantages over more externally controlled behavioral interventions (Elliott & Shapiro, 1990). With many self-management strategies, the targeted individual controls the contingency, which increases the probability of generalization and maintenance and may result in children taking more responsibility for their own behavior. Piersel and Kratochwill (1979) applied self-monitoring through a series of behavioral consultations for academic and behavioral problems. The self-observations of a second-grader and a ninth-grader both resulted in increased work completion and accuracy. Reliability checks indicated that the students were accurately recording their work completion rates. Interestingly, this series of studies employed a direct service variation of behavioral consultation: the teacher collected baseline data, and the consultant worked directly with the student during the intervention phase of consultation.

Kanfer's model of self-management procedures (1971, cited in Elliott & Shapiro, 1990) also includes self-evaluation and self-reinforcement strategies. Each of these components can be easily combined with self-monitoring. Self-management programs, which generally have focused on contingency management or cognitive-based interventions, such as self-instruction, have been shown to be effective with academic problems (Elliott & Shapiro, 1990).

Few researchers have applied behavioral consultation to the high school setting. Farber and Mayer (1972) conducted a multifaceted consultation study that used praise, ignoring, individual and group contingency reinforcers, and discriminative stimuli (cues, prompts) to increase work completion in a tenth-grade classroom. The authors employed an ABAB reversal design to assess intervention effectiveness. Treatment integrity checks were performed through classroom observations. The study found that average work completion increased from a baseline level of 18 percent to 74 percent after the treatment was reinstated. Thus, although further research at the high school level is needed, this study indicates that behavioral consultation can be effectively deployed with older students.

Although the treatment used in the Farber and Mayer study was effective in increasing work completion, it is not possible to discern which components of the treatment "package" accounted for the effect. Each of the components has been identified as effective in the literature. For example, group contingencies alone have been shown to increase academic performance (see, for example, Shapiro & Goldberg, 1986). Treatment packages, therefore, while they perhaps increase treatment strength, do not readily allow for analysis of the components of the package. It may well be that less intrusive methods, when used singularly, will produce the desired outcome.

Peer tutoring, a procedure that has frequently been used to enhance academic performance (Elliott & Shapiro, 1990), can be easily fostered within a consultation framework. In an excellent review of the use of peers as instructional agents, Hawryluk and Smallwood (1988) concluded that peer tutoring often results in enhanced academic and social learning. The preponderance of studies on peer tutoring have found it to be an effective treatment strategy for students experiencing academic difficulties.

School-home notes are another easily administered intervention technique. Kelley (1990) provides a comprehensive review of the efficacy of school-home notes and offers practical applications. She cites the following advantages of using this technique: it requires conjoint problem solving between teachers and parents; it provides parents with frequent feedback, thus facilitating communication between home and school; the small time commitment that it requires makes it likely that teachers will accept the procedure and use it with integrity; and because most school-home note procedures emphasize positive behaviors, their use may increase parental praise and attention, which may result in enhanced self-esteem and self-efficacy for children. Increased parental praise and involvement may also enhance treatment maintenance and generalization.

This discussion of treatments for academic performance problems has reviewed only a portion of the interventions cited in the literature. Studies using a behavioral consultation method, although limited by methodological flaws and few in number, have shown that interventions implemented through a behavioral consultation approach are effective in increasing academic performance. Other interventions, such as school-home notes and contingency management, can easily be adapted to the behavioral consultation format. As the literature base grows, behavioral consultation for pedagogical practices may also prove to be an effective means for enhancing students' academic performance (Berliner, 1988).

Externalizing Problems. Several of the interventions used for academic performance problems have been similarly applied to externalizing problems, such as disruptive behaviors and conduct problems. The studies on *self-monitoring* conducted by Piersel and Kratochwill (1979), for example, included a child who engaged in excessively loud and disruptive talk and a child described as hyperactive who spent time daily in a resource room for students with learning disabilities. Self-monitoring resulted in decreased disruptive verbalizations for the first child and decreased class interruptions for the second child.

Group contingencies have also been applied to externalizing problems. Zwald and Gresham (1982) used differential reinforcement of low rates of responding (DRL) with three junior high school students who engaged in negative verbal interactions during a fifty-minute resource room class. DRL involves reinforcing reductions in the performance of a target behavior. Reinforcers are delivered either for a reduction in overall response frequency within a particular period of time or for increased elapsed time between responses (interresponse time). The Zwald and Gresham study employed response frequency reinforcement, whereby the students earned reinforcers for five or fewer negative verbal interactions (for example, teasing, name-calling). Effectiveness was evaluated with a decelerating changing-criterion single-case design; the results indicate that the intervention successfully decreased the target behavior from a baseline average of twenty-six to only three negative verbal interactions per day.

This study provided evidence of the effectiveness of group contingencies with externalizing problem behaviors is one of the few studies that provide delineation of the behavioral consultation format used. Specifically, the authors describe the use of the behavioral consultation model proffered by Bergan (1977), which consists of four stages: problem identification, problem analysis, plan implementation, and plan evaluation. The intervention facilitated maintenance through the decelerating design and included the teacher's satisfaction with the treatment and perception of social significance to establish social validity.

Most of the strategies for remediating academic performance problems discussed above can easily be adapted to externalizing behavior problems. Classroom behavior management techniques, for example, have been used to increase on-task behavior and can be used to effect concomitant decreases in disruptive, off-task behaviors. Similarly, school-home notes can be used to target disruptive behaviors and to increase appropriate behaviors (Kelley, 1990).

Internalizing Problems. Internalizing problems are behaviors characterized as overcontrolled that usually result in greater difficulties for the individual than for others, such as social withdrawal and somatic problems. In a single-case study, Ajchenbaum and Reynolds (1981) reported using behavioral consultation to reduce the habitual finger-sucking behavior of a seven-year-old boy. The teacher and consultant devised an intervention employing a sticker reinforcement system during morning class time coupled with social praise from the teacher for behavior decreases. After the first week of implementation, the behavior was not observed during the morning, and the program was extended to include the entire day. At the same time, the child's parents began a similar program. At the end of the second week, the behavior had almost disappeared.

Behavioral consultation has also been used for alleviating tic behavior. In a study with a nine-year-old girl with a chronic motor tic, Pray, Kramer, and Lindskog (1986) used Bergan's behavioral consultation model (1977) in conjoint consultation with the child's teacher and mother. The treatment chosen focused on habit reversal and consisted of self-monitoring by the child, competing response practice, and social reinforcement. Procedural checks were made to enhance treatment integrity, and extensive social validation was included in the treatment evaluation. The treatment was evaluated with a simple AB single-case design, and thus it could not be concluded definitively that the treatment alone accounted for the behavioral change. The results indicate an absence of tic behavior at one-year follow-up, and, although the tic behavior began to recur after eighteen months, the frequency was described as below baseline rates.

The final study reviewed in this section compared conjoint (parent-teacher) and traditional (teacher-only) behavioral consultation for four socially withdrawn children ages nine to twelve at home and school (Sheridan, Kratochwill, & Elliott, 1990). This study used the four-stage behavioral consultation model originally conceptualized by Bergan (Bergan & Kratochwill, 1990; Kratochwill & Bergan, 1990) and a social skills treatment package designed to increase social interactions in two general phases: (1) goal-setting, self-report, and positive reinforcement and (2) self-monitoring and positive reinforcement. The number of treatment days ranged from twenty to twenty-one school days. For both the conjoint and the traditional conditions, teachers and parents were provided with treatment manuals to facilitate treatment integrity. Treatment integrity was assessed through audiotaping for the consultation process and through self-report rating scales from teachers and parents for the behavioral programs. Treatment assessment procedures consisted of direct observations, behavioral interviews, and behavioral checklists and rating scales (the Child Behavior Checklist, the Teacher Report Form, the Social Skills Rating System, and the Self-Perception Profile for Children). Finally, social validation was evaluated through comparison observations of nonwithdrawn children and through teacher and parent ratings.

The results of the treatment were analyzed via a combined series multiple-baseline design across subjects, which allows for comparisons between and within subjects. Follow-up assessments were conducted nine days after treatment termination and again at four months. All four children were reported as attaining the targeted level of social interaction. Social initiations at home were most apparent for children in conjoint consultation. Although treatment effects were maintained for all the children at follow-up, maintenance also was most notable for the children in conjoint consultation. The results from the behavioral checklists and rating scales also indicated improved social behavior.

The Sheridan et al. (1990) study stands out in the behavioral consultation treatment literature for several reasons. First, the study provides evidence for the efficacy of using behavioral consultation with socially withdrawn children, which few researchers have examined. Second, the study provides further evidence for the efficacy of conjoint behavioral consultation and the benefits that it offers (for example, generality). Finally, because the study employed nearly every facet of effective treatments, it represents the most exemplary behavioral consultation treatment research to date.

Social Skills Deficits. Children who persistently exhibit social skills deficits are at risk for negative short- and long-term consequences that are often precursors of more severe problems (Elliott & Busse, 1991). Since social skills deficits may be exhibited by children without interfering problem behaviors, this discussion focuses briefly on social skills deficits as a separate area for consultation.

A rather extensive literature exists regarding social skills training. Most social skills interventions focus on positive behaviors and use nonaversive methods, such as modeling, coaching, and reinforcement, which enhance treatment acceptability and treatment integrity. Because the treatment programs can easily be built into the existing structure of a home or classroom environment, several social skills treatments are highly appropriate for behavioral consultation (see, for example, Sheridan et al., 1990). Gresham and Elliott (1990) provide a classification scheme and suggested treatments for different types of social skills problems (see Exhibit 9.2). This schema differentiates between social skill acquisition and performance problems with and without interfering behaviors and provides possible interventions for each classification.

Most of the social skills interventions listed in Exhibit 9.2 can be used in consultation. Techniques such as modeling, coaching, and operant procedures are frequently used change methods. The use of peers to directly mediate change in target children, however, is rather unique to social skills and thus deserves some attention. Peer-mediated social skills interventions are based on the assumption that peers can be effective change agents for children who have performance deficits and do not interact with other children at acceptable rates. Using peers as intervention agents is argued to be cost-effective, as it minimizes adults' (consultants' and consultees') time in treating a target child. Further, peer confederates themselves are thought to benefit from the attention they receive and from interacting with handicapped or at-risk peers (Strain, 1985). The majority of studies of peer-mediated social skills intervention have demonstrated desired treatment effects of increased social interaction rates in the treatment setting; however, few of the interaction skills seem to generalize to new settings (Hendrickson, Strain, Tremblay, & Shores, 1982; Sisson, Van Hasselt, Hersen, & Strain, 1985).

Resources and Tactics for Discovering Effective Interventions

As this chapter has indicated, it is not enough for consultants to know about an array of effective interventions for changing children's behavior or academic functioning; they must also be sensitive to the skills and perceptions of their consultees and be able to clearly communicate treatment procedures so that they are implemented with integrity. To facilitate the communication between consultants and teacher consultees, Elliott and Gresham (1989, 1991) devel-

Exhibit 9.2. Linking Assessment to Intervention.

Once the analysis of the SSRS ratings has been completed, it is possible to develop general intervention strategies. Teaching students social skills involves many of the same methods as teaching academic concepts. Thus, effective interventions for both academic difficulties and social skills deficits often involve modeling correct behaviors, eliciting imitative responses, providing corrective feedback, and arranging opportunities for practice. While some social skills interventions require specialized training, most may be implemented in regular classrooms by teachers or at home by parents.

Three basic intervention approaches—operant, social learning, cognitive-behavioral—are commonly used to improve social behavior. These procedures are reviewed in detail in Chapter 4 of the Manual.

The use of the specific procedures depends on the severity of the social skills deficits and the existence of possible interfering problem behaviors. The more serious the social behavior deficit, the more involved and direct the intervention. The SSRS Analysis of Social Behaviors given on pages 4 and 5 of this AIR form categorizes the type of social skills problem. The following table suggests different kinds of interventions for various categories.

	No interfering problem behaviors	*Interfering problem behaviors*
Social skills Acquisition deficits	Direct instruction Modeling Behavioral Rehearsal Coaching	Modeling Coaching Differential Reinforcement of a Low Rate of Response (DRL) Differential Reinforcement of Other Behavior (DRO) Reductive procedures to decrease interfering problem behaviors
Social skills Performance deficits	Operant methods to manipulate antecedent or consequent conditions to increase the rate of existing behaviors	Operant methods to manipulate antecedent or consequent conditions to increase the rate of existing prosocial behaviors Differential Reinforcement of a Low Rate of Response (DRL) Differential Reinforcement of Other Behavior (DRO) Reductive procedures to decrease interfering problem behaviors
Social skills Strengths	Reinforcement procedures to maintain desired social behavior Use student as a model for other students	Reinforcement procedures to maintain desired social behavior Reductive procedures to decrease interfering problem behaviors

Source: Social Skills Rating System, test manual by Frank M. Gresham and Stephen N. Elliott. © 1990 American Guidance Service, Inc., Circle Pines, MN. All rights reserved.

oped the *Prereferral Behavior Inventory and Intervention Planning Record (PBI)* and the *Social Skills Intervention Guide (SSIG)*.

The *PBI* contains a variety of checklists and rating scales used to describe a target child, the self-report scale on effective teaching behaviors discussed earlier in this chapter, and a forty-item rating scale briefly describing interventions that can be rated on acceptability and use dimensions (see Exhibit 9.3). The forty brief descriptions can be conceptualized as the "building blocks" of basic interventions. By directly assessing a consultee's acceptance and perceptions of the ease of use of these basic intervention components, a consultant can gain a clearer sense of the type of interventions that a consultee might use with integrity. While no systematic research effort has as yet been undertaken to investigate the utility of the *PBI* in consultation, more than a thousand practicing school psychologists have used it to coordinate their prereferral data-collection efforts in states including Illinois, Louisiana, Wisconsin, Texas,

Exhibit 9.3. Sample Portion of the Intervention Selection and Planner from the Prereferral Behavior Inventory.

Regular Classroom Interventions

Teachers have a rather extensive repertoire of techniques for changing students' academic and social behaviors. Below is a list of over 30 possible techniques that could be used to change the target student's behavior. Please read each brief description of a technique and then rate (a) How much you like the technique and (2) How easy it is to use in *your* class with the target student.

		Like			Use		
	Intervention techniques	Do not like	OK	Like very much	Very hard	Possible	Very easy
1.	Touch student to demonstrate you like his/her behavior	1	2	3	1	2	3
2.	Require student to go to school office or place of detention outside of classroom	1	2	3	1	2	3
3.	Physically restrain or hold student firmly	1	2	3	1	2	3
4.	Model desired behavior for student	1	2	3	1	2	3
5.	Verbally threaten student with punishing consequences	1	2	3	1	2	3
6.	Use a gesture or verbal alert to signal student to stop inappropriate behavior	1	2	3	1	2	3
7.	Verbally promise reward for desired behavior	1	2	3	1	2	3
8.	Change task assigned to student to facilitate completion	1	2	3	1	2	3
9.	Move physically closer to student whose behavior is disturbing	1	2	3	1	2	3

and Michigan. Thus, at this time there appears to be high social validity for the *PBI* and its use with teachers.

The *SSIG* is a treatment manual designed to accompany the *Social Skills Rating System* (Gresham & Elliott, 1990). The *SSIG* was designed for use in direct treatment or small-group sessions with students in grades 3 through 12. However, material from the treatment planning section of the *SSIG* nicely illustrates the use of explicit treatment guidelines to enhance integrity of treatment implementation. Exhibit 9.4 presents the *SSIG*'s guidelines for using modeling and home-school notes. With a little effort, consultants can develop their own guidelines for other intervention techniques to use as communication tools with consultees and integrity checklists for monitoring treatment implementation.

Summary

The discussion in this section has touched on only a few of the myriad possible treatments for use within a behavioral consultation approach. Our purpose has been to offer a subset of potential treatment strategies that enjoy empirical support as effective techniques for positive behavioral change. Indeed, a number of other prereferral intervention studies that have used a behavioral consultation model have been published in the applied literature (see Bergan & Kratochwill, 1990, for further review). It is apparent that practitioners have many treatments from which to choose, and given the support that behavioral consultation has in the treatment literature, practitioners and researchers alike should find the behavioral consultation approach useful. Further support for the approach has come from applied programs incorporating a behavioral consultation model that have been recognized by the American Psychological Association and the National Association of School Psychologists. For example, the Amphitheater Public Schools in Arizona provide a continuum of psycho-educational services that include a behavioral consultation method of service delivery (Franklin & Duley, 1991); in Tennessee, Fuchs and Fuchs (1988) implemented a program of assistance teams based on the Bergan (1977) model of behavioral consultation.

Implications and Future Directions

As the consultation service delivery method gains further momentum, researchers and practitioners need to remain cognizant of the limitations in the current literature base and strive to redress these limitations. Researchers and practitioners need to focus more attention on the components of effective treatments, whether delivered through behavioral consultation or other forms of intervention. Treatment acceptability, integrity, maintenance and generaliza-

Exhibit 9.4. Sample Treatment Implementation Guidelines.

Guidelines for Using Modeling

1. Establish the Need to Learn the Skill. It is important to "sell" the social skill to students. Consider doing the following:
    a. Ask students why the skill might be important to them.
    b. Point out potential consequences of using the skill and not using the skill.
    c. Use examples from books, television, and the like in which characters used the skill.
    d. Identify situations in which the skill could come in handy for students.
2. Identify Skill Components. It is important that the social skill be task-analyzed for students. Students must know what steps and in what order the behaviors must be performed. Consider doing the following:
    a. Present a social skill (e.g., Starting a conversation).
    b. Ask students what they would have to do to start a conversation with someone else.
    c. Write *all* of their suggestions on a chalkboard or flip chart.
    d. Discuss the relevance of each suggestion with the group. Decide with the group what behaviors would be important and unimportant and why.
    e. Decide with the group the list of behaviors that would be most important in performing the skill.
    f. Decide with the group the order in which the behaviors should be performed. Identify potential problems that might occur in performing the skill (e.g., the other person ignores you).
3. Present the Modeling Display.
    a. Decide if you or another child will model the skill.
    b. Be sure to have each of the steps in performing the skill written in view of group members.
    c. Review the steps to be performed *before* presenting the modeling display.
    d. Instruct students to watch and see if each step is performed in the proper sequence.
    e. Model the skill for the group.
    f. After modeling, discuss with students what they say and have them evaluate the modeling sequence.
4. Rehearse the Skill. Have different students rehearse the modeled skill.
5. Provide Specific Feedback.
    a. Point out the correct things students did in performing the skill.
    b. Offer suggestions for how the performance could be improved. Remodel the skill if necessary and have students rehearse.
6. Program for Generalization.
    a. Use a number of different situations in role plays where the skill would be appropriate. Vary these situations as much as possible in terms of who, what, when, and where the skill will be performed.
    b. Teach a number of different ways in which the skill could be performed. For example, there are an infinite number of ways in which people can have a conversation. Teach a sufficient number of ways in which the skill could be performed.

Guidelines for Designing School-Home Notes

1. Schedule a conference between yourself, the teacher, and parent to discuss target behaviors and goals of the social skills training group.
2. Specifically define target behaviors that will be on the school-home note. These behaviors should be defined as specifically as possible so everyone involved will know what behaviors to expect. *Example:* Asked others before using their property. *Nonexample:* Respected others' property.
3. Design the school-home note to include child's name, date, teacher's signature, your signature, the target behaviors, and space for teacher to check whether or not the behaviors were performed.

(continued)

Exhibit 9.4, Sample Treatment Implementation Guidelines, Cont'd.

4. Keep the note simple and include no more than 3 or 4 target behaviors.
5. Establish the responsibilities of each party involved.
   a. Parent Responsibilities
      —Providing note to child each day before school
      —Providing or withholding rewards based on note results
   b. Child Responsibilities
      —Bringing note to school each day
      —Having note signed by appropriate persons
      —Bringing note home each day
   c. Teacher Responsibilities
      —Checking appropriate spaces on note
      —Signing note
   d. Social Skills Trainer's Responsibilities
      —Reviewing teacher's evaluation of behavior
      —Signing note
      —Using results of performance in group sessions
6. Decide with parents and child what level of behavioral performance will constitute a "good" note.
7. Assist parents and child in deciding what rewards or privileges will be made available contingent on a good note. Provide parents with a reinforcement menu for this purpose.
8. Emphasize to parents the importance of following through consistently with specified consequences for the child bringing home a "good" note.
9. Instruct parents *not* to ridicule or scold the child for not having a "good" note. Instead, instruct parents to simply withhold rewards and privileges. At the same time, instruct parents to use praise for the child bringing home a "good" note.
10. Arrange contingencies for the child's failure to meet his or her responsibilities (i.e., bringing note to and from school, having note signed, etc.). Lost or forgotten responsibilities *should result in the same consequences as not having a good note* (i.e., failure to earn rewards and privileges).
11. Gradually fade the note out as behavior improves. Fade from daily notes to weekly notes. *Do not abruptly withdraw the note system.*

Source: Social Skills Intervention Guide by Frank M. Gresham and Stephen N. Elliott. © 1991 American Guidance Service, Inc., Circle Pines, MN. All rights reserved.

tion, and evaluation are essential components of treatment effectiveness and should be introduced into research and practice. Continued neglect of these important treatment variables will undermine the knowledge base necessary for successful treatment selection and remediation of children's academic and behavior problems.

It should be apparent that identifying effective treatment strategies that are useful within a behavioral consultation delivery framework is a multifaceted process. The choice of treatment depends, of course, on the presenting problem, so problem assessment and definition are inextricably linked to intervention. Once the problem has been defined, there is a vast array of interventions from which to choose. One need only page through available sources such as the *Journal of Applied Behavior Analysis* and *Behavior Modification* to find treatments that enjoy empirical support as effective for a variety of problem behaviors. From there, it requires excellent communication and relationship skills and a bit of imagination and ingenuity to adapt treatments to a behavioral consultation approach.

Continued research on the application of interventions delivered through behavioral consultation is, of course, essential. Although much has been learned regarding effective behavioral consultation treatment strategies, researchers and practitioners must continue to explore and share information about effective treatments that fit into a consultation delivery system.

References

Ajchenbaum, M., & Reynolds, C. R. (1981). A brief case study using behavioral consultation for behavior reduction. *School Psychology Review, 10,* 407–408.

Alpert, J. L., & Yammer, M. D. (1983). Research in school consultation: A content analysis of selected journals. *Professional Psychology: Research and Practice, 14,* 604–612.

Bergan, J. R. (1977). *Behavioral consultation.* Columbus, OH: Merrill.

Bergan, J. R., & Kratochwill, T. R. (1990). *Behavioral consultation and therapy.* New York: Plenum Press.

Berliner, D. C. (1988). Effective classroom management and instruction: A knowledge base for consultation. In J. L. Graden, J. E. Zins, & M. J. Curtis (Eds.), *Alternative educational delivery systems: Enhancing instructional options for all students* (pp. 309–325). Silver Spring, MD: National Association of School Psychologists.

Cooper, J. O., Heron, T. E., & Heward, W. I. (1987). *Applied behavior analysis.* Columbus, OH: Merrill.

Cossairt, A., Hall, R. V., & Hopkins, B. L. (1973). The effects of experimenter's instructions, feedback, and praise on teacher praise and student attending behavior. *Journal of Applied Behavior Analysis, 6,* 89–100.

Elliott, S. N. (1988). Acceptability of behavioral treatments in educational settings. In J. C. Witt, S. N. Elliott, & F. M. Gresham (Eds.), *Handbook of behavior therapy in education* (pp. 121–150). New York: Plenum Press.

Elliott, S. N., & Busse, R. T. (1991). Social skills assessment and intervention with children and adolescents: Guidelines for assessment and training procedures. *School Psychology International, 12,* 63–83.

Elliott, S. N., & Gresham, F. M. (1989). *Prereferral behavior inventory and intervention planning record.* Unpublished scale, University of Wisconsin, Madison.

Elliott, S. N., & Gresham, F. M. (1991). *Social skills intervention guide.* Circle Pines, MN: American Guidance Service.

Elliott, S. N., & Shapiro, E. S. (1990). Intervention techniques and programs for academic performance problems. In T. B. Gutkin & C. R. Reynolds (Eds.), *Handbook of school psychology* (2nd ed., pp. 635–660). New York: Wiley.

Elliott, S. N., Turco, T. C., & Gresham, F. M. (1987). Consumers' and clients' pretreatment acceptability ratings of classroom-based group contingencies. *Journal of School Psychology, 25,* 145–154.

Farber, H., & Mayer, G. R. (1972). Behavior consultation in a barrio high school. *Personnel and Guidance Journal, 51,* 273–279.

Franklin, M. R., & Duley, S. M. (1991). Psychological services in the Amphitheater Public Schools. *School Psychology Quarterly, 6,* 66–80.

Fuchs, D., & Fuchs, L. S. (1988). Mainstream assistance teams to accommodate difficult-to-teach students in general education. In J. L. Graden, J. E. Zins, & M. J. Curtis (Eds.), *Alternative educational delivery systems: Enhancing instructional options for all students* (pp. 49–70). Silver Spring, MD: National Association of School Psychologists.

Gettinger, M. (1988). Methods of proactive classroom management. *School Psychology Review, 17,* 227–242.

Gresham, F. M. (1989). Assessment of treatment integrity in school consultation and prereferral intervention. *School Psychology Review, 18,* 37–50.

Gresham, F. M., & Elliott, S. N. (1990). *Social skills rating system.* Circle Pines, MN: American Guidance Service.

Gresham, F. M., & Kendell, G. K. (1987). School consultation research: Methodological critique and future directions. *School Psychology Review, 16,* 306–316.

Griest, D. L., & Wells, K. C. (1983). Behavioral family therapy with conduct disorders in children. *Behavior Therapy, 14,* 37–53.

Gutkin, T. B., Singer, J. H., & Brown, R. (1980). Teacher reactions to school-based consultation services: A multivariate analysis. *Journal of School Psychology, 18,* 126–134.

Hawryluk, M. K., & Smallwood, D. L. (1988). Using peers as instructional agents: Peer tutoring and cooperative learning. In J. L. Graden, J. E. Zins, & M. J. Curtis (Eds.), *Alternative educational delivery systems: Enhancing instructional options for all students* (pp. 371–389). Washington, DC: National Association of School Psychologists.

Hendrickson, J. M., Strain, P. S., Tremblay, A., & Shores, R. E. (1982). Interactions of behaviorally handicapped children: Functional effects of peer social interactions. *Behavior Modification, 6,* 323–353.

Hoge, R. D., & Andrews, D. A. (1987). Enhancing academic performance: Issues in target selection. *School Psychology Review, 16,* 228–238.

Idol, L. (1988). Theory of school consultation. In J. F. West (Ed.), *School consultation: Interdisciplinary perspectives on theory, research, training, and practice* (pp. 77–102). Austin, TX: Association of Educational and Psychological Consultants.

Jacobson, N. S., Follette, W. C., & Revenstorf, D. (1984). Psychotherapy outcome research: Methods for reporting variability and evaluating clinical significance. *Behavior Therapy, 15,* 336–352.

Jason, L. A., & Ferone, L. (1978). Behavioral versus process consultation interventions in school settings. *American Journal of Community Psychology, 6,* 531–543.

Kanfer, F. H. (1971). The maintenance of behavior by self-generated stimuli and reinforcement. In A. Jacobs & L. B. Sachs (Eds.), *The psychology of private events* (pp. 39–58). San Diego, CA: Academic Press.

Kazdin, A. E. (1988). *Child psychotherapy: Developing and identifying effective treatments.* Elmsford, NY: Pergamon Press.

Kelley, M. L. (1990). *School-home notes: Promoting children's classroom success.* New York: Guilford Press.

Kramer, J. J. (1990). Training parents as behavior change agents: Successes, failures, and suggestions for school psychologists. In T. B. Gutkin & C. R. Reynolds (Eds.), *The Handbook of school psychology* (2nd ed., pp. 683–702). New York: Wiley.

Kratochwill, T. R., & Bergan, J. R. (1990). *Behavioral consultation in applied settings: An individual guide.* New York: Plenum Press.

Kratochwill, T. R., Sheridan, S. M., & VanSomeren, K. R. (1988). Research in behavioral consultation: Current status and future directions. In J. F. West (Ed.), *School consultation: Interdisciplinary perspectives on theory, research, training, and practice* (pp. 77–102). Austin, TX: Association of Educational and Psychological Consultants.

Medway, F. J. (1979). How effective is school consultation? A review of recent research. *Journal of School Psychology, 17,* 275–282.

Paul, G. L. (1967). Strategy of outcome research in psychotherapy. *Journal of Consulting Psychology, 31,* 109–118.

Piersel, W. C., & Kratochwill, T. R. (1979). Self-observation and behavior change: Applications to academic and adjustment problems through behavioral consultation. *Journal of School Psychology, 17,* 151–161.

Ponti, C. R., Zins, J. E., & Graden, J. L. (1988). Implementing a consultation-based service delivery system to decrease referrals for special education: A case study of organizational considerations. *School Psychology Review, 17,* 89–100.

Pray, B., Kramer, J. J., & Lindskog, R. (1986). Assessment and treatment of tic behavior: A review and case study. *School Psychology Review, 15,* 418–429.

Pryzwansky, W. B. (1986). Indirect service delivery: Considerations for future research in consultation. *School Psychology Review, 15,* 479–488.

Randolph, D. L. (1979). The behavioral consultant in the school. *American Journal of Community Psychology, 7,* 353–356.

Randolph, D. L., & Hartage, N. C. (1972). Behavioral consultation and group counseling with potential dropouts. *Elementary School Guidance and Counseling, 7,* 204–209.

Randolph, D. L., & Wallin, K. R. (1973). A comparison of behavioral consultation with model-reinforcement group counseling for children who are consistently off-task. *Journal of Educational Research, 67,* 103–107.

Rhoades, M., & Kratochwill, T. K. (1992). Teachers' reactions to behavioral consultation: An analysis of language and involvement. *School Psychology Quarterly, 7,* 47–59.

Ritter, D. R. (1978). Effects of a school consultation program upon referral patterns of teachers. *Psychology in the Schools, 15,* 239–243.

Shapiro, E. S., & Goldberg, R. (1986). A comparison of group contingencies for increasing spelling performance among sixth grade students. *School Psychology Review, 15,* 546–557.

Sheridan, S. M., Kratochwill, T. R., & Elliott, S. N. (1990). Behavioral consultation with parents and teachers: Delivering treatment for socially withdrawn children at home and school. *School Psychology Review, 19,* 33–52.

Sisson, L. A., Van Hasselt, V. B., Hersen, M., & Strain, P. S. (1985). Peer interventions: Increasing social behaviors in multihandicapped children. *Behavior Modification, 9,* 293–321.

Stokes, T. F., & Baer, D. M. (1977). An implicit technology of generalization. *Journal of Applied Behavior Analysis, 10,* 349–367.

Stokes, T. F., & Osnes, P. (1989). An operant pursuit of generalization. *Behavior Therapy, 20,* 337–355.

Strain, P. S. (1985). Programmatic research on peers as intervention agents for socially isolated classmates. In B. H. Schneider, K. H. Rubin, & J. E. Ledingham (Eds.) *Children's peer relations: Issues in assessment and intervention.* (pp. 193–206). New York: Springer-Verlag.

Vernberg, E. M., & Reppucci, N. D. (1986). Behavioral consultation. In F. V. Mannino, E. J. Trickett, M. F. Shore, M. G. Kidder, & G. Levin (Eds.), *Handbook of mental health consultation* (DHHS Publication No. ADM 86-1466, pp. 49–80). Washington, DC: U.S. Government Printing Office.

Wolf, M. M. (1978). Social validity: The case for subjective measurement or how applied behavior analysis is finding its heart. *Journal of Applied Behavior Analysis, 11,* 203–214.

Zins, J. E. (1988). Examination of the conceptual foundations of school consultation practice. In J. F. West (Ed.), *School consultation: Interdisciplinary perspectives on theory, research, training, and practice* (pp. 17–34). Austin, TX: Association of Educational and Psychological Consultants.

Zwald, L., & Gresham, F. M. (1982). Behavioral consultation in a secondary class: Using DRL to decrease negative verbal interactions. *School Psychology Review, 11,* 428–432.

10

Implementing Consultation Programs in Child Service Systems

Joseph E. Zins, Robert J. Illback

Recent years have seen the development of an extensive array of validated interventions that can be applied for the resolution of child-related problems. Indeed, a plethora of effective treatments are available, most of which can be used in consultation (Martens & Meller, 1990; Witt, Elliott, & Gresham, 1988; see also Chapter Nine). A major challenge, therefore, is to influence organizations serving children to adopt consultation-based service delivery systems. However, surprisingly little has been written about the implementation of consultation methods to bring about systemic change (Lippitt, Langseth, & Mossop, 1985; Smith & Corse, 1986; Zins & Ponti, 1990). There remains a need for descriptions of such methods, as even the best program, "if poorly implemented, may prove ineffective" (Maher & Illback, 1985, p. 81).

This chapter discusses means by which consultation can be implemented so that the process becomes an essential element of an organization's daily functioning and routine. The primary focus is on system-level issues. Consultation is viewed as a program offered within an organization, just as schools have special education programs and community agencies have outreach programs. Consultation is considered as a planned organizational change effort designed to resolve system, group, and/or individual-level problems. A major focus of the discussion is on the entry process, and most of the

Note: Appreciation is extended to Edward S. Marks for his comments on an earlier draft of this chapter. Completion of the chapter was supported in part through research grants to the first author from the U.S. Department of Education (no. H023A20042) and from the University Research Council of the University of Cincinnati. The opinions expressed are solely those of the authors and may not represent the views of the U.S. Department of Education or the University of Cincinnati.

ideas apply to both internally and externally based consultants, although the primary emphasis is on the former. The chapter begins with a brief review of organizational change efforts, next discusses the major steps in implementing consultation, and concludes with suggestions for future research.

Consultation for Organizational Change

Our discussion of organizational change and the implementation of consultation programs is based on several assumptions. First, there is no one best method of organizational change. Successful efforts consider a complex array of factors, including people, procedures, products, and other mediating variables. Second, organizational interventions should reflect the fact that problems exist at multiple levels and often affect numerous constituencies, each of which must take ownership of the intervention plan. Third, although our focus is change in organizations, we must remember that change is brought about by individuals. Fourth, since organizations consist of interrelated and interdependent subsystems, change in one area usually results in change in another, which may be intended or unintentional. Finally, ongoing evaluation of the intervention program is essential to ensure adequate integrity of the effort (see Illback & Zins, 1984, for additional discussion).

New programs frequently take several years to become fully operational, and a commitment of at least three years is essential for implementation (Fullan, Miles, & Taylor, 1980; Hord, Rutherford, Huling-Austin, & Hall, 1987; Ponti, Zins, & Graden, 1988; Zins, 1992). Consultation programs are no exception, although it is common to overlook this point in the quest for immediate results.

Organizational change efforts often fail because the problem was not fully clarified or the organization's needs were not carefully considered; insufficient attention was given to the organization's readiness for the change process; the organization was not adequately involved in planning and developing the plans for change; intervention strategies were not well conceptualized or were too simplistic or limited; plans for evaluating the intervention program were not well developed or the outcomes of the evaluation were not utilized; there was insufficient or no follow-up; or insufficient time was allowed for the change to have an effect (Fullan et al., 1980). Of particular significance is that pressure to intervene prematurely must be resisted, even with an organization that is extremely dysfunctional.

The following section illustrates the application of these conceptual principles through a review of the steps involved in implementing consultation and presentation of examples from a case study.

Steps in the Consultation Process

Numerous approaches to conceptualizing the phases of the consultation process can be taken. Some authors (for example, Bergan & Kratochwill, 1990) focus primarily on the problem-solving component, while others (for example, Zins, Curtis, Graden, & Ponti, 1988) emphasize broad, systems-change issues. We believe that the following outline, which is a modification of the steps developed by Lippitt and Lippitt (1986), is helpful in examining the process. It includes five interrelated, multi-faceted phases:

Protocol for Implementing Consultation

Entry: Initial contact, relationship building, and contractual agreements
    Consultant and consultee familiarization
    Clarifying the need for change
    Contractual negotiations and agreements

Identifying problems through organizational analysis
    A. Methods
        Interviews
        Observations
        Product examination
        Questionnaires and rating scales
    B. Outcomes
        Understanding climate, health, boundaries, leadership styles, communication processes and patterns, external influences, and so on.

Goal setting and action planning
    Goal specification
    Gaining sanction:
      Administrative-level
      Staff/caregiver-level
    Identification of required resources
    Planning and scheduling program-related activities

Program implementation, management, and cycling feedback
    Integrating consultation into organizational routines
    Monitoring program implementation
    Marketing strategies to expand consumer groups
    Overcoming barriers and resistance

Program evaluation
    Inclusion in initial program planning
    Applications:
      Improve service delivery
      Expand service use

Listing the phases separately is artificial; it was done simply for discussion purposes. For example, the first three steps usually occur simultaneously. The specific circumstances of the organizational intervention somewhat dictate the order in which they are carried out.

Entry: Initial Contact, Relationship Building, and Contractual Agreements

The entry process and systems change begin as soon as interactions between the consultant and the organization are initiated, even before contractual agreements have been reached. Therefore, consultants should model the style of interpersonal interaction that they wish to promote as soon as they begin to discuss the consultation program with the organization.

Entry is not a single event but rather a lengthy process or series of activities that take place over an extended period of time (Hord et al., 1987; Zins & Curtis, 1984) as the consultant and the consultee system develop first impressions, become familiar with one another, and clarify the need for change. The consultant must understand the system's needs, history, expectations, manner of operating, resources, norms, structure, reward mechanisms, and so forth, while the organization must learn about the consultant's skills, style of interacting, philosophy, and limitations, as well as the benefits expected from consultation. Too often, however, we have seen instances in which consultants or consultee systems did not understand that this familiarization process must occur or devoted insufficient attention to it. Consultants sometimes expected consultees to intuitively understand the consultation process following a single, brief discussion; organizations sometimes believed that consultants could identify system needs "magically." Significant misunderstanding can result from such assumptions and hamper the consultation program.

Initial contact is usually initiated by the consultee system. It may begin during the process of hiring a professional such as a school psychologist who will provide consultation services, or when an external consultant, such as an organization development specialist, is called to assist in resolving a specific problem. A variety of factors can stimulate interest in the consultation process, including a desire for greater service efficiency, changes in funding, or new policies (Schaeffer, 1987).

Internal and external consultants usually deal with somewhat different issues with respect to entry, and each arrangement has its own strengths and limitations (Conoley & Conoley, 1982). Internal consultants may be more available to the consultee system and more easily establish referent power. Because of their familiarity with the organization, they may also be viewed as more credible. However, external consultants often have more expert power because they come from high-status institutions, such as universities, and have impressive credentials. Furthermore, internal consultants are often identified with certain subsystems within an organization, and thus may lose some of their influence with other groups and be unable to work as effectively with them (Conoley & Conoley, 1982). External consultants can face this same problem if they are perceived to have been called into the organization at the request of one group or are somehow identified with only one element. However, because they do not have long histories with the organization, external consultants usually can more easily avoid these situations.

While working as a psychologist in a community mental health center (CMHC), Zins (1992) had the opportunity to negotiate with a school district regarding its contractual agreement with the CMHC to provide psychological services. The CMHC, which had provided services to the schools for several years, hoped to expand those services to better meet the needs of the district. Beginning with his initial contacts with the district, Zins devoted significant attention to establishing a trusting and collaborative relationship, ensuring that he understood the consultee system's needs, actively listening to concerns and being nondefensive, and involving participants in planning and developing the services. These efforts were particularly important in this case because the district had previously had a negative experience with a consultant. By demonstrating a collegial and collaborative style of relating, Zins intended, among other things, to help organization members to better understand the interpersonal aspect of consultation, thereby facilitating the entry and relationship-building process.

To enable the completion of contractual agreements, it is desirable that negotiations take place between people with the power to ensure that terms of the agreement can actually be met. Otherwise, an additional step is created, and the potential for misunderstanding is increased. Another issue that should be addressed early in the process is whether the consultant and the consultee system are compatible enough to be able to work fruitfully together. Of course, compatibility is a somewhat different issue when it involves an internal consultant who is already part of the system. In that case, the compatibility issue should have been resolved when the consultant was initially hired. However, the internal consultant may not be the appropriate person to address a specific problem through consultation.

A needs assessment is helpful in developing the contractual agreement. When organizational needs are not clarified adequately, the contract may specify unnecessary goals or omit important ones. Periodic examination and renegotiation of the contractual agreements to address new concerns or to modify old ones are also important.

In the human service field, contractual arrangements may range from general, informal, and verbal to very specific, formal, and written. A contractual agreement is always needed, although the specific type depends on the situation. Even a "letter of understanding" written after a meeting between the consultant and the organization can serve to clarify the agreement. Each format has its own advantages and limitations. If the contract is too specific, some needs may not be met because they are outside the scope of the contract (Alpert & Associates, 1982). On the other hand, when no contractual agreements are reached, conflicts may result from misunderstandings about the terms.

Contracts should at a minimum describe the specific parameters of the relationship between the consultant and the organization. They may establish responsibilities and obligations of each party, specify areas and methods of intervention, outline acceptable activities, determine fees and time limits, list potential consumer groups for the service, identify the client and the targets of change, define the resources to be supplied by both parties, and clarify appropriate operational levels (for example, individual or systemwide) for the consultant. Goals usually are jointly established, with consideration given to the results of the needs assessment. At this point consensus may be achieved only on a general problem statement. Consultees also need to be informed about how the change may affect the organization or what it could mean to them individually. Confidentiality issues also should be explicitly discussed and its terms agreed upon. Once the contract has been accepted, it is a sign that the organization now sanctions this form of service delivery (Meyers, Parsons, & Martin, 1979).

To illustrate these points, we return to the case described by Zins (1992). In that case, a formalized contractual agreement was necessary, since Zins was an external consultant employed by an agency outside the school district. The contract was signed by the school superintendent and a CMHC director. It specified the number of hours each week that the psychologist would spend in each school, the remuneration to the CMHC, terms of payment, and procedures for discontinuing the agreement, and provided that a qualified professional would provide the services. It indicated that the contract was for "psychological services" but did not clarify specifically what they were. However, following verbal agreements, this information, as well as the dates and times when services would be provided, was included in a letter sent by the psychologist to the district. Other issues, such as confidentiality, record keeping, responsibility for obtaining parental permissions, changes in scheduling, and appropriate consultees were agreed to verbally.

After it has been determined that the match between the consultant and the system is a good one, the consultant must gain a greater understanding of the organization's methods of operation, its unique needs, and possible solutions to its problems. The process for gaining this information is described next.

Identifying Problems Through Organizational Analysis

Organizations may not even be aware of the specific problem that must be addressed or know how to deal with a certain situation (Conoley & Conoley, 1982). Consultants must know precisely how to focus their efforts to be most effective. For these reasons, specific problem identification is as important in consultation program implementation as in case-centered consultation. Although there is often an expectation that a consultant will make a quick and accurate diagnosis of problem situations, organizational assessment, like entry, is a long-term process and cannot be accomplished in a one-shot effort.

Systems issues are often ignored or neglected, even though they can significantly affect the consultation process. Failing to consider them, especially before introducing the new program, can lead to failure. Chesler, Bryant, and Crowfoot (1976) even suggest that meaningful personal change is often impossible without related systemic change. Thus, conducting an organizational assessment is necessary before any new program is introduced.

The organizational assessment, which builds on the initial needs assessment, is designed to help the consultant and the consultee to understand the organization as consisting of many interactive system variables, develop hypotheses about the organization's method of functioning based on an analysis of the data collected, determine what interventions are needed and what types might be appropriate, learn about the organization's receptivity to change, and plan actions in response to the assessment and according to contract goals (Harrison, 1987; Maher & Bennett, 1984; Maher, Illback, & Zins, 1984). At the end of the organizational assessment, there should be greater clarity about how the organization functions, the problems it is encountering, whether consultation is a potentially effective intervention, and the organization's interest in consultation services.

There are a variety of ways to learn about an organization. Each of these diagnostic methods has advantages and limitations (see Harrison, 1987). Organizational assessment should lead to better understanding of the organizational climate, health, boundaries, leadership styles, communication processes, power issues, and other characteristics. Factors external to the organization that may be influencing its functioning should also be examined. For example, a pending lawsuit or a new federal law can significantly affect communication and trust, which are essential to effective consultation programs. In addition, a historical perspective of the organization's problem-solving efforts will make it easier to identify organizational strengths, resources, and areas in need of change and to design system-level strategies to implement the consultation program. The following list offers examples of organizational factors that can be assessed:

Physical factors
    Physical plant condition
    Maintenance
    Facilities and supplies for staff (for example, restrooms, technology)

Organizational climate and health
    Staff relations
    Norms, values, traditions
    Communication (open, closed)
    Problem-solving patterns
    Integration of subsystems
    Morale
    Organizational trajectory
    Organizational boundaries
    Organizational goals

Leadership and power
    Relationship of power to competence and/or seniority
    Accessibility of administrators
    Formal and informal leaders
    Organizational structure (rigid versus flexible)
    Leadership style (authoritative versus participatory)
    Reward systems
    Lines of authority

External influences
    Community support
    Unions
    Laws
    Community status and trajectory

The issue of internal versus external consultants merits mention again. As a rule, internal consultants usually have the advantage of being more knowledgeable about the system and its resources, at least initially. External consultants may take longer to achieve the same level of understanding, depending on the extent and length of their involvement with the organization (Lippitt & Lippitt, 1986). However, because of their distance from the organization, they may have a more objective view of its functioning. Nevertheless, internal consultants still have an obligation to conduct an organizational assessment before introducing new programs such as consultation.

In the case in which Zins (1992) was involved, he engaged in a number of activities as part of the organizational assessment process. For instance, he was able to draw on the experience of several of his CMHC colleagues who had previously worked in the schools. In addition, he reviewed end-of-the-year reports published by the district, read recent issues of the community newspaper, and spoke with professionals in community agencies who had contacts with the schools. He also gained considerable understanding through interviews with school staff and observations in the building.

Through this data-gathering process, Zins learned that the district had a philosophical orientation supportive of consultation services, that consultative support would be needed because new federal and state mandates required regular education teachers to teach children with disabilities, and that more children, teachers, and parents would probably use psychological services if they were available.

Goal Setting and Action Planning

Initial goal setting occurs as part of contractual negotiations, although usually on a rather general level, with additional specificity and clarification added later. The diagnostic process discussed previously provides much direction in this regard (Lippitt & Lippitt, 1986).

During the goal-setting and action-planning phase, it is often helpful to devise a sequence of steps. In schools, consultation services could be implemented on a limited pilot basis or provided systemwide. Individual staff could provide services within their own domains or as part of a more coordinated systemwide intervention (Zins et al., 1988). Planning should address such issues as what consumer groups may use the service in the future and what substeps will enable the final goals to be achieved. A specific goal might be to develop consultation as an activity in which teachers must participate before a child can be referred for a special education evaluation.

Internal consultants sometimes have a vested interest in maintaining the status quo and may not be as willing to risk change as an external consultant would be (Alpert & Associates, 1982). Conversely, external consultants may try to ensure that their services continue to be needed by the organization and unwittingly attempt to make it dependent on them. These behaviors are not conducive to effective consultation. Although consultants have an obligation to try to influence the organization in which they are working, it is essential that they make their ideologies explicit to the consultee system.

Gaining Administrative-Level Acceptance. Without the active support of administrators who are involved with consultation on a daily basis, the program will not succeed and resistance may arise. This group may or may not be involved in the contractual negotiations or be aware of the specific terms of the agreement. Therefore, to obtain their support, several aspects of consultation need to be addressed explicitly. For example, the relationship between the needs assessment and the consultation program should be explained. Even when a formal consultation agreement has been reached with high-level administrators, such as superintendents, it is often necessary to negotiate the specific day-to-day operations with lower-level administrators, such as principals. When planning the program with administrators at any level, consultants should try to develop supportive organizational arrangements on such matters as policies, job descriptions, resource allocations, procedures, and planning. External consultants often have more leverage in requesting the involvement of top-level administrators than internal consultants do (Lippitt & Lippitt, 1986).

Consultation must be clearly defined and understood because there is so much confusion associated with the term. Modeling a collaborative interactive style may lessen the chance that misunderstandings will emerge. The rationale and potential benefits also should be explained. Administrators in particular are usually eager to learn that this service is a potentially cost-effective means of providing assistance to large numbers of caretakers and children. Finally, logistical issues, such as times and locations for consultative meetings, are usually decided on at this time.

During these discussions, open communication is a necessity. Differences in expectations are common and should be dealt with directly. Routine and structured mechanisms must be established to provide feedback and review contractual agreements. Information developed later in the implementation process may require a change in plans (Schaeffer, 1987).

Zins (1992) emphasized to the administrators with whom he worked several advantages of consultation: it makes the expertise of the consultant available to students and teachers, it focuses on early detection and intervention of problems, it helps consultees to make better use of their skills, and it provides a broad range of educational alternatives for students.

Gaining Staff- and Caregiver-Level Acceptance. Staff- and caregiver-level members of the organization need to know what to expect from the consultation process and how to become effective consultees. Sandoval, Lambert, and Davis (1977) observed that it takes time to become a good consultee. Consultees must learn to form realistic expectations about the consultation process; they need to know that consultants do not have all the answers, that they do not merely provide direct solutions to the problem without involving the consultee, and that they are not supervisors who evaluate consultee performance.

One technique that we have found to be effective in introducing consultation to a consultee system is the use of a formal presentation or in-service program. Organization members appear to be more receptive to new programs such as consultation that they understand than to those they do not (Reimers, Wacker, & Koeppl, 1987). Areas addressed include a description of the consultation process, anticipated goals and outcomes, and expectations for consultee involvement. Usually, consultation is described as one of many services provided. Such an introductory or entry presentation can be outlined as follows:

Delivery guidelines
Adapt contents to audience and use precise, readily understandable language
Engage audience in the presentation and build motivation to participate

Introduce the consultation process
Describe purposes of presentation
Briefly review professional qualifications and background; establish credibility and sell yourself
Emphasize that consultation is intended to help children and to provide supportive assistance to consultees

Define consultation
Explain what consultation is (for example, a joint problem-solving process) and is not (for example, counseling, supervision)
Describe and provide examples of appropriate and inappropriate issues to address; share brief case example of consultation

Review rationale and emphasize potential benefits
More immediate assistance for consultees and their clients
Successful resolution of presenting problems
Ecological/systems perspective
Prevention and skills-building components
Potential indirect benefit to other children

Discuss characteristics of consultant/consultee relationship
Joint, collaborative process; emphasize your respect for consultees' expertise and knowledge

Voluntary, in terms of both initiating consultative interactions and continuation of relationship
Responsibilities of each participant
   To client and each other
   To problem-solving process
Confidentiality and trust
Need for consultee involvement in problem solving
Behavioral expectations of each participant
Consultee makes decision to accept or reject suggestions

Describe problem-solving steps
   Problem identification
   Problem analysis
   Treatment implementation
   Treatment evaluation

Demonstrate consultation process
   Use videotape or role-play simulation
   Discuss observations of consultation process

Address logistical and practical issues
   Access to services
   Availability of services
   Record keeping
   Relationship of consultation to other services

Answer questions and summarize key points

Bergan and Kratochwill (1990), Gutkin and Curtis (1990), and Zins and Ponti (1990) include explanations of most of these aspects of consultation. Other psychological or educational services available from the consultant are usually also described during this presentation. This type of presentation can also be used with parents and other constituencies.

To demonstrate support for and understanding of the program and to address procedural problems, administrators should attend the initial presentation on consultation. Discussion of the confidentiality issue with them in attendance is particularly essential (Zins et al., 1988).

Following the in-service training program, it continues to be necessary to address many related issues during individual consultation sessions and to encourage consultee involvement. Consultees need to be supported for engaging in consultation, and their efforts to change should be recognized in a nonevaluative manner. A prime area for possible misunderstanding is the differing expectations for consultation that consultants and consultees frequently have; for example, consultees may expect to directly receive specific solutions for their problems, while consultants seek to develop solutions jointly (Piersel & Gutkin, 1983). Further, as Martens, Lewandowski, and Houk (1989) argue, the process is simply too complex to be explained or demonstrated in detail in a brief presentation. In addition, an infinite number of issues can arise that need to be dealt with individually. Thus, continued monitoring of the consultation process and of both participants' performance is essential to successful implementation and program integrity.

We have also learned that it is beneficial to prepare consultees to participate in consultation (Kratochwill, Sheridan, Carrington-Rotto, & Salmon, in press; Ponti & Zins, 1990). Sandoval et al. (1977) suggested that such training will result in more effective interactions and greater satisfaction with consultation outcomes. Kratochwill et al. (in press), for example, instructed consultees in the use of behavioral strategies such as specific observational assessment skills and target behavior identification techniques. Ponti and Zins (1990) assisted consultees in the development of consultation process skills such as joint problem solving and team strategies. Both groups of investigators reported that positive outcomes resulted from their efforts, but a combination of the two approaches may be most productive (Zins, in press).

Two additional steps also need to be taken. First, resources required to implement the consultation program have to be identified. For instance, are new ones needed, or can existing ones be reallocated to the program? Second, consultation-related implementation activities must be carefully planned and scheduled to maximize the probability of success.

In the case that we have been following, Zins (1992) conducted an inservice program for teachers in each school, following an outline similar to that presented above. In addition, he made a presentation regarding his role in general and consultation in particular at the orientation for new teachers each year. These sessions were followed by individual meetings with each new teacher.

Program Implementation, Management, and Cycling Feedback

The assessment process discussed earlier should have identified any needed human, informational, technological, physical, and financial resources necessary to implement the consultation program successfully. Informing administrators and caretakers about the consultation process should also have helped to lay the foundation for implementation. When the consultation program is actually implemented, it can be done on a case-by-case basis (the traditional approach) or on a systemic level, as with prereferral intervention and intervention assistance programs (see Zins et al., 1988). Both approaches are discussed later in this section.

Integrating Consultation into Organizational Routines. Crucial to having consultation adopted is moving the primary focus from direct to indirect services. Significant resistance to this effort is common, as there is a widespread belief among helping professionals that problems and pathologies are best treated directly. Many of these people were trained according to psychodynamic models that emphasize internal disorders and do not pay adequate attention to environmental variables. Furthermore, in many mental health, educational, and human service agencies, there is a strong press for direct services and minimal attention to preventive approaches. Consultation is not viewed favorably, not only because of theoretical orientation but also because it is often difficult to collect payments for indirect services. Consumers and decision makers must understand what consultants *can* do in providing services before they decide what they *will* do (Curtis & Zins, 1986). However, consumer expectations should not be confused with desires (Zins & Curtis, 1981). Although consumers might not expect consultation to be provided, there is considerable evidence suggesting that teachers, parents, and administrators desire such assistance (Manley & Manley, 1978).

Formal policies and practices that promote consultation are effective means of incorporating it into organizational routines. In some schools, for instance, teachers might be required to implement three interventions developed through consultation before they can refer a child for a psychoeducational assessment. The job description of a child-care worker in a residential setting might specify that the worker will engage in consultation to develop appropriate behavioral goals for residents. In both cases, there is a clear administrative mandate as well as sanction to participate in consultation. However, consideration must be given to ensuring that participation in consultation remains voluntary, although organization members are encouraged to continue to use the service.

Most professionals in the human service field do not engage solely in consultation but also provide psychological assessments, counseling, or other services. However, to promote the consultation model, we have found it helpful to always consult on every case, even if the primary service being provided is not consultation (Zins et al., 1988). With an adolescent counseling case, for example, consulting with parents, teachers, juvenile court workers, and so forth may facilitate behavioral change and enhance the effectiveness of the counseling. When psychoeducational assessments are conducted, parents and teachers should always be consulted as part of the process.

As mentioned earlier, it is most effective and parsimonious to integrate consultation into organizational routines systemically. A systemic approach recognizes the value of introducing and bringing about change throughout the organization rather than on a piecemeal basis. In schools, for example, this process has been accomplished through programs such as prereferral intervention and intervention assistance—systemwide consultation programs designed to provide early intervention assistance to prevent problems or to keep them from becoming more serious.

With this approach, consultation is provided by individual consultants and/or a problem-solving team, usually consisting of regular educators and special services staff. Before students can be referred for a multidisciplinary assessment and special education consideration, consultation must occur as part of the intervention assistance process. All teachers, administrators, and parents have access to the service, so that early intervention can be provided. The program is supported by school philosophies, policies, and procedures, is adopted systemically, and therefore becomes part of the school's organizational routines (Zins et al., 1988).

Monitoring Program Implementation. As noted several times, the use of consultation services should be systematically monitored through objective data-collection methods, as well as through less formal means, to determine whether goals are being met and to identify areas in need of modification. These data and observations should be shared with those responsible for the consultation program. For instance, if it is known that a certain group is not engaging in consultation, changes can be made to increase their participation. Misconceptions about consultation might be found, the consultant might not be accessible to some consumers, or there may be a need to increase program promotion efforts.

In addition to learning about how effectively the consultation program is meeting its intended goals, consultants should direct specific attention to any unplanned outcomes that may result. Some of these may be positive, and it may be possible to make changes to ensure that they continue. If they are negative, corrective action should be taken as necessary.

Marketing Strategies to Expand Consumer Groups. Our focus here is on efforts to expand use of consultation that can be undertaken once the program has been implemented. The availability of the service should be broadcast to potential consumer groups on a continuing basis, and this process should be undertaken in concert with the monitoring efforts described above. Initially, it may be decided to focus on a specific target group until the consultation program is well established. Gradually, this group can be expanded through additional promotional efforts. We have found, too, that consumers are ideal promoters of the program: those who believe that consultation was beneficial let others know about their success, thereby generating more interest.

The initial in-service presentation is usually a first step in introducing consultation to consumers, but to maximize the number of people using consultation and to ensure that it is used appropriately, significant energy must be directed to additional marketing techniques. Written and verbal announcements originating from the consultant as well as from relevant administrators can be given to organization members and other consumers, such as parents. These might include announcements at staff meetings or in newsletters, presentations at meetings of parent organizations or at churches, and follow-up sessions to the initial in-service presentation.

Consultation can also be promoted during interactions with individual staff. When providing other services, consultants can mention that consultative assistance is available, be sure to use a collaborative interaction style, and show genuine concern and regard for the problems experienced by consultees. In addition, consultees can be reinforced whenever they engage in the consultation process. Initial consultation sessions in particular should be made as positive and successful as possible, with misunderstandings addressed quickly.

Overcoming Barriers and Resistance. A variety of barriers to consultation can be identified; several representative ones are described briefly here. A more detailed discussion of this topic is contained in Chapter Eight.

Significant resistance often arises when organization members are given little opportunity to participate in the change process; if they feel that consultation is being imposed on them, they will feel little ownership of it (Fullan et al., 1980; Zins et al., 1988). As Sarason (1982, p. 79) notes, "to the extent that the effort at change identifies and meaningfully involves all those who directly or indirectly will be affected by the change, to that extent the effort stands a chance to be successful." The issues outlined in this chapter emphasize the importance of involving organization members as consultation is implemented.

Even when facing problems, most people resist or have a low tolerance for change and strive to maintain the status quo (Margolis, Fish, & Wepner, 1990). Change is often associated with stress and discomfort, which are not reinforcing (Piersel & Gutkin, 1983). In fact, resistance to change is natural. Anticipating and recognizing it are first steps in overcoming it and can be starting places for improving commitment and understanding. Margolis et al. (1990) offer a number of suggestions for building trust that can reduce resistance.

Confusion or miscommunication about the consultation program may also result in difficulties with program implementation. Therefore, consultants need to assess whether their intended messages have been communicated effectively and understood accurately (Margolis et al., 1990). A single in-service program is usually insufficient for accomplishing this goal, and we therefore recommend that multiple efforts be made to ensure that organization members understand the consultation process.

In the Zins (1992) case, there was initially significant resistance in the organization, primarily because of a lack of understanding of what constitutes consultation. A mental health professional who had previously provided services to the schools had used the term *consultation* to refer to the "sensitivity training groups" that she conducted, with the result that teachers and administrators had very negative reactions when Zins proposed that consultation services be made available. However, because he was aware of this misunderstanding, he was able to address this source of resistance directly.

Program Evaluation

Evaluation too often is added as an afterthought or to meet some type of external requirements well after a consultation program has been in operation. Program evaluation plans should be developed when the consultation program is first conceptualized. They should document progress toward the intended consultation goals and the overall impact of the program. Specific program evaluation methods are discussed in Chapter Twelve; here we focus on uses that can be made of the information gathered.

A primary application of program evaluation data is in improving the delivery of consultation services. They can also be used to market the program to decision makers and consumers, who must know that the program is effective and is achieving its intended goals if they are to fully support it (Zins et al., 1988).

Program evaluation information may also be helpful in expanding the consultation program. Zins (1992) was able to demonstrate that providing program effectiveness data to the school board and administration in his district led to an increase in the psychological services available. The data illustrated that there were great demands for the service and that it was having a positive impact in the schools.

There is debate over whether internal or external consultants are most accountable to an organization. Alpert and Associates (1982) seem to believe that internal consultants by definition are more accountable, since they must answer to the administration on a daily basis and are under its direct supervision. On the other hand, external consultants can be easily removed or their contracts not renewed if they do not perform satisfactorily. In any case, a decision needs to be made on the degree to which the consultant should be given responsibility for the program evaluation efforts, not whether this person should be involved.

Research Issues

As should be clear by now, research on the implementation of consultation programs in human service organizations is sparse. Much of the literature that addresses the implementation process is based on case study reports rather than carefully controlled and executed experimental designs. There is a pressing need for empirical studies of consultation program implementation.

Among the issues needing study is identification of specific aspects of organizations that make one more receptive to consultation than another and that lead to successful outcomes. Issues such as organizational climate and health, staff morale and training, and administrator leadership styles, for instance, may exert influence on the process, and it is therefore important to examine these factors to understand the effects that altering them may have. In a current study, we are looking at the relationship among consultants' perceptions of organizational climate, consumer satisfaction with consultation, and outcomes for students. Clarification is also needed regarding what steps should be followed to most efficiently implement consultation services; Lippitt and Lippitt (1986) and Schaeffer (1987) offer differing approaches. It is also important to determine whether approaches to program implementation described in the literature actually work in the field. A systemic approach is often suggested, but is it always the best method? Are team approaches such as prereferral intervention the most efficient means to make a program part of organizational routines?

The preparation of professionals to deliver and receive consultation services also requires additional attention. There have been few field-based studies demonstrating effective methods of developing consultation skills or improving participant performance in the process (see Zins, in press, for discussion of consultee training). And the few reports available do not indicate whether the training programs result in actual long-term change in participants' daily job functioning or whether they spend more time engaging in consultation.

As a final note, we believe that if more practitioners engaged in program evaluation efforts, our knowledge concerning the outcomes of consultation would be expanded significantly, as would our understanding of the components of effective practice. Thus, it is likely that more children would benefit from the vast array of potentially helpful intervention procedures that we have available to address the many challenging issues facing us today.

References

Alpert, J. L., & Associates. (1982). *Psychological consultation in educational settings: A casebook for working with administrators, teachers, students, and community.* San Francisco: Jossey-Bass.

Bergan, J. R., & Kratochwill, T. R. (1990). *Behavioral consultation and therapy.* New York: Plenum Press.

Chesler, M., Bryant, B., & Crowfoot, J. (1976). Consultation in schools: Inevitable conflict, partisanship, and advocacy. *Professional Psychology, 7,* 637–645.

Conoley, J. C., & Conoley, C. W. (1982). *School consultation: A guide to practice and training.* Elmsford, NY: Pergamon Press.

Curtis, M. J., & Zins, J. E. (1986). The organization and structuring of psychological services within educational settings. In S. Elliott & J. Witt (Eds.), *The delivery of psychological services in schools* (pp. 109–138). Hillsdale, NJ: Erlbaum.

Fullan, M., Miles, M. B., & Taylor, G. (1980). Organization development in schools: The state of the art. *Review of Educational Research, 50,* 121–183.

Harrison, M. I. (1987). *Diagnosing organizations.* Newbury Park, CA: Sage.

Hord, S. M., Rutherford, W. L., Huling-Austin, L., & Hall, G. (1987). *Taking charge of change.* Alexandria, VA: Association for Supervision and Curriculum Development.

Illback, R. J., & Zins, J. E. (1984). Organizational interventions in educational settings. In C. A. Maher, R. J. Illback, & J. E. Zins (Eds.), *Organizational psychology in the schools* (pp. 21–52). Springfield, IL: Thomas.

Kratochwill, T. R., Sheridan, S., Carrington-Rotto, S., & Salmon, D. (in press). Preparation of school psychologists in behavioral consultation service delivery. In T. R. Kratochwill, S. N. Elliott, & M. B. Gettinger (Eds.), *Advances in school psychology* (Vol. 8). Hillsdale, NJ: Erlbaum.

Lippitt, G. L., Langseth, P., & Mossop, J. (1985). *Implementing organizational change: A practical guide to managing change efforts.* San Francisco: Jossey-Bass.

Lippitt, G., & Lippitt, R. (1986). *The consulting process in action* (2nd ed.). San Diego, CA: University Associates.

Maher, C. A., & Bennett, R. E. (1984). *Planning and evaluating special education services.* Englewood Cliffs, NJ: Prentice-Hall.

Maher, C. A., & Illback, R. J. (1985). Implementing school psychological service programs: Description and application of the DURABLE approach. *Journal of School Psychology, 23,* 81–89.

Maher, C. A., Illback, R. J., & Zins, J. E. (1984). Applying organizational psychology in the schools: Perspectives and framework. In C. A. Maher, R. J. Illback, & J. E. Zins (Eds.), *Organizational psychology in the schools: A handbook for professionals.* (pp. 5–20). Springfield, IL: Thomas.

Manley, T., & Manley, E. (1978). A comparison of personal values and operative goals of school psychologists and school superintendents. *Journal of School Psychology, 16,* 99–109.

Margolis, H., Fish, M., & Wepner, S. B. (1990). Overcoming resistance to prereferral classroom interventions. *Special Services in the Schools, 6*(1/2), 167–187.

Martens, B. K., Lewandowski, L. J., & Houk, J. L. (1989). The effects of entry information on the consultation process. *School Psychology Review, 18,* 225–234.

Martens, B. K., & Meller, P. J. (1990). The application of behavioral principles to educational settings. In T. B. Gutkin & C. R. Reynolds (Eds.), *The handbook of school psychology* (2nd ed., pp. 612–634). New York: Wiley.

Meyers, J., Parsons, R. D., & Martin, R. (1979). *Mental health consultation in the schools: A comprehensive guide for psychologists, social workers, psychiatrists, counselors, educators, and other human service professionals.* San Francisco: Jossey-Bass.

Piersel, W. C., & Gutkin, T. B. (1983). Resistance to school-based consultation: A behavioral analysis of the problem. *Psychology in the Schools, 30,* 311–320.

Ponti, C. R., & Zins, J. E. (1990, April). *Changes in consultee problem clarification skills and attributions following direct training in problem-solving techniques.* Paper presented at the annual meeting of the National Association of School Psychologists, San Francisco.

Ponti, C. R., Zins, J. E., & Graden, J. L. (1988). Implementing a consultation-based service delivery system to decrease referrals for special education: A case study of organizational considerations. *School Psychology Review, 17,* 89–100.

Reimers, T. M., Wacker, D. P. & Koeppl, G. (1987). Acceptability of behavioral interventions: A review of the literature. *School Psychology Review, 16,* 212–227.

Sandoval, J., Lambert, N. M., & Davis, J. M. (1977). Consultation from the consultee's perspective. *Journal of School Psychology, 15,* 334–342.

Sarason, S. B. (1982). *The culture of the school and the problem of change* (2nd ed.). Needham Heights, MA: Allyn & Bacon.

Schaeffer, M. (1987). *Implementing change in service programs.* Newbury Park, CA: Sage.

Smith, K., & Corse, S. (1986). The process of consultation. In F. V. Mannino, E. J. Trickett, M. F. Shore, M. G. Kidder, & G. Levin (Eds.), *Handbook of mental health consultation* (DHHS Publication No. ADM 86-1446, pp. 247–278). Washington, DC: U.S. Government Printing Office.

Witt, J. C., Elliott, S. N., & Gresham, F. M. (Eds.). (1988). *Handbook of behavior therapy in education.* New York: Plenum Press.

Zins, J. E. (1992). Implementing school-based consultation services: An analysis of five years of practice. In R. K. Conyne & J. O'Neil (Eds.), *Organizational consultation: A casebook* (pp. 50–79). Newbury Park, CA: Sage.

Zins, J. E. (in press). Enhancing consultee problem-solving skills in consultative interactions. *Journal of Counseling and Development.*

Zins, J. E., & Curtis, M. J. (1981). Teacher preferences for differing consultation models. In M. J. Curtis & J. E. Zins (Eds.), *The theory and practice of school consultation* (pp. 184–189). Springfield, IL: Thomas.

Zins, J. E., & Curtis, M. J. (1984). Building consultation into the educational service delivery system. In C. A. Maher, R. J. Illback, & J. E. Zins (Eds.), *Organizational psychology in the schools: A handbook for professionals* (pp. 213–242). Springfield, IL: Thomas.

Zins, J. E., Curtis, M. J., Graden, J. L., & Ponti, C. R. (1988). *Helping students succeed in the regular classroom: A guide for developing intervention assistance programs.* San Francisco: Jossey-Bass.

Zins, J. E., & Ponti, C. R. (1990). Strategies to facilitate the implementation, organization, and operation of system-wide consultation programs. *Journal of Educational and Psychological Consultation, 1,* 205–218.

Part Three

EVALUATION OF PROCESS AND OUTCOME

11

Conducting
Consultation Research

Terry B. Gutkin

Enthusiasm for consultative approaches to educational and clinical services for children appears to be growing with each passing year. Evidence to support this notion is plentiful and exemplified by the publication of this volume and the *Journal of Educational and Psychological Consultation,* a recently initiated scholarly outlet devoted solely to the topic of consultation services. Unfortunately, although interest has been accelerating for years, many perceive that the demands of practice have far outstripped the science on which that practice should be based (Gresham & Kendell, 1987; Reynolds & Clark, 1984). That is, the empirical base of research to support consultation services has not kept pace with the field-based demand for these services.

The gap between research and practice has led some practitioners to turn away from empirical research as a guidepost for professional practice (Bardon, 1987; Morrow-Bradley & Elliott, 1986); they may even see it as irrelevant and unnecessary. In the eyes of this author, however, this is a most unproductive stance. Given the complexity of psychological and educational problems facing contemporary society, it would seem that a growing base of research-generated knowledge is essential if human service personnel are to have any realistic hope of increasing the quality of their practice.

Although it would be very misleading to suggest that practitioners can glean "perfect" and "guaranteed" solutions to their daily professional challenges from the pages of research articles and books (Phillips, 1989, 1990; Stoner & Green, 1992), it would be unprofessional for these same practitioners to work with their clients without the benefit of current research findings to inform their actions. The scientist-practitioner model (Raimy, 1950), reaffirmed at the 1990 National Conference on Scientist-Practitioner Education and Training for the Professional Practice of Psychology (Belar & Perry, 1992), must continue as the foundational bulwark of professional actions for those in the human service delivery fields. Progress in the practice of psychological consultation in educational and clinical settings is inextricably tied to progress in consultation research. The primary purpose of this chapter is to explore research methodologies for consultation services to children, with particular emphasis on approaches that can be used to address important future research questions.

Methodological Critique of Previous Research

Since the mid 1970s, there have been a number of critical reviews of consultation research methodologies (for example, Bergan & Kratochwill, 1990; Gresham & Kendell, 1987; Kratochwill, Sheridan, & VanSomeren, 1988; Medway, 1979, 1982; Meyers, Pitt, Gaughan, & Freidman, 1978; Pryzwansky, 1986; West, 1988; see also Chapter Twelve). A review of these collective works reveals a startling level of agreement among the various authors. The following discussion is a synthesis of issues raised by these reviewers that, in the opinion of this author, remain active problems for consultation researchers.

Operational Specification of Consultation Processes

One of the primary shortcomings of consultation research has been its failure to describe consultation processes in sufficient detail. The result is that one is never completely sure what is meant by the term *consultation*. Although there is general agreement on the broad conceptualization that consultation is an indirect service in which a consultant works with a consultee for the benefit of a third party (client), too little detail typically is provided in research articles for one to discern the specifics of how this broad conceptualization was operationalized in any particular study. Lacking such information, it is extremely difficult to build a systematic body of organized knowledge regarding consultation services because of the limited external validity of most consultation research and problems in replicating consultation interventions.

In an attempt to arrive at a greater level of operational specificity, a number of different consultation models have been delineated in the literature. One of the earliest efforts along these lines was completed by Reschly (1976), who attempted to differentiate among mental health, behavioral, and organizational models of consultation. More recently, West and Idol (1987) described ten different models of consultation in terms of underlying theory, knowledge base, goals, stages or steps, and responsibilities of the consultant and consultee. Although work such as this makes important theoretical contributions to the field, it has not brought us to the level of operational specificity necessary to address the research methodology problems discussed above. Even for behavioral consultation, the most highly operationalized of the consultation models, Kratochwill et al. (1988) report that there remains a considerable range of heterogeneous practice and conceptualization. These authors have gone so far as to call for "a moratorium on the comparative outcome research where unspecified models of consultation are evaluated (e.g., behavioral vs. mental health)" (p. 93).

Future consultation research must describe consultation interactions in greater operational detail. Merely indicating that consultation occurred or that a particular model of consultation was used, is no longer sufficient. As discussed by Kazdin (1986), there is a logical developmental progression of research methodologies for the investigation of social science treatments, such as psychotherapy and consultation. Initially, a treatment package strategy can be employed in which the treatment is examined in toto with little delineation of its specific elements. Once shown to be effective, however, the treatment package strategy should give way to a variety of more refined research methodologies (for example, dismantling, constructive, parametric research strategies) addressing the efficacy of specific treatment elements. We appear to be at a developmental crossroads in the field of consultation research. Meta-analyses and other research literature reviews (Mannino & Shore, 1975; Medway & Updyke, 1985) have shown consultation to be an effective technique. It is now time to move beyond the treatment package strategies employed in previous research efforts toward more advanced approaches that will help us learn which specific elements of the total package are most important (Witt & Elliott, 1983). To make this developmental leap, however, will require a much higher degree of operational specification than has been characteristic of most previous research efforts.

Treatment Integrity of Consultation Processes

Closely related to the need for improved definition and specification of consultation interactions is the need for increased attention to the treatment integrity of consultation processes that occur during research (Gresham, 1989; Kratochwill et al., 1988). Very few research projects have included any systematic checks to determine whether consultants in a study were providing consultation services as they were intended to be provided. Given the inherent complexity and subtleties of consultation, one cannot assume that consultation services are being delivered as intended simply because consultants honestly try to do so and believe that they have succeeded. For the very same reasons that we collect direct observational data to determine whether client behavior has changed as a result of consultation rather than simply relying on the word of well-intentioned consultees and/or clients, it is essential to determine empirically whether consultants serving in consultation research have, in fact, carried out consultation treatments correctly. Without assurances of treatment integrity for the consultation process, it is not possible to determine what intervention process is actually being examined in any given study.

Treatment Integrity of Consultation Interventions

Consonant with the need for increased scrutiny of treatment integrity of consultation processes is the parallel need for increased scrutiny of treatment integrity of consultation interventions (Gresham, 1989; Kratochwill et al., 1988). Whereas the former issue addresses whether consultation models are implemented appropriately by the consultant, the latter issue focuses on whether the interventions arising from consultation interactions are implemented appropriately by the consultee. As with treatment integrity of consultation processes, very few consultation studies have utilized systematic procedures to assess the treatment integrity of consultation interventions. As a result, when outcome data regarding client change are collected, it is not possible to determine whether observed changes (or the lack of changes) are, in fact, the result of treatments agreed on during consultation. For example, following consultation, a teacher might agree to provide contingent social reinforcement to a child for appropriate on-task behavior. Should that intervention fail, however, treatment integrity data are necessary to determine whether the planned intervention was ineffective or was simply never implemented correctly.

Behavioral Versus Attitudinal Data

One of the most consistent and long-standing criticisms of consultation research has been directed at the types of data that are collected. Many have pointed out that there has been an excessive reliance on self-report, questionnaire, and attitudinal data rather than direct observation of behavioral change in consultants, consultees, and clients. Although an argument could be made that there is value in learning about the *subjective* perceptions of consultants, consultees, and clients (Gutkin, 1986), and thus that paper-and-pencil measurements may have an important role to play, it is clear that these types of data are inferior to direct behavioral observation when one wishes to know *objectively* what has happened either during or as a result of consultation. It is clear, for example, that the mere fact that consultees say that they are going to do or have done an intervention does not mean that they will actually do or have done it. Likewise, reports of successful intervention efforts or verbal reports of consultee satisfaction may or may not be congruent with the reality of client behavioral change. In light of overwhelming empirical evidence from the social psychology research literature that attitudinal and behavioral changes are not always consistent (Raven & Rubin, 1983), it is imperative that direct observation become the dominant form of data collection in future consultation research efforts.

Multivariate Versus Univariate Research Designs

It would seem to be self-evident that consultation research requires multivariate rather than univariate methodologies. If, as Reynolds, Gutkin, Elliott, and Witt (1984) recommend, one adopts a reciprocal determinism model (Bandura, 1978) for conceptualizing consultation services for children, then it becomes clear that consultation processes and outcomes are the result of complex interactions among and between the individual characteristics, behavior, and environments of the client, consultee, and consultant. To make matters even more complex, each one of these specific dimensions is multivariate in and of itself. The environment of a classroom teacher serving as a consultee, for instance, would include but not be limited to variables such as the number of students in the class; the characteristics of those students; the curriculum approaches used in class; the nature of the physical space in the classroom; relationships with parents, particularly those of a referred child; relationships with other teachers in the school; the leadership style of the school's principal; the organizational climate of the school; local, state, and federal policies; and local community values and political pressures.

In light of the complexity of consultation services, many previous research efforts seem inappropriately univariate. In general, variables have been studied in isolation from each other with research designs and statistical analyses that are inadequate to address the interactions among multiple independent and dependent variables. Exemplifying this general perception are the recommendations of Kratochwill et al. (1988, p. 93) calling on future research efforts "to be multifaceted, involving multiple target behaviors (e.g., academic and social), different methods of assessment (e.g., self-report, direct observation), and different settings (e.g., school, home community), and different perspectives across these settings (e.g., teacher, parent, child, peers)."

Long-Term Follow-Up

Although research reviews have consistently indicated that consultation services are generally effective (Mannino & Shore, 1975; Medway, 1979; Medway & Updyke, 1985), a closer examination of these reviews reveals that what we know pertains almost exclusively to the short-term impact of consultation. Medway (1979), for example, found only five of the twenty-nine consultation studies he examined to include follow-up data addressing long-term impact, while Medway and Updyke (1985, p. 498) reported that "few studies had follow-up measures." Particularly in light of existing knowledge pertaining to difficulties commonly associated with maintenance and generalization of behavioral change (Cooper, Heron, & Heward, 1987; Kratochwill, Elliott, & Rotto, 1990), it is clear that previous research efforts have paid far too little attention to whether the short-term gains brought about by consultation are maintained by clients or consultees across time, settings, and behaviors. These data are critical to assessing the true efficacy of consultation services and helping us learn how to intervene in ways that promote long-term and far-reaching behavioral change.

Representativeness of Consultation Research

One of the most recently raised issues regarding consultation research has been its representativeness (Bergan & Kratochwill, 1990; Kratochwill et al., 1988). Specifically, since there are almost no data describing how consultation services are carried out in the field under normal circumstances, there is virtually no way of knowing the extent to which the consultation procedures being researched bear any resemblance to actual contemporary consultation practices. Ideally, there would be a close congruence between research and field practices, although one might argue that research procedures ought to be "out in front" of typical practice. Clearly, however, it is difficult to know with any reasonable degree of precision what implications consultation research holds for practice if we have inadequate data describing the nature of contemporary practices in the field.

Promising Methodologies for Future Research

The following methodologies are among those that could make the greatest contributions to consultation research in the immediate future.

Small-N Methodologies

Although there is not unanimous agreement (for example, Medway, 1982), there is a growing consensus (for example, Bergan & Kratochwill, 1990; Gresham & Kendell, 1987; Kratochwill et al., 1988; Meyers et al., 1978; Pryzwansky, 1986; West, 1988) that previous consultation investigations have relied too heavily on traditional large-n, between-groups research designs and have made insufficient use of small-n approaches such as withdrawal-reversal, multiple-baseline, multitreatment, alternating-treatment, simultaneous-treatment, and changing criterion designs (Cooper et al., 1987; Hersen & Barlow, 1976;

Kratochwill, 1978; Tawney & Gast, 1984). Among the problems noted with large-n methodologies have been difficulties in randomly assigning subjects to treatment groups, finding sufficient numbers of homogeneous subjects (consultants, consultees, and clients) to form treatment groups, designing adequate control and placebo conditions, applying group data to clinical decision making for individual clients, and revising treatment plans for individual clients in midstream in response to formative evaluation data.

Of particular importance to consultation researchers, however, is that small-n designs may reasonably be used to respond to all the methodological shortcomings noted in the previous section of this chapter. Specifically, by investigating only small numbers of consultation cases in each individual study (generally ranging from one to three), researchers will find it much easier to define in greater detail the specific consultation processes used during consultation interactions; collect data pertaining to the integrity of the consultation processes that were employed during consultation; collect data pertaining to the integrity of treatment interventions resulting from consultation; gather direct observational data for consultants, consultees, and clients; assess a much broader (multivariate) range of consultant, consultee, and client data; conduct long-term follow-up of cases after the completion of consultation; and determine whether the consultation processes under investigation are representative of the approaches used naturally in the field by practitioners. Basically, by dramatically limiting the number of consultants, consultees, and clients in a study, small-n designs allow researchers to gather a substantially richer array of information about each consultation interaction. Examples of small-n approaches to consultation research include studies conducted by Meyers, Freidman, and Gaughan (1975), Workman, Kindall, and Williams (1980), and Robbins and Gutkin (in press).

The primary methodological complaint against small-n designs has been that they are less robust than large-n approaches in terms of external validity. That is, since the number of subjects involved in each study is so low, it is very difficult to generalize the results of any individual study to other consultants, consultees, and clients. While this may be an accurate criticism when comparing a single small-n study to a single large-n study, it is not a particular problem if one considers the total body of small-n research, which often contains large numbers of replications.

Despite the strengths of small-n approaches for consultation research, they are not without their own unique set of problems. For example, the need for a baseline period may be difficult for consultees to accept, since they want to begin alleviating client problems at the earliest possible opportunity. This can be a particularly thorny issue with multiple-baseline designs, in which a consultee might have to wait weeks before treatments can be applied to problem clients or behaviors (Robbins & Gutkin, in press). Likewise, the withdrawal or reversal of treatment effects, which is often necessary to attain adequate internal validity in many small-n designs, can be quite uncomfortable for many consultees.

Lag Sequential Analysis   *Cross-lag panel*

Although not a new data-analysis technique (Bakeman & Gottman, 1986), the potential value of lag sequential analysis has only recently been recognized in regard to consultation research (Gutkin & Curtis, 1990). At the heart of this approach is an examination of temporally contiguous events to determine whether one particular type of behavior follows another particular type of behavior more or less frequently than would be expected by chance. Given a sufficient quantity of data (for formulas, see Bakeman & Gottman, 1986), researchers should be able to investigate and identify long chains of sequential consultant and consultee behaviors occurring during consultation interactions. An excellent conceptual description of the lag sequential analysis technique is provided by Bus and Kruizenga (1989) in their study of diagnostic problem-solving behaviors among expert practitioners in the field of learning disabilities.

The primary advantage of lag sequential analysis is that it permits researchers to develop an empirical "moving picture" of consultation interactions rather than the "still photographs" produced by more traditional research methodologies (Benes, Gutkin, & Kramer, 1990). While one might use ANOVA (analysis of variance) or regression methodologies, for example, to examine whether the total number of specification statements made by a consultant is related to the total number of inference statements made by a consultee during the course of a problem-identification interview, these research approaches would not shed light on the sequential pattern of verbal interactions occurring between consultants and consultees. With lag sequential analysis, however, we can discern meaningful sequences of interactional behavior, such as whether a consultee is most likely to respond to a consultant's use of a specification statement with an inference statement and whether the consultant is most likely to respond to the consultee's inference statement with a positive validation.

To date, although lag sequential analysis has been employed successfully in other areas of research (see, for example, Gottman, Markman, & Notarius, 1977), only a few studies addressing consultation have appeared (Benes et al., 1990; Martens, Deery, & Gherardi, 1990). Even these early efforts, however, demonstrate how lag sequential analysis can be used to address meaningful questions and, in particular, assist in the process of providing further operational specification of consultation processes. The findings of Benes et al.

(1990), for example, indicate that the three-event sequence mentioned above (consultant specification statements leading to consultee inference statements, which in turn lead to consultant positive validation statements) was not supported, although there was a statistically significant probability that consultee specification statements would immediately follow consultant specification, consultant elicitor, consultant positive validation, consultee positive validation, and consultee inference statements. Future researchers should consider using lag sequential analysis in experimental as well as descriptive research designs, so that we can begin to investigate how consultants might manipulate their own behavior to produce specified outcomes in the communication behaviors of their consultees.

Standardizing and Validating Consultation Processes

Suggestions to standardize consultation processes represent another important methodological direction for future consultation researchers. As noted earlier, problems with operational specificity impede progress by severely reducing external validity and our ability to replicate research findings. Bergan and Kratochwill (1990) argue that standardization would help to address these problems, improve our ability to train student consultants effectively (by making consultation a more competency-based procedure), and increase the use of consultation methodologies by field-based practitioners (by clarifying how one goes about serving as a consultant). The calls to increase the standardization of consultation processes are congruent with developments in the field of psychotherapy, where the same general suggestions are being given regarding therapy techniques for many of the very same reasons (Kazdin, 1986; Luborsky & DeRubeis, 1984).

Although significant progress has been made in this regard, particularly for the behavioral consultation model (Kratochwill & Bergan, 1990; Kratochwill et al., 1990), much work remains to be done. Particularly important is research investigating the *validity* of standardized approaches once they are designed and implemented. Obviously, the successful implementation of ineffective consultation processes will be of little service to anyone. Reliability (consistency of treatment) should be viewed as a necessary but not sufficient precursor to validity (effectiveness of treatment). Once consultation procedures have been sufficiently standardized (which, with few exceptions, they have not yet been), it will be essential to modify them as necessary in response to empirical investigation. Thus, while Kratochwill and Bergan (1990) have provided an excellent manual detailing, for example, the five essential elements of problem identification (establishing objectives, selecting measures of client performance, collecting data, displaying data, and assessing discrepancies between current and desired performance), it will be important for future researchers to further advance our knowledge by investigating the validity of these five elements.

Case Studies and Analogue Research Strategies

There is a great need to place more emphasis on studying "live" consultation interactions. A reasonable argument could be made that too much of the consultation literature describes laboratory and analogue approximations of real consultation. Clearly, what is true under simulated, analogue, and laboratory conditions may or may not be true in "live" practice. Currently, we know far too little about the actual delivery of consultation services in the field.

Given this need for gaining greater access to "live" data, consultation researchers should place increasing emphasis on case study methodologies. By detailing the specifics of "live" consultations, case studies can provide a valid picture of the natural ecology of consultation services. As Kratochwill et al. (1988) point out, there is much we need to know. For example: How long do typical consultation sessions last? How many consultation sessions are usually necessary to resolve a presenting problem? What proportion of consultees and clients demonstrate clinically significant improvement following consultation? What is the average financial cost of a consultation case? And even though case studies typically lack adequate experimental control and thus cannot be used to draw scientifically valid inferences, they can serve a number of valuable functions beyond more description, such as "casting doubt on general theories, generating hypotheses about treatment and clinical dysfunction, evaluating rare phenomena, [and] providing opportunities for new applications of existing treatments" (Kazdin, 1986, p. 38). Interested readers are referred to Kratochwill (1985) for a discussion of the effective use of case study research.

Having made the argument for placing increased emphasis on studies of "live" consultation, it is important that we note that analogue studies are a necessary complement that must not be overlooked by researchers (Huebner, 1991). Whereas precise experimental control is often impossible in "live" situations, it is quite achievable in the "laboratory." In fact, many of the dismantling, constructive, and parametric research strategies (see Kazdin, 1986) so essential to increasing the operational specification of consultation processes can be conducted only under highly controlled and artificial circumstances. Although one must always be cautious about overgeneralizing analogue findings to "live" clinical and educational settings, it would be equally incorrect to dismiss categorically the relevance for practitioners of analogue research. One need only recall that all of B. F. Skinner's foundational work was done with animals in a laboratory setting to be reassured that analogue research can have profound and direct implications for "live" practice. Furthermore, the only consultation study to directly examine the degree of congruence between consultant behaviors in and out of the "laboratory" found a "high degree of consistency between . . . performance during simulated and real-life consultation experiences" (Rieke & Curtis, 1981, p. 338). Thus, it is recommended that consultation researchers not lose sight of "tinkering" and "playing in the laboratory" (Gendlin, 1986, p. 133) as a means for generating ideas and hypotheses that ultimately can be tested under more natural conditions in the field.

Important Research Directions and Questions for the Immediate Future

There is a seemingly endless array of unanswered questions needing attention by consultation researchers. Those discussed below are among those that many perceive to be the most pressing issues that could and should be addressed in the next five to ten years.

Theory Base for Organizing Research Efforts

To make significant progress in the immediate future, it will be important for consultation researchers to adopt a theoretical base on which they can build an integrated and coherent body of knowledge. Because "science depends upon theory as much as it depends upon data" (Forsyth & Strong, 1986, p. 117), atheoretical research will be of only limited value to the field.

Traditionally, psychodynamic (Caplan, 1970) and behavioral (Bergan, 1977) conceptualizations have dominated the field. More recently, models such as reciprocal determinism (Bandura, 1978; Reynolds et al., 1984) and ecobehaviorism (Gutkin, 1993) have begun to attract attention. In particular, recent analyses have stressed the importance of expanding the traditional focuses of researchers on the intrapsychic life of the client and consultee and the microenvironmental elements of the classroom to include the natural ecology and systems that encompass clients, consultees, and consultants alike (Gutkin & Conoley, 1990; Martens & Witt, 1988; Witt, 1990b; Witt & Martens, 1988). Taken together, these perspectives suggest that the impact of micro-, meso-, exo- *and* macrosystems will have to be addressed if we are to understand many of the complex phenomena associated with consultation services (Christenson, Abery, & Weinberg, 1986). Although research along these lines will not be accomplished easily, both the systems-ecological and reciprocal determinism models should help researchers to frame significant research questions and identify independent and dependent variables of consequence.

Adopting systems-ecological and reciprocal determinism models of consultation most assuredly has important implications for research methodology. Clearly, designs that are univariate will typically prove to be less than adequate. Researchers must develop tools that will provide a view of consultation services that is both richer and more complete than has been typical in the past. In addition to the suggestions made throughout this chapter, path analysis (Keith, 1988a, 1988b) and qualitative research methods (Maanen, 1986–1988; Pryzwansky & Noblit, 1990) would seem to be among those potentially useful approaches that have thus far been substantially underutilized.

Descriptive Studies of Successful Consultants

We know far too little about how successful consultants actually consult (Kratochwill et al., 1988). In the research literature, "experts" too often turn out to be students who are in the process of training to become consultants (Pryzwansky, 1986). Consistent with Gendlin's suggestion that we create a "bank of clearly successful cases" (1986, p. 131) as a means for improving the psychotherapy research literature, a parallel data base of successful consultation interactions would likewise be extremely useful. Case study and small-n methodologies would seem to be the keys to reaching this modest but important goal.

Examination of Core Consultation Concepts

Although there is a core of accepted assumptions undergirding consultation practice (Gutkin & Curtis, 1990), the research support for most of these is less than sufficient. For example, on the basis of his review of the literature, Witt (1990a) recently labeled as a "myth" the assumption that consultant-consultee relationships should be collaborative. His argument rests primarily on research indicating positive outcomes when consultants are directive in the consultation relationship (Erchul, 1987; Erchul & Chewning, 1990) and the lack of convincing empirical evidence that collaborative methodologies are superior. Although there are, in fact, both empirical and theoretical arguments that could be mounted in defense of the collaborative position (Babcock & Pryzwansky, 1983; Erchul, 1992; Sheridan, 1992; Tyler, Pargament & Gatz, 1983), Witt (1990a) is essentially correct that this "most hallowed of consultative dictums" (p. 367) is in need of greater empirical investigation.

Similar arguments could be made regarding the foundational assumptions of Caplan's work (1970) in the area of mental health consultation. After reviewing the literature, Gresham and Kendell (1987, p. 311) concluded, "There is no empirical support for the hypothesis that *theme interference* seriously impedes consultees' professional objectivity nor is there empirical support for the techniques suggested . . . to reduce theme interference." Beyond this, in one of the few empirical investigations of mental health consultation, Gutkin (1981) reports that most consultee-centered case consultations appear to revolve around issues pertaining to consultee lack of knowledge, skill, and self-confidence rather than objectivity. This finding is completely contrary to Caplan's assumption that "in a well-organized institution or agency in which there is an effective personnel system, good administrative control, and a well-developed supervisory network, most cases that present themselves for consultee-centered case consultation fall into the [lack of objectivity] category" (1970, p. 131). Although Caplan has recently modified his position on this issue somewhat, arguing that lack of objectivity would be a major problem only "if you were dealing with a competent group of consultees" (Erchul, 1991, p. 18), the absence of any substantive research data to support his fundamental premises remains a serious problem.

In the interest of space, additional examples of inadequate empirical support for foundational assumptions in consultation theory will not be given (although many could have been). The point is simply that if we are to build sophisticated consultation methodologies, we must first be sure that our most basic operating assumptions are accurate. It is essential that we articulate this list of assumptions and determine which of them do not have adequate empirical support. Studies addressing these points must be among the highest of our research priorities.

Microanalysis of Communication Behavior

Few things would appear to be more central to consultation than the topic of interpersonal communication. As Gutkin and Curtis (1982) wrote, "At its most basic level, consultation is an interpersonal exchange. As such, the consultant's success is going to hinge largely on his or her communication and relationship skills" (p. 822). These authors note that although "there appears to be a broad consensus concerning the effectiveness of various specific communication techniques . . . there has been little empirical work in this area" (p. 822). With some recent noteworthy exceptions (for example, Benes, Gutkin, & Kramer, 1990, 1991; Erchul, 1987; Erchul & Chewning, 1990; Henning-Stout & Conoley, 1987; Martens, Lewandowski, & Houk, 1989a), this statement is as true today as it was a decade ago. Despite the excellent work of Bergan and his colleagues in the late 1970s and early 1980s (Bergan & Neumann, 1980; Bergan & Tombari, 1976), we have not yet progressed nearly far enough. Microanalyses of the functional patterns of consultant and consultee communication behaviors (both verbal and nonverbal) are needed. As noted earlier in this chapter, techniques such as lag sequential analysis should be of great assistance in this regard.

Entry Processes and Resistance

Although human service personnel such as school psychologists (Fisher, Jenkins, & Crumbley, 1986; Meacham & Peckham, 1978), speech therapists (Secord, 1990), and special educators (West, 1988) generally appear to agree that they would like to spend more time consulting, many are frustrated by their inability to accomplish this goal (Gutkin & Conoley, 1990). Despite a broad range of useful theoretical analyses (Canter, 1982; Hughes, 1983; Hughes & Falk, 1981; Kratochwill & VanSomeren, 1985; Piersel & Gutkin, 1983; Pipes, 1981; Witt, 1986; Zins & Ponti, 1990), there are almost no data-based investigations of either consultation entry processes or consultee resistance to consultation services (for exceptions, see Gutkin & Hickman, 1990; Mann, 1972; Martens, Lewandowski, & Houk, 1989b). This is, unfortunately, yet another glaring hole in the consultation research literature, for there would appear to be little value in developing effective methods of consultation if we are unable to figure out how to get human service personnel to employ these approaches. Adopting a systems-ecological mind-set will undoubtedly be vital to furthering our understanding of these issues.

Group Consultation

With the passage of Public Law 94–142 (the Education of Handicapped Children Act) and the growing popularity of prereferral intervention procedures (Graden, Casey, & Bonstrom, 1985; Gutkin, Henning-Stout, & Piersel, 1988; Ponti, Zins, & Graden, 1988), it would appear that more and more consultations are occurring in group settings. In all likelihood, this trend will continue and perhaps accelerate for at least the next decade. In light of this fact, it is distressing to note the paucity of empirical research investigating group consultation methodologies (for an exception, see Wilcox, 1980). Obviously, the dynamics of group and individual consultations will vary, probably quite dramatically in many instances. Generalizing research knowledge gained from interactions involving single consultees to consultations conducted in group settings seems risky, at best. If we are to avoid "flying by the seat of our pants," it will be necessary to develop significant research efforts in this area. Empirical research and theory gleaned from social psychology (Brehm, 1976; Medway & Cafferty, 1990; Tingstrom, Little, & Stewart, 1990), organizational development (Schmuck, 1990), and group therapy (Corey, 1990; Napier & Gershenfeld, 1989; Yalom, 1985) may provide particularly useful starting points.

Conclusion

Consultation service for children is an area of great importance. It is essential that we operationalize the scientist-practitioner model and move beyond reliance on personal experience and clinical intuition. Practice must be informed by science (Bardon, 1987; Phillips, 1990; Stoner & Green, 1992). Although research efforts have a long way to go, as has been documented throughout this chapter, they nonetheless already have much to offer the practitioner.

The field has arrived at a developmental crossroads. Previous research programs have succeeded in identifying the broad defining elements of consultation services and demonstrating the global effectiveness of this approach. In the future, we must shift to qualitatively more refined and sophisticated levels of research. It is no longer sufficient, for example, to proclaim the importance of collaboration unless we can define with more precision what we mean by this term and then demonstrate empirically that it is, in fact, an important facilitative element in the consultation process. Clearly, it is time to expand the research agenda beyond the question of whether consultation is effective. We must develop and utilize research strategies that will move us closer to answering questions such as what forms of consultation are most effective with which types of consultees having what kinds of clients with which sort of problems under what sets of circumstances (Conoley & Conoley, 1981; Kazdin, 1986; Paul, 1967).

Although the road in front of us is long, the possibilities are exciting. I hope that this chapter will help some readers to move research methodologies and focuses in our field in constructive and progressive directions.

References

Babcock, N. L., & Pryzwansky, W. B. (1983). Models of consultation: Preferences of educational professionals at five stages of service. *Journal of School Psychology, 21,* 359–366.

Bakeman, R., & Gottman, J. M. (1986). *Observing interaction: An introduction to sequential analysis.* New York: Cambridge University Press.

Bandura, A. (1978). The self-system in reciprocal determinism. *American Psychologist, 33,* 344–358.

Bardon, J. I. (1987). The translation of research into practice in school psychology. *School Psychology Review, 16,* 317–328.

Belar, C. D., & Perry, N. W. (1992). National conference on scientist-practitioner education and training for the professional practice of psychology. *American Psychologist, 47,* 71–75.

Benes, K. M., Gutkin, T. B., & Kramer, J. J. (1990, August). *A functional analysis of communication behaviors in a consultation environment.* Paper presented at the annual meeting of the American Psychological Association, Boston.

Benes, K. M., Gutkin, T. B., & Kramer, J. J. (1991). Micro-analysis of consultant and consultee verbal and nonverbal behaviors. *Journal of Educational and Psychological Consultation, 2,* 133–149.

Bergan, J. R. (1977). *Behavioral consultation.* Columbus, OH: Merrill.

Bergan, J. R., & Kratochwill, T. R. (1990). *Behavioral consultation and therapy.* New York: Plenum Press.

Bergan, J. R., & Neumann, A. J., III. (1980). The identification of resources and constraints influencing plan design in consultation. *Journal of School Psychology, 18,* 317–323.

Bergan, J. R., & Tombari, M. L. (1976). Consultant skill and efficiency and the implementation and outcomes of consultation. *Journal of School Psychology, 14,* 3–14.

Brehm, S. S. (1976). *The application of social psychology to clinical practice.* New York: Wiley.

Bus, A. G., & Kruizenga, T. H. (1989). Diagnostic problem-solving behavior of expert practitioners in the field of learning disabilities. *Journal of School Psychology, 27,* 277–287.

Canter, L. A. (1982). Developing a consultative contract. In J. L. Alpert & Associates, *Psychological consultation in educational settings: A casebook for working with administrators, teachers, students, and community.* (pp. 8–32). San Francisco: Jossey-Bass.

Caplan, G. (1970). *The theory and practice of mental health consultation.* New York: Basic Books.

Christenson, S., Abery, B., & Weinberg, R. A. (1986). An alternative model for the delivery of psychological services in the school community. In S. N. Elliott & J. C. Witt (Eds.), *The delivery of psychological services in schools: Concepts, processes, and issues* (pp. 349–391). Hillsdale, NJ: Erlbaum.

Conoley, J. C., & Conoley, C. W. (1981). Toward prescriptive consultation. In J. C. Conoley (Ed.), *Consultation in schools: Theory, research, procedures* (pp. 265–293). San Diego, CA: Academic Press.

Cooper, J. O., Heron, T. E., & Heward, W. L. (1987). *Applied behavior analysis.* Columbus, OH: Merrill.

Corey, G. (1990). *Theory and practice of group counseling* (3rd ed.). Pacific Grove, CA: Brooks/Cole.

Erchul, W. P. (1987). A relational communication analysis of control in school consultation. *Professional School Psychology, 2,* 113–124.

Erchul, W. P. (1991, March). An interview with Gerald Caplan. *Communique,* p. 18.

Erchul, W. P. (1992). On dominance, cooperation, teamwork, and collaboration in school-based consultation. *Journal of Educational and Psychological Consultation, 3,* 363–366.

Erchul, W. P., & Chewning, T. G. (1990). Behavioral consultation from a request-centered relational communication perspective. *School Psychology Quarterly, 5,* 1–20.

Fisher, G. L., Jenkins, S. J., & Crumbley, J. D. (1986). A replication of a survey of school psychologists: Congruence between training, practice, preferred role, and competence. *Psychology in the Schools, 23,* 271–279.

Forsyth, D. R., & Strong, S. R. (1986). The scientific study of counseling and psychotherapy: A unificationist view. *American Psychologist, 41,* 113–119.

Gendlin, E. T. (1986). What comes after traditional psychotherapy research? *American Psychologist, 41,* 131–136.

Gottman, J. M., Markman, H., & Notarius, C. (1977). The typology of marital conflict: A sequential analysis of verbal and nonverbal behavior. *Journal of Marriage and the Family, 39,* 461–477.

Graden, J. L., Casey, A., & Bonstrom, O. (1985). Implementing a prereferral intervention system: Part II. The data. *Exceptional Children, 51,* 377–384.

Gresham, F. M. (1989). Assessment of treatment integrity in school consultation and prereferral intervention. *School Psychology Review, 18,* 37–50.

Gresham, F. M., & Kendell, G. K. (1987). School consultation research: Methodological critique and future research directions. *School Psychology Review, 16,* 306–316.

Gutkin, T. B. (1981). Relative frequency of consultee lack of knowledge, skill, confidence, and objectivity in school settings. *Journal of School Psychology, 19,* 57–61.

Gutkin, T. B. (1986). Consultees' perceptions of variables relating to the outcomes of school-based consultation interactions. *School Psychology Review, 15,* 375–382.

Gutkin, T. B. (1993). Moving from behavioral to ecobehavioral consultation: What's in a name? *Journal of Educational and Psychological Consultation, 4,* 95–99.

Gutkin, T. B., & Conoley, J. C. (1990). Reconceptualizing school psychology from a service delivery perspective: Implications for practice, training, and research. *Journal of School Psychology, 28,* 203–223.

Gutkin, T. B. & Curtis, M. J. (1982). School-based consultation: Theory and techniques. In C. R. Reynolds & T. B. Gutkin (Eds.), *The handbook of school psychology* (pp. 796–828). New York: Wiley.

Gutkin, T. B., & Curtis, M. J. (1990). School-based consultation: Theory, techniques, and research. In T. B. Gutkin & C. R. Reynolds (Eds.), *The handbook of school psychology* (2nd ed., pp. 577–611). New York: Wiley.

Gutkin, T. B., Henning-Stout, M., & Piersel, W. C. (1988). Impact of a district-wide behavioral consultation prereferral intervention service on patterns of school psychological service delivery. *Professional School Psychology, 3,* 301–308.

Gutkin, T. B., & Hickman, J. A. (1990). Relationship of consultant, consultee, and organizational characteristics to consultee resistance to school-based consultation: An empirical analysis. *Journal of Educational and Psychological Consultation, 1,* 111–122.

Henning-Stout, M., & Conoley, J. C. (1987). Consultation and counseling as procedurally divergent: Analysis of verbal behavior. *Professional Psychology: Research and Practice, 18,* 124–127.

Hersen, M., & Barlow, D. H. (1976). *Single case experimental designs: Strategies for studying behavior change.* Elmsford, NY: Pergamon Press.

Huebner, E. S. (1991). Bias in special education decisions: The contribution of analogue research. *School Psychology Quarterly, 6,* 50–65.

Hughes, J. N. (1983). The application of cognitive dissonance theory to consultation. *Journal of School Psychology, 21,* 349–357.

Hughes, J. N., & Falk, R. S. (1981). Resistance, reactance, and consultation. *Journal of School Psychology, 19,* 134–142.

Kazdin, A. E. (1986). The evaluation of psychotherapy: Research design and methodology. In S. L. Garfield & A. E. Bergin (Eds.), *Handbook of psychotherapy and behavior change* (3rd ed., pp. 23–68). New York: Wiley.

Keith, T. Z. (1988a). Path analysis: An introduction for school psychologists. *School Psychology Review, 17,* 343–362.

Keith, T. Z. (1988b). Using path analysis to test the importance of manipulable influences on school learning. *School Psychology Review, 17,* 637–643.

Kratochwill, T. R. (Ed.). (1978). *Single subject research: Strategies for evaluating change.* San Diego, CA: Academic Press.

Kratochwill, T. R. (1985). Case study research in school psychology. *School Psychology Review, 14,* 204–215.

Kratochwill, T. R., & Bergan, J. R. (1990). *Behavioral consultation in applied settings: An individual guide.* New York: Plenum Press.

Kratochwill, T. R., Elliott, S. N., & Rotto, P. C. (1990). Best practices in behavioral consultation. In A. T. Thomas & J. Grimes (Eds.), *Best practices in school psychology* (2nd ed., pp. 147–169). Washington, DC: National Association of School Psychologists.

Kratochwill, T. R., Sheridan, S. M., & VanSomeren, K. R. (1988). Research in behavioral consultation: Current status and future directions. In J. F. West (Ed.), *School consultation: Interdisciplinary perspectives on theory, research, training, and practice* (pp. 77–102). Austin, TX: Association of Educational and Psychological Consultants.

Kratochwill, T. R., & VanSomeren, K. R. (1985). Barriers to treatment success in behavioral consultation: Current limitations and future directions. *Journal of School Psychology, 23,* 225–239.

Luborsky, L., & DeRubeis, R. J. (1984). The use of psychotherapy treatment manuals: A small revolution in psychotherapy research style. *Clinical Psychology Review, 4,* 5–14.

Maanen, J. V. (Ed.). (1986–1988). *Qualitative research methods series* (Vols. 1–12). Newbury Park, CA: Sage.

Mann, P. A. (1972). Accessibility and organizational power in the entry phase of mental health consultation. *Journal of Consulting and Clinical Psychology, 38,* 215–218.

Mannino, F. V., & Shore, M. F. (1975). Effecting change through consultation. In F. V. Mannino, B. W. MacLennan, & M. F. Shore (Eds.), *The practice of mental health consultation* (pp. 25–46). New York: Wiley.

Martens, B. K., Deery, K., & Gherardi, J. (1990, August). *The effects of summarization statements on consultee verbal behavior.* Paper presented at the annual meeting of the National Association of School Psychologists, San Francisco.

Martens, B. K., Lewandowski, L. J., & Houk, J. L. (1989a). Correlational analysis of verbal interactions during the consultative interview and consultees' subsequent perceptions. *Professional Psychology: Research and Practice, 20,* 334–339.

Martens, B. K., Lewandowski, L. J., & Houk, J. L. (1989b). The effects of entry information on the consultation process. *School Psychology Review, 18,* 225–234.

Martens, B. K., & Witt, J. C. (1988). Expanding the scope of behavioral consultation: A systems approach to classroom behavior change. *Professional School Psychology, 3,* 271–281.

Meacham, M. L., & Peckham, P. D. (1978). School psychologists at three-quarters century: Congruence between training, practice, preferred role and competence. *Journal of School Psychology, 16,* 195–206.

Medway, F. J. (1979). How effective is school consultation? A review of recent research. *Journal of School Psychology, 17,* 275–282.

Medway, F. J. (1982). School consultation research: Past trends and future directions. *Professional Psychology, 13,* 422–430.

Medway, F. J., & Cafferty, T. P. (1990). Contributions of social psychology to school psychology. In T. B. Gutkin & C. R. Reynolds (Eds.), *The handbook of school psychology* (2nd ed., pp. 175–197). New York: Wiley.

Medway, F. J., & Updyke, J. F. (1985). Meta-analysis of consultation outcome studies. *American Journal of Community Psychology, 13,* 489–505.

Meyers, J., Freidman, M. P., & Gaughan, E. J. (1975). The effects of consultee-centered consultation on teacher behavior. *Psychology in the Schools, 12,* 288–295.

Meyers, J., Pitt, N. W., Gaughan, E. J., & Freidman, M. P. (1978). A research model for consultation with teachers. *Journal of School Psychology, 16,* 137–145.

Morrow-Bradley, C., & Elliott, R. (1986). Utilization of psychotherapy outcome research by practicing psychotherapists. *American Psychologist, 41,* 188–197.

Napier, R. W., & Gershenfeld, M. K. (1989). *Groups: Theory and experience* (4th ed.). Boston: Houghton Mifflin.

Paul, G. L. (1967). Strategy of outcome research in psychotherapy. *Journal of Consulting Psychology, 31,* 109–118.

Phillips, B. N. (1989). Role of the practitioner in applying science to practice. *Professional Psychology: Research and Practice, 20,* 3–8.

Phillips, B. N. (1990). Reading, evaluating, and applying research in school psychology. In T. B. Gutkin & C. R. Reynolds (Eds.), *The handbook of school psychology* (2nd ed., pp. 53–73). New York: Wiley.

Piersel, W. C., & Gutkin, T. B. (1983). Resistance to school-based consultation: A behavioral analysis of the problem. *Psychology in the Schools, 20,* 311–320.

Pipes, R. B. (1981). Consulting in organizations: The entry problem. In J. C. Conoley (Ed.), *Consultation in schools: Theory, research, procedures* (pp. 11–33). San Diego, CA: Academic Press.

Ponti, C. R., Zins, J. E., & Graden, J. L. (1988). Implementing a consultation-based service delivery system to decrease referrals for special education: A case study of organizational considerations. *School Psychology Review, 17,* 89–100.

Pryzwansky, W. B. (1986). Indirect service delivery: Considerations for future research in consultation. *School Psychology Review, 15,* 479–488.

Pryzwansky, W. B., & Noblit, G. W. (1990). Understanding and improving consultation practice: The qualitative case study approach. *Journal of Educational and Psychological Consultation, 1,* 293–307.

Raimy, V. (Ed.). (1950). *Training in clinical psychology.* Englewood Cliffs, NJ: Prentice-Hall.

Raven, B. H., & Rubin, J. Z. (1983). *Social psychology* (2nd ed.). New York: Wiley.

Reschly, D. (1976). School psychology consultation: "Frenzied, faddish, or fundamental?" *Journal of School Psychology, 14,* 105–113.

Reynolds, C. R., & Clark, J. H. (1984). Trends in school psychology research: 1974–1980. *Journal of School Psychology, 22,* 43–52.

Reynolds, C. R., Gutkin, T. B., Elliott, S. N., & Witt, J. C. (1984). *School psychology: Essentials of theory and practice.* New York: Wiley.

Rieke, S. L., & Curtis, M. J. (1981). The consistency between consultant performance during simulated and real-life consultations. In M. J. Curtis & J. E.

Zins (Eds.), *The theory and practice of school consultation* (pp. 335–340). Springfield, IL: Thomas.

Robbins, J. R., & Gutkin, T. B. (in press). Consultee and client remedial and preventive outcomes following consultation: Some mixed empirical results and directions for future researchers. *Journal of Educational and Psychological Consultation.*

Schmuck, R. A. (1990). Organization development in schools: Contemporary concepts and practices. In T. B. Gutkin & C. R. Reynolds (Eds.), *The handbook of school psychology* (2nd ed., pp. 899–919). New York: Wiley.

Secord, W. A. (Ed.). (1990). *Best practice in school speech-language pathology—collaborative programs in the schools: Concepts, models, and procedures.* San Antonio: TX: Psychological Corporation.

Sheridan, S. M. (1992). What do we mean when we say "collaboration"? *Journal of Educational and Psychological Consultation, 3,* 89–92.

Stoner, G., & Green, S. K. (1992). Reconsidering the scientist-practitioner model for school psychology practice. *School Psychology Review, 21,* 155–166.

Tawney, J. W., & Gast, D. L. (1984). *Single subject research in special education.* Columbus, OH: Merrill.

Tingstrom, D. H., Little, S. G., & Stewart, K. J. (1990). School consultation from a social psychological perspective: A review. *Psychology in the Schools, 27,* 41–50.

Tyler, F. B., Pargament, K. I., & Gatz, M. (1983). The resource collaborator role: A model for interactions involving psychologists. *American Psychologist, 38,* 388–398.

West, J. F. (1988). *School consultation: Interdisciplinary perspectives on theory, research, training, and practice.* Austin, TX: Association of Educational and Psychological Consultants.

West, J. F., & Idol, L. (1987). School consultation (part I): An interdisciplinary perspective on theory, models, and research. *Journal of Learning Disabilities, 20,* 388–408.

Wilcox, M. R. (1980). Variables affecting group mental health consultation for teachers. *Professional Psychology, 11,* 728–732.

Witt, J. C. (1986). Teachers' resistance to the use of school-based interventions. *Journal of School Psychology, 24,* 37–44.

Witt, J. C. (1990a). Collaboration in school-based consultation: Myth in need of data. *Journal of Educational and Psychological Consultation, 1,* 367–370.

Witt, J. C. (1990b). Complaining, precopernican thought and the univariate linear mind: Questions for school-based behavioral consultation research. *School Psychology Review, 19,* 367–377.

Witt, J. C., & Elliott, S. N. (1983). Assessment in behavioral consultation: The initial interview. *School Psychology Review, 12,* 42–49.

Witt, J. C., & Martens, B. K. (1988). Problems with problem-solving consultation: A re-analysis of assumptions, methods, and goals. *School Psychology Review, 17,* 211–226.

Workman, E. A., Kindall, L. M., & Williams, R. L. (1980). The consultative merits of praise-ignore versus praise-reprimand instruction. *Journal of School Psychology, 18,* 373–380.

Yalom, I. D. (1985). *The theory and practice of group psychotherapy* (3rd ed.). New York: Basic Books.

Zins, J. E., & Ponti, C. R. (1990). Strategies to facilitate the implementation, organization, and operation of system-wide consultation programs. *Journal of Educational and Psychological Consultation, 1,* 205–218.

12

Documenting the Effectiveness of Consultation Outcomes

Frank M. Gresham, George H. Noell

Consultation is a potentially effective method through which intervention services are delivered in school and home settings (Bergan & Kratochwill, 1990; Gresham & Kendell, 1987; Kratochwill, Elliott, & Rotto, 1990; Medway & Updike, 1985; Zins & Ponti, 1990). Except for minor variations, most reviews of the consultation literature have agreed on what is known empirically about school consultation.

Alpert and Yammer (1983) report that 30 percent of the studies that they reviewed dealt with the *outcomes* of consultation. Medway (1979, 1982) indicated that behavioral consultation has been shown to be more effective than mental health or organization development consultation models. Dependent or outcome measures in school consultation research typically have included changes in consultee and client behavior (Bergan & Kratochwill, 1990; Medway, 1979, 1982), in consultees' knowledge and attitudes (Gresham & Kendell, 1987), and in consultation utilization (Graden, Casey, & Christensen, 1985; Pryzwansky, 1986).

In spite of the numerous reviews of consultation outcomes, the state-of-the-art research methodology in consultation is elementary. Gresham and Kendell (1987) suggest that most consultation research is descriptive research in which researchers describe training practices, survey attitudes toward consultation, or assess utilization of consultation by practitioners. By comparison, the sophistication of our knowledge base in assessment and intervention far exceeds that of the consultation literature (Lentz, 1988; Shapiro, 1987).

The thesis of this chapter is that consultation research is infrequently used by practitioners. It is suspected that practitioners regard consultation outcome research as irrelevant in their daily practice of consulting with parents and teachers. A survey of clinical practitioners (Morrow-Bradley & Elliott, 1986) concerning the use of psychotherapy research by practicing psychotherapists indicated that research questions addressed in research are not clinically relevant; the variables studied are not representative of typical clinical practice; the forms in which results are reported (for example, mean differences, *F* ratios) do not represent clinically important changes or differences; single-case research is infrequent; and practical or relevant measures of psychological change often are not used. In short, practitioners are relatively unaffected by psychotherapy research and do not find it valuable in their daily practice.

Currently, there are no data for this same phenomenon in consultation. However, the authors strongly suspect that consultation practitioners may hold the same low regard for consultation research. Why would practitioners hold such a low opinion of consultation research? An unlikely explanation is that practitioners fail to keep up with a literature that supposedly has much to offer them in their practice of consultation. A more likely explanation is that the way we market research outcomes is often alien, incomprehensible, and irrelevant, speaking little to the practical significance of a particular research finding. As Barlow (1981) suggests in his criticisms of psychotherapy research, perhaps the literature itself is to blame for the underutilization of clinical research by practitioners.

The purpose of this chapter is to provide a critical analysis of methods for reporting consultation outcomes. An overview of basic research design strategies is presented along with a discussion of dependent variables used in consultation research. Particular attention is focused on single-case experimental and case study designs. Traditional indices of consultation outcomes, such as parametric statistics, effect size estimates, and visual inspection, are discussed. Newer methods for reporting outcomes, such as indices of social validation, reliable change, regression analysis of single-case data, and percentage of nonoverlapping data points, are described. In addition, recent work in a variation of cost-benefit analysis known as functional outcome analysis is discussed. The chapter concludes with recommendations for conducting consultation outcome research and making it more relevant and useful for consultation practitioners.

Overview of Consultation Research Designs

Similar to psychotherapy research, consultation research has employed three types of research design strategies: group experimental designs, single-case experimental designs, and case study designs (see also Chapter Eleven). These designs have taken various forms and levels of complexity. Generally speaking, it is safe to say that sophistication and degree of experimental control in consultation research are far below those of psychotherapy research. Gresham and Kendell (1987) characterize consultation research as univariate, nonexperimental, atheoretical, and unsophisticated.

Group Experimental Designs

It is unusual to find consultation research that exceeds a one-way design strategy in complexity. This, of course, does not allow for an evaluation of potentially important interaction effects that probably exist in applied settings. The typical research strategy in consultation is to expose some consultees to consultation method A and others to consultation method B and assess differences between the methods using a single dependent variable. This type of design arrangement is an oversimplification of what transpires daily in the practice of consultation. The following are examples of key variables that may influence the outcomes of consultation, most of which have not been combined in a single study in the consultation literature (Gresham & Kendell, 1987):

Consultant variables
  Level of training
  Experience
  Theoretical orientation
  Verbal behavior in consultation
  Demographics
  Previous success rate in consultation

Consultee variables
  Level of training
  Experience
  Classroom management style
  Attitudes toward consultation
  Knowledge of classroom interventions
  Referral rates for special education
  Referral rates for consultation
  Demographics

Client variables
  Age and grade
  Gender
  Prior history of school problems
  Severity of prior school problems
  Family background variables
  Demographics

Consultation plan variables
  Acceptability
  Time required
  Type of treatment
  Reported effectiveness
  Integrity of plan
  Goals of consultation
  Strength of treatment

Ecological variables
  Classroom variables
  School variables
  School system variables
  Setting events
  Behavioral interrelationships
  Environmental context of consultation

These variables could be used as either independent or dependent variables in studying consultation. Moreover, many of them could be used as either covariates or blocking variables to study their effects on other variables.

One of the major methodological flaws cited in reviews of consultation research is the paucity of studies using control or comparison groups. Medway (1979) indicates that only 60 percent of consultation studies conducted between 1972 and 1979 used control groups. Alpert and Yammer (1983) reviewed 132 consultation studies and found that only 31 percent (41 studies) used control or comparison groups. The failure to include control or comparison groups in group experimental designs presents numerous threats to the internal validity of these designs and thus compromises any conclusions that might be drawn from these studies (see Cook & Campbell, 1979; Kerlinger, 1986).

No studies could be located in the consultation literature that used the types of comparison or control groups typically found in the psychotherapy literature, such as attention-placebo, wait-list, or best-alternative control groups. Attention-placebo control groups have the advantage of ruling out internal validity threats as well as controlling for reactivity effects (Kendall & Norton-Ford, 1982). A huge disadvantage of attention-placebo control groups in consultation research is the questionable ethics of providing consultees and clients with an *inert* intervention for referral problems.

Wait-list control groups are an alternative to attention-placebo control groups. In a wait-list control condition, subjects are assessed on dependent measures exactly as are the treatment group subjects to control for reactive effects of testing, and their scores on dependent measures are compared to those of the treatment group. Disadvantages of wait-list controls include problems in finding enough subjects comparable to the treatment group for comparison purposes, emergencies that may arise for these subjects that require immediate attention, and the possibility that the treatment that they are waiting for is ineffective.

O'Leary and Borkovec (1978) described another type of comparison group, called the *best alternative intervention* control group. This arrangement involves presenting subjects with the most effective or best-validated alternative treatment and comparing their dependent measure outcomes to those of the experimental group. Kendall and Norton-Ford (1982) suggest that this type of control group has several advantages: it controls for attention and placebo effects; it circumvents the ethical problems encountered in withholding or delaying treatment; and it allows for comparisons among alternative or competing intervention strategies.

To summarize, group experimental designs in consultation outcome research typically are simplistic and unimaginative. The most devastating aspect of this literature is the low number of studies that even include a control or comparison group. Furthermore, no studies could be found that used alternative control group arrangements such as attention-placebo, wait-list, or best alternative intervention groups. The failure to include control groups creates numerous threats to the internal validity of experimental designs and thereby limits conclusions that might be drawn from research.

Single-Case Experimental Designs

Relatively few studies in the consultation literature have used single-case experimental design strategies (Gresham & Kendell, 1987). As previously stated, a large percentage of consultation outcome studies have failed to include control groups of any kind, thereby compromising the internal validity of these designs. Single-case experimental designs do not require control groups because subjects serve as their own controls.

There are a number of internally valid single-case experimental designs in which the effectiveness of consultation could be demonstrated (see Barlow & Hersen, 1984, for a comprehensive treatment). These designs include multiple-baseline, reversal, changing-criterion, and alternating-treatment designs. Hayes (1981) has organized all single-case design strategies into three categories: within-series strategies, between-series strategies, and combined-series strategies.

Single-case experimental designs are true experiments in that they control for most threats to internal validity. However, these designs do not provide adequate controls for *external validity* threats. Given that single subjects are used, the demonstration of an experimental effect on a subject does not ensure that similar effects would be observed on other subjects in other settings. Single-case researchers often advocate replication of treatment effects across several subjects to bolster external validity (Barlow & Hersen, 1984; Johnston & Pennypacker, 1980). (Chapter Eleven provides a detailed analysis of single-case strategies.)

Case Study Designs

Case studies have frequently been used in the consultation literature to describe the processes and outcomes of consultation. Case study methodology typically is an uncontrolled and subjective description of a single case (Bergan & Kratochwill, 1990). As such, case studies are *preexperimental* in that they lack the necessary controls to ensure the internal validity of the design (Campbell & Stanley, 1963).

Bergan and Kratochwill (1990) suggest that case studies do not necessarily have to be uncontrolled or subjective and that they have several advantages over formal group or single-case experimental designs. First, case studies allow for investigation of novel interventions or variations of established interventions that would be expensive and difficult to conduct using group designs. Case studies often uncover unique variables or effects that have not been realized or anticipated. Consistent case study findings of a new technique can set the stage for more controlled investigations of the phenomenon using group or single-case experimental designs.

Second, case studies can be used by practitioners who want to be involved in research as part of their daily activities (Kratochwill, 1985). Case studies have the advantage of not requiring the necessary experimental restrictions of group or single-case designs and avoid many ethical problems in experimental designs, such as delaying or withholding treatment (Bergan & Kratochwill, 1990).

Finally, case studies can be conducted in a manner that does control for many internal validity threats, allowing for firm conclusions regarding treatment effects. For example, Harris and Jenson (1985) argue that the use of AB case study designs with replication across subjects provides for an amount of control similar to that in multiple-baseline designs. Unlike multiple-baseline designs, AB designs with replication do not require that treatments be applied sequentially across subjects or that baselines be of different lengths. Hayes (1981) refers to this design as a natural multiple-baseline design, and Watson and Workman (1981) label it a "non-concurrent multiple baseline design." Harris and Jenson (1985) present convincing evidence that this design adequately controls for historical sources of invalidity and is very easy to implement in applied settings.

Table 12.1. Characteristics of Adequate and Inadequate Case Study Designs.

Methodological factor	*Adequate*	*Inadequate*
Type of data	Objective	Subjective
Assessment occasions	Repeated	Pre-post
Independent variable	Manipulated	Not manipulated
Effect size	Large	Small
Effect impact	Immediate	Delayed
Number of subjects	$N = 1$	$N > 1$
Diversity of subjects	Heterogeneous	Homogeneous
Standardization of assessment and treatment	Nonstandardized	Standardized
Integrity assessment	Monitored	Not monitored
Impact of treatment	Multiple	Single
Formal design structure	Minimal A/B	No design
Social validation	Validation	No validation
Analysis of results	Formal analysis	No analysis
Generalization and follow-up	Assessment	No assessment

Source: Adapted from Kratochwill, 1985.

Kratochwill (1985) discusses a number of methodological factors that facilitate the drawing of valid inferences from case studies. Table 12.1 provides a comparison and contrast between inadequate and adequate case study methodologies presented by Kratochwill. An adequate case study can be characterized as using objective data, repeated measurement of the dependent variable, manipulation of the independent variable, replication across subjects, monitoring of treatment integrity, the maintenance of a formal design structure, and social validation of treatment effects. A more detailed discussion of these factors can be found in Bergan and Kratochwill (1990) and Kratochwill (1985).

Future Directions in Consultation Research Design

As mentioned earlier, the sophistication of research designs in consultation is far below that of the psychotherapy research literature. Relatively few studies use control or comparison groups, making definitive conclusions regarding the effects of specific consultation strategies difficult. Few consultation researchers use control group variations such as wait-list, attention-placebo, or best-alternative control groups, which are common in the psychotherapy literature (Kendall & Norton-Ford, 1982; O'Leary & Borkovec, 1978).

The use of group experimental designs with adequate internal validity is difficult in school settings. The organization nature of schools makes random assignment of consultants, consultees, and clients to groups difficult. Moreover, ethical considerations make withholding or delaying treatment a questionable practice.

Given the difficulty of randomization in school settings, it is surprising that there have been few consultation research studies that have used *hierarchical designs* to get around the randomization problem. These designs may be useful in consultation research studies because different classrooms can be nested within different treatments (consultation strategies). There are a number of variations of these designs, such as completely randomized hierarchical and randomized blocks hierarchical designs, that could be used to answer important research questions in consultation (see Kirk, 1982, for a complete description).

      The use of single-case experimental designs is an efficient way of dealing with the issue of experimental control and randomization in consultation research. Given that subjects serve as their own controls, the issue of randomization is moot with these designs. While they possess adequate internal validity, the biggest problem in interpretation of single-case experimental data is external validity. Replication of treatment effects across subjects decreases external validity threats; however, this is rarely done systematically in consultation research. Case study designs are a more user-friendly means of incorporating some aspects of scientific research into the daily practice of consultation. However, these designs have insufficient controls over internal validity threats to warrant definitive conclusions regarding effects of consultation.

      What is the relationship among these methodologies in consultation research? What should be the sequence of research methodology in consultation outcome studies? We believe that all three methodologies can contribute valuable information regarding consultation. Case study designs could be a rich source of hypotheses concerning effects of certain consultation strategies. These designs are an economical and efficient means of replicating treatment effects and thereby providing external validity evidence for consultation treatments. Following a series of case study designs generating certain hypotheses and replication of treatment effects, the next step would be to focus on internal validity. Thus, single-case experimental designs using within-, between-, or combined-series strategies could be used to establish functional relationships between independent and dependent variables. These experiments could be replicated across settings, consultees, and clients to build external validity evidence. Finally, using the above sequence of investigation, large-scale validation studies using group designs (for example, hierarchical designs) could be conducted to provide stronger evidence for consultation strategies.

Dependent Variables in Consultation Research

Dependent measures used in consultation outcome research have included changes in consultees' and clients' behavior, changes in consultees' knowledge, perceptions, and attitudes, changes in the frequency of consultation utilization, changes in referral rates, and changes in consultants' verbal behavior (Bergan & Kratochwill, 1990; Gresham & Kendell, 1987; Gutkin & Curtis, 1982; see also Chapter Eleven). In spite of the wide variety of dependent variables used in consultation research, relatively few studies have used multiple dependent measures to assess consultation outcomes.

In a seminal article on school-based consultation, Witt (1990) argues that many consultants have a "univariate linear mind" in that they identify *the problem* to be fixed in consultation. The success or failure of consultation hinges on whether *the problem* was solved. According to Witt, "the 'fixing' of problems for the teacher (i.e., case centered consultation) has enormous appeal to the linear, univariate mind. . . . But most teachers do not have just one problem. They often have many problems. And for each problem there is not just one cause, there are many causes. And for each intervention there is not just one effect, there are many effects. Thus, the teacher lives in a multivariate world where events occur simultaneously and effects are synergistic" (p. 375). This argument is compelling. One reason that consultation research perhaps has little effect on consultation practice is that dependent variables used are limited in scope, univariate, and ecologically invalid.

Ecological invalidity of dependent variables is addressed in a review by Martens and Witt (1988) concerning expanding the scope of consultation practices. According to these authors, many consultants fail to consider "side effects" of consultation—collateral changes in behaviors not targeted for change in consultation. Willems (1974) maintains that the term *side effects* is a misnomer in that all effects are main or principal effects given the interdependency among behaviors in applied settings. More than sixty studies conducted since 1980 have reported collateral behavioral changes as a function of intervention (Evans, Meyer, Kurkjian, & Kishi, 1988). Martens and Witt (1988) suggest that the failure to consider multiple effects of consultation interventions often results in mismatching of interventions to target behaviors.

In summary, much consultation research and practice suffers from a univariate approach to problem solving. This is not only simple-minded, it is often ecologically invalid. Gresham (1983, 1985) argues for measurement of variables using the *principle of multiple operationalism*. That is, behaviors should be measured from a variety of perspectives using a number of assessment methods and information sources. The idea of multiple operationalism has come to be known as the multitrait-multimethod (MTMM) approach to construct validation (Campbell & Fiske, 1959).

Multiple operationalism acknowledges the fact that any given assessment method may reflect the method used in the assessment as much as the behaviors being measured. The MTMM approach is an attempt to separate method from behavioral variance such that convergent validity of a particular construct can be evaluated (Gresham, 1984). It is also possible that interventions might affect multiple dependent variables in multiple ways, so that convergent validity should not be expected. In addition, measurement of dependent variables has been shown to be affected by situational influences on behavior (Achenbach, McConaughy, & Howell, 1987; Gresham & Elliott, 1990).

That consultation researchers often do not adopt a multivariate perspective in reporting the outcomes of consultation is perplexing, given the well-known complexities of school settings and the multiple effects that interventions produce. A welcome exception to this univariate approach to consultation research is reported by Sheridan, Kratochwill, & Elliott, 1990), who document the outcome of behavioral consultation for socially withdrawn children using multimethod assessments including direct observations, behavioral interviews, checklists, behavior ratings scales, and child self-reports. This type of research should serve as a model for future investigations of consultation for school-age children and youth.

Traditional Indices of Consultation Outcomes

Conventional methods for reporting consultation research outcomes have relied primarily on parametric statistics. Although parametric statistics have contributed to our understanding of consultation, these methods have some drawbacks, particularly their failure to provide information about individuals and their lack of practical significance. This section briefly outlines some major criticisms of their use in consultation research and discusses two other traditional ways to evaluate consultation outcomes: effect size and visual analysis of data.

Parametric Statistics

Research outcomes using parametric statistical criteria necessarily involve averaging of results. If group A's mean is different from group B's mean, then the researcher concludes that A is different from B. This averaging, however, obscures the fact that the performance of some subjects in group A may have been the same as that of some subjects in group B. That is, there is no difference between A and B treatments for these subjects. Group mean comparisons ignore the frequent finding in outcome research that some subjects improve, some stay the same, and some deteriorate (Barlow & Hersen, 1984).

Conventional statistical methods test the significance of between-group differences by using within-group differences as error. If between-group differences are large relative to within-group differences, then statistical significance is achieved. The probability of finding a significant result depends in part on the homogeneity of variance within groups (that is, small error term). It is unusual to find consultants, consultees, and clients in consultation research who are homogeneous on dependent variables of interest and who are affected by treatment in similar ways.

Treating individual differences as error throws away potentially important information about how individuals respond to different experimental conditions. In criticizing this conception of "error," Johnston and Pennypacker (1980, p. 203) state, "To a considerable degree, there is a requirement for 'error variance' against which to assess the variability imposed by treatments. The dogmatic insistence in some quarters that all experiments be performed on large samples almost seems to be a statement tactically reifying intrinsic variability in order to preserve the legitimacy of prescientific conceptions of the causes of behavior." In short, Johnston and Pennypacker argue for treating individual variability as a legitimate focus of study rather than subsuming it under the misnomer of "error." In their view, individual variability has a cause and therefore can be explained.

Statistical significance is also highly dependent on sample size. As sample size increases, less difference between groups means is required for statistical significance. Sample size is directly related to the *power* of an experiment—the probability of its disproving a null hypothesis, which decreases the probability of a type II error (retention of a false null hypothesis).

Baer (1977) suggests that the goal of group comparison research designs is to uncover "weak" treatment effects, when it should be to discover strong effects. The primary difference between single-case experiments and group design experiments is that the former have relatively high rates of type II errors (concluding that no effect exists when an effect does exist) and very low rates of type I error (concluding that an effect exists when one does not). In contrast, those who conduct group experiments are willing to accept 5 percent of their findings as type I errors ($p < .05$) and thereby control their rates of type II errors.

Finally, research findings based on statistical significance often are not socially relevant. There is frequently no relationship between statistical significance and practical significance, particularly when statistical significance is a function of large sample size rather than strong effects of independent variables (Baer, 1977; Barlow & Hersen, 1984; Gresham, 1991; Jacobson, Follette, & Revenstorf, 1984). This is probably the main reason that consultation research does not affect consultation practice in a meaningful way. Establishing the practical significance of research findings, or social validation (Kazdin, 1977; Wolf, 1978), is discussed later in this chapter.

Effect Sizes

A relatively recent statistical development that is used to evaluate the efficacy of intervention procedures is meta-analysis. Developed by Glass (1976), meta-analysis provides a quantitative synthesis of a particular research literature. Although there are several minor variations, the basic procedure in meta-analysis is transforming the results of each study into an *effect size*. Effect size is calculated by subtracting the mean score on the dependent variable for the control group from the mean score of the experimental group and dividing this difference by the standard deviation of the control group.

Effect sizes are interpreted as standard deviation units expressed in terms of z scores. Thus, effect sizes are positive when the experimental group scores higher than the control group and negative when the control group scores higher than the experimental group. For example, an effect size of + 1.00 would indicate that the experimental group scored 1 standard deviation higher on the dependent variable than the control group. Thus, we could say that the mean score of the control group is only at the sixteenth percentile of the experimental group.

Two studies were located that used meta-analysis to summarize the efficacy of consultation. Medway and Updyke (1985) reviewed fifty-four studies that compared behavioral, mental health, and organization development consultation with a control group. The meta-analysis revealed that consultation (collapsed across the three consultation models) provided an effect size of .55 on dependent measures of consultee attitudes and behavior and an effect size of .39 on dependent measures of client attitudes and behavior. Contrary to previous qualitative reviews, the three models of consultation produced similar effect sizes. The meta-analysis by Sibley (1986) produced results that differed from the Medway and Updyke (1985) meta-analysis. Sibley reviewed sixty-three studies and found larger effect sizes for clients (.91) and consultees (.60). These findings indicate that effect sizes calculated from different studies can greatly alter our interpretation of a particular research literature.

Meta-analysis has a number of limitations. First, the quantification of an entire literature with a single number is deceptively simple. The way in which meta-analysis is conducted involves the averaging of results of many studies, calculating effect sizes, and then averaging the effect sizes. This process removes us further and further from the original data on which the individual effect sizes are based.

Second, the problems with traditional parametric statistics (F ratios, t tests, and so on) discussed in the previous section are even greater with meta-analysis. Recall that F ratios and t tests are based on averages and comparisons of between-group variances to within-group variances. As such, within-group variability is treated as error, and we lose sight of how a given individual performs under a given treatment condition. Meta-analysis compounds this problem by averaging the results of averages and producing a number than may have little meaning other than a broad statement that something produces a larger number than something else.

A third problem with meta-analysis is that while studies often use different dependent variables, meta-analysis ignores these differences and treats dependent variables as the same. Given differences in reliability and validity of dependent measures, the results of a meta-analysis often boil down to a comparison of apples and oranges.

Finally, meta-analysis lives and dies by the dictum that all studies are created equal. In other words, well-controlled, internally valid studies receive the same weighting in a meta-analysis as poorly controlled studies with many threats to internal validity. Obviously, we should trust the results of internally valid studies more than the results of internally invalid studies. Slavin (1986) provides an alternative to traditional meta-analysis, which he terms "best-evidence synthesis," that selects only studies that meet high standards of internal validity (high-quality studies) and then performs a meta-analysis and narrative review of these studies.

Visual Analysis of Data

Visual inspection of graphed data is the most common method of analyzing single-case research (Barlow & Hersen, 1984). Effects of intervention are determined by comparing baseline levels of performance to postintervention levels to detect treatment effects. Unlike complex statistical analyses, this method uses the "interocular" test of significance. Visual inspection of graphed data has been criticized on the grounds that it is an insensitive method of determining treatment effects (Kazdin, 1984); that is, it identifies only large effects and fails to detect subtle changes in the dependent variable. Also, research demonstrates that even highly trained behavior analysts cannot obtain consensus in evaluating single-case data through visual inspection (Center, Skiba, & Casey, 1985–86; Knapp, 1983).

Although there are technical problems associated with visual inspection, it may be a more useful way of determining the *practical significance* of treatment effects than statistical analysis. Baer (1977) maintains that the use of statistical analysis with single-case data does nothing but uncover weak treatment effects. His logic is simple: if you need a statistical test to know whether your treatment worked, you should assume that it did not (that is, risk a type II error).

The purpose of consultation is to identify and implement *strong* interventions that have a large effect of behavior. It is not likely that consultees will be convinced that consultation was effective in cases where the behavioral problem of the client remains but the consultant presents them with data showing that the intervention was effective at the .05 level.

In spite of the simplicity of the visual inspection approach to evaluating consultation outcomes, there are several technical problems associated with its use. As mentioned earlier, the interjudge agreement regarding treatment effects using visual inspection is low. Second, visual analysis of graphed data does not lend itself to a quantitative synthesis using meta-analysis. Third, interventions can produce large effects discernible through visual analysis yet not produce socially valid results.

Alternative Indices of Consultation Outcomes

As we have seen, there are a number of methodological and interpretative problems with traditional methods for reporting consultation outcomes. There are, however, several viable alternatives available to consultation practitioners and researchers for evaluating the effects of consultation. These include social validation, reliable changes in behavior, quantification of single-subject effects, and cost-effectiveness analysis.

Social Validation

Social validity concerns, in part, the *social importance* of effects produced by interventions (Kazdin, 1977; Wolf, 1978). Social validation establishes the clinical or practical importance of behavioral change—that is, how much difference that change makes in an individual's functioning.

Jacobson et al. (1984) suggest that most behavioral problems vary on a continuum of functioning involving a range of scores. Some approaches to social validation (for example, Kazdin & Wilson, 1978) contend that a result is socially validated if the problem is successfully resolved. This approach leads to thinking about outcomes in terms of false dichotomies (problem present versus problem absent) (Jacobson et al., 1984). For example, it would be unlikely that short-term consultation with a teacher for a child's academic difficulties would result in complete resolution of the deficiency.

One solution to this dilemma would be to conceptualize academic functioning as belonging to either a *functional* or a *dysfunctional* distribution. One way to socially validate a consultation intervention for academic problems would be to demonstrate that the child moved from a dysfunctional to a functional range of academic performance. This could be established statistically by calculating the probabilities that the child's academic scores belonged to functional versus dysfunctional distributions. Jacobson et al. (1984) correctly point out that this approach to social validation is problematic because it requires a normative data base for both functional and dysfunctional populations. Many of our dependent variables in consultation do not have a normative data base, and fewer still have separate norms for "functional" and dysfunctional" populations.

Kazdin (1977) suggests more practical approaches to social validation. Kazdin recommends three general approaches: social comparisons, subjective evaluation, and combined social validation procedures. Social comparison involves comparing an individual's behavior after intervention with the behavior of relevant peers. For example, if a target child's behavior after intervention is similar to that of nonreferred peers, then one can conclude that the effects of intervention were socially valid. Walker and Hops (1976) present an excellent example of how this can be applied to classroom settings. This procedure involves establishing local "micronorms" against which behavior of referred and nonreferred peers can be judged (Nelson & Bowles, 1975).

Subjective evaluation consists of having people familiar with the child in a particular setting rate qualitative aspects of the child's behavior. These global evaluations of behavior assess how well the child is functioning and provide an overall assessment of performance (Kazdin, 1977). Subjective evaluations need not be limited to the quality of behavioral change in children. Virtually all of the research concerning teachers' acceptability of classroom-based interventions uses subjective judgments of treatment acceptability (Elliott, 1988; Witt & Elliott, 1985; see also Chapter Nine). Subjective judgments could be used to evaluate the quality of consultants' behavior in consultation sessions and the quality of consultees' behavior in applied settings.

Combined social validation procedures perhaps represent the "best practice" in social validation. That is, the practical significance of consultation outcomes would be bolstered if we could demonstrate that: clients' behavior moved into the same normative range as that of nonreferred peers and that consultees felt that consultation had produced socially important changes in behavior. This combined approach captures not only how much behavior changed (a quantitative criterion) but also how consumers of consultation services view that change (a qualitative criterion).

Reliable Changes in Behavior

We have previously noted that the major problem with group-design statistics is reliance on mean differences between groups of subjects to determine treatment effectiveness. This averaging masks the effects of interventions for individual clients and ignores potentially valuable information. Although we could compute the percentage of clients who "improved" in a group design, this improvement may not represent statistically reliable improvement. It is entirely possible for the change in an individual's scores from a dysfunctional to a functional distribution to be within the range of measurement error (Jacobson et al., 1984).

Nunnally and Kotsche (1983) propose a *reliable change index* (RC) to determine the effectiveness of intervention. RC is defined as the difference between pretest and posttest scores divided by the standard error of measurement: $RC = X2 - X1/SEM$ where $X2$ = a subject's posttest score, $X1$ = a subject's pretest score, and SEM = that standard error of measurement.

An RC of ± 1.96 ($p < 0.5$) would be statistically significant, and given this value, one could conclude that an intervention produced reliable changes in behavior. This metric for reporting intervention outcomes has the following advantages: data are reported for individuals rather than groups, reliable changes from pretest to posttest for individuals are indexed by the standard error of measurement, and confidence intervals can be constructed around change scores to avoid overinterpretation of a particular result (Jacobson et al., 1984).

RC is affected by the reliability of the dependent measure used in research studies. For example, if a measure is highly reliable (.90 or greater), then small changes in behavior may be considered statistically reliable but not socially important. In contrast, if a measure has low reliability, then large changes in behavioral functioning may be socially important but not considered statistically reliable. Thus, using the dual criteria of social validation (combined social validation procedures) and RC should provide practitioners and researchers with a means of documenting educationally and statistically significant changes in behavior as a function of intervention.

Quantification of Single-Case Effects

As previously discussed, visual inspection of graphed single-case data is the most common method of analysis. However, this method yields relatively low interjudge agreements of treatment effects and does not lend itself to quantitative synthesis via meta-analysis. At least two alternatives have been proposed for the quantitative synthesis of single-case data: regression analysis (Center et al., 1985–86) and percentage of nonoverlapping data points between baseline and treatment phases (Mastropieri & Scruggs, 1985–86).

Center et al. (1985–86) argue for the use of piecewise regression procedures to estimate change *level* (changes in behavior at the point of intervention) and *slope* (changes in trend among phases). This analytical technique, while potentially valuable, has limitations. First, it is fairly complex and thus not particularly user-friendly. Second, fitting regression models to data with relatively few data points often yields inaccurate results because it is often impossible to meet the statistical assumptions of regression. Third, the piece-wise regression model yields three effect sizes—level, baseline trend, and slope of intervention phases—rather than the one effect size yielded by a traditional meta-analysis. Finally, the interpretation of effect size measures with the regression approach is the percentage of variance accounted for by the intervention expressed as standard errors of estimate (prediction errors from the regression model) (Center et al., 1985–86). This is a more complex interpretation than the traditional meta-analysis, which quantifies effect sizes as differences between experimental and control groups expressed in standard deviation units.

An easier and perhaps equally valid approach to synthesizing single-case data from multiple studies is computing the percentage of nonoverlapping data points between baseline and treatment phases (Mastropieri & Scruggs, 1985–86). This procedure is easy to compute, yields an adequate measure of treatment effectiveness, and gets around potentially troublesome statistical problems, such as baseline variability and changes in slope.

Percentage of nonoverlapping data points is computed by indicating the number of *treatment data points* that exceed the *highest baseline data point* in an expected direction and dividing by the total number of data points in the *treatment phase* (Mastropieri & Scruggs, 1985–86). This method can be used to aggregate data across studies to determine the effectiveness of particular intervention techniques. The chief advantages of this method for consultation are the quantitative synthesis of single-case consultation research and its easy application by practitioners to individual cases. Although there are situations in which this method would not be appropriate (for example, with inappropriate baseline trends, nonorthogonal slope changes, floor and ceiling effects), by and large, it is a reasonable estimate of treatment effectiveness in single-case research designs.

Cost-Effectiveness Analysis

Cost-effectiveness analysis (CEA) is based on the premise that intervention effectiveness is an inadequate criterion by which to judge intervention success (Levin, 1975). CEA adds the additional criterion that interventions represent the efficient use of consumers' resources (Wortman, 1983). The core element of CEA is the comparison of intervention costs to benefits. Interventions are considered successful when benefits exceed costs and unsuccessful when costs exceed benefits.

Within a CEA framework, costs are typically assessed in monetary terms (Yates, 1985): the funds devoted to personnel, facilities, and materials are totaled to yield cost. Intervention benefits may also be assessed in monetary terms: increased income and savings resulting from an intervention. Income benefits might result from an intervention decreasing a person's time away from work due to child misbehavior; avoiding special education placement might represent income benefits for a school district.

Some intervention benefits, particularly those of a social or psychological nature, cannot be expressed in monetary terms. Intervention benefits such as increased arithmetic skills, increased social skills, or decreased depression may not have direct monetary correlates. In these cases, the cost data are reported relative to the types of benefits of interest. Cost and benefit data are typically reported in terms of absolute level and ratio of benefit to cost (Wortman, 1983; Yates, 1985).

Functional Outcome Analysis. Functional outcome analysis (FOA) has been proposed as an alternative approach to consultation and intervention evaluation (Noell & Gresham, in press). FOA derives from CEA and the principles of ecological behavior analysis (Martens & Witt, 1988). Within this framework, the functional relationship between resources invested in consultation activities and outcomes is examined. FOA is designed to permit efficiency-based evaluation in consultation with the goal of developing more efficient, ecologically valid interventions.

Consultation "costs" can be conceptualized along two dimensions: objective and subjective. Objective costs consist of time and money. Within a FOA framework, time would be employed as the primary objective cost metric to enhance the utility of results. Time data would permit evaluation of interventions for settings with differing personnel costs. Time data would also permit evaluation of feasibility of interventions in settings in which personnel costs represent not new personnel but rather new time demands on existing personnel. Material costs would be reported in monetary terms.

Subjective costs are the phenomenological costs (for example, hassle, discomfort, inconvenience) of implementing an intervention. Subjective costs may also be conceptualized as the response cost to the intervention provider for carrying out the intervention. Subjective cost data may be collected through rating scales or by interview.

Benefits may also be conceptualized as objective and subjective. Objective benefits can be either increases in available resources or desired behavioral changes. In cases of child behavioral problems, the most probable resource increase is in available time. The time a teacher or parent no longer spends dealing with inappropriate behavior represents an objective benefit (that is, increased available resources). Behavioral change benefits might include increased time on task, decreased aggression, and improved grades. For behavioral changes to meaningfully be referred to as benefits, however, they should be socially validated (Kazdin, 1977; Wolf, 1978).

Subjective benefits are also phenomenological in nature. These benefits might include reduced stress, decreased depression, increased happiness, and the like. Both the child and consultees may be beneficiaries of subjective benefits. Subjective benefits, like costs, could be assessed through rating scales, observations, and interviews. Subjective benefits and costs should be assessed using the same method with similar scaling properties to permit comparison of results.

Efficiency Ratios. The consumer's return on investment is a central element of an efficiency-based strategy for documenting the relationship between costs and benefits. This return on investment is expressed as an efficiency ratio (ER)—the ratio of benefits to costs. An ER describes the amount of return per unit of investment, similar to an interest rate. An ER above 1 indicates that the intervention was profitable (benefits exceeded costs), whereas an ER of less than 1 means that the intervention was unprofitable (costs exceeded benefits).

In most cases, consultation-based interventions will have multiple ERs. Because objective and subjective costs represent conceptually different domains, separate ERs would be computed for each. The objective efficiency ratio (OER), the ratio of objective benefits to objective costs, is ordinarily computed by comparing time savings to time costs. Where necessary, time data may be converted to money data (based on salary) to permit computation. As a result, the OER normally has no units, as time and money appear in both the numerator and the denominator. In this sense, the OER is like an interest rate.

An OER may also be computed by comparing time invested in behavioral change. OERs computed in this fashion may be useful for comparing interventions, but they do not represent absolute efficiency. These OERs are dependent on the units specified. Levin and Meister (1986) provide an example of this type of reporting in which they showed the ratio of gain in achievement to $100 expended per student.

The subjective efficiency ratio (SER) is the ratio of subjective benefits to subjective costs. Both costs and benefits are computed according to phenomenological ratings. It is important that the instruments used to collect these data have similar measurement properties. Instrument artifacts such as restriction of range or ceiling effects can artificially inflate or deflate the SER.

The costs and benefits of particular intervention may be distributed among various individuals (Yates, 1985; Wortman, 1983). Time and monetary costs may be borne by teachers, parents, school systems, and nontargeted peers. This presents the possibility that an intervention may be cost-effective from one perspective but not from others. Cost and benefit data should be collected from the perspective of various people contributing to the intervention. This will permit computation of ERs relevant to different consumers.

The OER and SER are intended to help guide the ongoing evaluation of interventions during consultation and at their conclusion. The ERs relevant to an intervention should be computed and graphed on an ongoing basis. Interventions showing negative trends may need to be modified. Interventions that are objectively efficient (OER > 1) but noxious to the consumer (SER < 1) may need to be modified to find a more acceptable treatment with roughly equal objective benefits.

While FOA is a potentially useful approach to conceptualizing and evaluating consultation outcomes, there are no empirical studies specifically employing FOA in the consultation literature. A liability of FOA is that no specific technology for subjective cost and benefit assessment has been developed. The chief advantage of FOA in our view is that it considers the resource demands and gains of consultation. This provides a framework for determining when consultation is an efficient use of consumers' finite resources and when it is not.

Conclusions

Consultation research potentially has much to offer practitioners in terms of "best practices" in consultation in applied settings. However, because of the way in which this research is reported, it often has little or no impact on consultation practice. Our hypothesis regarding why this may be the case is that traditional indices or methods of reporting consultation outcomes are not readily comprehensible to practitioners, are frequently irrelevant, lack in social validity or practical significance, and are based on outcomes for groups rather than individuals.

Alternative indices of reporting consultation outcome research discussed in this chapter hold promise for increased use of research findings by practitioners. Social validation of outcomes ensures the clinical or practical significance of research findings. Using combined social validation procedures of subjective judgments and social comparisons is a means of documenting practical significance of interventions.

Quantification of single-case design outcomes using percentage of non-overlapping data points is an easy, quick way of demonstrating the effectiveness of interventions developed in consultation. This method is preferable to using piecewise regression techniques because of the technical difficulties associated with regression approaches and the somewhat cumbersome metric in which this method reports outcomes (that is, standard errors of estimate).

Demonstrating reliable changes in behavior for individuals is an alternative to traditional significance testing. Reliable changes in behavior are indexed by the standard error of measurement and thus are highly dependent on the reliability of dependent measures used in consultation research. We recommend the combined use of social validation and reliable changes in behavior to document consultation outcomes.

Finally, functional outcome analysis (a variant of cost-efficiency analysis) may be the most socially valid means of reporting consultation outcomes. Calculating both objective and subjective costs and benefits makes it possible to calculate the efficiency of different consultation strategies so that consultation programs can be modified and refined.

The goal of applied research is to base practice on scientifically validated methods and techniques. As we have seen, however, applied research does not affect practice to a significant degree. This chapter argues that the primary reason for the lack of research utilization by practitioners is their perception that specific research investigations are irrelevant and the frequent user-unfriendliness of data reported in consultation studies. This chapter has presented viable alternatives to traditional methods of reporting research outcomes. It is our hope that consultation research will begin to adopt some of the procedures to ensure that we are addressing socially significant goals in consultation, using socially acceptable intervention methods that produce socially important, reliable, and cost-beneficial changes in behavior.

References

Achenbach, T., McConaughy, S., & Howell, C. (1987). Child/adolescent behavioral and emotional problems: Implications of cross-informant correlations for situational specificity. *Psychological Bulletin, 101,* 213–232.

Alpert, J. L., & Yammer, M. D. (1983). Research in school consultation: A content analysis of selected journals. *Professional Psychology: Research and Practice, 14,* 604–612.

Baer, D. (1977). "Perhaps it would be better not to know everything." *Journal of Applied Behavior Analysis, 10,* 167–172.

Barlow, D. (1981). On the relation between clinical research and clinical practice: Current issues, new directions. *Journal of Consulting and Clinical Psychology, 49,* 147–155.

Barlow, D., & Hersen, M. (Eds.). (1984). *Single case experimental designs* (2nd Ed.). Elmsford, NY: Pergamon Press.

Bergan J., & Kratochwill, T. (1990). *Behavioral consultation and therapy.* New York: Plenum Press.

Campbell, D., & Fiske, D. (1959). Convergent and discriminant validation by the multitrait-multimethod matrix. *Psychological Bulletin, 56,* 81–105.

Campbell, D., & Stanley, J. (1963). *Experimental and quasi-experimental designs for research.* Skokie, IL: Rand McNally.

Center, B., Skiba, R., & Casey, A. (1985–86). A methodology for the quantitative synthesis of intra-subject design research. *Journal of Special Education, 19,* 387–400.

Cook, T., & Campbell, D. (1979). *Quasi-experimentation: Design and analysis issues for field settings.* Skokie, IL: Rand McNally.

Elliott, S. N. (1988). Acceptability of behavioral treatments in educational settings. In J. C. Witt, S. N. Elliott, and F. M. Gresham (Eds.), *Handbook of behavior therapy in education* (pp. 121–150). New York: Plenum Press.

Evans, I., Meyer, L., Kurkjian, J., & Kishi, G. (1988). An evaluation of behavioral interrelationships in child behavior therapy. In J. C. Witt, S. N. Elliott, & F. M. Gresham (Eds.), *Handbook of behavior therapy in education* (pp. 189–216). New York: Plenum Press.

Glass, G. (1976). Primary, secondary, and meta-analysis of research. *Educational Researcher, 5,* 3–8.

Graden, J., Casey, A., & Christensen, S. (1985). Implementing a prereferral intervention system: Part I. The model. *Exceptional Children, 51,* 377–384.

Gresham, F. M. (1983). Multitrait-multimethod approach to multifactored assessment: Theoretical rationale and practical application. *School Psychology Review, 12,* 26–33.

Gresham, F. M. (1985). Behavior disorder assessment: Conceptual, definitional, and practical considerations. *School Psychology Review, 14,* 495–509.

Gresham, F. M. (1991). Moving beyond statistical significance in reporting consultation outcome research. *Journal of Educational and Psychological Consultation, 2,* 1–14.

Gresham, F. M., & Elliott, S. N. (1990). *Social skills rating system.* Circle Pines, MN: American Guidance Service.

Gresham, F. M., & Kendell, G. K. (1987). School consultation research: Methodological critique and future research directions. *School Psychology Review, 16,* 306–316.

Gutkin, T. B., & Curtis, M. J. (1982). School-based consultation: Theory and techniques. In C. R. Reynolds & T. B. Gutkin (Eds.), *The handbook of school psychology* (pp. 796–828). New York: Wiley.

Harris, F., & Jenson, W. (1985). Comparisons of multiple-baseline across persons designs and AB designs with replication: Issues and confusion. *Behavioral Assessment, 7,* 121–127.

Hayes, S. C. (1981). Single case experimental design and empirical clinical practice. *Journal of Consulting and Clinical Psychology, 49,* 193–211.

Jacobson, N. S., Follette, W. C., & Revenstorf, D. (1984). Psychotherapy outcome research: Methods for reporting variability and evaluating clinical significance. *Behavior Therapy, 15,* 336–352.

Johnston, J., & Pennypacker, H. (1980). *Strategies and tactics for human behavioral research.* Hillsdale, NJ: Erlbaum.

Kazdin, A. (1977). Assessing the clinical or applied significance of behavior change through social validation. *Behavior Modification, 1,* 427–452.

Kazdin, A. (1984). Statistical analysis for single-case experimental designs. In D. Barlow & M. Hersen (Eds.), *Single case experimental designs* (2nd ed., pp. 285–324). Elmsford, NY: Pergamon Press.

Kazdin, A., & Wilson, G. T. (1978). *Evaluation of behavior therapy: Issues, evidence, and research strategies.* New York: Ballinger.

Kendall, P., & Norton-Ford, J. (1982). Therapy outcome research methods. In P. Kendall & J. Butcher (Eds.), *Handbook of research methods in clinical psychology* (pp. 429–459). New York: Wiley.

Kerlinger, F. (1986). *Foundations of behavioral research* (3rd ed.). New York: Holt, Rinehart & Winston.

Kiresuk, T. J., & Sherman, R. E. (1968). Goal attainment scaling: A general method for evaluating comprehensive community mental health programs. *Community Mental Health Journal, 4,* 443–453.

Kirk, R. E. (1982). *Experimental design: Procedures for the behavioral sciences* (2nd ed.). Pacific Grove, CA: Brooks/Cole.

Knapp, T. (1983). Behavior analysts' visual appraisal of behavior change in graphic display. *Behavioral Assessment, 5,* 155–164.

Kratochwill, T. R. (1985). Case study research in school psychology. *School Psychology Review, 14,* 204–215.

Kratochwill, T. R., Elliott, S. N., & Rotto, P. C. (1990). Best practices in behavioral consultation. In A. T. Thomas & J. Grimes (Eds.), *Best practices in school psychology* (2nd ed., pp. 147–169). Silver Spring, MD: National Association of School Psychologists.

Lentz, F. E. (1988). Reductive techniques. In J. C. Witt, S. N. Elliott, & F. M. Gresham (Eds.), *Handbook of behavior therapy in education* (pp. 439–468). New York: Plenum Press.

Levin, H. (1975). Cost-effectiveness analysis in evaluation research. In M. Guttentag & E. Struening (Eds.), *Handbook of evaluation research* (vol. 2). Newbury Park, CA: Sage.

Levin, H. M., & Meister, G. R. (1986). Is CAI cost effective? *Phi Delta Kappan, 67,* 745–749.

Martens, B. K., & Witt, J. C. (1988). Expanding the scope of behavioral consultation: A systems approach to classroom behavior change. *Professional School Psychology, 3,* 271–281.

Mastropieri, M., & Scruggs, T. (1985–86). Early intervention for socially withdrawn children. *Journal of Special Education, 19,* 429–441.

Medway, F. J. (1979). How effective is school consultation? A review of recent research. *Journal of School Psychology, 17,* 275–282.

Medway, F. J. (1982). School consultation research: Past trends and future directions. *Professional Psychology, 13,* 422–430.

Medway, F. J., & Updyke, J. F. (1985). Meta-analysis of consultation outcome studies. *American Journal of Community Psychology, 13,* 489–505.

Morrow-Bradley, C., & Elliott, R. (1986). Utilization of psychotherapy outcome research by practicing psychotherapists. *American Psychologist, 41,* 188–197.

Nelson, R., & Bowles, P. (1975). The best of two worlds: Observation with norms. *Journal of School Psychology, 13,* 3–9.

Noell, G. H., & Gresham, F. M. (in press). Functional outcome analysis: Do the benefits of consultation and prereferral intervention justify the costs? *School Psychology Quarterly.*

Nunnally, J., & Kotsche, W. (1983). Studies of individual subjects: Logic and methods of analysis. *British Journal of Clinical Psychology, 22,* 83–93.

O'Leary, K. D., & Borkovec, T. (1978). Conceptual, methodological, and ethical problems of placebo groups in psychotherapy research. *American Psychologist, 33,* 821–830.

Pryzwansky, W. B. (1986). Indirect service delivery: Considerations for future research in consultation. *School Psychology Review, 15,* 479–488.

Shapiro, E. (1987). Intervention research methodology in school psychology. *School Psychology Review, 16,* 290–305.

Sheridan, S. M., Kratochwill, T. R., & Elliott, S. N. (1990). Behavioral consultation with parents and teachers: Delivering treatment for socially withdrawn children at home and school. *School Psychology Review, 19,* 33–52.

Sibley, S. (1986). *A meta-analysis of school consultation research.* Unpublished doctoral dissertation, Texas Woman's University, Denton.

Slavin, R. (1986). Best-evidence synthesis: An alternative to meta-analysis and traditional reviews. *Educational Researcher, 15,* 5–11.

Walker, H., & Hops, H. (1976). Use of normative peer data as a standard for evaluating classroom treatment effects. *Journal of Applied Behavior Analysis, 9,* 159–168.

Watson, P. J., & Workman, E. A. (1981). Non-concurrent multiple-baseline across individuals design: An extension of the traditional multiple-baseline design. *Journal of Behavior Therapy and Experimental Psychiatry, 12,* 257–259.

Willems, E. P. (1974). Behavioral technology and behavioral ecology. *Journal of Applied Behavior Analysis, 7,* 151–165.

Witt, J. C. (1990). Complaining, precopernican thought, and the univariate linear mind: Questions for school-based behavioral consultation research. *School Psychology Review, 19,* 367–377.

Witt, J. C., & Elliott, S. N. (1985). Acceptability of classroom intervention strategies. In T. Kratochwill (Ed.), *Advances in school psychology* (Vol. 4, pp. 251–288). Hillsdale, NJ: Erlbaum.

Wolf, M. M. (1978). Social validity: The case for subjective measurement or how applied behavior analysis is finding its heart. *Journal of Applied Behavior Analysis, 11,* 203–214.

Wortman, P. M. (1983). Evaluation research: A methodological perspective. *Annual Review of Psychology, 34,* 223–260.

Yates, B. T. (1985). Cost-effectiveness analysis and cost-benefit analysis: An introduction. *Behavioral Assessment, 7,* 207–234.

Zins, J. E., & Ponti, C. R. (1990). Best practices in school-based consultation. In A. T. Thomas & J. Grimes (Eds.), *Best practices in school psychology* (2nd ed., pp. 673–694). Silver Spring, MD: National Association of School Psychologists.

Part Four

EFFECTIVE PRACTICE

13

Consulting in Elementary and Secondary Schools

Charlene R. Ponti, Janette Cahill Flower

The need for consultation services in elementary and secondary schools has increased in recent years. Motivation for adopting this form of service delivery stems from a number of forces, including current educational reforms, changes in beliefs about service delivery to children, and community pressures. The trend toward intervention assistance programs (Zins, Curtis, Graden, & Ponti, 1988) and the regular education initiative (Lloyd, Singh, & Repp, 1991), for example, have stimulated the use of consultation as a sanctioned means of providing supportive assistance to regular and special education teachers and increasing collaboration among school staff.

Conceptualizations of psychological and educational service delivery in the schools have also expanded, with increased recognition of schools as logical settings for primary prevention efforts (Branden-Muller & Elias, 1991; Zins & Forman, 1988). Consultation itself has a preventive orientation in that it often addresses problems before they become serious and emphasizes enhancing consultee skills to more effectively solve similar problems in the future (Gutkin & Curtis, 1990). Further, through consultation, more interventions and schoolwide programs that focus on empowering students and enhancing their competencies and coping strategies are now being implemented (Elias, 1987). Finally, events such as the Los Angeles riots (Youngstrom, 1992), the Persian Gulf crisis (Gibelman, 1991), violence in schools (Dillard, 1989), and natural disasters (Alderman, 1989) have stimulated requests for consultation in schools.

Note: Appreciation is extended to Cora Coulter and Kathy MacNeil for assistance with data collection for this chapter.

Although consultation can be carried out on many organizational levels, the purpose of this chapter is to illustrate how it can be applied to resolve individual student-related problems. The chapter begins with a brief description of how consultation services can be conceptualized and integrated into the overall educational service delivery system. Two case examples are then presented to illustrate major issues in consulting in elementary and secondary school settings. The behavioral consultation model, described in more detail in Chapter Four of this volume and in Bergan and Kratochwill (1990), underlies the procedures followed in both cases. Implementation issues are discussed in more detail in Chapter Ten.

Conceptual Framework

Consultation is most effective when it is an integral component of the entire educational service system (Zins & Ponti, 1987). Many schools implement the approach by adopting programs variously termed *intervention assistance, student or teacher assistance teams,* or *prereferral intervention.* These terms refer to a consultation-based method of service delivery aimed at facilitating collaborative problem solving among staff and providing prompt intervention for students experiencing mild behavioral or learning problems (Zins et al., 1988).

Within the model developed by Zins et al. (1988), consultation is viewed as the overarching framework from which all other services flow. Assessment activities are considered part of problem clarification, and direct instruction and counseling are conceptualized as interventions resulting from consultation (Zins, 1992).

Consultation is provided by individual practitioners or an intervention assistance team, generally comprising special services staff (for example, a psychologist, a speech/language therapist, and a counselor), special and regular education teachers, and a building administrator. Teachers can also serve as consultants or as peer collaborators (Pugach & Johnson, 1990).

When student-related problems occur, the regular education teacher requests a meeting with an individual consultant or with the intervention assistance team. If a team approach is used, one or more primary consultants are selected to work with the teacher, depending on the situation (for example, a psychologist for a behavioral problem). The primary consultant and the teacher engage in collaborative problem solving (see Bergan & Kratochwill, 1990). The main components of the process are outlined in Figure 13.1. Follow-up is generally done by the primary consultant; however, the entire team may be involved if further problem clarification or new intervention approaches need to be considered.

Figure 13.1. Flow Chart for Problem Analysis and Intervention Planning.

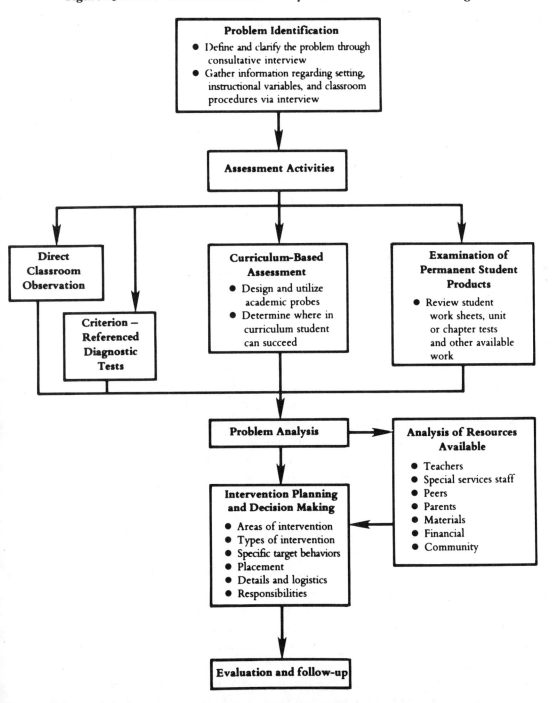

Source: Based on Lentz (1987). Reprinted from Zins et al. (1988), *Helping students succeed in the regular classroom.* Copyright 1988, Jossey-Bass Publishers, Inc., San Francisco. Reprinted with permission.

Case Illustrations

Two examples of school-based consultation illustrate the specific steps of the process. The first focuses on an elementary school student; the second involves one in high school. Several points of interest are highlighted, including collaboration among teachers, parents, and special services personnel and organizational factors that influenced the process.

Case Study: Elementary School

The first case involved a first-grader, John, whose school used an intervention assistance model similar to that described above. The school psychologist served as the primary consultant in the case; parents and other school personnel were active in the problem-solving process at various stages.

   Problem Identification and Analysis. Substantial attention was given to problem identification, as the success of problem solving is linked to how well a problem has been clarified (Bergan & Tombari, 1976). During the initial consultation session, teachers said that John was experiencing difficulty staying on task, following directions, learning classroom and lunchroom routines, and mastering basic math facts, sight words, and letter blends. It became evident that general consultation goals would first need to be established to provide a framework for organizing and conceptualizing more specific performance objectives for John (Kratochwill & Bergan, 1990). Teachers were assisted in clarifying and prioritizing their concerns. Two general long-range goals were then developed for John: improving attentional skills and increasing mastery of addition facts. Because John was already receiving remedial reading instruction through the Chapter 1 program and help with following directions in language therapy, these areas were not initially identified as priorities for additional intervention.

   John's teachers had held a number of conferences with his parents to inform them of their concerns. Because consultation is enhanced when parents are involved actively (Sheridan, Kratochwill, & Elliott, 1990), another meeting was held with John's parents to explain the consultation process, gather additional information about attentional and academic skills at home, and obtain permission to use further assessment strategies, such as behavioral observations and curriculum-based probes of his math skills. The specific information obtained through these procedures aided in target behavior selection.

   A third consultative meeting focused on John's attentional skills. It was revealed that he did not possess many basic prerequisite skills for attending, such as looking at the teacher during instruction and following on the correct page, and that he was not staying on task when asked to complete classwork independently. Several direct observations were completed in the classroom to gain a baseline of John's on-task behavior. Data also were collected on randomly selected peers to determine a class norm for on-task behavior. An interval recording procedure was used, and on-task behavior was observed over a period of several days during both instructional and seatwork periods. John was on task in 38 percent of the intervals during instruction but only 13 percent of the intervals during independent seatwork. On average, he was on task 25 percent of the time, in contrast to an average of 83 percent for comparison peers, a discrepancy large enough to warrant further problem solving (Kratochwill & Bergan, 1990). When off task, John was usually engaged in some type of motor activity, such as moving his chair, playing with objects, or tapping on his desk.

A structured teacher interview was conducted to gain additional information about the math curriculum, instructional procedures used in the classroom, contingencies in effect for accuracy and work completion, and John's math performance compared with the class norm (see Shapiro, 1989, for a more detailed description and examples). Data from this interview suggested further assessment needs and possible modifications of the instructional environment. Single-digit addition probes were then administered to gain a baseline of John's performance. The probes indicated that he accurately completed one single-digit addition problem within a two-minute period, suggesting that John had a skills deficit. However, it was unclear to what degree his attentional problems were related to his lack of mastery of basic math facts.

The accumulated data were used to specify performance objectives for John and as a means of monitoring his progress (Shapiro, 1989). His math goal was subdivided into two objectives: improving sight recognition of addition facts to ten and increasing fluency with addition facts to ten. The teachers expressed the need for additional intervention agents, so the school psychologist enlisted the aid of two practicum students from a nearby university to help in implementation. With parental permission, they were assigned to work with John and one other first-grade student needing intervention.

During the next consultative meeting, the language therapist was asked to participate in the problem-solving process. Two objectives were identified to improve John's attentional skills: increasing the amount of time during which he attended to the teacher during instructional periods and increasing time on task during independent seatwork periods. The first objective was then broken down into more specific performance skills to be taught, including looking at the person who is talking or instructing and looking at the correct page when appropriate.

Plan Implementation: Improving Attentional Skills. This phase focused on selecting the most appropriate intervention and specifying the details of implementation. John's parents and school personnel collaboratively generated a number of intervention ideas and chose to begin with the most parsimonious and least intrusive intervention. The language therapist taught John to look at the speaker (an individualized education plan goal) and reinforced this behavior in her small group for a few weeks. The teachers and parents began verbally prompting this behavior and reinforcing occurrences in the classroom and at home with social praise. Progress was evaluated with event recording for three weeks, but no significant change in attending behavior occurred. Consequently, all personnel met again, analyzed the intervention, and developed a more structured plan.

Two goals were developed for John that were reviewed with him each morning: to look at the teacher while she was talking and to follow along on the correct page. Two fifteen-minute instructional periods were selected each day during which behavior was monitored. A response-cost procedure was used whereby each time John had to be reminded by the teacher to attend, a face would be crossed off his monitoring sheet. If he had three of six faces left by the end of the fifteen-minute interval, he received a special treat at home that night. The teachers continued to verbally praise him in the classroom when he was on task.

Plan Implementation: Improving Mastery of Math Facts. This intervention consisted of John being tutored for thirty minutes three times a week by a university practicum student. Tutoring focused on mastery of addition facts to ten and then proceeded to addition teen facts. A stimulus-delay procedure (Touchette & Howard, 1984) was used to teach math facts. Initially, John was shown flash cards, immediately provided with the answers, and then asked to model the tutor's response. After two trials, a three-second delay was introduced before the answer was provided. Finally, a six-second delay was introduced. Consistent incorrect responses led to a shortening of the delay. John was to provide the answer before the tutor did and received reinforcement for the number of flash cards mastered each session. Flash cards mastered were reviewed periodically, and any facts not recognized within five seconds were returned to the drill.

Evaluation and Follow-Up. This crucial phase focused on evaluating the effectiveness of the plan. As shown in this case, it is often necessary to return to previous stages of consultation to reevaluate and refine the intervention (Kratochwill, Elliott, & Rotto, 1990). John's progress in the areas of mastery of and fluency in addition facts was measured by continual use of curriculum-based probes. To promote generalization, the probes initially were similar to the two-minute timed tests taken in class (100 typed problems). Correct digits per minute were counted and graphed to monitor progress (see Shapiro, 1989). John earned points for each correct digit, which could be exchanged daily for items from a treasure chest or for time at the water fountain.

Follow-up indicated that, although John was mastering flash cards during the tutoring sessions, there was little carry-over of this knowledge in written form on the probes. After seven weeks, he demonstrated no significant progress on the addition probes (see Figure 13.2) or in the classroom. It was more difficult for the tutor to keep John focused during the two-minute probe than during oral tutoring drill. It was hypothesized that the problem might be with the written response format of the probes, so the probe sheet was reduced to fifty problems. However, John continued to have difficulty attending during the written probe and still made no noticeable progress in the classroom. Although the instructional procedure seemed to be effective, the conditions that would maximize the probability that he could translate his knowledge into written form still needed to be identified.

After further analysis and problem solving, the following changes were introduced into the intervention procedure. The tutor continued to use a stimulus-delay procedure; however, the number of flash cards to be mastered was reduced from ten to five. The probe was reduced to only twenty-five problems and handwritten with colored pens instead of typed, to catch John's attention. A self-instructional component was added. Before each probe was administered, the tutor told John to go slowly, think before he wrote, and concentrate on getting more problems correct. An effect was seen almost immediately after these modifications were implemented. Correct digits per minute began to increase, while incorrect digits per minute decreased significantly (see Figure 13.2). John was able to maintain improved performance throughout the remainder of the school year. Similar modifications in required response format were implemented in the classroom, and John demonstrated improvement there as well.

The intervention to improve John's attentional skills was moderately successful. He achieved his goals 82 percent of the time during the fifteen-minute intervals. However, these intervals were not increased substantially over the school year.

Case Study: Secondary School

Provision of consultation services in secondary schools is somewhat different from its elementary counterpart. While the fundamentals of collaborative partnership, problem solving, and accountability remain constant across settings, the nature of the secondary school and the population that it serves create distinct differences in how consultation is carried out.

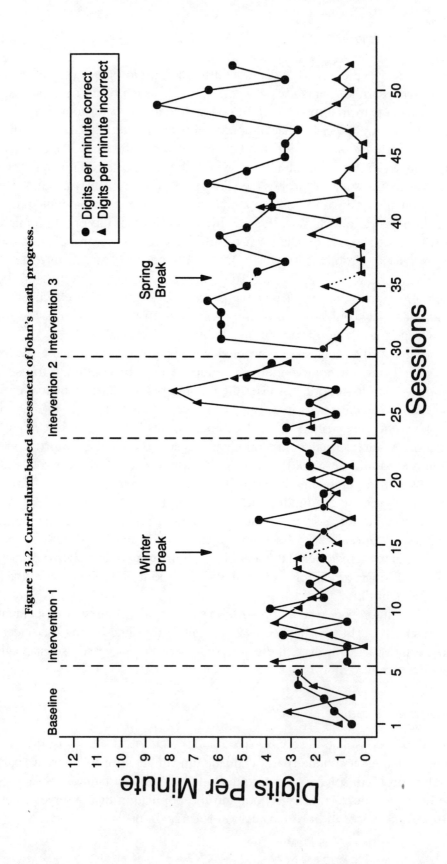

Figure 13.2. Curriculum-based assessment of John's math progress.

Secondary schools are generally larger in size and more complex in layout than those housing younger students. Typically, space is divided into areas with specific functions and specializations, and teachers consequently tend to be physically distant from those who do not share their curriculum area, which may inhibit communication (Nagle & Medway, 1982). This physical isolation is complemented by the organizational structure of the secondary school. A large number of teachers, assistants, and others usually staff the school, and each individual specializes in one or two subject areas. Teachers see a different group of students during each of five or six periods throughout the day, often teaching 100 to 150 different students every day. Further, high school administrative structures tend to be fairly autocratic, and teachers have little involvement in decision making. As a consequence of their specialization and isolation, high school teachers tend to view their job responsibilities more narrowly than do elementary teachers (Nagle & Medway, 1982). They are less likely to feel responsible for or take ownership of problems related to an individual student and consequently may not request student-centered consultation as frequently.

Problem Identification and Analysis. In this case, consultation was initiated by the parents of a fifteen-year-old girl who expressed concerns about her academic progress. Parents are often the initiators of services for their adolescent children (Fisch, Weakland, & Segal, 1982), which may be due in part to the organizational variables discussed previously. Holly was described as struggling academically since seventh grade, earning five grades of D and one F during her freshman year. Her mother felt that Holly was putting forth little effort in class or on homework. She reported that after two quarters, her daughter was continuing to receive poor grades and was in danger of failing several classes.

Holly was enrolled in a large rural high school where teachers had until recently met infrequently for planning or for staff meetings. The provision of consultation was particularly difficult because of the specialization and relative isolation of the teachers and resistance to such services from a number of more experienced teachers.

In responding to Holly's parents' concerns, the school psychologist-consultant's first step was to identify and clarify the problem. Holly and each of her teachers were interviewed. Adolescents' increasing capacity for abstract thought and problem solving, as well as their desire for independence from adult authority, suggests their inclusion in the consultation process (Keating, 1980). Interventions designed exclusively by adults that exclude students from the decision-making process may be sabotaged. Holly's participation turned out to be critical in devising an acceptable intervention. Holly reported a dislike of schoolwork and said that her parents' attempts at motivating her, such as verbal reprimands and grounding, made her angry. Her response was to refuse to do any work. At the conclusion of the interview, Holly expressed interest in improving her grades so that college might be an option and agreed to cooperate in the intervention process.

Individual consultations with Holly's teachers revealed concerns that generalized across classes. These included lack of effort in class and failure to take notes or to do homework consistently. All teachers perceived her as capable of achieving at least a B in their class, although she in fact was earning one C, two D's, and two F's.

During the second meeting with Holly's parents, problems were further clarified. Her parents agreed that their motivational strategies had been unsuccessful and that consequences had been applied inconsistently. Holly's father was quick to ground Holly for poor grades, while her mother tended to excuse Holly's behavior and allow her to escape her father's punishments. Further, a consistent study time had not been established at home. Holly's parents then met with their daughter and the consultant to jointly identify goals and intervention strategies. The identified problems, Holly's lack of effort and work completion and parental inconsistency, were reviewed, and the consultant then moderated negotiations between Holly and her parents regarding goals (Shapiro, 1976).

Plan Implementation. After mutually agreeable goals had been identified, intervention strategies were discussed. A written behavioral contract was negotiated specifying Holly's goals and the consequences of meeting or failing to meet expectations. A goal of achieving A or B grades in all subjects on her report card was established. A ninety-minute study period was instituted at home six days per week. If homework was completed early, Holly was to read or do extra-credit work for the remainder of the study period. She was also required to have her teachers complete a progress checklist each Friday and to give it to her parents. If Holly completed her responsibilities and achieved at least 90 percent on her checklist, she could go out or have a friend over on Friday. Achievement of all A or B grades on the next report card would be rewarded with permission to begin dating, while a D or F would result in grounding.

Several comments concerning the contract are warranted. First, the consultant believed that achievement of all A and B letter grades was an unrealistic goal for Holly, whose present performance ranged from C to F. It was suggested that more realistic grade goals be established or that only one or two subject areas initially be addressed and that a multiple-baseline design be used, adding other subject areas at a later time (Gresham & Kendell, 1987). However, Holly's parents were opposed to these recommendations. The school psychologist met with each of Holly's teachers, explained the contract and checklist, and responded to concerns. The rewards specified in the contract were of Holly's choosing.

Finally, the progress checklist was used to increase Holly's sense of responsibility for her own behavior. It also provided a means of collecting data regarding intervention effectiveness and informed Holly's parents of her progress on a weekly basis, thereby keeping them involved.

Evaluation and Follow-Up. Holly's academic behavior improved following implementation of the contract. She achieved her 90 percent behavioral goal for each of the first five weeks of the intervention. Her grades at the end of the term reflected behavioral change but were not as high as had been hoped. She raised her grades in four of the five problem areas by one letter grade or more. At this time, the consultant suggested another problem-solving meeting with Holly, her parents, and her teachers. All of Holly's teachers participated with the exception of the typing teacher, who was a long-term faculty member (individual meetings with him were scheduled later). Teachers at the meeting shared the perception that Holly had improved in her performance, but not to optimal levels. Several teachers stated that Holly was not bringing the progress checklist to them consistently, so the contract was modified accordingly. Holly was to receive a minus each time she failed to bring the progress checklist to any teacher. In addition, more realistic grade expectations were established for Holly, requiring her to earn B and C grades on her report card to earn her reward.

Holly's parents acknowledged an occasional failure to follow the terms of the contract; twice they did not provide the reward specified, and they were also inconsistent in enforcing study time. They recognized that their failure to adhere to the contract might have contributed to Holly's failure to meet her goals and took steps to be more consistent in the future.

The intervention was more successful in some classes than in others. Although Holly initially did not meet the stated overall grade goal, she improved her grades in all but one class. The intervention further provided Holly's family with an experience in negotiation to achieve goals, thus empowering them to better resolve difficulties in the future (Witt & Martens, 1988). It also increased collaboration and problem solving among the majority of Holly's teachers and established a more effective parent-educator partnership. The results might have been more positive if this group had convened more frequently and if all of Holly's teachers had actively participated.

Conclusion

The case studies presented in this chapter illustrate a number of important points with respect to consulting in schools:

1. Consultation and intervention development require comprehensive analysis and problem solving on the part of the participants. Both cases illustrate that the steps of solving problems are fluid and not always sequential. In the follow-up phase, consultants and consultees had to return to problem analysis on more than one occasion.
2. All interventions should be evaluated through some method of data collection. For example, the first case demonstrated how data were used to make decisions about student progress and about modifications in instructional strategies and response formats needed to promote acquisition of attentional skills and math facts.
3. In developing interventions, it is important to explore existing resources and to identify alternative intervention agents. In the first case, university practicum students were trained to implement the intervention. However, parents, grandparents, or peer tutors can all be effective, particularly when the goal is to teach basic skills.
4. A careful assessment should be made of the training necessary for consultees or other intervention agents. It is often unrealistic to simply describe a procedure and then expect it to be carried out. Training through demonstration and role playing may be necessary. In addition, agents should be taught to collect and graph data and appropriately administer reinforcement.
5. In choosing intervention strategies, those that are empirically validated deserve primary consideration. Still, modification will likely be necessary to ensure success in each unique situation.
6. The second case demonstrated the importance of allowing older students to become more active participants in consultation and highlighted the parent-professional relationship.

Consultation is rapidly becoming a preferred model of service delivery in schools for special services staff. It provides a means for these professionals to organize their services efficiently and to effectively meet the many problems encountered by today's schools and the students who attend them. As stated previously, consultation can be provided most effectively when it is established as an integral component of the educational system and well integrated with other services.

Further research into the consultation process and the impact of consultation on student outcome variables could contribute to the enhancement of services. Development and evaluation of alternative formats for in-service training would also be beneficial. Finally, increased collaboration between field practitioners and university-based researchers could provide a stimulus for creative new ideas, identification of effective practices, and more account-ability. It is our hope that this chapter will be associated with enhanced practice and research in these stimulating settings.

References

Alderman, G. (1989). Disaster team works during crisis. *NASP Communique, 18*(3), 24.

Bergan, J. R., & Kratochwill, T. K. (1990). *Behavioral consultation and therapy.* New York: Plenum Press.

Bergan, J. R., & Tombari, M. L. (1976). Consultant skill and efficiency and the implementation and outcomes of consultation. *Journal of School Psychology, 14,* 3–14.

Branden-Muller, L. R., & Elias, M. J. (1991). Catalyzing the primary prevention revolution in schools: The role of school psychologists. *Journal of Educational and Psychological Consultation, 2*(1), 73–88.

Dillard, H. (1989). Winnetka: One year later. *NASP Communique, 17*(9), 17–20.

Elias, M. J. (1987). Establishing enduring prevention programs: Advancing the legacy of Swampscott. *American Journal of Community Psychology, 15,* 539–553.

Fisch, R., Weakland, J. H., & Segal, L. (1982). *The tactics of change: Doing therapy briefly.* San Francisco: Jossey-Bass.

Gibelman, M. (1991). NASP responds to Operation Desert Storm: Project underway with DoDDS. *NASP Communique, 19*(5), 1–2.

Gresham, F. M., & Kendell, G. K. (1987). School consultation research: Methodological critique and future research directions. *School Psychology Review, 16,* 306–316.

Gutkin, T. B., & Curtis, M. J. (1990). School-based consultation: Theory, techniques, and research. In T. B. Gutkin & C. R. Reynolds (Eds.), *The handbook of school psychology* (2nd ed., pp. 577–611). New York: Wiley.

Keating, D. (1980). Thinking processes in adolescence. In J. Adelson (Ed.), *Handbook of adolescent psychology* (pp. 211–246). New York: Wiley.

Kratochwill, T. R., & Bergan, J. R. (1990). *Behavioral consultation in applied settings: An individual guide.* New York: Plenum Press.

Kratochwill, T. R., Elliott, S. N., & Rotto, P. C. (1990). Best practices in behavioral consultation. In A. T. Thomas & J. Grimes (Eds.), *Best practices in school psychology* (2nd ed., pp. 147–169). Silver Spring, MD: National Association of School Psychologists.

Lentz, F. E. (1987). *Functional assessment of academic problems.* Workshop presented for the Hamilton County Office of Education, Cincinnati, OH.

Lloyd, J. W., Singh, N. N., & Repp, A. C. (Eds.). (1991). *The regular education initiative: Alternative perspectives on concepts, issues, and models.* Sycamore, IL: Sycamore.

Nagle, R. J., & Medway, F. J. (1982). Issues in providing psychological services at the high school level. *School Psychology Review, 11,* 359–369.

Pugach, M. C., & Johnson, L. J. (1990). Meeting diverse student needs through peer collaboration. In W. Stainback & S. Stainback (Eds.), *Support networks for inclusive schooling* (pp. 123–138). Baltimore, MD: Brookes.

Shapiro, D., Jr. (1976). Altering school truancy and petty theft. In J. D. Krumboltz & C. E. Thorenson (Eds.), *Counseling methods* (pp. 47–56). New York: Holt, Rinehart & Winston.

Shapiro, E. S. (Ed.). (1989). *Academic skills problems: Direct assessment and intervention.* New York: Guilford Press.

Sheridan, S. M., Kratochwill, T. R., & Elliott, S. N. (1990). Behavioral consultation with parents and teachers: Delivering treatment for socially withdrawn children at home and school. *School Psychology Review, 19*(1), 33–52.

Touchette, P. E., & Howard, J. S. (1984). Errorless learning: Reinforcement contingencies and stimulus control transfer in delayed prompting. *Journal of Applied Behavioral Analysis, 17,* 175–188.

Witt, J. C., & Martens, B. K. (1988). Problems with problem-solving consultation: A re-analysis of assumptions, methods, and goals. *School Psychology Review, 17,* 211–226.

Youngstrom, N. (1992). Psychology helps a shattered L.A. *APA Monitor, 23*(7), 1, 12.

Zins, J. E. (1992). Implementing school-based consultation services: An analysis of five years of practice. In R. K. Conyne & J. O'Neil (Eds.), *Organizational consultation: A casebook* (pp. 50–79). Newbury Park, CA: Sage.

Zins, J. E., Curtis, M. J., Graden, J. L., & Ponti, C. R. (1988). *Helping students succeed in the regular classroom: A guide for developing intervention assistance programs.* San Francisco: Jossey-Bass.

Zins, J. E., & Forman, S. G. (Eds.). (1988). Primary prevention: From theory to practice [Special issue]. *School Psychology Review, 17*(4).

Zins, J. E., & Ponti, C. R. (1987). Prereferral consultation: A system to decrease special education referral and placement. *The Community Psychologist, 20,* 10–12.

14

Behavioral Consultation in Hospital Settings

Keith J. Slifer, Marilyn Cataldo,
Roberta L. Babbitt, Michael F. Cataldo

Pediatric psychology has evolved as a unique discipline over the past twenty-five years. The primary activities of the pediatric psychologist have included developmental evaluation, consultation to parents on child-rearing techniques, and either direct treatment or consultation with medical professionals concerning how to manage behavioral and psychological manifestations of physical illness. A more comprehensive discussion of the scope and history of the field can be found elsewhere (Roberts, 1986; Routh, 1988; Wright, Schaefer, & Solomons, 1979).

Behavioral pediatrics is a subspecialty that is closely related to pediatric psychology. While there is considerable overlap between the two, behavioral pediatrics emphasizes an empirical approach to the assessment and treatment of behavioral phenomena in relation to medical variables. Measuring observable behavior and demonstrating the effects of behavioral variables on biological events (and vice versa) are the primary defining characteristics of the field (Russo & Varni, 1982; Sugai & Luiselli, 1989). Addressing these issues through consultation to medical staff has been an important focus in recent years.

Rationale for a Consultation Approach

The majority of patients seen by pediatricians present with problems that are, at least in part, psychological in nature (Drotar, Benjamin, Chwast, Litt, & Vajner, 1982; Duff, Rowe, & Anderson, 1973). Lacking the training and the time to address these concerns, many pediatricians refer patients to consulting psychologists. Referrals in the hospital ordinarily focus on facilitating child and family adaptation to illness and hospitalization, preparing the child for medical procedures, ensuring the child's cooperation with medical treatment and unit routines, and helping the child cope with pain, fear, separation from parents, and the psychosocial consequences of chronic illness (Mesibov & Johnson, 1982). In addition, many referrals focus on the special needs of children with developmental disabilities who are confronting these same problems in the medical setting. Many pediatric psychologists work in a comprehensive medical care center where they provide direct and indirect services to both inpatients and outpatients. In this type of setting, as in educational settings, the demand for direct services far exceeds available resources. Therefore, indirect methods of service provision have become essential.

Models of Consultation

Approaches to the provision of consultation in pediatric and other applied settings, which have been referred to as "models," are described in detail elsewhere (Drotar et al., 1982; Kratochwill & Bergan, 1990; Roberts, 1986; Sugai & Luiselli, 1989; see also Chapter Two). The models most relevant to consultation in pediatric hospitals are summarized below.

When following the *independent functions* (Roberts, 1986) or *noncollaborative* (Drotar et al., 1982; Stabler, 1979) model, the psychologist practices as an independent professional who receives referrals from physicians, provides psychological diagnosis and treatment, and shares information with the referring physician. The *indirect model* describes a primarily educational approach to consultation in which the psychologist teaches at seminars, rounds, conferences, or individual "supervision" (tutorial) sessions. The psychologist may have no direct contact with the patient, instead training or advising individual medical professionals or the staff of a particular unit (Burns & Cromer, 1978; Roberts, 1986; Stabler, 1979). In the *collaborative team* (Burns & Cromer, 1978; Roberts, 1986) or *process consultation* (Stabler, 1979) model, the psychologist functions as a regular member of a multidisciplinary team. Finally, *consultation liaison* refers to an approach in which there is an ongoing and relatively long-term relationship between the consultant and a particular staff member or unit involving a combination of approaches to service delivery (Sugai & Luiselli, 1989).

The Behavioral Psychology Consultation Service

The Behavioral Psychology Consultation Service is a group of psychologists and behavior analysts who provide specialized consultation and related services (involving behavioral measurement and management) to medical staff within the Johns Hopkins medical institutions. The authors are the faculty members responsible for this service.

For more than fifteen years, psychologists and behavior analysts in our setting have been consulting with a variety of medical specialty units, including neurorehabilitation, pulmonary disease, clinical research, psychiatry, developmental disabilities, pediatric surgery, neurology, neurosurgery, oncology, genetics, dentistry, gastroenterology, and occupational and physical therapies. The reasons for referral have been noncompliance with medical regimens (21 percent), food refusal or selective eating (19 percent), disruptive behavior (19 percent), self-injury or other stereotypies (14 percent), physical aggression (9 percent), toilet training (6 percent), ingestion of nonfood material (5 percent), social withdrawal or mutism (2 percent), impulsiveness (2 percent), noncompliance with caregiver instructions (2 percent), and sleep disturbance (1 percent).

Collaborative Consultation in an Academic Medical Setting

The conceptual model followed by our service is *behavioral* and *ecological,* with particular emphasis on measurement of observable behavior and environmental variables and on a systematic analysis of the relationship between the two. While intrapsychic and biological variables are considered and targeted when appropriate and possible, interventions depend primarily on manipulation of the physical and social environment.

The *process* of consultation in our setting is similar to that described by Bergan and Kratochwill (1990; see also Chapter Four). The consultant and the referring physicians engage in a joint, systematic problem-solving effort that extends over a period of months to years, proceeding through problem identification, problem analysis, treatment implementation, and evaluation. The process occurs on two levels: (1) on a case-by-case basis and (2) through the development of innovative, unitwide intervention programs that evolve over time and span many cases. At times, the focus is on solving problems related to a specific case. At other times, a broader perspective is taken, with the collaboration focusing on programmatic or systems-level issues. There are repeated contacts between consultant and consultee to evaluate the feasibility, effectiveness, acceptability (to patient, family, and medical staff), and cost of the interventions developed. Both individual case data (using single-subject, repeated-measures research designs) and treatment outcome data (using group statistical and experimental designs) are evaluated during this process. The primary steps in this consultation approach can be summarized as follows:

1. Consultant meets with medical staff to operationally define the problem, select target behavior of children and staff, and select a method of data collection.

2. Skills to be taught children or staff are task analyzed.
3. Baseline data are obtained, unless medically precluded.
4. Consultants propose potential intervention protocol.
5. Consultant and medical staff review and revise protocol.
6. Consultants demonstrate intervention with "test cases."
7. Consultant and medical staff review results of test cases to identify problems and determine whether large-scale application is feasible.
8. Large-scale application is jointly implemented by consultant and medical staff, and treatment outcome data are recorded.
9. Treatment outcome data are reviewed with medical staff, and if they are favorable, protocol is adopted.
10. Medical staff are intensively trained and assume responsibility for protocol implementation.
11. Consultant continues to treat complex cases and assists with periodic program evaluation.

A consultation service of this type requires a combination of direct and indirect services, with increasing emphasis on the indirect as both the relationship and the technology develop over time. The initial work is case-oriented; by working directly with difficult cases, the consultant identifies the variables in the medical setting controlling problem behavior. There are many similarities across cases, and eventually a standard approach to a particular type of problem is developed. As this occurs, greater emphasis is placed on teaching medical staff to implement these procedures themselves. As the consulting relationship evolves, the consultee changes from individual patient to individual medical staff to groups of medical staff and, finally, to a particular unit or department.

In the following examples, we highlight some areas of collaboration and integration at our institution. As a result of these experiences, we have discovered obstacles that are not inherent in the particular subject matter but related to the dissemination of knowledge, the coordination of care, and the management of patients' responses to medical stimuli. For example, hospital settings themselves can cause or exacerbate maladaptive behavior in children. The absence of structured daily routines, inconsistency among the responses of multiple caregivers to child behavior, and hospital staff with no training in systematic approaches to behavior management all interact to create a setting in which the child has little opportunity to predict or control either positive or negative events. In response, children typically develop elaborate repertoires of avoidant or disruptive behavior, such as crying, tantrums, aggression, lethargy, and excessive sleep. Social withdrawal, separation anxiety, loss of self-care skills, and sleep and feeding disturbances frequently emerge, even in children with good premorbid adjustment. In our work with these patients, we have demonstrated that the inclusion of routine behavior management strategies such as behavioral contracts, token economy point systems, and self-monitoring can quickly reverse these problem behaviors. Through the consultation process described above, we have integrated behavior management systems into many of these settings, with the ultimate goal of preventing the emergence of behavioral problems.

Consultation with Pediatric Oncology

Our service has a well-established consulting relationship with the children's cancer services. We have directly treated children who present major disruptive behavior problems and later trained the unit staff to implement behavior management protocols themselves. Staff have been taught to make the environment as positive and predictable as possible by separating painful procedures physically and temporally from "safe" activities of the day. They have also been instructed to praise appropriate behavior, particularly compliance with medical and daily care routines, and to ignore disruptive and noncompliant behavior while prompting and demonstrating cooperative behavior. The percentages of noncompliant behavior for each of three children treated during the demonstration phase of consultation with the cancer unit staff using this approach are presented in Figure 14.1. The children's behavior was scored as compliant if they allowed staff to conduct necessary medical procedures without disruption (screaming, hitting, kicking, and so on) and noncompliant if such disruption occurred. Both staff and child behavior was measured when staff used standard cancer unit procedures and after they had been trained to implement the behavioral protocol. Staff members' behavior was scored as appropriate or not as they were observed to follow or deviate from the protocol. Data were recorded using a time-sample format in which the child and staff were observed briefly and their behavior coded at regular intervals.

In these cases, a single-subject experimental design (multiple baseline across patients) was used to systematically demonstrate the effects of training unit staff to implement basic behavior management recommendations. Results indicate that staff behavior changed markedly from a mean of less than 20 percent correct performance in baseline to 97 percent correct during treatment. The behavior of the three children dramatically improved, with noncompliance decreasing from an overall mean of 69 percent during standard unit procedures to 7 percent when treatment was implemented. After this type of consultation, the unit staff and medical directors better recognize the need for incorporating behavioral technology into pediatric environments. For this to be done effectively, however, experts in behavior analysis need to be integrated into the teams that plan, design, and operate these environments. They

**Figure 14.1. Percentages of Noncompliant Child Behavior
Before and After Staff Training.**

Behavioral psychology consultation with pediatric cancer unit staff

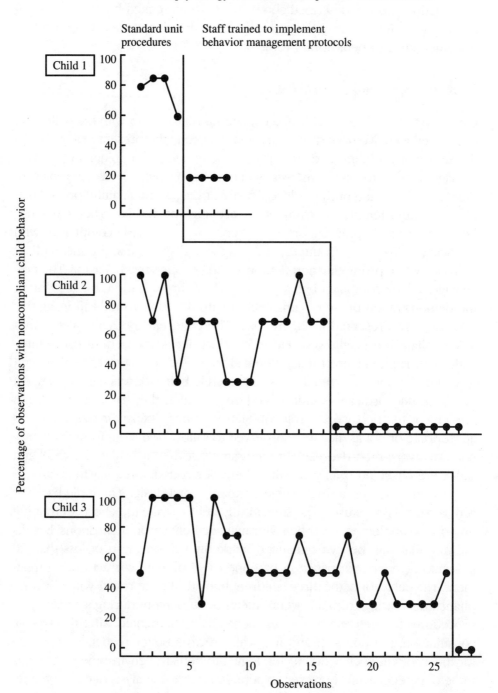

must also be routinely included in the educational programs that train the medical staff.

Preparing Children to Cooperate with "High-Tech" Procedures

Another of our programs has focused on training children to cooperate with high-tech procedures such as brain scans, radiation therapy for tumors, brain electrical activity tests, breathing tests, and cardiac exercise stress tests. We have demonstrated that with a combination of environmental changes and behavioral teaching procedures, even young and behavior-disordered children can learn to cooperate with such nonpainful but nevertheless frightening procedures. Even many preschoolers can be taught to meet the demands for cooperation and strict motion control required for these procedures without sedation. However, for this to occur, several features of the medical setting must be altered. First, the environment, which is dominated by large, frightening equipment, must be modified to be "child-friendly" and to minimize fear and avoidance. Second, ample access to the equipment must be provided to allow for gradual and systematic desensitization of the child to it. Third, tangible and social reinforcers (rewards) must be available and provided contingent on cooperation. Fourth, the child must be given the opportunity to practice the behavior necessary for cooperation. This requires some redesign of the physical environment and the system for managing referrals and patient flow. Fifth, the child must be referred early to allow for coordination and provision of behavioral training. Finally, trained staff must be available to implement reinforcement procedures during waiting room and treatment times. Waiting areas need to be designed to prevent long waits and to provide positive events that compete with anticipatory anxiety. While we have shown that many improvements can be introduced to existing medical settings, they could be incorporated more efficiently if given consideration during design, construction, or renovation of facilities.

Our protocols for preparing children for brain scans and radiation treatment have shown that children can learn to lie motionless for up to seventy-five minutes for diagnostic imaging, given adequate training and reinforcement contingencies (Slifer, Cataldo, Cataldo, & Burke, 1989). Exhibit 14.1 shows how behavior required to cooperate with radiation therapy was "task analyzed" into a series of steps or behavioral components. An observer using this form can code whether the child performs the steps described without physical guidance, vigorous protest, or attempts to escape.

Our protocol for desensitizing preschoolers to radiation therapy equipment and for shaping the necessary motion control to avoid sedation involves gradually introducing the child to the equipment. Demands for cooperation

Exhibit 14.1. Radiation Therapy Task Analysis.

Date:_____	Time:_____	Session no:_____	Observer:_____
Step	Description		Outcome (+, −, na)

Step	Description	Outcome
1	Child enters the practice, simulation, or treatment room without crying or attempting to escape (may hold an adult's hand or be carried).	
2	Child sits on patient support or examination table. Child may be lifted or assisted by an adult but does not cry or attempt to get down.	
3	Child lies in supine or prone position on table (in body cast if required for treatment) for brief practice session (two to five minutes) without crying or attempting to get up.	
4	Child lies in position as described in step 3 above for extended practice session (six to ten minutes).	
5	Child lies in position (in body cast when required) on simulator without moving while head is aligned, cranial x-rays are taken, developed, and checked, and landmarks are drawn on body with an indelible pen (approximately twenty minutes).	
6	Child lies in position as described in number 5 above while body is aligned, spinal x-rays are taken, developed, and checked, and spinal landmarks are drawn (approximately twenty minutes).	
7	Child lies in position as described above while cranial radiation treatment is administered (five to ten minutes)	
8	Child lies in position as described above while spinal radiation is administered (five to ten minutes)	

Steps required today _____
Steps achieved today _____
Percentage   _____

and motion control are gradually increased while these experiences are paired with a high density of social and tangible reinforcement (praise, hugs, stickers and other prizes). The child practices on the inactive machine and gradually progresses from sitting on a chair near it while holding a parent's hand, to sitting and then lying on it while having a Polaroid snapshot taken, to lying in the required position for increasing intervals. Children develop a history of reinforcement in the presence of the equipment, master the required skills, and learn that the procedures are not painful.

Figure 14.2 presents data on the percentage of required steps that were performed by two preschoolers who received the behavioral training. "Jack" was a four-and-a-half-year-old boy with cancer in his neck who responded to efforts to administer radiation treatment with noncompliance, tantrums, aggression, and self-injury. "Don" was a five-year-old boy with leukemia who wan noncompliant, cried, and attempted to escape from the radiation therapy

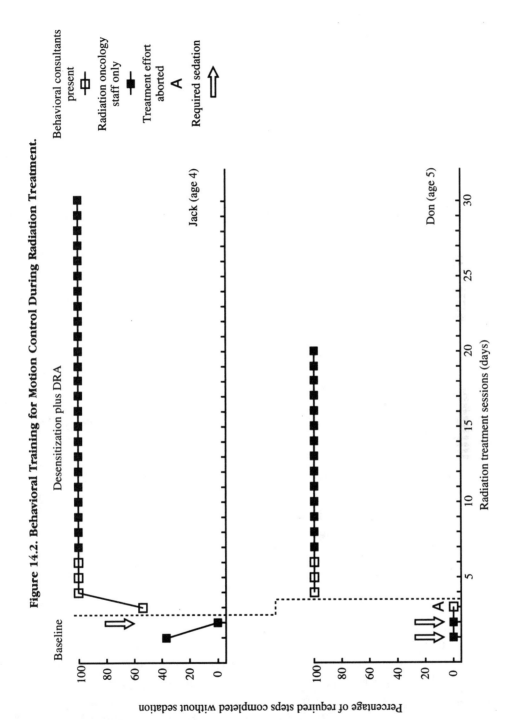

Figure 14.2. Behavioral Training for Motion Control During Radiation Treatment.

equipment. Consultation staff first demonstrated the procedures to establish initial cooperation in these children, thereby modeling teaching and motivational techniques for medical staff. Implementation of the procedures was then transferred to medical staff over the course of two to three treatment sessions. Both boys quickly learned to eagerly anticipate the social interactions with the radiation treatment staff, and both were able to complete their course of treatment without the need for sedation. The effectiveness of the behavioral intervention and the relative ease with which staff can be trained to carry out the intervention are highlighted by the multiple-baseline experimental design shown in Figure 14.2, which was used to demonstrate control of the boys' behavior by the intervention.

The above cases illustrate that behavioral problems related to medical procedures can often be managed with a brief but intensive behavioral consultation format. Once cooperative child behavior is established by behavioral consultants, control of teaching and motivational contingencies can be transferred to medical staff. As a result of this type of consultation and staff training over the course of a half dozen demonstration cases, the radiation technologists and nurses have now fully adopted this protocol and rarely require direct intervention by behavioral consultants.

Teaching Children to Swallow Oral Medication

In a different project, we have shown that children who must take life-sustaining medication can be taught to routinely swallow large capsules or distasteful liquids. This process requires that they be provided with systematic training using differential consequences to shape the ability to swallow these items without gagging or vomiting. It also requires timely behavioral training before an extensive history of conditioned vomiting and escape-avoidance behavior is established. The following is an example of a training program designed to teach routine pill and capsule swallowing to developmentally disabled children diagnosed with chronic illnesses (Babbitt, Parrish, Brierley, & Kohr, 1991).

Initially, baseline probes were conducted to determine whether the children could swallow the necessary-sized capsules before training. No programmatic contingencies were applied during baseline. Training consisted of verbal instruction, demonstration, reinforcement for swallowing candies or capsules progressively larger in size, ignoring mild inappropriate behavior, and gradually providing less guidance and structure.

"Jane" was a seven-year-old diagnosed with moderate mental retardation and partial ornithine transcarbamylase deficiency (an inborn error of metabolism). She had been prescribed four different medications requiring her to swallow twenty-four 23.7-millimeter capsules per day. Figure 14.3 displays the percentage of presented stimuli swallowed by Jane. She quickly mastered the candies and, eventually, practice (inert) pills and capsules of gradually increasing size. Total training time for this child was approximately forty-two minutes, and she was able to take her medication with supervision thereafter.

The results of this and multiple other cases support the premise that training children (including those with developmental disabilities) to accept and self-administer oral medications is a cost-efficient and relatively straightforward task that nurses and other medical staff can be trained to implement with the use of a consultation approach.

Ecological Considerations in the Hospital Environment

Our consultation work with medical units where children are admitted for extended hospitalizations has taught us that case-by-case consultation is usually not enough to produce lasting programmatic changes in medical staff behavior. These units benefit most from long-standing liaison relationships through which the behavioral technology of antecedent control and teaching by consequences is designed into the physical environment and the training curriculum. Medical staff need to be taught that children can learn even complex skills if provided with structured and developmentally appropriate training. Given the opportunity to learn before the medical procedure or medication is "forced upon them," children can and do learn to cooperate with medical technology. However, it is essential that medical staff be taught to recognize the types of cooperative and self-care skills that children can learn and that staff become familiar with the nature and timing of the required training protocols. Space for mock equipment is needed for preparing and desensitizing children. Actual equipment can be modified or camouflaged to appear less frightening and can be used for behavioral training when not in use for actual procedures. Reinforcement for cooperation can be incorporated into imaging and treatment routines. Patient scheduling and waiting room routines can be modified to decrease "downtime" during which children wait anxiously and become disruptive in an attempt to avoid feared medical treatment. The behaviorally trained consultant who maintains a long-term liaison relationship with the medical staff can help ensure that behavioral and psychological technologies are considered during key opportunities and incorporated into new programs.

Directions for Future Research

While the process of consultation has been researched at length in other settings, as detailed elsewhere in this volume, little attention has been given

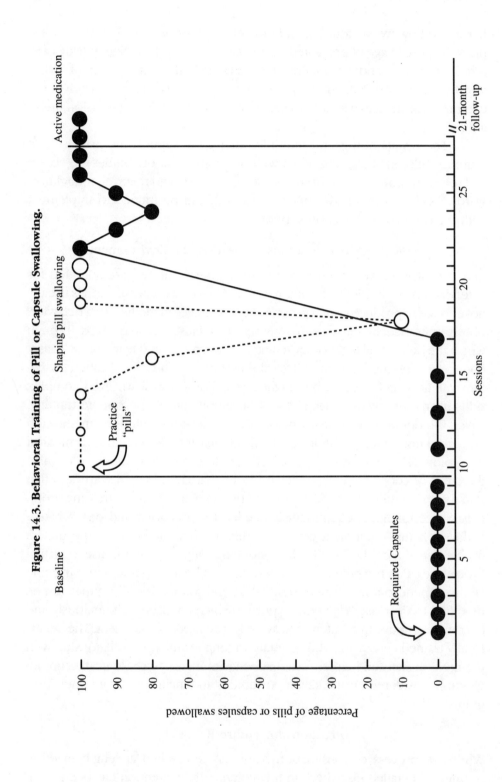

Figure 14.3. Behavioral Training of Pill or Capsule Swallowing.

to consultation research in pediatric medical settings. Others have researched intervention techniques for specific presenting problems (see Krasnegor, Arasteh, & Cataldo, 1986; Russo & Kedesdy, 1988; for many examples), and research on the child's response to hospitalization is extensive (Thompson, 1985). Considerable research has also been conducted on "psychological" preparation for surgery and medical procedures (see, for example, Melamed, Robbins, & Graves, 1982). This research on preparation for medical procedures has emphasized the effects of providing *information* about medical procedures to children awaiting medical treatment. Relatively little attention has been devoted to studying the types and complexity of cooperative child behavior required to meet the demands of medical diagnosis, treatment, and hospital routines. Some of the work described in this chapter highlights a preventive and educative approach in which children are taught specific skills required for benefiting from medical technology. More systematic research into the feasibility and limits of such an approach is an important priority. Finally, systematic study of the "process" of consultation (timing, method of communication and teaching, administrative organization, and so on) in relation to important medical outcome measures is needed. Demonstrating more efficient and effective strategies (both direct and indirect) for incorporating knowledge from the behavioral sciences into the provision of medical treatment and the administration of medical facilities is an important research objective for our field.

References

Babbitt, R. L., Parrish, J. P., Brierley, P. E., & Kohr, M. A. (1991). Teaching developmentally disabled children with chronic illness to swallow prescribed capsules. *Journal of Developmental & Behavioral Pediatrics, 12*(4), 229–235.

Bergan, J. R., & Kratochwill, T. R. (1990). *Behavioral consultation and therapy.* New York: Plenum Press.

Burns, B. J., & Cromer, W. W. (1978). The evolving role of the psychologist in primary health care practitioner training for mental health services. *Journal of Clinical Child Psychology, 7,* 8–12.

Drotar, D., Benjamin, P., Chwast, R., Litt, C., & Vajner, P. (1982). The role of the psychologist in pediatric outpatient and inpatient settings. In J. M. Tuma (Ed.), *Handbook for the practice of pediatric psychology* (pp. 229–250). New York: Wiley Interscience.

Duff, R. S., Rowe, D. S., & Anderson, F. P. (1973). Patient care and student learning in a pediatric clinic. *Pediatrics, 50,* 839–846.

Krasnegor, N. A., Arasteh, J. D., & Cataldo, M. F. (Eds.). (1986). *Child health behavior: A behavioral pediatrics perspective.* New York: Wiley.

Kratochwill, T. R., & Bergan, J. R. (1990). *Behavioral consultation in applied settings: An individual guide.* New York: Plenum Press.

Melamed, B. G., Robbins, R. L., & Graves, S. (1982). Preparation for surgery and medical procedures. In D. C. Russo & J. W. Varni (Eds.), *Behavioral pediatrics: Research and practice* (pp. 225–267). New York: Plenum Press.

Mesibov, G. B., & Johnson, M. R. (1982). Intervention techniques in pediatric psychology. In J. Tuma (Ed.), *Handbook for the practice of pediatric psychology* (pp. 110–164). New York: Wiley.

Roberts, M. C. (1986). *Pediatric psychology.* Elmsford, NY: Pergamon Press.

Routh, D. K. (1988). *Handbook of pediatric psychology.* New York: Guilford Press.

Russo, D. C., & Kedesdy, J. H. (1988). *Behavioral medicine with the developmentally disabled.* New York: Plenum Press.

Russo, D. C., & Varni, J. W. (1982). Behavioral pediatrics. In D. C. Russo & J. W. Varni (EDs.). *Behavioral pediatrics: Research and practice* (pp. 3–24). New York: Plenum Press.

Slifer, K. J., Cataldo, M. F., Cataldo, M. D., & Burke, J. C. (1989). Preparation for medical diagnostic imaging. Paper presented at the meeting of the American Psychological Association, New Orleans, LA.

Stabler, B. (1979). Emerging models of psychologist-pediatrician liaison. *Journal of Pediatric Psychology, 4,* 307–313.

Sugai, D. P., & Luiselli, J. K. (1989). Behavioral medicine consultation. In J. K. Luiselli (Ed.), *Behavioral medicine and developmental disabilities* (pp. 199–225). New York: Springer-Verlag.

Thompson, R. H. (1985). *Research on pediatric hospitalization.* Springfield, IL: Thomas.

Wright, L., Schaefer, A., & Solomons, G. (1979). *Encyclopedia of pediatric psychology.* Baltimore, MD: University Park Press.

15

Collaborating with the Community

Olga Reyes, Leonard A. Jason

As pointed out in Chapter One, consultation is defined in countless and varied ways. The authors of this chapter also have their own definition, borrowed largely from Caplan's conceptualization (1970) of mental health consultation. As it is discussed in the context of this chapter, consultation is a process of interaction between two professionals: the consultant, who is the presumed specialist, and the consultee, who seeks the consultant's advice or help with a work-related problem (Caplan, 1970). In the specific type of consultation discussed here, the consultee is an institution that is represented by the administrator and other personnel of that setting.

Within the parameters of this definition, the authors adopt a community psychology orientation in their approach to consultation, emphasizing such values as empowerment, prevention, competence, and an ecological focus (Heller, Price, Reinharz, Riger, & Wandersman, 1984). Like the authors of Chapter One, who also stress a preventive focus in consulting, we recognize that consultation affords the greatest potential benefit when it is used before serious problems may develop (Parsons & Meyers, 1984). Along these lines, our consulting approach aims for maximum client impact. That is, whenever possible, we attempt to intervene at a level within the system that allows for the maximum number of clients in the system to benefit. To this end, rather than focusing directly on the clients, as the authors of Chapter One do, we use an indirect service method in our consultative approach: clients are served indirectly by the consultant through the consultee.

The ecology of the setting is also taken into account. We appreciate the complex interplay between setting and clients and between setting and consultant. That is, organizational contextual factors are considered both in the design of interventions that serve the clients and in the approach used in providing consultation. Similarly, within that context, the consultant must also understand the setting "atmosphere," including its physical, social, and political character (Caplan, 1970). This information is used by the consultant to create the best possible climate for facilitating change.

Finally, empowerment and competence are important aspects of our consultation approach. Rather than "dictating" our expertise to consultees, we adhere to an approach that involves the mutual input of both consultant and consultee in a joint problem-solving process. The expertise of the consultee is accorded status equal to that of the consultant. The relationship between consultant and consultee is thus an egalitarian one that is respectful of the consultee's needs, opinions, and expertise. Ultimately, we aim to enhance a consultee's feelings of competence in the area for which consultation was sought. We also endeavor to empower consultees through the new knowledge imparted in the consultation and through the feelings of competence and self-efficacy engendered by our cooperative, mutually respectful, and collegial style.

Important components of a successful consultation include achieving the intended goals of the consultation, benefiting relevant parties (program, consultees, clients) in a measurable way, and providing consultees with useful and practical skills or knowledge. As with the definition of collaboration, there is no commonly defined sequence of steps in the consultation process, although the various conceptualizations of the process are more similar than different. Though some or all of these steps have been discussed in the consultation literature (Bergan & Kratochwill, 1990; Caplan, 1970; Meyers, Parsons, & Martin, 1979), five basic stages are common among the many definitions of this process: (1) gaining entry into the system, (2) identifying goals, (3) defining goals, (4) planning and implementing the intervention, and (5) assessing the impact of the consultation. Terminating the consultation relationship is sometimes seen as a part of this process as well. Implicit in and critical to the consultation process is the development of the relationship between the consultant and the consultee (Caplan, 1970).

The following case example describing a school consultation uses the framework of Parsons and Meyers (1984) to illustrate basic stages in the consultation process. It also draws on Caplan's work (1970) to discuss the process of building the consultant-consultee relationship. Caplan highlights the importance of this process, observing its often complex and lengthy nature. The prolonged nature of the relationship-building process in the present case illustration is captured in recalling entry into that system. The process of fostering a cooperative and collaborative atmosphere is also discussed.

Setting and Historical Context.

Many problems plague the predominantly Hispanic low-income inner-city high school served in this consultation, including high dropout rates, teen pregnancy, substance abuse, gangs, and violence. Because of its many social problems, the school has great appeal to researchers. However, researchers' disregard for the school's privacy and dignity in their handling of research findings has left school personnel very suspicious and reluctant to be involved in research. For example, one researcher who documented some of the school's serious problems divulged the damaging data to local newspapers without the school's permission. Researchers frequently try to gain access to this school, but the school's administrators respond by turning them away. It was in this atmosphere of hypervigilance and distrust that the first author had her initial contact with the school.

Gaining Entry and Establishing a Relationship

The first author and the principal had initially worked together on a project that involved identifying factors accounting for high-risk students' success in this setting (Reyes & Jason, 1993). In the project, students who were succeeding in the school were compared to those who were failing. The variables that differentiated the two groups were gang involvement and satisfaction with school.

Early in her initial visits to the school, as the staff learned of her purpose there, the consultant saw evidence of their suspiciousness. Some were frank in their reasons for distrust, specifically citing the publicized study that portrayed their school negatively. For example, in her exchange with the first author, one teacher annoyingly wondered, "Oh, are you going to study us and tell the world what a mess we are, too?" It was clear that establishing trust and acceptance would be a challenge. However, the consultant had the principal as her ally, and her interactions with him were conflict-free. For example, the consultant found it easy to see or call him with questions relevant to the project. Despite the fact that there were many others competing for his time, the consultant managed to gain access to the principal readily. The principal made it clear to the consultant that this informal meeting arrangement was acceptable.

As the manager of his hectic schedule, the principal's secretary was most concerned about his busy work life. The secretary guarded his time fiercely. She handled many "crisis" situations on her own, sparing the principal any unnecessary waste of his time. Her reward for the smooth and efficient management of her boss's overcommitted professional life was the deference accorded to her by the students, parents, other support staff, administrators, and the principal. Unknown to the consultant, the secretary resented the consultant's frequent bypassing of her carefully structured routine. On one unplanned visit during a chaotic day, the secretary sternly denied the consultant permission to see the principal. During her next visit to the school, the consultant stopped first at the secretary's desk and asked whether she could see the principal. Somewhat surprised at the consultant's deference, the secretary found a way to accommodate the consultant in spite of the principal's full schedule.

This experience proved to be an important lesson in identifying key members of the communication network. Caplan (1970) cites this as an important part of the process of building channels of communication. A key person who has easy access to other principal figures within the system can serve as a communication bridge between the consultant and those figures (Caplan, 1970). In this case, the secretary was such a person, with her ready access to the highest authority in that system and to other important office heads. The consultant thought that she was in an advantageous position because of her excellent relationship with the school's principal, the presumed source of power at the school. However, the secretary knew more about the school than even the principal did. She was a major resource and a powerful and influential figure, and her disapproval of something or someone carried great weight.

After this confrontation and the consultant's subsequent demonstrated respect of the secretary's authority, the secretary and the consultant began working cooperatively with each other. With the development of the more trusting relationship, the consultant began to notice that she had more friends in the school. Other support staff started smiling at her, calling her by name, recognizing her voice over the telephone, and generally being more helpful. The rest of that first consultation project went smoothly, aided the entire way by the unfailing assistance of the principal's secretary.

The consultant maintained her relationship with the school even after the project ended. She often provided informal consultation to the school and attended various school functions. Two years after this first formal project, the principal invited the consultant back to the school to conduct an evaluation of a school-based dropout prevention program (Reyes & Jason, 1991). Though the consultant knew many people in the school by this time, she had not had an opportunity to get to know the teachers who had created the dropout program very well, if at all. This consultation process is discussed next.

Collaborative Consultation

To initiate evaluation of the dropout prevention program, the principal arranged a meeting between the consultant and the teacher coordinator who had developed the program, recruited teacher participation, and secured the necessary administrative support. The dropout program consisted of two primary components: redefining the role of the homeroom teachers in order to extend greater, more substantive support to students and reducing the overall complexity of the setting for students by modifying the environmental structure. The latter component was also designed to facilitate greater peer support among program participants. The teacher coordinator was interested in determining how effective her program was in keeping students from dropping out of school.

Meetings with other program teachers did not take place until the beginning of the school year, because the program coordinator did not want to impose on teachers during their summer break. The teachers were in the process of renegotiating their contracts with the school board, and there was a strong likelihood of a teachers' strike. The summer was a critical time, because many issues surrounding the dropout prevention program evaluation were discussed and formulated at that time. The consultant was concerned that the program teachers were not involved in the consultation process from its inception.

Gluckstern and Packard (1977) advise using the team approach to bridge the consultant-consultee relationship, particularly in settings where outsiders, especially social scientists, are viewed with suspicion, as in the present case. The approach includes at least one insider from the setting, whose involvement in the consultation process serves to bring legitimacy to the activities of the consultation team. Rappaport, Seidman, and Davidson (1979) additionally observe that consultations generated in a collaborative atmosphere are more likely to be "truly adopted" than those that are imposed by professionals. Finally, a program is more likely to be adopted if its characteristics, practices, and values correspond with those of the setting (Rhodes & Jason, 1991). In the present case, the possibility of involving more than one person was precluded by teachers' unavailability. However, the teacher coordinator indicated that she could represent the interests of the program teachers.

As events developed, the teachers did strike, delaying the school's opening a record thirty days. In an unprecedented move, students picketed the school, vociferously criticizing the school system and teachers. When the parties finally resolved the dispute, the salary demands of the teachers were met, but only as a result of the dismissal or demotion of junior colleagues. This event marked the beginning of the school year both for teachers, whose morale was depressed by the strike outcome, and for program students, who felt resentful about the nature of their introduction to high school. In this atmosphere, the consultant finally met the team of teachers. To make matters worse, as the consultant had suspected, the teachers were unaware of the principal's request for consultation and the teacher coordinator's support of it. Immediately there was skepticism and suspicion about the consultant, the principal, and even the teacher coordinator, a possible consequence that the consultant had mentioned to the teacher coordinator.

Though teachers had been unaware of the request for consultation, the concept of program evaluation was not new to them. In fact, the previous year, an in-house evaluation had been conducted by a nonprogram teacher. This evaluation did not involve program teachers' input and drew negative conclusions about the prevention program. Not surprisingly, there was reluctance to have another evaluation conducted.

The program teachers who had been recruited by the teacher coordinator had over the past year become committed to the prevention program. The consultant did not want to disrupt this loyalty, because prevention programs "owned" by those who create and implement them are most likely to be maintained (Gartner & Reissman, 1977). The emotional and physical investment of the program developers in such ventures are what often facilitate a positive outcome. Teachers were clearly invested in their program.

After considerable discussion with the teachers, the consultant began developing a positive and trusting relationship with them. She showed her respect for teachers' expertise about the school and emphasized an interchange between professional colleagues and an avoidance of hierarchical relationships (Gutkin & Curtis, 1990). This was not always an easy task. Influenced by their own preconceptions of what such a consultation relationship should be like, several teachers tried to create an expert role for the consultant. Caplan (1970) refers to this process as "one-downmanship" and suggests that such behavior should be responded to with deference, which was exactly the consultant's approach. She was non-threatening and respectful of their views, without being patronizing. The consultant genuinely appreciated information that was shared with her, especially the privileged information that increasingly was provided to her as school personnel began to trust her. She conveyed genuineness, empathy, and respect, important qualities for facilitating the consultant-consultee relationship. Researchers have found that the best predictor of consultees' satisfaction with consultation is their perception of these facilitative characteristics in the consultant (Schowengerdt, Fine, & Poggio, 1976). The consultant's success in this process is evidenced by the fact that following the preliminary meetings, the teachers decided to pursue an evaluation of the program.

A potential obstacle in the consultation was the teachers' and the consultant's different value systems regarding evaluation. The teachers believed that an evaluation of the intervention could rely on subjective criteria—the teachers' personal feelings about the program. However, the consultant believed that the program evaluation would be improved if more standardized instruments and a tighter experimental design were used.

Flexibility was needed for both sides to develop an evaluation that was useful to the teachers and methods that could result in an objective assessment. The consultant recognized teachers' values, interests, and emotional investment (Parsons & Meyers, 1984) and emphasized an egalitarian and collaborative approach. The consultant and teachers designed the evaluation to include more subjective criteria as well as more standardized scientific procedures.

Understanding the Setting's Culture and Values

One element of the consultant's approach that greatly facilitated her work at the school was her knowledge and understanding of the setting's culture. The consultant-consultee relationship is affected by the norms of the setting in which the relationship takes place (Parsons & Meyers, 1984). Over the years the consultant spent working at the school, she had the opportunity to get to know the setting well. She learned about the various gatekeepers at the school and about the school's policies and procedures, both explicit and implicit. More importantly, she came to know the residents of the setting and their values and beliefs. Although she had known the principal prior to her introduction to the school, this relationship was only moderately helpful in facilitating entry to the school. As illustrated above, gatekeepers proved to be more central in this process.

As suggested by Caplan (1970), two principal ways for building relationships with school personnel and getting to know the setting were used: (1) establishing "spontaneous proximity" and (2) holding formal interviews. Establishing spontaneous proximity means that the consultant finds informal situations in which to casually meet and talk with consultees. In previous work at the school, the consultant had needed to examine students' school records, which had required her to contact all the guidance counselors individually. The time spent in the individual counselors' offices gathering this information provided an informal context for the consultant and the counselors to get to know one another. For the consultant, this included learning about the school as well. More formal interviews involved talks with the principal and the teacher coordinator. Through these informal and formal contacts with school personnel, the consultant was able to gain their confidence and trust.

Politics were also a part of the school culture, usually involving the gatekeepers of the school. The consultant learned that there were many gatekeepers within the school, with their own domains of power, routines, and sets of rules, policies, and procedures, and came to understand the system's communication network. With the principal's secretary as her ally, the consultant had access to the secretary's extensive history with these other gate-keepers. The secretary prompted the consultant on dealing with the gate-keepers, including when and how certain gatekeepers should be approached, how the needed information could be secured most efficiently, and when the secretary should act as a liaison between the consultant and other gatekeepers. Negotiations with these individuals went much more smoothly as a result.

Another dimension of school politics involved the school system itself and the teachers' strike. The teachers' strike had all the potential for creating an additional barrier between the consultant and teachers. It was in the consultant's best interest to remain as neutral as possible regarding the strike. She needed the teachers' cooperation and trust to carry out the program evaluation. Without trust, research and consultation activities are often hindered, resulting in participants' failure to respond to the intervention or consultation process. Rhodes and Jason (1991) provide an illustration of this in their experience with a group of teachers who admitted to deliberately withholding information because of their lack of trust. In the present case, an atmosphere of distrust already existed. It was therefore especially important that the consultant's sympathies in either direction on the school strike issue be carefully contained. The consultant negotiated this fine line carefully, opting to be empathically supportive of teachers in a noncommittal way and without criticizing the board of education.

Goal Identification

When it came to establishing goals, the consultant and teachers worked collaboratively. Together, the teachers, teacher coordinator, and consultant reviewed the advantages and disadvantages of an evaluation. The teachers discussed what an evaluation meant to them and shared their concerns about what extra work might be involved beyond their regular duties. They also discussed their feelings about the previous evaluation of the intervention, dismissing it as invalid. Finally, the group resolved that an evaluation could serve as a means of constructive feedback and of identifying effective program components that were worth teachers' continued investment of time and effort. To this end, the group established several evaluation goals that centered on identifying the strengths and weaknesses of their program.

Intervening: Roles for Consultees and the Professional

In much the same way as goals were identified, program development was also approached collaboratively. The teachers and the consultant brainstormed about ways to improve or modify the existing program and the evaluation.

The consultant was supportive of teachers' intervention ideas and encouraged their input. The teachers' relative comfort in the process of working collaboratively was demonstrated in the program implementation phase. At mid-semester, team teachers decided that the student progress reports, sent to parents as a part of the program's feedback component, required too much detail and took too much time to complete at the agreed-upon biweekly rate. The fact that teachers felt free to modify a program component that had been contributed by the consultant suggested to her that she had succeeded in creating an atmosphere where teachers felt comfortable enough to develop procedures and strategies that everyone felt were effective and worthwhile.

Assessment

In spite of all the obstacles, an evaluation of the dropout prevention program was carried out. It served the intended purpose of informing team teachers of the program's strengths and weaknesses, and it was in this context that feedback was provided. Although political problems continued to dominate the school atmosphere, teachers were able to remain invested in the program and even responded to some of the consultant's recommendations for modifying the program on the basis of the evaluation outcome. For example, one suggestion made by the consultant concerned restructuring the school environment so that most participating students' classes would be located in one section of the school. Many of the freshmen who were new students to the school experienced the setting as large and overwhelming. They had classes throughout a heavily congested eight-story building. The following year, the school restructured the setting so that program students attended most of their classes on one floor of the building.

Terminating the Relationship

In terminating the consultation relationship, the consultant can encounter a number of problems. These problems mainly center on consultees' concerns about the consultant becoming unavailable to consultees in the event of future problems (Parsons & Meyers, 1984). In the consultation described above, from the outset, the consultant respectfully deferred to the teachers who had developed the program. In addition, she recognized that teachers had expertise concerning their school and their students that she did not have. The understanding between the teachers and the consultant was that each brought something to the consultation, no one being superior to another. This is one strategy that can be used to help foster cooperation and decrease dependency (Caplan, 1970). And when teachers did show some deference in the discussion of research design—an area in which they felt less experienced—this was offset by a subsequent set of relevant questions about the school that reestablished them as experts in their own right. Furthermore, throughout the consultation, the consultant assumed a participant role. The teachers and consultant functioned as a unit in the consultation process. That is, the consultant's ideas were not granted any more status than teachers'. Generally, the process was egalitarian and nonauthoritarian, with the consultant reinforcing teachers' autonomy as a group throughout. Both of these approaches helped to decrease the development of consultee dependency.

Another aspect of the project that facilitated termination was teachers' ownership of the program. Although the consultant made contributions, the program was conceived and implemented by the teachers themselves. When it came time to terminate the consultation, the teachers still felt in control of their program; their investment in it remained intact. They did not feel abandoned. They were left with a program that they cared for and in which they had pride.

Conclusion

As evidenced in the case described here, it is important when entering a setting in a consultation relationship to be sensitive to the social codes of that setting. Insensitivity to contextual issues can compromise one's ability to accomplish the defined tasks. One might even be excluded from the setting, as was illustrated in the incident involving the secretary. Had the consultant not realized some of the setting's important social norms, she might not have been able to continue her work there.

Even if one survives in a setting, if social norms have been violated, the relationship between the consultant and the consultees might be so damaged that the outcomes are useless (Kelly, 1986). This damage may result in consultees disregarding, devaluing, or distrusting information produced by the consultation. Therefore, it is important for consultants to cultivate respectful, cooperative relationships. This cooperative process is more likely to ensure that a useful and culturally sensitive product is developed and used. The approach described here also has empowering effects. Respect and equality accorded by an individual who is typically viewed as an authority figure enhance consultees' sense of importance and efficacy, reinforce their sense of commitment, and strengthen their resolve to contribute.

In consulting in complex systems, one confronts multifaceted ecological constraints, sometimes making it difficult to adopt the consulting approach described here. For instance, how does one plan a project when there is a teachers' strike? What does one do when events occur that prevent necessary dialogue from taking place? Sometimes the people central to a consultation process are not available to participate in the development of the project. Such issues present obstacles to using the consulting approach described here.

In addition, there are often time limits with which to contend. The pacing of events in the latter consultation was quick, and the consultant and consultees had to develop specific interventions and procedures without the benefit of a stable, lengthy relationship. However, this was offset by the previous work with the consultee setting also described here, in which other key relationships at the school had been nurtured at a slower and more natural pace. Relationships fostered in such a manner could provide for even better processes that allow for the development of mutually beneficial goals.

The concept of collaboration between consultants and consultees is not a new one. However, its potential benefits are perhaps not fully realized. For example, consultants are often unaware of the empowering nature of an egalitarian, cooperative approach in consulting. The promise of collaboration is particularly appealing to community-oriented consultants, who have recently begun to develop models that emphasize even greater collaboration between consultants and consultees (Bond, 1990; Serrano-Garcia, 1990). Consultation efforts that maximize the understanding of people, their settings, and the rich interactions between the two offer perhaps the best chance at producing useful and meaningful consultations.

References

Bergan, J. R., & Kratochwill, T. R. (1990). *Behavioral consultation and therapy*. New York: Plenum Press.

Bond, M. (1990). Defining the research relationship: Maximizing participation in an unequal world. In P. Tolan, C. Keys, F. Chertok, & L. A. Jason (Eds.), *Researching community psychology: Issues of theory and methods* (pp. 183–185). Washington, DC: American Psychological Association.

Caplan, G. (1970). *The theory and practice of mental health consultation*. New York: Basic Books.

Gartner, A., & Reissman, F. (1977). *Self-Help in the human services*. San Francisco: Jossey-Bass.

Gluckstern, N. B., & Packard, R. W. (1977). The internal-external change agent team: Bringing change to a "closed institution." *Journal of Applied Behavioral Science, 13,* 41–52.

Gutkin, T. B., & Curtis, M. J. (1990). School-based consultation: Theory, techniques, and research. In T. B. Gutkin and C. R. Reynolds (Eds.), *The handbook of school psychology* (2nd ed., pp. 577–611). New York: Wiley.

Heller, K., Price, R. H., Reinharz, S., Riger, S., & Wandersman, A. (1984). *Psychology and community change: Challenges of the future*. Homewood, Il: Dorsey Press.

Kelly, J. (1986). Context and process: An ecological view of the interdependence of practice and research. *American Journal of Community Psychology, 14,* 581–589.

Meyers, J., Parsons, R. D., & Martin, R. (1979). *Mental health consultation in the schools: A comprehensive guide for psychologists, social workers, psychiatrists, counselors, educators, and other human services professionals.* San Francisco: Jossey-Bass.

Parsons, R. D., & Meyers, J. (1984). *Developing consultation skills: A guide to training, development, and assessment for human services professionals.* San Francisco: Jossey-Bass.

Rappaport, J., Seidman, E., & Davidson, W. (1979). Demonstration research and manifestation versus true adoption: The natural history of a research project to divert adolescents from the legal system. In R. F. Muñoz, L. R. Snowden, J. G. Kelly, & Associates, *Special and psychological research in community settings: Designing and conducting programs for social and personal well-being* (pp. 101–144). San Francisco: Jossey-Bass.

Reyes, O., & Jason, L. A. (1991). An evaluation of a high school dropout prevention program. *Journal of Community Psychology, 19,* 221–230.

Reyes, O., & Jason, L. (1993). Pilot study examining factors associated with staying in school for the Hispanic high school student. *Journal of Youth and Adolescence, 22*(1), 57–71.

Rhodes, J. E., & Jason, L. A. (1991). Community health assessment. In H. Schroeder (Ed.), *New directions in health psychology: Assessment* (pp. 159–173). New York: Hemisphere Press.

Schowengerdt, R. V., Fine, M. J., & Poggio, J. P. (1976). An examination of some bases of teacher satisfaction with school psychological services. *Psychology in the Schools, 13,* 269–275.

Serrano-Garcia, I. (1990). Implementing research: Putting our values to work. In P. Tolan, C. Keys, F. Chertok, & L. A. Jason (Eds.). *Researching community psychology: Issues of theory and methods* (pp. 171–182). Washington, DC: American Psychological Association.

Serrano-Garcia, I., Lopez, M. M., & Rivera-Medina, E. (1987). Toward a social-community psychology. *Journal of Community Psychology, 15*(4), 431–446.

16

Providing Consultation Services in Business Settings

Charles A. Maher

As a method of psychoeducational service delivery, consultation is a much researched approach (see Chapter One). It is generally defined as an interactive process between a professional consultant and someone who wants to help a third party (Morsink, Thomas, & Correa, 1991); within educational and mental health systems, it is a means for assisting administrators and teachers in better serving their ultimate clients, children and adolescents (Conoley & Conoley, 1992). This chapter focuses on a relatively new area for educational and psychological consultation: private business. In this setting, consultants help consultees, such as corporate human resource directors, to identify and resolve employees' problems in meeting the educational and psychological needs of their children.

Employers in business and industry seek consultation for the benefit of their employees' children in order to enhance productivity, profitability, and the quality of work life. Increasingly, owners of small to mid-size businesses as well as executives of large corporations are recognizing that work performance is greatly affected by their employees' personal lives; how well employees focus on their work is related to how well they are able to coordinate it with other dimensions of their lives (Berlinger, Glick, & Rogers, 1988). For instance, when children of employees are not achieving as expected in school, parental attention will be directed to those matters. Single parents, whose numbers continue to grow, face special difficulties in attempting to balance work with home life (Heatherington & Camara, 1984), particularly in finding adequate

Note: James Plunkett is acknowledged for preparation of material for an earlier version of this chapter.

time and social support to make informed decisions about the health, education, and general well-being of their children. Naturally, such nonwork concerns become priorities for these parents. Research results described by Stackel (1989–90) illustrate the productivity problems resulting from these concerns:

- A 1985 survey report by Child Care Systems, Inc., a consulting firm in Lansdale, Pennsylvania, found that problems such as the illness of a caregiver, school holidays, and difficulties with transportation force working parents to be off the job approximately eight days a year.
- A survey by PAL Corporate Child Care, Inc., of employees of twenty-two companies in northern Virginia found that businesses lost an average of $1,800 a year for each employee who was the parent of a preschooler because of time spent on the phone or away from the office to deal with child-related problems.
- In a survey of its employees, AT&T found that caring for a sick child was the reason given for missing work by 56 percent of the women and 33 percent of the men who were absent one to three times during 1985. The same study revealed that more than half the women and a third of the men spent unproductive time at work dealing with child-care concerns.

If problem-solving assistance is readily available in the workplace for employees with children, some of these productivity problems may be overcome (Repetti, 1985).

Educational and psychological consultation to clients in business and industry may be valuable in other respects as well. The changing nature of workplace routines and the projected declines in the numbers of skilled workers (Hudson Institute, 1987; Carnivale, Gainer, & Meltzer, 1990) make it important for companies to retain valued employees. Child-care assistance programs that reinforce workers for self-initiated learning and personal problem solving can provide positive incentives for employees to remain with their companies (Smith, 1988).

Rapid changes in the commercial and industrial sectors, especially corporate downsizing and mergers, have brought increasing mobility of families as parents must relocate to take up new employment positions (World Bank, 1987). Employee assistance programs can help support workers who are transferred in making the transition from one school and community setting to another.

This chapter offers direction for both consultants and companies that wish to engage in consultation services to benefit employees' children. First, it outlines the qualities needed in consultants who wish to provide such services.

Second, it describes a systems approach to determining how such services may be provided and to what clients. Third, because this is a relatively new area for consultation, the chapter provides guidelines for assessing a company's readiness for engaging in consultation. Finally, since there are virtually no applied research or program evaluation data available on this promising new area of consultation, the chapter provides an outline for future research and development.

The examples and applications discussed in this chapter are drawn largely from the author's professional experiences working with a range of private businesses, including General Motors, Johnson & Johnson, Ford Motor Company, General Electric, IBM, and General Foods, as well as a number of small and mid-size companies.

Important Qualities of the Consultant

A vast literature has developed during the past fifteen years about characteristics of educational and psychological consultants who serve children and their families (Conoley & Conoley, 1992; see also Chapter One). In almost all instances, however, extant literature bases have described characteristics needed by consultants in public schools, related educational settings, and mental health clinics; no empirical research appears to have been published about consultants serving clients in business and industry for the benefit of employees' children.

Despite the lack of empirical research, however, it is possible to identify some important qualities necessary for a consultant to be successful in the area discussed in this chapter. One such essential quality may be entrepreneurship—the ability to create value by recognizing new professional opportunities, managing risks associated with those opportunities, and following through with value-added services (Kao, 1989; Kao & Stevenson, 1984). Even though consultation in organizations, including private businesses, is a well-developed area (Schein, 1985), the opportunity to consult with company clients to help them with employees' concerns about meeting the educational and psychological needs of their children is indeed a new opportunity. The consultant with an entrepreneurial desire and approach is likely to be able to sustain the professional efforts necessary to implement a successful consultation arrangement in this area (Csikszentmihalyi, 1990).

Timmons et al. (1985) reviewed more than fifty empirical studies of new business and professional ventures and identified a range of qualities that are related to the success of consultation-oriented entrepreneurs:

- *Commitment, determination, and persistence*—necessary because this type of consultation is relatively uncharted

- *Desire to achieve*—without which, the consultant may quickly lose interest in providing services within a competitive business environment
- *Taking initiative*—important because the need for services may not be perceived by employers or employees
- *Seeking and using feedback*—essential to continuous improvement of the quality and effectiveness of new services
- *Risk taking and risk seeking*—necessary to initiate actions toward new ventures, where how to proceed may not be as clear as it usually is in more established areas of consultation in business (for example, financial services consultation).

While this is by no means an exhaustive list, these qualities are likely to be important for the professional consultant who is interested in providing services to clients in business and industry where the ultimate beneficiaries of those services are children of employees. Moreover, most of these qualities are also likely to be important for consultants in schools and related settings. My own consultation experiences, as well as research on organizational consultation in private workplaces (Gunn, 1984; Moos, 1986; Shaiken, 1985), suggest some additional important qualities for consultants to businesses:

- Understanding of target marketing principles, including methods of getting appointments, sales presentation approaches, and closing techniques
- Knowledge of the nature of the specific business and industry in which proposed consultation services are to be provided
- Understanding of the needs and interests of prospective clients (for example, employers, human resource professionals)
- Procedures and methods for designing, implementing, and evaluating programs, products, policies, and services
- Technical competence in the particular areas in which consultation services will be provided

The next section describes a framework for consultants to use to provide valuable services to clients.

Systems Approach

A systems approach to providing consultation in business and industry for the benefit of employees' children enables the consultant to focus on both broad and narrow factors, both internal and external to the company, that must be considered if consultation is to be considered as valuable by clients and employees. This approach consists of three separate yet interrelated dimensions: the levels of consultation assistance, the process of client involvement in consultation, and the methods of consultation.

Levels of Consultation Assistance

The first dimension of the systems approach is deciding what assistance may be valuable to employees with respect to their children and at what levels of the company—organizational, group, and individual.

Organizational Level. At the organizational level of consultation assistance, the client is likely to be a manager or director of human resources. At this level, the consultant can assist the client in the areas of needs assessment, policy development, and program design.

In the area of needs assessment, consultation focuses on helping the client to identify specific and relevant needs of employees for promoting their children's educational and psychological well-being. For example, employees may need information about how they can help their children succeed in school; about the normal development of children and adolescents; and about life events that may precipitate problems in the development of their sons and daughters, such as death, divorce, and peer pressure to use drugs. This kind of needs assessment information will serve as a basis for dissemination of information to employees by means of brochures, company-sponsored seminars, or other programs.

The consultant can also assist the client in developing policies as to how and when parents will have access to psychological and educational information, what type of programs are appropriate for the company, and how employee educational programs will be coordinated with other company services, such as an employee assistance program (EAP).

Finally, the consultant can help the client to design, implement, and evaluate particular employee programs and services in accordance with needs assessment data and company policies. Most such companywide programs will be voluntary and informational, rather than targeted counseling or skill development programs.

Group Level. At the group level of consultation assistance, the client may be the manager or director of human resources or, in large corporations, a trainer responsible for design and implementation of specific programs or an EAP coordinator. The client at this level will probably have less companywide and more targeted interests than one at the organizational level, focusing on particular parents or perhaps even on children themselves. Thus, at this level, consultation can focus on identifying particular groups that may benefit from programs and services such as the following:

- Day care of preschool children provided through an on-site program, a contractual arrangement with an outside day-care facility, or a voucher system covering employees' child-care expenditures.

- Social support of the children and families of company employees who are relocating to new communities and thus subject to psychological stress and concomitant physical problems
- Supplemental instruction of adolescents with learning disabilities
- Counseling of families with children with disabilities

Individual Level. At the individual level of consultation assistance, the client is likely to be a professional associated with the company's EAP. Clients at this level may seek a consultant's help in meeting the needs of such individuals as a parent who desires a second opinion when a child has been diagnosed by the school system as educationally handicapped; a high school junior who is interested in learning more about the range of available college options; or a child of an employee who has experienced the loss of a parent.

Process of Client Involvement in Consultation

Client involvement in the consultation process is organized in four phases: clarification, design, implementation, and evaluation.

Clarification. This phase consists of three steps. First, the consultant identifies the particular level of consultation assistance that is being targeted, the particular client within that level, and the individual, group, or company unit that will be served by educational and psychological consultation. If the target for the consultation is not delineated precisely and clearly, the consultant, the client, and the company are likely to experience confusion, frustration, and waste of resources, both human and otherwise. Second, the consultant and client assess and validate employees' needs for development of knowledge and skills through interviews; reviews of permanent products, such as annual reports, technical reports, and office records; and testing or other observational procedures. Finally, the consultant and client interpret the needs assessment data in relation to the organization's goals, employees, strategy, and so on, and place the identified needs into relevant social, linguistic, work, and related contexts.

Design. Using the information that has been gathered in the clarification phase, the consultant and client decide what the consultation is to accomplish and how and establish specific consultation goals. The goals should be stated in terms of anticipated outcomes or accomplishments, preferably results that can be documented. Maher and Bennett (1984) recommend what they call SMART goals: goals that are *specific* (and thus meaningful to employees and their children); *measurable* (worthy of inclusion in a consultation service document and investment of a company's resources); *a*ttainable (fair to employees and their children); *r*elevant (justifiable to others); and *t*ime-referenced (clear as to when they are to be attained).

Once the purpose and goals of the consultation have been established, the consultant recommends interventions and procedures that the client can use to realize the goals. The consultant and the client then reach an agreement about the nature, scope, and timing of the consultation, preferably putting the agreement into writing as an action plan.

Implementation. The implementation of the action plan developed by the consultant and client first requires the marketing of the program or service to participants, potential participants, and other relevant audiences. It is important that the consultant and client understand the concerns of other people in the company with respect to their part in the program and build positive expectations for it, through their own enthusiasm.

Evaluation. The purpose of this phase is to gather and analyze data about each consultation episode (including particular programs) so that judgments can be made about the value of consultation to the client. This processing can be usefully guided by the following evaluation questions:

1. What have been *reactions* of the client to the consultation?
2. What has the client *learned* as a result of the consultation?
3. What has the client *applied* to the work setting that was learned during the consultation?
4. What has been the *contribution* of the consultation to the company?

Data to answer these questions can be gathered through a range of evaluation methods, instruments, and procedures, including interviews, rating scales, checklists, testing, record review procedures, and naturalistic observational schemes.

Methods of Consultation

Although the process of consultation is the same for each client at each level of assistance, the particular methods and procedures for consultation will vary. The following list provides examples of methods and procedures that can be used for each phase of the consultation process:

Clarification

- Market surveys—instruments to gather information about the nature of the target population (for example, employees with high school-age children) and their interests in participating in programs or services

- Focus group discussions—gathering groups of employees to discuss their needs, concerns, or problems in relation to their children and their workplace activities
- Needs assessments—interviewing members of a work group about their needs, problems, and concerns regarding their school-age children

Design

- Goal attainment scaling—measuring the degree of goal attainment for a consultation transaction
- Brainstorming of interventions—conceptualizing alternative ways to view the problems to be addressed by a program or service
- Writing program design documents and agreements—specifying how to provide the resources needed to provide a consultation service, including charting information, program personnel, budget, facilities, methods, and materials

Implementation

- Discussions with company officials—meetings with key management personnel to inform them about the progress of consultation, troubleshoot potential problems, and revise time lines for consultation activities
- Implementation training sessions—meetings with employees to inform them about methods being used, such as behavior management approaches or effective parenting skills
- Monitoring implementation—determining how well management has followed through with commitments such as providing after-school tutors for children of employees

Evaluation

- Reaction evaluation—using a survey to gather information on whether the employees and client felt that the service they received was helpful to them
- Assessment of learning—interviewing the client to establish the extent of changes in knowledge and skills that were goals of the consultation
- Observation of postconsultation application—examining group attendance and productivity records of work groups that participated in the program to determine changes in frequency or quality of results
- Client and participant forum—a meeting with management and program participants to communicate evaluation results and brainstorm about improvement of future consultation services

Assessing Organizational Readiness for Consultation

Assessing the organizational readiness of a company for consultation will give consultants a better understanding of how to position themselves with clients or prospective clients and make them better able to design consultation proposals that will be positively received by key company officials. This type of preparation will increase consultants' confidence and thus their ability to interest clients and obtain consultation contracts.

Maher and Bennett (1984) provide an organizational readiness assessment framework adapted from the work of Davis & Salasin (1975) that is a proven, practical way for the consultant to complete a useful assessment. The framework consists of a set of questions organized under the categories of *ability, values, idea, circumstances, timing, obligation, resistance,* and *yield;* thus, Maher and Bennett call their method the AVICTORY framework. Through interviews, permanent product reviews, and participant observational procedures, the consultant answers the following questions:

Ability

1. To what extent can the company commit the following types of resources to educational and psychological consultation in the service of children of employees: targeted personnel, including interns or consultants; funds; necessary physical facilities; and planning time for company managers?

Values

2. What has been the company's tradition with respect to providing innovative employee benefits and related benefit packages to workers?
3. Do company officials value their employees comprehensively and personally?

Idea

4. What does the idea of educational and psychological consultation mean to employees? Company officials?
5. Are the programs, products, and services that can be offered to employees with children really perceived as needed? By whom in the company? To what extent?

Circumstances

6. Does the company appear sound enough that it will be in existence during the foreseeable future?
7. Will company personnel who are supportive of the consultant remain with the company?

Timing

8. What is the most appropriate time line for gaining approval of and implementing consultation in this company?
9. What is the proposed time line's implications for consultation service delivery?

Obligation

10. Who in the company really wants to champion the consultation idea and help it become a reality?

Resistance

11. Who in the company is likely to resist the consultation idea?

Yield

12. Who in the company will benefit, and in what ways, from such consultation services?

The consultant can use the answers to these questions as a basis for deciding whether and to what extent the company is a viable prospect for worthwhile consultation.

Directions for Research and Evaluation

The systems approach to consultation described in this chapter is at a formative stage of development. Although it has been used by the author to assist clients in private business and industry in ways reported by clients and measured by him as worthwhile, the value of this kind of approach with respect to the educational and psychological consultation domain has yet to be determined. Toward that end, empirical inquiry is clearly warranted. The following suggestions are offered as a basis for research and evaluation in this area:

1. Data could be gathered and analyzed to provide information about perceived needs of prospective clients in private business and industry for child-focused educational and psychological consultation.
2. The issue of organizational readiness for this form of consultation could be systematically assessed, via survey instrumentation, with representative groups of companies.
3. Studies could be conducted to determine the kinds of help considered most desirable by clients at the different levels of consultation assistance.
4. A study of the involvement of company clients in the child-focused consultation process could generate information about potentially effective consultation methods.
5. Systematic program evaluation of the implementation of the systems approach to consultation could be conducted.

Individual consultants and consulting groups could pursue these research directions in conjunction with university researchers and company officials.

Summary

The information contained in this chapter is intended to serve heuristic purposes for educators and psychologists who are considering whether they can serve children of employees in business and industrial settings. The systems approach described herein is meant to guide professionals in learning more about themselves and markets of opportunity for their expertise. The field will benefit if educational and psychological consultants report results of their ventures into the private commercial sector of the economy.

References

Berlinger, L. R., Glick, W. H., & Rodgers, R. C. (1988). Job enrichment and performance improvement. In J. P. Campbell, R. J. Campbell, & Associates, *Productivity in organizations: New perspectives from industrial and organizational psychology.* San Francisco: Jossey-Bass.

Carnevale, A. P., Gainer, L. J., & Meltzer, A. S. (1990). *Workplace basics: The essential skills employees want.* San Francisco: Jossey-Bass.

Conoley, J. C., & Conoley, C. W. (1992). *School consultation: Practice and training* (2nd ed.). New York: Macmillan.

Csikszentmihalyi, M. (1990). *Flow: The psychology of optimal experience.* New York: HarperCollins.

Davis, H. T., & Salasin, S. E. (1975). The utilization of evaluation. In E. L. Struening & M. Guttentag (Eds.), *Handbook of evaluation research* (Vol. 1). Newbury Park, CA: Sage.

Gunn, C. E. (1984). *Workers' self management in the United States.* Ithaca, NY: Cornell University Press.

Heatherington, E. M., & Camara, K. A. (1984). Families in transition: the processes of dissolution and reconstitution. In R. D. Parke (Ed.), *The family: Review of child development research* (Vol. 7, pp. 398–439). Chicago: University of Chicago Press.

Hudson Institute. (1987). *Workforce 2000 executive summary.* Indianapolis, IN: Author.

Kao, J. (1989). *Entrepreneurship, creativity, and organization.* Englewood Cliffs, NJ: Prentice-Hall.

Kao, J., & Stevenson, H. (1984). *Entrepreneurship: What it is and how to teach it.* Cambridge, MA: Harvard Business School, Division of Research.

Maher, C. A., & Bennett, R. E. (1984). *Planning and evaluating special education services.* Englewood Cliffs, NJ: Prentice-Hall.

Moos, R. (1986). Work as a human context. In M. S. Pallak and R. S. Perloff (Eds.), *Psychology and work: Productivity, change, and employment* (pp. 5–52). Washington, DC: American Psychological Association.

Morsink, C. V., Thomas, C. C., & Correa, V. I. (1991). *Interactive teaming: Consultation and collaboration in special programs.* Columbus, OH: Merrill.

Repetti, R. L. (1985). *The social environment at work and psychological well being.* Unpublished doctoral dissertation, Yale University, New Haven, CT.

Schein, E. H. (1985). *Organizational culture and leadership.* San Francisco: Jossey-Bass.

Shaiken, H. (1985). *Work transformed: Automation and labor in the computer age.* New York: Holt, Rinehart & Winston.

Smith, R. M. (1988). *Theory building for learning how to learn.* Chicago: Educational Studies Press.

Stackel, L. (1989–90, Winter). Employment relations programs. *Employment Relations Today,* pp. 355–357.

Timmons, J., et al. (1985). *New ventures creation.* Homewood, IL: Irwin.

World Bank. (1987). *World Bank report 1987.* New York: Oxford University Press.

17

Ethical Consultation Practice

Walter B. Pryzwansky

If one takes the position that consultation is an indirect service delivery approach, as opposed to a separate profession, as some would claim, then the complexity of the question of what standards or ethics should guide practice becomes most apparent. As an indirect service, consultations' parameters are as loosely defined as those of another prevalent intervention employed by mental health workers, "therapy." Standards and ethics, then, become inextricably intertwined with factors such as the professional background of the practitioner (for example, educator, psychologist, social worker), the model of consultation that is adopted (mental health, medical, behavioral), the focus (individual, group, organizational), the context in which the consultant operates (for example, internal versus external origins), and the setting (for example, schools, private or public agencies, businesses). Each of these factors alone may dictate a particular perspective that, if not in conflict with the alternative options within that factor, will combine in unique ways with other factors to influence "best-practice" decision making. Such questions, then, as "Is this consultation information confidential?" can be more comprehensively addressed.

It should not be surprising that when we review the writings of others on this topic of ethics, we find that they turn for guidance to the various codes of the professions associated with the consultation activity. Yet these codes lack even references to consultation practice, much less dealing with specific issues and dilemmas of concern to them as consultants. Therefore, it seems prudent to begin this chapter with a basic question: Is there a need for a separate ethical code and/or standards for professionals practicing consultation? From that starting point, the chapter addresses the process of ethical decision making and then presents reflections on some next steps that need attention.

A Separate Code of Ethics?

One critical defining feature of a profession is whether its members abide by an enforceable set of ethical principles, standards, or guidelines. By definition, such statements represent the values of that professional group, be it an association or a society. Brown, Pryzwansky, and Schulte (1991, p. 354) point out that codes that are well developed "delineate the responsibility of the professional to society, the profession, and to specific client groups. They also identify specific practices to be followed in certain areas deemed most critical by the profession, for example, confidentiality of client-practitioner communication." Not only do professionals such as lawyers, physicians, counselors, and psychologists have a moral obligation to subscribe to professional ethics; legally, they have a *fiduciary* obligation to do so (Haas & Malouf, 1989). A fiduciary obligation implies a special commitment to care for the welfare of the client, as Haas and Malouf illustrate with the concept of loyalty: the expectations for the professional's loyalty to a person in need is quite different from the ordinary citizen's responsibility.

Ethical codes should challenge and inspire practitioners to give the best service that they can offer rather than simply serving as yardsticks by which to judge behavior, or even constraining collections of statements to be used against the professional whenever a mistake is made. Ethical statements can range from the minimal acceptable standard (mandatory) to the ideal (aspirational), and it is important that practitioners recognize that distinction. That distinction is made quite explicit in the revision of the 1982 Ethical Principles of Psychologists (American Psychological Association [APA], 1992). While the earlier format presents ethical *principles,* defined as "aspirational norms which guide psychologists toward the highest ideals of psychology" (APA, 1992, p. 1598), the revision offers ethical *standards,* which, while broadly stated to apply to psychologists in varied roles, are nonetheless designed to be *enforceable.* Thus, in this proposed revision of the APA code, ethical standards are clearly minimum criteria by which alleged violations can be judged. Nonetheless, it is important to note that ethical codes usually leave room for a reasonable degree of practitioner judgment.

Thus, as we have seen, an ethical code serves to inform the public, the members of a profession, and their clients about what the profession stands for and how it proposes to protect the public welfare. Such a code provides the criteria by which a professional organization will judge complaints of impropriety against one of its members; in essence, how it will police itself. Ethical codes also provide practitioners with guidelines for decision making in difficult situations involving ethical questions, maintain intra- and intergroup harmony among professionals, and guard a profession against external (for example, governmental) regulation (Brown et al., 1991).

Yet, in spite of their laudable objectives and, in some cases, products, these codes are not without their critics. As Snow and Gersick (1986) report, codes of ethics have been seen not only as not very useful but, in some instances, as simple window dressing. These criticisms seem to be based primarily on the fact that professional organizations have few sanctions to use against members who violate their codes and, more basically, the charge that organizations are sometimes too passive in policing themselves. In the case of consultation, critics observe that "consultants" come from a variety of professions, and a particular code may have little relevance for or inspire little loyalty in professions other than the one for which it was written. Similarly, since codes generally do not take into account the fact that some professionals may be salaried employees of organizations, the special circumstances of internally based professionals whose role involves consultation are not addressed.

Kitchener (1984, p. 45) notes that while ethical codes can be "the first line of ethical justification to which we may appeal to evaluate our moral intuitions," they can also offer contradictory and ambiguous guidelines for action. Furthermore, the problem of the applicability or relevance of a code is made more complicated if the consultant is a member of several professional organizations each with its own code. Kitchener also points out that professional codes tend to be conservative documents because they reflect what most of the profession can agree on. While most codes are broadly based to apply to a variety of circumstances, that advantage becomes a drawback for practitioners who look to a code for direction in a specific assessment or intervention area, such as consultation. For example, the Ethical Principles of Psychologists (APA, 1981) makes only four references to consultation and consulting relationships (Robinson & Gross, 1985), and the proposed 1992 draft is equally silent on the process.

Gallessich (1982) expressed concern about the paucity of references to consultation ethics at a time when malpractice among consultants was becoming a concern. This lack of attention to ethics may have been an index of the sudden attractiveness of the use of consultation outdistancing its conceptual base, while the prestigious title of "consultant" was being used indiscriminately. To address this problem, Gallessich proposed a comprehensive code of ethics for consultants. Drawing on several professional codes and the recommendations of colleagues, Gallessich (1982, pp. 397–405) developed the following twenty-eight principles:

1. Consultants' clients are the agencies that hire them.
2. Consultants are responsible for safeguarding the welfare of their consultees and client organizations.
3. Consultants present their professional qualifications and limitations accurately in order to avoid misinterpretation.
4. Consultants are careful to present their knowledge accurately.
5. When consultants perceive a consultee to behave in an unethical manner, they express their observations and the reasons for their concern to the person involved.
6. Consultants avoid involvement in multiple roles and relationships that might create conflicts of interest and thus jeopardize their effectiveness in the consultant role.
7. Consultants avoid manipulating consultees. Instead they seek to increase consultees' independence and freedom of choice.
8. Consultants accept contracts only if they are reasonably sure that the client agency will benefit from their services.
9. Consultants establish clear contracts with well-defined parameters.
10. Consultants fulfill their contracts and remain within contractual boundaries.
11. Consultants strive to evaluate the outcomes of their services.
12. Consultants assume responsibility for assisting administrators in establishing confidentiality policies to govern consultation and communicating these policies to the staff members involved in consultation activities.
13. Consultants acquire the basic body of knowledge and skills of their profession. They keep abreast of new theoretical, empirical, and technical developments related to consultation.
14. Consultants know their professional strengths, weaknesses, and biases.
15. Consultants are aware of personal characteristics that predispose them to systematic biases.
16. Consultants are alert to differences between their own social and political values and interests and those of client organizations.
17. Consultants regularly assess their strengths and weaknesses in relation to current and future work.
18. When advertising or otherwise promoting their services,

consultants are careful to describe them accurately and to avoid fraudulent information or claims.

19.   Consultants serve public interests through offering a proportion of their time to agencies that are financially unable to pay for consultation services.

20.   Consultants contribute to the growth of knowledge through their own research and experimentation.

21.   Consultants are alert to the public's welfare.

22.   Consultants contribute to the training of less experienced consultants.

23.   Consultants behave so as to protect the reputation of their profession.

24.   Consultants cooperate with other consultants and with members of other professions.

25.   Consultants acquaint themselves with the current fee standards in their area of expertise and in the agency's geographic location.

26.   When a consultant observes another professional to behave in an apparently unethical way, the consultant goes to that person to discuss these perceptions.

27.   Consultants contribute to their profession by participating in the activities of peer associations and supporting their standards.

28.   Consultants take active steps to maintain and increase their effectiveness.

Beyond the acknowledgment in subsequent writings of the code proposed by Gallessich, little has been done to extend or refine her suggestions or to propose alternative codes specifically for consultants.

Principles of Ethical Consultation Practice

Other authors have taken at least two different approaches to advancing the ethical practice of consultants. One is an attempt to identify higher-level guidelines or norms of practice to guide the decision making of consultants. A second approach, while it may embrace the proposition that generic principles are needed, emphasizes and deals directly with ethical dilemmas faced in the consultation relationship and advocates the development of principles based on consensus. Examples of these two approaches are presented below.

Principles as Guidelines

Davis and Sandoval (1982) argued for the use of "democratic ethics" in school-centered consultation approaches. Building on the work of Benne (1961), they constructed a set of five principles, or norms, to be used as guidelines in dealing with consultees and clients. First, they argue that the consultative process must be collaborative, that what emerges from the professional contact is a result with which both the consultant and consultee can feel comfortable. Setting aside the confusion that sometimes arises between the terms *consultation* and *collaboration* (Pryzwansky, 1990), this principle seems to tie the consultant to the philosophical underpinnings of the change model (that is, collaboration) that is employed. It is an important and useful one, provided that the consultant understands the implications of the decision to select that model for the underlying problem-solving approach (for a description of the collaboration model, see Pryzwansky, 1974).

Second, Davis and Sandoval (1982) argue that consultation has an educational objective: to prepare the consultee to better deal with subsequent challenges, especially ones similar to those for which consultation has been sought. Third, they argue that a strong evaluative bias should guide practice in that whatever ideas or intervention are generated need to be carefully monitored and changes made when warranted by the data. Fourth, they view consultation as task- and client-centered. This principle is particularly important given that change in the consultee is considered only in relation to the consultee's work with the client. Finally, they advocate for the protection of client rights.

Principles as Norms

Kitchener (1984) summarizes the writings of authors who resolved the inadequacies of professional codes by including higher-level norms. In her model, principles serve as the foundation of codes or even moral rules and "constitute a rationale for the choice of items in the code itself." The most critical in terms of ethical questions in psychology are the principles of autonomy, beneficence, nonmaleficence, justice, and fidelity.

According to Kitchener (1984, p. 46), the principle of *autonomy* involves the right of both the consultant and the consultee to act autonomously. Respect for others' rights, including that of choice, is valued. A profession's commitment to informed-consent policies is one practical application of this principle. However, as with all principles, there are limitations or restrictions on its application. For example, the competence of the consultee to make decisions, versus the prohibition against infringing on the rights of others, constrains this principle so that it is not completely binding in each instance of its application.

The principle of *beneficence* results in not just preventing harm but also promoting benefit for the client. Very often, however, it requires a balancing with the autonomy objective. Kitchener (1984) suggests that, above all, no harm should be inflicted on others in the delivery of service—the principle of *nonmaleficence.* While in some instances, actions such as the use of diagnostic labels may illustrate the negative consequences of an assessment service, Kitchener does point out that *harm* is such an ambiguous term that there will always be dilemmas in situations where this principle is applied.

Another important principle is that professionals are encouraged to offer services and in general behave professionally with fairness, or *justice.* Equal treatment to all is among the most timely of the issues that face our society today.

Finally, *fidelity* seems especially relevant to consultation, a service often engaged in voluntarily by the consultee, so that loyalty and truthfulness become the cornerstone of the relationship. Of course, confidentiality, clearly a commitment on which all writers in the area of consultation agree, is most relevant here.

Consensus

Another strategy for generating overarching principles that can guide consultation practice is an examination of the current professional codes of ethics. In fact, one such approach was used to derive a set of principles from the APA's 1981 Ethical Principles of Psychologists and the AACD's 1988 Ethical Standards (Brown et al., 1991). Six principles emerged from this analysis, regarding competence, protection of the welfare of clients, maintaining confidentiality of disclosures, responsibilities involved with making public statements, ethical and moral responsibility, and relationships with other consultants. These principles seem to adequately cover the many ethical dilemmas that could confront consultants.

The first principle, that regarding *competence,* requires that consultants aspire to a high degree of knowledge of their area of consultation practice, particularly since external standards for a well-trained consultant remain poorly defined in the literature. Given the fact that consultees are "at risk because no guidelines exist to aid them in selecting consultants" (Brown et al., 1991, p. 357), it is most important that the professional be held accountable in this regard. Similarly, the principle dealing with the *welfare of the consultee and client groups* needs to be considered whenever interventions are selected. These authors find internal consultants especially burdened when honoring this principle, since actions of the organization must also be taken into account. Consultees' freedom of choice is implied in this principle, as is the avoidance of a dependency relationship. Sensitivity to multicultural issues is also important in cross-cultural consultation cases. Of course, the principle of *confidentiality* is a part of this formulation. Responsibilities regarding *public statements* are particularly relevant in the case of external consultants, although internal consultants must also take responsibility for what they say about their services.

As these authors note, the literature indicates that a large number of the ethical pitfalls facing consultants arise out of conflicts between the needs of the consultant and those of the consultee. Thus, self-awareness is again viewed as an important attribute of the consultant to ensure *ethical and moral responsibility*. Consultants not only must be aware of their personal needs and problems that can impair their functioning, but also must be prepared to take action to eliminate such factors in their practice. The sixth and final principle deals with *intergroup and interprofessional relationships*. These consultation relationships should be conducted so that they facilitate the growth of the consultee and do not take advantage of the consultee or client.

Ethical Dilemmas

Yet another strategy employed in the literature to spell out the consultant's ethical responsibilities has been to identify ethical issues or dilemmas. Such a strategy can reveal resources that can be tapped by a consultant facing a professional challenge, expand one's appreciation of the complexity of such issues, and reinforce the need for a flexible orientation that incorporates different perspectives on the issue. Three examples of this strategy are presented below.

Five Challenges

Snow and Gersick (1986) center their attention on five areas of ethical responsibility and the ethical dilemmas that could arise within each area. The first set of challenges that they identify originates from the *nature of the consultation agreement* itself. For example, questions immediately arise when one sector of an organization arranges for consultation to be offered to another sector. To whom is the consultant accountable? Under what rules of confidentiality are decisions made? An equally challenging area involves the ambiguity that arises when there is a conflict in *loyalty and responsibility* between the organization and its clients (or between consultee and client). "Ethical dilemmas may arise from the conflicting agenda of multiple levels in the consultee organization and from ambiguity within the consultant organization concerning the autonomy of the staff consultant" (Snow & Gersick, 1986, p. 402). Another group of issues are likely to arise from *value choices related to intervention techniques* and the openness with which consultants identify their values. Wittingly or unwittingly, consultants can become wedded to a particular intervention or philosophical orientation; on the other hand, they can become "choice increasers" and facilitate independent decision making on the part of the consultee. The degree to which consultants identify their own biases to the consultee, the timing of that sharing, and the compatibility between the values orientation of the consultant and that of the consultee are the subject of a wide range of opinion and guidance in the literature. (See Chapter Nine for additional discussion of intervention issues.)

The *use and limits of confidentiality* present a fourth set of challenges to the consultant: the boundaries of confidentiality, the limits of what will be shared and with whom and in what way, and the ramifications of disclosure. How well issues in this area will be resolved depends on the consultant's competencies, resources, and motivations.

The final set of challenges posed by Snow and Gersick (1986) involve the *degree of responsibility for outcomes to be assumed by the consultant.* Here, the specific concerns involve accountability for recommendations, proposed solutions, evaluation, and negative actions of the consultee. Is the consultant to be primarily a facilitator of the problem-solving process, a problem solver, or the advocate of a solution? The answer to this question suggests how much alternative solutions and their risks will be emphasized, as well as who will be responsible for the impact of the changes and for follow-up.

Snow and Gersick (1986) also present a conceptual framework from which to deal with ethical issues. They point out that it is the context of consultation that creates change in the organization. The *environment* definitely affects one's perspective. Their focus is clearly "ecological": ethical issues should be considered in terms of their relevance to the real world and their relationship to political, economic, and organizational contexts. Factors that they consider important here include the characteristics of the consultant and the consultee, the relationship between the consultant and the consultee system, and the relationship between the consultant and consultee system and the community.

The framework presented by Snow and Gersick (1986) illustrates the necessity for the consultant to consider the choices presented by each dilemma in order to be prepared to offer consultation. That is not to say that making conscious choices of where to operate on the continuum represented by each dilemma area will eliminate all ethical problems. However, it does seem that consultant self-awareness should reduce potential ethical problems and their complications, while alerting the consultant to points within the process where such issues are most likely to arise.

Six Value Confrontations

In their discussion of applied ethics for school-based consultants, Davis and Sandoval (1982, p. 547) identify six typical situations involving value confrontations in the schools: "confidentiality, contractual clarity, evaluation and role confusion, client welfare, values versus techniques, and knowing and sharing one's own limitations." The overlap between the issue areas discussed above and these six concerns is obvious, but the particular examples and illustrations vary. All the examples used by Davis and Sandoval pertain to school situations, but they have obvious relevance for other settings. For example, in discussing confidentiality, Davis and Sandoval warn against sharing of information that is obtained in a discussion where explicit or implicit constraints have been promised, although they recognize that this restraint is often one-sided, so that the consultee is free to share information. They also warn of the problems that can arise if an internal consultant wears too many hats in the organization; dual roles can cause role misunderstanding on the part of the consultee. Such dual roles require that professionals be especially careful to avoid gossiping or rumor spreading. They should also avoid taking on evaluation responsibilities more appropriate to a supervisor or program evaluator.

A noteworthy aspect of these authors' perspective is their position that the school-based consultant's client is almost always the pupil, and not the consultee, as in Caplan's model (Caplan, 1979, p. 125). They strongly encourage consultants to practice introspection as a way to ensure that the role of personal values is always evident to the consultant. Finally, they argue against providing service without the necessary level of expertise or in the absence of supervision.

Competency Attributions

Robinson and Gross (1985, p. 446) argue that in the absence of codes of ethics for consultation, "the ethical issues surrounding consultation might be viewed in terms of the competencies that the consultant takes upon himself or herself as he or she provides service to the client/consultee." They identify consultants' responsibilities as presenting qualifications accurately and ethically, conducting negotiations with honesty and integrity; respecting client rights, conducting assessment and using data according to professional standards, and carrying out research and evaluation with sensitivity to ethical standards.

Technical Standards Versus Principles

While calling for revision of the APA code to accommodate practice in organizations, Lowman (1985) acknowledges that the principles in that code are general and broad enough to cover a diversity of situations, including consultation. While he notes that the ethical concerns identified by Robinson and Gross (1985) are not unique to consultation, he agrees with others that the field does need a set of detailed technical standards to guide this very specific and rather narrow area of practice. Since, however, the casework necessary to allow application to this area of practice has yet to be produced, Lowman considers that it would be "inappropriate and unrealistic" to develop ethical principles or guidelines when the parameters of good professional practice have yet to be accepted, particularly in organizations.

Consultant, Consultee, and Client Rights

Yet another way to view ethical dilemmas is in terms of the rights of the three parties involved in the consultation process—in the case of school-based consultation, the student, the consultee, and the consultant. Concentrating on the school psychologist as consultant, Hughes (1986) first considered ethical issues related to the rights of the pupil and parents, followed by the rights of the consultee and finally the rights of the school.

Hughes argues that the school psychologist as an agent of the school shares responsibility with consultees (teachers, parents, counselors) for the well-being of the students; the consultant is ultimately committed to student welfare, notwithstanding the focus of the mental health consultation model, which is to focus on the consultee. Consultants are obligated to take unilateral action if necessary to resolve conflicts between their responsibilities to the consultee and their responsibilities to the school.

Regarding parents' rights, Hughes discusses legal issues concerning parental consent and access to notes taken by the consultant during interviews. Among consultee rights, Hughes lists compatibility of goals to be reached between the consultee and the consultant; privacy and confidentiality, including being fully informed of any limits or constraints on confidentiality; participation in all stages of consultation; and full information about their obligations. Finally, schools have the right to hold consultants accountable for their actions and to be fully informed about a consultant's educational philosophy or approach.

In an interesting addition to her discussion of ethical issues, Hughes addresses the particular models of consultation that can be employed and the potential problems associated with each approach. For example, the issue of manipulation and control arises when consultation is viewed as an interpersonal influence attempt (consultee-centered consultation). Given the fact that consultants operating from this framework are likely to encourage the consultee to choose the client intervention, the consultee must be given every opportunity to agree or disagree with the consultant. When behavioral consultation is used, the goals of the intervention may be influenced by the consultant's eagerness to demonstrate effectiveness; similarly, the match of the consultee's philosophy about change practices with this theoretical approach may be overlooked as a consideration by the consultant. By contrast, process consultants are likely to be involved in group work and must guard against unmonitored self-disclosures, as well as carefully considering how to deal with loyalty issues between the administrator and consultee. Hughes occasionally draws on legal statutes and ethical codes to suggest answers to dilemmas in these areas.

Ethics in Different Contexts

In his review of literature addressing the ethics of consultation in two contexts (human service delivery and government or private business settings), Tokunaga (1984) found similar concepts and solutions discussed by writers on both areas. While they addressed different populations, their recommendations for training and identification of clients did not differ much. He did conclude that among psychology specialties, "the potential for ethical behavior and accountability would appear to be much higher in clinical or school consultation than in consultation offered by industrial/organization psychologists" (p. 820). Ultimately, Tokunaga concluded, the solution to ethical problems is the responsibility of the consultant.

Ethical Decision Making

Perhaps the most valuable suggestion for enhancing the ethical practice of consultants is the use of an ethical decision-making strategy. How one processes the details of a situation involving ethical questions is as important as the resources brought to bear in arriving at the solution. While decision-making strategies are not intended to be models that are slavishly followed in each instance, they do provide a useful aid for analyzing a dilemma and choosing a course of action.

The Flow Chart Approach

Haas and Malouf (1989) point out three areas in which practitioners must gather information before undertaking the decision-making process. First, it is important that the situation be analyzed to answer the question "What makes this an ethical dilemma?" The posing of this question will help the consultant determine whether the problem is really a technical challenge or legal constraint rather than an ethical issue. On the other hand, the situation may actually pose multiple ethical questions. Second, it is critical that the consultant identify all parties (for example, parents, third-party payers, a clinic) that have a legitimate stake in the outcome of the problem resolution and take their preferences into account. Finally, existing codes of ethics and standards for practice

Figure 17.1. The Decision-Making Flow Chart.

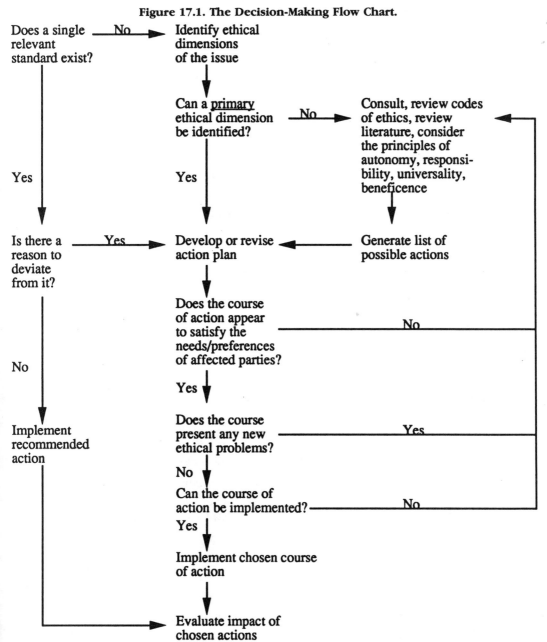

Source: Keeping up the Good Work: A Practitioner's Guide to Mental Health Ethics by L. J. Haas & J. L. Malouf. Copyright 1989 by Professional Resource Exchange, Inc., P. O. Box 15560, Sarasota, FL 34277–1560. Reprinted by permission of the publisher.

should be consulted; in some cases, such codes and standards may provide sufficient guidance.

Haas and Malouf point out that consultation with colleagues and professional resource units, such as an ethics committee or licensing board, can prove extremely helpful to consultants facing ethical dilemmas. Such reaching out helps to reduce the feelings of isolation and overwhelming burden that can accompany ethical dilemmas. In addition, peer consultation is in itself a sign of sound, responsible action and is likely to enhance a consultant's reputation for good judgment, rather than, as some consultants fear, making them appear either incompetent or guilty. A record of such consultation is evidence of professionally sound judgment in coping with a problem objectively and responsibly.

Haas and Malouf (1989, p. 8) propose a decision-making process based on three underlying presumptions: "the dignity and free will of the individual (autonomy); the obligation of professionals to respect the existing standards and expectations of the society that legitimizes their activities (responsibility); and the duty to avoid special or self-serving interpretations or situations (universality)." Their framework for decision making is presented in Figure 17.1. Action flows from the answers to the two basic questions presented in the figure: Is there a relevant legal or professional standard that could mandate an answer? Is there a reason to deviate from that standard?

Hierarchical Model of Ethical Justification

Kitchener (1984) has developed a model of ethical justification, presented in Figure 17.2, that is based on the premise that there are "different levels of moral reasoning and that they are hierarchically related" (p. 45). At the basic intuitive level is a set of ethical beliefs that represent prior ethical knowledge and experience. These beliefs are critical for developing everyday ethical decisions when time constraints prevent long deliberation. However, because moral intuition is not enough, we need to move to a more reflective level, representing the best critical thinking that can be mustered. Within this second level, there are three sublevels of increasingly general and abstract forms of justification: professional codes and laws, ethical principles, and ethical theory. One moves to each of these sublevels as needed to reach a decision.

Ethical Decision-Making Process

Nagle (1987) has proposed a process based on a distillation of several frameworks that had previously been proposed (Keith-Spiegel & Koocher, 1987; Tymchuk, 1981). Nagle suggests the following process for ethical decision making:

1. Gather information from individuals or parties involved and define potential ethical issues.
2. Consult appropriate ethical and legal guidelines, if available, that may apply to resolution of issues.
3. Determine the rights, responsibilities, and well-being of all parties involved.
4. Formulate possible alternative decisions for each issue raised.
5. Evaluate the various possible consequences of each decision.
6. Estimate the probability of occurrence of each consequence.
7. Review information with affected parties.
8. Implement the decision.
9. Monitor, review, and follow up the decision.

Nagle (1987) argues that strategies that permit a systematic evaluation of a situation, including factors that could influence a decision, force the consultant to evaluate many important issues. It is obvious that following such a step-by-step process will require information gathering and peer consultation. In the end, it can also serve as a self-evaluative mechanism.

Figure 17.2. A Model of Ethical Justification.

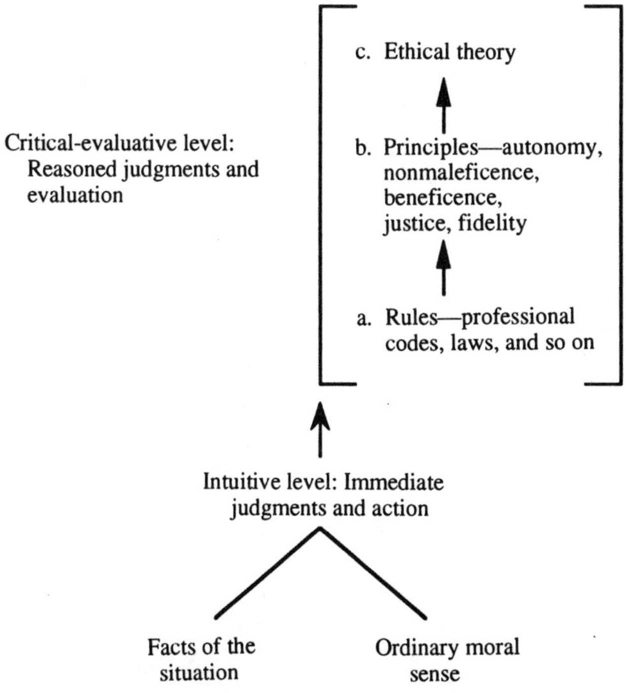

Critical-evaluative level:
Reasoned judgments and
evaluation

c. Ethical theory

b. Principles—autonomy,
nonmaleficence,
beneficence,
justice, fidelity

a. Rules—professional
codes, laws, and so on

Intuitive level: Immediate
judgments and action

Facts of the
situation

Ordinary moral
sense

Source: Kitchener, 1984.

Conclusion

It is prudent to remind ourselves that there are limitations on any decision-making strategy; such schemes are not foolproof. For example, frameworks such as that proposed by Haas and Malouf (1989) are based on a rational mind-set and thus are susceptible to self-serving rationalizations. In addition, their approach does not take into account legal liability or existing legal precedent as Nagle's and Kitchener's do; they emphasize the purely ethical and moral aspects of a situation. As they do point out, the guidelines make no allowances for ambiguity or mistakes; the actions that consultants take in attempting to resolve ethical challenges are likely to play as important a part in how their performance is judged as are other aspects of their practice.

Where Do We Go from Here?

The future of ethical guidelines for consultation practice depends primarily on the degree to which consultation is considered a profession rather than an indirect service intervention. As noted earlier, Gallessich (1982) began with the premise that consultation has developed into a profession when she developed her twenty-eight principles. After examining the themes developed in a handbook on mental health consultation, Levin, Trickett, and Kidder (1986, p. 509) concluded that "the increasing knowledge base, the assertion that ethical issues in consultation are not easily clarified by the ethical standards of other professional roles, and the clear evidence that consultation activities are proliferating across populations and settings argues that the preconditions for consultation as a primary professional identity are discernible"; their argument lends support to the position taken by Gallessich.

Somewhat sidestepping the question of the maturity of the consultation profession, Snow and Gersick (1986) note the absence of clearly defined basic principles to help consultants deal with the varying contexts in which they practice and recommend three steps toward building consensus. First, they recommend a general code of ethics for consultants, although they do not address how that should be developed. Second, they encourage collaboration among professional associations, state licensing bodies, and the legal system to develop methods for review and enforcement. Third, in spite of the discouraging results of their review, they advocate a more concerted emphasis on training in all phases of professional development.

The absence of evidence for ethical abuses among consultants means that there is no need for an alarmist call for the development of a code or a summit meeting of professionals to take action. In fact, the literature seems to indicate that professionals engage in no more unethical conduct when they are engaged in consultation than when they offer other services. If this conclusion is sound, one might ask why there is such an interest in ethics. One obvious answer to this question is that the existing professional codes do not specifically mention consultation or mention it only in passing. Second, any serious student of consultation recognizes the different models of consultation prevalent in the literature and the differences in emphasis and attention given to certain issues in each model. Thus, the ethical challenges of each model need to be appreciated by the consultant who uses an eclectic approach. Third, practice may vary according to the professional backgrounds of different consultants and the nature of the problems that they deal with. As a result, some commonly agreed upon standards of practice would be welcomed. From a purely cognitive standpoint, ethical awareness should be as important a component of the intervention process in consultation as should the steps of the process or obligations for accountability.

However, it may still be premature to call for a separate code of ethics for consultation. After all, if consultation is an indirect service approach practiced by experts, it should be the professional experts' code of ethics that takes precedence when professional behavior is involved. Codes of ethics seem most appropriate for professionals because it is here that consensus regarding acceptable practices has been achieved and at least some degree of enforcement is available. The above arguments notwithstanding, consultation seems to be not a "profession" but rather a technique practiced by professionals from a number of disciplines. Given its popularity in several fields (see, for example, Idol & West, 1987; Kurpius, 1985), it would seem reasonable to expect these professions or specialties to formulate guidelines that the respective professionals could refer to in their practice. We could expect relatively few areas of difference among them. For example, all of the authors cited in this chapter identified confidentiality as an important issue, and most of them cited the competence of the consultant. Of the other areas of concern addressed, only conflict over values between the consultant and the consultee approximated the level of attention received by confidentiality and consultant competence. Clearly, an interaction of several facets of the consultation process has influenced the contributions that have been made to the literature in this area. What is needed is an explicit explanation of what facets were influential in the formulation of the specific discussions.

One dimension of consultation surely to influence ethical practice is the operational base of the consultant; that is, whether the professional is an external consultant or is employed by the same organization as the consultee. (See Chapter Ten for a discussion of this issue.) Beginning with this one dimension, guidelines can be drawn up regarding best practices. Obviously, the issues involved in the negotiation of a contract will be different for external and internal consultants. In fact, the conceptualization of the "contract" will likely differ greatly because of the perspective of each consultant. Conflicts may also arise between the consultant and organizational policies.

Another important dimension is the model of consultation followed by the consultant and, to a certain extent, the reason that model is being employed. For example, collaborating with another professional suggests that the consultant must assume greater responsibility for the intervention than would be expected in the case of a mental health consultation. It is this type of consideration that must begin to permeate training, supervision, and the scholarly literature. The permutations are numerous when just consultation model, consultant locus, setting, and problem interact, before taking into account such variables as the characteristics of the consultant, the consultee, and the client. Consultants should keep in mind examples of such interactions as they think through situations.

It would seem obvious that didactic and supervised training in consultation should include focused attention on ethical practice. A separate section of a course should be targeted for presentation and discussion of relevant professional codes and similar guidelines. The use of a case instructional methodology is one of the most promising strategies for ensuring both a cognitive and an affective involvement with ethics and, more importantly, for dealing with application issues. Ethical applications in supervision also need systematic attention. Supervisors should consciously critique each supervising session to ensure that potential consultant-consultee conflicts and professional dilemmas are considered by the consultee. Anticipation of problem areas that can arise with particular consultees may be among the most valuable types of preparation that a supervisor can provide. Crego (1985) suggests that exposure within a systematic training program to a multiplicity of models and a variety of consulting environments could foster generalization of skills and promote ethical consultation practice.

Finally, we must recognize the solitary nature of the consultant's practice and its implications for the provision of objective, high-quality service. Consultants need mechanisms that not only support them in providing effective service but also keep them accountable. A variety of continuing education opportunities are available, and their numbers seem to be increasing each year. A more important area in need of attention is the provision of service in a critical-evaluative manner (Kitchener, 1984). The use of peer consultation seems to be a viable approach. In this instance, the internally based consultant may have an advantage in access to peer consultation in which colleagues critique each other's cases (the external consultant in a group practice would also have this advantage). Peer support groups are a promising means of facilitating professional development; the case example presented by Zins, Maher, Murphy, and Wess (1988) illustrates one strategy for accomplishing it. Otherwise, such interchanges might have to be arranged at professional conferences or whenever the two parties could get together personally or through teleconferencing.

Another option for the truly isolated consultant—and for others as well—is the presentation of cases at professional meetings or for publication. Again, the public sharing of cases ensures the self-reflective attitude that is the basis of a sound ethical orientation. It would also provide a secondary benefit for practitioners and researchers. The consultation literature suffers from the paucity of case studies, and such input and involvement from practitioners would promote the development of consultation training and research.

Ethical consultation practice is a complicated topic that practitioners from many fields have begun to address. There is a clear need for model builders to address the unique facets of their approaches that will challenge the consultant. For trainers, the goal is to foster an attitude of problem anticipation that goes beyond the do's and don'ts of some codes and reinforces the self-examination and decision making encouraged by the profession that the consultant represents. For consultants, the goal is to ensure that ethical issues are considered as routinely as other aspects of the consultation enterprise in their deliberations.

References

American Psychological Association. (1981). Ethical principles of psychologists. *American Psychologist, 36,* 633–638.

American Psychological Association. (1992). *Ethical principles of psychologists and code of conduct,* 47(12), 1597–1611.

Benne, K. D. (1961). Democratic ethics and engineering. In. K. D. Benne, W. Bennis, & R. Chin (Eds.), *The planning of change.* New York: Holt, Rinehart, & Winston.

Brown, D., Pryzwansky, W. B., & Schulte, A. C. (1991). *Psychological consultation: Introduction to theory and practice* (2nd ed.). Needham Heights, MA: Allyn & Bacon.

Caplan, G. (1970). *The theory and practice of mental health consultation.* New York: Basic Books.

Crego, C. A. (1985). Ethics: The need for improved consultation training. *The Consulting Psychologist, 13,* 473–476.

Davis, J. M., & Sandoval, J. (1982). Applied ethics for school-based consultants. *Professional psychology, 13,* 543–551.

Gallessich, J. (1982). *The profession and practice of consultation: A handbook for consultants, trainers of consultants, and consumers of consultation services.* San Francisco: Jossey-Bass.

Haas, L. J., & Malouf, J. L. (1989). *Keeping up good work: A practitioner's guide to mental health ethics.* Sarasota, FL: Professional Resource Exchange.

✓ Hughes, J. N. (1986). Ethical issues in school consultation. *School Psychology Review, 15*(4), 489–499.

Idol, L., & West, J. F. (1987). Consultation in special education (part II): Training and practice. *Journal of Learning Disabilities, 20,* 474–494.

Keith-Spiegel, P., & Koocher, G. P. (1985). *Ethics in psychology: Professional standards and cases.* New York: Random House.

Kitchener, K. S. (1984). Intuition, critical evaluation and ethical principles: The foundation for ethical decisions in counseling psychology. *The Counseling Psychologist, 12*(3), 43–55.

Kurpius, D. J. (1985). Consultation interventions: Successes, failures and proposals. *The Counseling Psychologist, 13,* 368–389.

Levin, G., Trickett, E. J., & Kidder, M. G. (1986). The themes, promise, and challenges of mental health consultation. In F. V. Mannino, E. J. Trickett, M. F. Shore, M. G. Kidder, & G. Levin (Eds.), *Handbook of mental health consultation* (DHHS Publication No. ADM 86-1446, pp. 505–520). Washington, DC: U.S. Government Printing Office.

Lowman, R. L. (1985). Ethical practice of psychological consultation: Not an impossible dream. *The Consulting Psychologist, 13,* 466–472.

Nagle, R. J. (1987). Ethics training in school psychology. *Professional School Psychology, 2*(3), 163–171.

Pryzwansky, W. B. (1974). A reconsideration of the consultation model for delivery of school-based psychological services. *American Journal of Orthopsychiatry, 44,* 579–583.

Pryzwansky, W. B. (1990). The nature of consultation vs collaboration. *The Consulting Edge, 2,* 1–2.

Robinson, S. E., & Gross, D. R. (1985). Ethics in consultation: The Canterville Ghost revisited. *The Counseling Psychologist, 13,* 444–465.

Snow, D. L., & Gersick, K. E. (1986). Ethical and professional issues in mental health consultation. In F. V. Mannino, E. J. Trickett, M. F. Shore, M. G. Kidder, & G. Levin (Eds.), *Handbook of mental health consultation* (DHHS Publication No. ADM 86-1446, pp. 393–431). Washington, DC: U.S. Government Printing Office.

Tokunaga, H. T. (1984). Ethical issues in consultation: An evaluative review. *Professional Psychology: Research and Practice, 15,* 811–821.

Tymchuk, A. J. (1981). Ethical decision-making and psychological treatment. *Journal of Psychiatric Treatment and Evaluation, 3,* 507–513.

Zins, J. E., Maher, C. A., Murphy, J. J., & Wess, B. P. (1988). The peer support group: A means to facilitate professional development. *School Psychology Review, 17,* 138–146.

Part Five

TRAINING ISSUES

18

Preservice Education and Professional Staff Development

Lorna Idol

The intent of this chapter is to describe how educational consultants can be prepared in both preservice preparation programs and inservice professional development programs. The recommendations in this chapter were developed over several years of using expert- and field-validated approaches to developing preparatory curricula for educational consultants at both the preservice and the inservice levels of personnel development. The chapter begins by examining the need for this type of professional preparation, clarifying several different and relevant terminologies. It then discusses the specific types of scientific and artful skills needed by educational consultants; examines preparatory education at the preservice level for educational consultants; reports on efforts to provide professional staff development opportunities in school consultation; and considers the similarities and differences between preservice and inservice staff development efforts. The chapter concludes with suggestions for future research directions.

Need for Formal Preparation

The major thrust of this chapter is to lay out a plan for how the skills of educational consultants can be developed through preservice and inservice preparatory training. The underlying premise is that effective educational consultants are not "born" but are the result of a finely tuned combination of well-executed training experiences and practical experience in the field. As we explore the need for this combination, it will be helpful to clarify certain terms and conceptualizations of educational consultation.

351

First, although much has been written about the use of consultation in the school setting, I have been unable to locate a precise definition of *educational consultation*. For the purposes of this chapter, *educational consultation* is defined as an interactive decision-making and problem-solving process undertaken among school professionals, focusing on school-related problems and using a structured problem-solving framework in which one or more of the professionals involved has been trained in consultation.

The specific consultation model used depends on the training and preferences of the professionals involved. For instance, in a review of the school consultation literature, Idol (1988a) described ten different models of consultation reported in the literature, including mental health, behavioral, process, advocacy, two different types of organizational consultation, collaboration, clinical, and program and education-training models. Conoley and Conoley (1982) offer detailed descriptions of the four primary consultation models: mental health, behavioral, advocacy, and process. Suffice it to say that any of these models, with some adaptation in certain cases, could be applied within the context of educational consultation and relevant training efforts. Serious consideration must be given to a key training issue: whether to expose trainees to several different models of consultation or to provide in-depth training in a single model. In the training efforts described in this chapter, trainees are provided with descriptions of the various models but are expected to master only the collaborative model.

All the models of consultation have two primary goals: to provide remedial problem-solving services for presenting problems and to increase consultees' skills so that they can prevent or respond more effectively to similar problems in the future (Gutkin & Curtis, 1990). In determining training needs of school professionals, my colleagues and I have found it useful to ask those professionals to complete a consultation model preference scale (Babcock & Pryzwansky, 1983), which helps them to determine the model or models that they currently are using and/or prefer to use. This chapter emphasizes embedding the collaborative model of consultation within the context of educational consultation.

Skills Needed by Educational Consultants

Educational consultants need skill development in two areas: scientific skills and artful skills (see Idol, 1988b, 1990). The scientific skills of school consultation are the *content* or technical teaching and intervention strategies used to solve work-related problems. The artful skills consist of the *process* skills of consultation, including the various communicative, interactive, problem-solving, and decision-making skills used in the consultative process.

Artful and Scientific Bases of Consultation

In this view of educational consultation, as in effective teaching, there is both an artful base and a scientific base. For example, effective educational consultation requires both a knowledge of specific and related content for solving problems and a knowledge of how to influence the process of consultation in a positive manner. These are referred to respectively as the scientific and artful bases of consultation.

The scientific base is the content or knowledge base that the consultant brings to the consulting process. Possession of this knowledge base is usually the primary reason a consultant is brought in to work with a consultee to help solve a problem. In education, this knowledge usually consists of a wide range of content pertaining to technical teaching interventions, materials modifications, and child-management strategies (Idol, 1990, p. 5).

The artful base of consultation is the way in which the consultant works with consultees in solving problems. This base is often referred to as the process skills of consultation. It is a demonstrable knowledge of how to bring about effective decision making, to solve problems with others, and to interact and communicate effectively with others (Idol, 1990, p. 5).

These two types of consultative skills have been further studied by Cannon, Idol, and West (1992) and West and Cannon (1988) to articulate the precise types of skills thought by experts to be essential for effective school-based consultants. Both of these survey studies employed a futures forecasting technique using a Delphi voting process (Helmer, 1983; Linstone & Turoff, 1975) to obtain the ratings from experts in the areas of study. Basic assumptions of this technique are that consensus indicates a high probability of an accurate forecast, recognized experts in the field are good predictors, and anonymity is a valuable attribute of accurate prediction (Weatherman & Swenson, 1974).

West and Cannon (1988) examined consulting skills, and Cannon et al. (1992) studied instructional and management skills. Both studies used the following procedures. First, an extensive search of the interdisciplinary literature base of the subject was conducted. Second, competency areas that were described with an accompanying research base were written into specific skill statements for professionals. Third, the statements were sent to a nationally representative panel of experts for Delphi voting as to the essentialness of each statement. Fourth, panelists returned their ballots, and the researchers compiled basic statistics for each statement, including a comparison of the rating of the individual panelist with the overall group rating. Fifth, this information was returned to the panelists, and they were required to change or provide a rationale for any outlying ratings. Sixth, after these responses had been returned, the researchers compiled a final set of ratings, considering those to be essential that had both high mean ratings (3.5 and above on a scale of 4.0) and a high degree of consensus among panelists (at least 75 percent of the ratings falling within the panel range of consensus, ± 1.64 SD).

The scientific base of the educational consultant must be a rich knowledge from which to draw practical and workable solutions to the many teaching and child-management problems that arise during school consultation (Idol, 1990). One of the above-mentioned surveys was conducted nationally with both general and special educators (Cannon et al., 1992) to validate a number of essential teaching and management competencies for both general and special educators collaborating to educate students who have mild learning and behavioral problems or are at risk for failure in the classroom. These competency statements were obtained by reviewing the interdisciplinary research literature on effective educational practices. Then, the educational futures forecasting technique described earlier was used. A 105-member interdisciplinary expert panel, representing both general and special education and evenly divided between university- and field-based experts from thirty-five states, was formed. The panel reached consensus on ninety-six competencies thought to be essential for effective teaching of such students. These competencies were arranged in six categories: (1) assessment and diagnosis, (2) instructional content, (3) instructional practices, (4) managing student behavior, (5) planning and managing the teaching and learning environment, and (6) monitoring and evaluation. Although the focus of this study was educators, it is assumed that effective educational consultants would draw on a similar scientific knowledge base. Idol and West (1993) have developed a training program for these skills.

To aid in understanding the artful skills, West and Cannon (1988) conducted an extensive interdisciplinary review of the literature on consultation (school psychology, counseling, general education, special education) to determine some of these process-oriented skills. The skills were then validated by a 100-member panel of experts on school consultation from forty-seven states to determine those skills that were viewed as essential to the consultation process. This study also used the futures forecasting technique; forty-seven of the skills met these experts' standards for being essential. The skills are contained in a training curriculum for developing communicative, interactive, and problem-solving skills (West, Idol, & Cannon, 1988), which is described later in this chapter and in Idol (1990). They are listed in Table 18.1.

Other Types of Skills and Knowledge

In addition to scientific and artful skills, educational consultants also need to develop skills in empowering people, as well as certain types of cognitive skills. The skills to empower people include skills in advocacy, networking,

Table 18.1. Essential Skills for the Process of Consultation.

Consultation Theory/Models

1. Practice reciprocity of roles between consultant and consultee in facilitating the consultation process.
2. Demonstrate knowledge of various stages/phases of the consultation process.
3. Assume joint responsibility for identifying each stage of the consultation process and adjusting behavior accordingly.
4. Match consultation approach(es) to specific consultation situation(s), setting(s) and need(s).

Research on Consultation Theory, Training and Practice

5. Translate relevant consultation research findings into effective school-based consultation practice.

Personal Characteristics

6. Exhibit ability to be caring, respectful, empathic, congruent and open in consultation interactions.
7. Establish and maintain rapport with all persons involved in the consultation process, in both formal and informal interactions.
8. Identify and implement appropriate responses to stage of professional development of all persons involved in the consultation process.
9. Maintain positive self-concept and enthusiastic attitude throughout the consultation process.
10. Demonstrate willingness to learn from others throughout the consultation process.
11. Facilitate progress in consultation situations by managing personal stress, maintaining calm in time of crisis, taking risks, and remaining flexible and resilient.
12. Respect divergent points of view, acknowledging the right to hold different views and to act in accordance with convictions.

Interactive Communication

13. Communicate clearly and effectively in oral and written form.
14. Utilize active ongoing listening and responding skills to facilitate the consultation process (e.g., acknowledging, paraphrasing, reflecting, clarifying, elaborating, summarizing).
15. Determine own and others' willingness to enter consultative relationship.
16. Adjust consultation approach to the learning stage of individuals involved in the consultation process.
17. Exhibit ability to grasp and validate overt/covert meaning and affect in communications (perceptive).
18. Interpret non-verbal communications of self and others (e.g., eye contact, body language, personal boundaries in space) in appropriate context.
19. Interview effectively to elicit information, share information, explore problems, set goals and objectives.
20. Pursue issues with appropriate persistence once they arise in consultation process.
21. Give and solicit continuous feedback which is specific, immediate, and objective.
22. Give credit to others for their ideas and accomplishments.
23. Manage conflict and confrontation skillfully throughout the consultation process to maintain collaborative relationships.
24. Manage timing of consultation activities to facilitate mutual decision-making at each stage of the consultation process.
25. Apply the principle of positive reinforcement to one another in the collaborative team situation.
26. Be willing and safe enough to say "I don't know ... let's find out."

(*continued*)

Table 18.1, Essential Skills for the Process of Consultation, Cont'd.

Collaborative Problem-Solving

27. Recognize that successful and lasting solutions require commonality of goals and collaboration throughout all phases of the problem-solving process.
28. Develop a variety of data collection techniques for problem identification and clarification.
29. Generate viable alternatives through brainstorming techniques characterized by active listening, nonjudgmental responding and appropriate reframing.
30. Evaluate alternatives to anticipate possible consequences, narrow and combine choices, and assign priorities.
31. Integrate solutions into a flexible, feasible and easily implemented plan of action relevant to all persons affected by the problem.
32. Adopt a "pilot problem-solving" attitude, recognizing that adjustments to the plan of action are to be expected.
33. Remain available throughout implementation for support, modeling and/or assistance in modification.
34. Redesign, maintain, or discontinue interventions using data-based evaluation.
35. Utilize observation, feedback, and interviewing skills to increase objectivity and mutuality throughout the problem-solving process.

Systems Change

36. Develop role as a change agent (e.g., implementing strategies for gaining support, overcoming resistance).
37. Identify benefits and negative effects which could result from change efforts.

Equity Issues and Values/Beliefs Systems

38. Facilitate equal learning opportunities by showing respect for individual differences in physical appearance, race, sex, handicap, ethnicity, religion, SES or ability.
39. Advocate for services which accommodate the educational, social and vocational needs of all students, handicapped and nonhandicapped.
40. Encourage implementation of laws and regulations designed to provide appropriate education for all handicapped students.
41. Utilize principles of the least restrictive environment in all decisions regarding handicapped students.
42. Modify myths, beliefs and attitudes which impede successful social and educational integration of handicapped students into the least restrictive environment.
43. Recognize, respect and respond appropriately to the effects of personal values and belief systems of self and others in the consultation process.

Evaluation of Consultation Effectiveness

44. Insure that persons involved in planning and implementing the consultation process are also involved in its evaluation.
45. Establish criteria for evaluating input, process and outcome variables affected by the consultation process.
46. Engage in self-evaluation of strengths and weaknesses to modify personal behaviors influencing the consultation process.
47. Utilize continuous evaluative feedback to maintain, revise, or terminate consultation activities.

Source: West, J. F., Idol, L., & Cannon, G. (1989). *Collaboration in the schools: Interacting, communicating, and problem solving.* Austin, TX: PRO-ED. Reprinted with permission from the publisher.

and team building. According to Idol, Paolucci-Whitcomb, and Nevin (1993), "*Empowerment,* a term meaning actions or sanctions that *enable* certain persons to make decisions, is currently being applied in school reform efforts centered around site-based management. In this example, certain teachers are empowered to work with the building principal in making site-based management decisions. The idea behind this movement is the legitimization of power, such as the empowerment of decision making given to those who are most directly involved in the areas for which the decisions are being made."

Empowerment skills are associated with the advocacy model of consultation (Chesler, Bryant & Crowfoot, 1981), which is expected to be used in conjunction with other models of consultation. Skills typical of the advocacy consultant include knowledge of educational law, organization of people, organization of events, media use, negotiation, parent partnerships, persuasive writing and speaking, building of support networks, and tolerance for ambiguity and conflict (see Conoley & Conoley, 1982; Idol, 1988a).

In contrast, the cognitive skills are drawn from the cognitive instruction literature. Although these skills are described primarily as aids for teaching students thinking and studying skills (Derry, 1990; Bransford, Vye, Kinzer, & Risko, 1990), they apply quite aptly to the preparation of both teachers and education consultants. An important quality of an educational consultant is the ability to use different strategies for different types of knowledge within the context of a consultative problem-solving process. The cognitive learning theories of Gagne (1985) and Anderson (1983) suggest three types of knowledge relevant for educational consultants: declarative knowledge, procedural knowledge, and conditional knowledge. The development of preparatory programs should include consideration of how educational consultants need to use these three types of knowledge.

Declarative knowledge, sometimes referred to as "knowledge that," is the organized collection of facts and concepts that make up the scientific base of a discipline, such as educational methodologies and techniques. In educational consultation, this declarative knowledge base means a mastery of a repertoire of specific solutions to certain types of problems. Another example is when educational consultants learn to use specific techniques for enhancing communication, interaction, and group problem solving.

For illustrative purposes, consider what happens cognitively when we train an educational consultant to use a series of stages in problem solving. These stages, which commonly are accepted in the consultation literature, would be considered a "knowledge that" and would consist of having a knowledge of the following stages:

1. Determining the goal of the consultation, including specification of roles and responsibilities

2. Identifying the problem
3. Exploring possible alternative solutions to the problem
4. Developing implementation recommendations consisting of a specific plan of action
5. Determining how the implementation plan and interventions will be evaluated
6. Completing a follow-up session to determine whether the plan of action has been successful or should be redesigned

The declarative knowledge in this case is the educational consultant's knowledge of what is to be done in each of the stages in the problem-solving process.

Procedural knowledge, or "knowledge how," consists of "performance capabilities involving symbol manipulation, such as the ability to write, read, or solve algebra problems" (Derry, 1990, p. 350). In the case of preparing educational consultants to use the stages of problem solving listed above, an important procedural knowledge is the ability to use a problem-solving sequence. This would involve the cognitive ability to know when to shift to subsequent stages in the problem-solving process, depending upon the progress of the problem-solving team.

A third type of knowledge, which is important for the ability to spontaneously retrieve information is based on *conditional knowledge,* "knowledge about the conditions under which knowledge is applicable" (Bransford et al., 1990, pp. 389–390). Basically, procedural knowledge is knowing *when* to do *what.* In using stages of problem solving, conditional knowledge would indicate when to contribute certain types of information, interactive communication skills, and resources in the appropriate stage in the problem-solving process.

The learned ability to use a formal problem-solving process in the three ways described above is a basic and essential component in the preparation of educational consultants. In addition to these basic components, a sound preparatory program, whether preservice or inservice, should also include a careful analysis of the appropriate artful and scientific skills and the people-empowerment skills discussed earlier.

All relevant skills are taught at three levels of learning: acquisition, supervised practice, and application. This teaching sequence helps to develop skills that may be applied as declarative, procedural, or conditional knowledge, depending on what is appropriate.

The next two sections of this chapter provide a more detailed examination of how educational consultants can be prepared in preservice and professional development programs. These descriptions are followed by a comparative discussion of the two types of preparatory efforts.

Consultant Preparation at the Preservice Level

The discussion in this section is based on several years of experimentation to determine effective ways of preparing resource and consulting special education teachers at the master's level (see Idol, 1983, 1990; Idol-Maestas, 1981; Idol-Maestas, Lloyd, & Lilly, 1981; Idol-Maestas & Ritter, 1985). This research has resulted in a basic framework for preparatory experiences for educational consultants with two primary components: a core course in consultation, including both presentation of course content and supervised and simulated practice, and a supervised internship, consisting of practical experiences and the completion of a series of independent field studies.

The Core Course

Within the core course, two levels of learning are used as opportunities for graduate students to master consulting skills: acquisition and supervised practice. Students first acquire a core set of information for each skill that is being explored. Then, when they have demonstrated mastery of a concept, the level of instruction is moved to *supervised practice,* where students are expected to practice using the particular skills under instructor supervision. This practice is almost always undertaken in small groups of students, who provide feedback to each other.

The core course consists of four subcomponents: (1) demonstrations and discussions of different types of school consultation projects, (2) demonstrated student mastery of a basic set of core skills related to efficient and effective problem solving, (3) further student development of specific interpersonal communication and interaction skills, and (4) independent student completion of computer-simulated problems reflecting typical school consultation situations (Lloyd & Idol-Maestas, 1983).

The first subcomponent, demonstrations of different types of school consultation projects, consists of presentation and group discussion of the actual field-based consultation projects described in Idol (1992). These projects are organized into the following types:

1. Helping students in transition from a resource or supplementary educational program to a general classroom program (see Idol, 1992, chaps. 4 and 5)
2. Helping students experiencing academic problems in the classroom (see Idol, 1992, chaps. 6 and 7)
3. Helping students experiencing behavioral problems in the classroom (see Idol, 1992, chap. 8)
4. Working with families of problem students (see Idol, 1992, chap. 9)

5. Furthering staff development among school faculties (see Idol, 1992, chap. 10; West, Idol, & Cannon, 1989, instructor's manual).

In their internship in the field, students are eventually required to complete a field-based project for each of these five types.

The second subcomponent of this course consists of mastery of a basic set of skills. While a nationwide panel of experts in school consultation has identified as many as forty-seven essential communicative, interactive, and problem-solving skills (West & Cannon, 1988), my colleagues and I have found a particular set of skills to be especially important in the practice of school consultation and have incorporated them into the various modules of our training curriculum (West et al., 1989). As evidence of their mastery of these skills, students are expected to:

1. Demonstrate knowledge of various stages and phases of the consultation process (module 2)
2. Demonstrate tacit knowledge of four basic models of consultation (module 2) and mastery of the collaborative model
3. Use active, ongoing listening and responding skills (for example, acknowledging, paraphrasing, reflecting, clarifying, elaborating, and summarizing) to facilitate the consultation process (module 14)
4. Interview effectively to elicit information, share information, explore problems, and set goals and objectives (module 19)
5. Develop skills in systematic identification of problems (module 28; also see Idol et al., 1986, chap. 3; Idol, Nevin, & Paolucci-Whitcomb, 1986)
6. Generate viable alternatives through brainstorming techniques characterized by active listening, nonjudgmental responding, and appropriate reframing (module 29)
7. Evaluate intervention alternatives to anticipate possible consequences, narrow and combine choices, and assign priorities (module 30)
8. Integrate solutions into a flexible, feasible, and easily implemented action plan relevant to everyone affected by the problem (module 31)

In the third subcomponent of the course, students complete a needs assessment instrument (West et al., 1989, app. A) to determine where they need improvement in personal characteristics, interactive communication, effectiveness as a change agent, equity issues, and values and belief systems and then sign a personalized contract with the course instructor identifying the particular skills on which they wish to improve. Skills selected by a number of students are discussed in class, and students are then required to target these skills for practice during simulated group problem-solving sessions in the classroom. These skills are also earmarked as ones on which to concentrate when the actual field internships are completed.

The fourth subcomponent of the course focuses on independent use of computerized and simulated problem-solving opportunities. Students are required to work through a series of nine simulated problems on computers, either individually or in pairs. The program allows them to compare their responses and solutions to various consultation problems to those of experts. During our experimental phase, these experts were graduates of preparatory programs in school consultation who were working in the field at the time the simulation program was developed (see Lloyd, 1984; Lloyd & Idol-Maestas, 1983, for related research in program content validation and expert responses). After the completion of each set of three problems, students gather for discussion of the program content and their reactions and thoughts regarding the preferred solutions to the various problems.

For each skill that is taught in the second and third subcomponents, an instructional module plan is used to determine the instructional tasks, the required demonstrations of student mastery, and the materials needed for instruction. An example of such an instructional module plan is presented in Table 18.2. Note that this sample module plan is designed to facilitate learning and skill acquisition at three levels of learning: acquisition, supervised practice, and application. For each level of learning, the table lists how the skill is taught, how learner performance and skill acquisition are evaluated, and the resources needed to facilitate each level of the lesson.

Supervised Internship

In the third component of this training effort, students preparing for the consultant role are required to conduct an internship in a school or other educational setting. During this internship, students are expected to complete the first five types of field-based projects listed above. The evaluation process is a collaborative one, involving the trainee, an experienced consultant at the school site, a field supervisor from the university, and the internship program coordinator.

The interns are evaluated by four methods: direct observation, continuous monitoring, formal evaluation, and completion of the projects. First, direct observations are provided by the field supervisors on a weekly basis. These supervisors use data sheets to remind themselves to evaluate particular targeted skills for the intern. The experienced consultant offers biweekly feedback concerning the intern's progress.

Second, for continuous monitoring, each of the people involved in evaluation has a copy of a booklet listing the particular skills that the intern is

Table 18.2. Instructional Module Plan for Demonstrating Knowledge of Various Phases of the Consultation Process.

■ CONSULTATION SKILL 2 Demonstrate knowledge of various stage/phases of the consultation process.		■ SKILL AREA Consultation Theory/Models

Learning experience	Performance evaluation (criteria, method)	Materials/Resources*
■ ACQUISITION Using lecture/readings, the instructor exposes learners to each of the stages and gives examples of each stage.	Learners complete the Consultation Process Outline, giving examples of each stage. Learners may draw examples from the lecture and/or readings.	Readings (see References and Resources in Module Knowledge Base) Module Knowledge Base for lecture Summary of Four Consultation Models at Five Stages of the Consultation Process (West, 1985) Consultation Process Outline
■ PRACTICE Learners view or listen to segments of a complete consultation episode, identifying the stages. The stages could be presented in random order to strengthen skill in identifying stages.	Given a consultation episode, learners, as a group, delineate stages.	Segments of a complete consultation situation (through all stages) as depicted on the accompanying videotape
■ APPLICATION Given a consultation case study, learners analyze each relationship by identifying the specific stages in the consultation process.	Learners accurately identify specific stages in the consultation process.	Case Study (see List of References of Consultation Case Studies)

Source: West, J. F., Idol, L., & Cannon, G. (1989). *Collaboration in the schools: An inservice and preservice curriculum for teachers, support staff, and administrators.* Austin, TX: PRO-ED. Reprinted with permission of the publishers.

* The Consultation Model Preference Scale in Appendix B could be used as an additional resource for this module.

working to master. As the intern initiates, works on, and completes each performance objective, evaluators record this information in their booklets. Upon completion of each objective, the intern's performance is rated on a three-point Likert scale; the field supervisor records all ratings on a master copy that is submitted to the intern program coordinator three times during the period of the internship.

Third, formal evaluations are conducted three times during the period of the internship. The intern, the experienced consultant, and the field supervisor complete evaluation forms and then meet to collaboratively examine the results of the evaluations, making certain to discuss and understand any discrepancies among them.

Fourth, for completion of the five types of projects, the evaluation team provides feedback on the intern's progress at three critical points in the preparatory process: at the initiation of the project, at some point during the project, and at the termination of the project. As the projects are finished, reports are submitted to the program coordinator. Examples of typical completed projects can be found in Idol (1992).

Program Evaluation and Course Restructuring

An integral part of an effective preservice preparatory program is continuous redesign based on consumer feedback. Evaluative feedback should be periodically collected from the cooperating teachers, the consultees, and the trainees themselves. In earlier efforts, we have accomplished this by surveying program graduates, the graduates' supervisors, and the graduates' former cooperating teachers after the first and fifth years after program completion, as well as by conducting in-depth interview studies of the graduates (Idol & Ritter, 1987; Idol-Maestas & Ritter, 1985).

Using the survey method, we have asked graduates to rate their mastery of each of the skills acquired in their preparatory program at three times: prior to program entry, after program completion, and after working in the field. With the interview method, we have conducted structured interviews with the program graduates over the telephone. We have used as interviewers people not affiliated with the program in the hopes of obtaining candid responses. Through these two types of feedback, survey and interview, program developers are able to determine which aspects of the program have been successful, which require improvement, and which are not relevant.

Summary

Students enrolled in advanced studies in school consultation can be provided with opportunities to master consultation skills by engaging in three levels of learning: acquisition, supervised practice, and field applications. The study experience includes a core course and a field internship, with ongoing program evaluation and revision. The course of study includes completion of different types of school consultation projects and mastery of communicative and interactive skills, individual problem-solving skills, and group problem-solving skills. Throughout the experience, emphasis is placed on collegial and reciprocal collaboration with other professionals.

Professional Staff Development

In the field-validation process that we used to build the training curriculum for *Collaboration in the Schools* (West et al., 1989), we developed a structure for preparing school staffs. This structure consists of several components, described in this section.

Selection of Program Participants

A training effort such as this should be focused on interdisciplinary groups of professionals representing school administration, general education, school psychology, special education, guidance and counseling, speech and language services, and related services. One of our most successful efforts to bring about change in schools has been training building-based leadership teams prepared in group decision making, collaborative team building, and effective communication and group interaction skills. These teams offer similar training experiences to the entire school staff.

The first member of a team is the building principal, who is recruited on a voluntary basis. The principal selects or the staff nominates key staff as leadership team members. These team members then select a small core of classroom teachers who are influential among the school staff. These teachers may or may not be the most effective instructors in the building, but they are often professionals to whom other teachers turn for guidance. The team next recruits support staff such as resource and special program teachers who are responsible for auxiliary instruction for particular at-risk, remedial, and/or mildly handicapped students. Finally, other key support staff who would enhance the development of the leadership team are selected. Depending on the needs of the team, these people may include staff such as school psychologist, guidance counselor, speech and language clinician, or social worker.

Needs Assessment

It is important to administer a needs assessment to all staff who are to be involved in training. This recommendation is based on three important findings from a comprehensive review of the inservice staff development literature in education (Nicholson, Joyce, Parker, & Waterman, 1976):

1. School-based programs in which teachers participated as helpers and planners of inservice activities were more likely to be successful than programs planned and conducted without teachers' assistance.
2. Teachers were more likely to benefit from programs in which they chose

their own goals and activities than from program in which goals and activities were preplanned.
3. Teacher self-initiated and self-directed activities were seldom used in in-service educational programs; however, when used, they were successful in accomplishing objectives.

The assessment instrument should include a listing of the various skills that could be offered in training and allow staff members to select areas in which they feel they need more training opportunities. (We use the needs assessment instrument in app. A of West et al., 1989.)

Organization of the Staff Development Program Agenda

On the basis of the needs assessment data, staff development program developers construct a tentative agenda containing training modules in areas that the majority of the staff have indicated as having high priority. In addition, the consultants and staff members responsible for staff development efforts determine whether there are skill areas that have not been indicated as high priorities but that are essential to developing effectively functioning teams. If there are any of these, they are usually added to the training program. For example, our curriculum includes key modules on using a systematic structure for group problem solving (modules 29, 30, 31) and using the commonly accepted stages of problem solving of school consultation (modules 2 and 4, West, Idol, & Cannon, 1989; see also Idol & Baran, 1992; Idol, Nevin, & Paolucci-Whitcomb, 1986); if the focus of the training is building problem-solving teams of professionals, these areas are included in the training program.

Program Design

In our efforts to prepare building-based teams, we have used the *Collaboration in the Schools* training curriculum (West et al., 1989), which was designed to develop essential communicative and interactive interpersonal skills and collaborative problem-solving skills. It is a complete curriculum for providing professional and preservice training experiences for classroom teachers, remedial and special education teachers and other support staff, and school administrators in the artful process of collaborative consultation and effective teaming. The major purpose of collaborative consultation is to stimulate collaboration among classroom teachers, special education teachers, other support staff, and building administrators who are jointly responsible for the education of exceptional and at-risk students. Its use is intended to aid in prevention of serious learning or behavioral problems in at-risk students and to improve coordination of instruction and remediation for exceptional and at-risk students.

The curriculum consists of forty-seven training modules based on the essential collaborative consultation skills described in Table 18.1. Each training module provides three levels of adult learning experiences designed for inservice and preservice learners: acquisition of knowledge, supervised practice and mastery, and field and/or simulated application. The acquisition-level experiences provide learners with a basic knowledge of each skill. Instructors use various modes of information giving and sharing, such as lectures, readings followed by discussion, brainstorming, large- and small-group discussions, video presentation demonstrating a skill, and individual self-appraisal.

At the level of supervised practice and mastery, learners are provided with opportunities to practice each skill in a controlled, supervised learning environment. These often involve practicing the targeted skill through individual activities; group or team activities; role plays; triadic interactions, with one member serving as observer and providing feedback, coupled with role rotation; problem-solving exercises; and development of a plan of action to address a given problem. Integral features of this level of learning experience are instructor modeling, evaluative and corrective feedback, and suggestions for improvement by both peers and instructors.

For the third level of learning experience, field and/or simulated application, particular attention has been given to the design of learning experiences for both preservice and inservice learners. Learning experiences at this level emphasize "real-life" situations encountered by the learner in the school environment. Extensive use is made of simulated problem solving, as well as actual field experiences designed to apply the targeted skill under "real" conditions. Evaluation of skill mastery at this level includes self-appraisal, field supervisor or peer feedback, learner development and field testing of a permanent product followed by feedback and sharing with fellow learners, and, of course, instructor observation and feedback. Again, emphasis is given to the use of peer and supervisor or instructor evaluative feedback and suggestions for further improving the learner's competence in the targeted skill.

Field Visitations and Follow-Up Evaluations

An important element of effective professional development efforts is field visitations to determine the impact of training activities on what is actually occurring in the field. Probably one of the biggest criticisms of inservice staff development programs is that they place people in passive learning situations without opportunities for direct learning and application experiences. We have found that supplying these opportunities is still not enough. Follow-up field visitation is important for a number of reasons. First, support may be given lip service during training but not actually provided once the professionals involved are back in the schools. Second, new barriers to implementation that may be encountered may seem so overwhelming that all projected plans for change are forgotten. Third, the team of trained professionals may fail to carry through with whole-staff training and may instead function as a singular and independent unit within the school. Fourth, the trainees may have focused on certain singular aspects of their training and forgotten other information that would help them to expand their efforts. Fifth, if individual team members who assumed considerable initial leadership have left the team, the entire team may have floundered. These are all examples of problems that we have encountered when conducting field visitations after training.

On a more positive note, we have also visited teams that have trained the entire school staff, implemented new and improved service delivery systems, developed some of their own training videotapes, and so on. What we have found with these teams is a very human need for reinforcement: for their former instructors to encourage them, to praise them, and to help them attack new problems. They always seem to need more encouragement to document and evaluate their efforts. Several of our field-based sites have received national recognition in the form of published reports, workshops, and invited speeches at national meetings. We have also found considerably better implementation and follow-through when trainees expect and receive a forthcoming field visitation.

Preservice and Inservice Education: Similarities and Differences

While the preceding discussion seems to reveal more similarities than differences between the preservice and inservice preparation of professionals for educational consultation, a careful analysis reveals that the list of differences is considerably more extensive.

Similarities

The primary similarity between these two types of preparatory efforts lies in the *content* of what is being taught to these school consultants. Both types of trainees receive opportunities to develop a basic core of skills essential for effective school consultation and collaboration. This content was derived primarily from a developed training curriculum covering research-based and expert-validated skills in group problem solving, communication, and interaction. In addition, both types of programs give trainees opportunities to evaluate themselves and one another and to apply learned concepts in the field.

Differences

The differences, although less reflective of the bulk of what is mastered, are considerable. First, there appears to be a much higher level of completion of field-based projects—the application level of learning—in the preservice efforts. With the professional inservice groups, completion of field-based projects depends primarily on the individual motivation of those involved in training efforts. We have encountered no school districts that provide financial incentives to personnel who actually implement the content of training programs.

Second, the preservice programs emphasize developing the ability to make sound decisions on the basis of the technological knowledge that the consultant in training has acquired. This is done through the use of independent student completion of simulated and computerized consultation problems, followed by group discussion of results and comparison of trainees' decisions with those of experts in school consultation. We have not experimented with this type of procedure in inservice staff development programs, and it seems unlikely to be used in that context, where there is little leverage to ensure completion of such independent tasks and often little time provided to conduct such work.

Third, professional staff development programs provide considerably more opportunities for working in real interdisciplinary teams with group feedback. This is more difficult to accomplish in preservice programs. There have been some initial efforts to require interdisciplinary cooperation among university departments in such areas as elementary and secondary education, educational psychology, special education, school administration, social work, guidance and counseling, and speech and language services. The literature provides descriptions of coordinated course efforts in elementary education and social work (Pugach and Allen-Meares, 1985) and educational psychology and special education (Sheridan and Welch, 1990). However, practice simulations in preservice preparation generally do not provide opportunities for students to practice with certificated and field-based professionals, which are an important part of professional development.

Fourth, there is much better program evaluation in preservice than in inservice programs. University instructors whose participation in evaluation activities is likely to improve their chances for promotion and tenure are therefore likely to see such efforts to their completion. In school districts, on the other hand, it is difficult to get anyone to take responsibility for evaluation activities unless they are required for a specifically funded project or are the specified domain of an evaluation department. It cannot be assumed that people responsible for staff development and the promotion of change within a system are necessarily committed to ongoing evaluation efforts. Such people may be accustomed to gathering evaluative data on training sessions at the time of training but much less accustomed to or motivated for gathering information over time. It is the latter that is needed.

Fifth, a hard reality is that the reason most people enroll in a preservice preparatory program is to obtain certification or credentials. By joining a particular program, they give their consent to complete the required tasks, projects, assignments, and so on and submit themselves to serious evaluation efforts. The same outcomes are considerably more difficult to achieve with inservice populations, because they have often not been involved in selecting the content of the training program (although we make efforts to do this through needs assessment surveys for certain skills), there is often no requirement or leverage for them to complete field-based applications (unless they consent individually to be part of particular pilot projects), and they often feel uncomfortable with individual evaluation efforts.

Sixth, program implementation is expected in inservice professional development efforts, whereas the single outcome goal of preservice programs is to produce qualified individuals. Professional attitude, availability of funding, commitment of key people, time for consulting, a specified plan of service delivery, the need to train the entire school staff, and turnover of key staff are all important variables that contribute to program implementation that are also discussed esoterically in preservice programs. Idol (1988) and West and Idol (1990) provide more detailed discussions of these key considerations for effective development and implementation of consultation programs.

Thus, both types of preparatory efforts are challenging; in some key and concrete ways, they are very similar. I suspect that the lack of effective staff development efforts has been due primarily to two erroneous assumptions: (1) that course content would need to be vastly different for inservice efforts and (2) that staff development is a singular effort, consisting of a few hours of training, rather than multiple contact hours.

It is also true that there are a considerable number of differences between preservice and inservice efforts. The discussion of six of these differences above, is likely to convince most readers that they could be minimized if efforts were made to assist school personnel in reconceptualizing what staff development is: rather than separate and isolated "inservice sessions" or "presentations," a series of ongoing professional learning and application activities that help prepare staff for the future.

Directions for Future Research

An exciting and challenging future lies ahead for research on the preparation of professionals for school consultation. One challenging area is the list of interpersonal, interactive, and problem-solving skills. The skills listed in Table 18.1 cover forty-seven different topics. This list needs to be condensed into a more compact enumeration of the most essential skills. Another area is the personal attitudes that the consultant brings to the problem-solving process, which are certain to affect outcomes. We have gained some insight into these attitudes from our personal experiences and years of preparing school consultants (see Idol, Paolucci-Whitcomb, & Nevin, 1993); definitive research in this area would be most helpful.

A third challenging area is developing a better understanding of how best to offer preservice preparation to school consultants, creating learning environments where they can be trained with preservice candidates from other disciplines, such as elementary and secondary education, guidance and counseling, special education, school administration, speech and language, and so on. When these professionals are employed in the school systems, they will be expected to engage in collaborative problem solving. Why not create such learning environments to give practice in the kinds of real environments in which they will eventually be consulting and collaborating with one another?

References

Anderson, J. R. (1983). *The architecture of cognition.* Cambridge, MA: Harvard University Press.

Babcock, N. L., & Pryzwansky, W. B. (1983). Models of consultation: Preferences of educational professionals at five stages of service. *Journal of School Psychology, 21,* 359–366.

Bransford, J. D., Vye, N., Kinzer, C., & Risko, V. (1990). Teaching thinking and content knowledge: Toward an integrated model. In B. F. Jones & L. Idol (Eds.), *Dimensions of thinking and cognitive instruction* (pp. 381–414). Hillsdale, NJ: Erlbaum.

Cannon, G., Idol, L., & West, J. F. (1992). Educating students with mild handicaps in general classrooms: Essential teaching practices for general and special educators. *Journal of Learning Disabilities, 25*(5), 300–317.

Chesler, M. A., Bryant, B. I., Jr., Crowfoot, J. E. (1981). Consultation in schools: Inevitable conflict, partisanship, and advocacy. In M. J. Curtis & J. E. Zins (Eds.), *The theory and practice of school consultation.* Springfield, IL: Thomas.

Conoley, J. C., & Conoley, C. W. (1982). *School consultation: A guide to practice and training.* Elmsford, NY: Pergamon Press.

Derry, S. J. (1990). Learning strategies for acquiring useful knowledge. In B. F. Jones & L. Idol (Eds.), *Dimensions of thinking and cognitive instruction* (pp. 347–380). Hillsdale, NJ: Erlbaum.

Gagne, R. M. (1985). *The conditions of learning* (4th ed.). New York: Holt, Rinehart & Winston.

Gutkin, T. B., & Curtis, M. J. (1990). School-based consultation. In T. B. Gutkin & C. R. Reynolds (Eds.), *The handbook of school psychology* (2nd ed., pp. 577–611). New York: Wiley.

Helmer, O. (1983). *Looking forward: A guide to futures research.* Newbury Park, CA: Sage.

Idol, L. (1992). *Special educator's consultation handbook* (2nd ed.). Austin, TX: PRO-ED.

Idol, L. (1988a). Theory of school consultation. In J. F. West (Ed.), *School consultation: Interdisciplinary perspectives on theory, research, training, and practice* (pp. 1–16). Austin, TX: Association of Educational and Psychological Consultants.

Idol, L. (1988b). Training in special education consultation. In J. F. West (Ed.), *School consultation: Interdisciplinary perspectives on theory, research, training, and practice* (pp. 105–126). Austin, TX: Association of Educational and Psychological Consultants.

Idol, L. (1990). The scientific art of consultation. *Journal of Education and Psychological Consultation, 1,* 3–22.

Idol, L., & Baran, S. (1992). Elementary school counselors and special educators consulting together: Perilous pitfalls or opportunities to collaborate. *Elementary School Guidance and Counseling, 26*(3), 202–213.

Idol, L., Nevin, A., & Paolucci-Whitcomb, P. (1986). *Models of curriculum-based assessment.* Austin, TX: PRO-ED.

Idol, L., Paolucci-Whitcomb, P., & Nevin, A. (1986). *Collaborative consultation.* Rockville, MD: Aspen.

Idol, L., Paolucci-Whitcomb, P., & Nevin, A. (1993). *Collaborative consultation* (2nd ed.). Austin, TX: PRO-ED.

Idol, L., & Ritter, S. A. (1987). Data-based instruction: Do teachers use it? *Teacher Education and Special Education, 9*(1), 65–70.

Idol, L., & West, J. F. (1987). Consultation in special education (part II): Training and practice. *Journal of Learning Disabilities, 20,* 474–494.

Idol, L., & West, J. F. (1993). *Effective instruction of difficult-to-teach students.* Austin, TX: PRO-ED.

Idol-Maestas, L. (1981). A teacher training model: The resource/consulting teacher. *Behavioral Disorders, 6*(2) 108–121.

Idol-Maestas, L., Lloyd, S., & Lilly, M. S. (1981). Implementation of a noncategorical approach to direct service and teacher education. *Exceptional Children, 48*(3), 213–219.

Idol-Maestas, L., & Ritter, S. A. (1985). A follow-up study of resource/consulting teachers: Factors which facilitate and inhibit teacher consultation. *Teacher Education and Special Education, 8*(3), 121–131.

Linstone, H., & Turoff, M. (1975). *The Delphi method: Technique and applications.* Reading, MA: Addison-Wesley.

Lloyd, S. R. (1984). *The development of a computer simulation for consulting teachers.* Unpublished doctoral dissertation, University of Illinois, Urbana-Champaign.

Lloyd, S., & Idol-Maestas, L. (1983). Consulting teacher simulation program. *Teacher Education and Special Education, 6*(3), 179–185.

Meyers, C. E. (1973). The school psychologist and mild retardation. *Mental Retardation, 11,* 15–20.

Nicholson, A., Joyce, B. R., Parker, D., & Waterman, F. T. (1976). *The literature on inservice teacher education: An analytic review* (ISTE Report III). Palo Alto, CA: National Center for Education Statistics and Teacher Corps. (ERIC Document Reproduction Service No. ED 129 734).

Pugach, M., & Allen-Meares, P. (1985). Collaboration at the preservice level. *Teacher Education and Special Education, 8*(1), 3–11.

Sheridan, S. M., & Welch, M. (1990). An interdisciplinary course in educational problem-solving and conflict management. *The Consulting Edge, 2*(2), 3–7.

Weatherman, R., & Swenson, K. (1974). Delphi techniques. In S. P. Hencley & J. R. Yates (Eds.) *Futurism in education: Methodologies* (pp. 97–114). Berkeley, CA: McCutchan.

West, J. F., & Cannon, G. S. (1988). Essential collaborative consultation competencies for regular and special educators. *Journal of Learning Disabilities, 21,* 56–63.

West, J. F., Idol, L., & Cannon, G. (1989). *Collaboration in the schools: Communicating, interacting and problem solving.* Austin, TX: PRO-ED.

19

Educating Consultants for Applied Clinical and Educational Settings

Sylvia Rosenfield, Todd A. Gravois

As interest in consultation as a helping process grows across a number of human service fields, there is concurrent interest in developing skillful consultants through training. Because of this shift in practice within applied settings toward use of consultation, there is a need for both preservice and in-service consultation training. While acknowledging that different consultation models (for example, mental health, organizational, behavioral), have different assumptions and focuses, this chapter is responsive to the developing perception that there are similarities among the major theoretical perspectives in both the content and the process of consultation (Alpert & Associates, 1982; Gallessich, 1985). If this perception is accurate and similarities do exist, we believe that a basis for consultation training in core skills can be established, whatever the theoretical perspective. These core skills represent the foundation for practice and should be incorporated into all training programs, although particular consultation models may require additional competencies.

A major thrust of this chapter is a search for the essential elements of consultation—those skills and competencies that transcend theoretical models—and methods for educating skillful consultants. Given the current state of our understanding of consultation, the empirical base for developing training models is still limited. Nonetheless, a small literature on educating consultants exists, and it is reviewed here (additional discussion can be found in Chapters Eighteen and Twenty). In addition, the chapter includes a discussion of issues to consider in conceptualizing the training process.

Defining Consultation

Consultation is typically defined as a relationship between two or more individuals. A more comprehensive definition of consultation acknowledges this relationship but also addresses the individual who assumes the role of consultant. This section focuses on both the consultative relationship and the consultant as an individual.

The Consultative Relationship

Consultation has been defined across a number of disciplines, (such as education, business, organization development, and psychology) by a number of professionals in each field (Carter, 1989; Dougherty, 1990; French & Anderson, 1983; Gallessich, 1974, 1985; Gutkin & Curtis, 1990; Idol, Paolucci-Whitcomb, & Nevin, 1986; Kratochwill & VanSomeren, 1985; Meyers, 1981; see also Chapter Seven). Consultation is most consistently defined to include the following aspects: it is a voluntary relationship between professionals, one identified as a consultant and the other identified as a consultee; the goal of the consultative relationship is the resolution of some work-related problem presented by the consultee; and it teaches the consultee additional skills that will help facilitate problem solving in future situations (see the related discussion in Chapter One). Such a definition follows the trend toward conceptualizing consultation more and more as a vehicle or device by which services (such as knowledge, technical expertise, information, and support) can be delivered, rather than a thing in itself (see, for example, Zins & Ponti, 1990).

A majority of consultation definitions rely on earlier literature, which included the proposition that consultation is a triadic model (Caplan, 1970; Tharp & Note, 1988), with the main focus of the relationship between consultant and consultee being problem solving for the benefit of a third person. Generally, the consultee maintains responsibility for the client and controls the implementation of interventions. However, another conception of consultation focuses on collaboration (Pryzwansky, 1977) and sharing of responsibility for the outcome between the consultant and consultee. In training, the nature of the consultation relationship along the continuum from expert to collaborative and collegial needs to be considered.

The Consultant

While the relationship-focused definitions of consultation presented above are often helpful to guide initial behaviors of trainees by offering a schema of how consultation looks, trainers must have a fuller definition of consultation. Defining consultation for the purpose of training requires an exploration of the type of consultant that will result from training, whether the consultant is defined as having a "bag of tricks" or as an expert in both the content and process of complex interpersonal experiences.

Typically, expertise is defined in terms of the specific tasks performed by professionals, and the role of training programs is to teach these specific skills (Kennedy, 1987). This technical-skills view of expertise is based on three assumptions: essential skills can be identified; they can be transmitted to practitioners through training; and, once trained, such skills can be drawn on in practice (Kennedy, 1987). However, problems tend to arise not in identifying competencies but in delimiting their number and/or establishing agreement on the list. Moreover, complex competencies raise questions as to which contributing elements are essential.

The strongest criticism of the technical-skills approach has focused on its failure to consider professional practice as a complex process. The difficulty in the real world arises when practitioners are asked to "solve problems and make decisions in ambiguous situations . . . to see the relationship between general principles and the particular situations they will encounter in practice" (Kennedy, 1987, pp. 138–139). The issue for trainers is to enable novice consultants to combine expertise in skills with the ability to recognize situations in which these skills are appropriate. Thus, it is critical to attend to the heuristics that determine when and whether principles are applied.

This leads to another level of expertise, that of professionals who can analyze situations in the context of their work, and assumes a reciprocal interaction between analysis and action. The recent work by Schön (1987) on educating reflective practitioners, who analyze and reflect on their own performance and modify their behavior accordingly, is an example of this model of expertise. Gambrill (1990) also approaches the problem of critical thinking in clinical practice, suggesting how clinicians could improve their understanding of their own behavior. Such conceptual models of expertise as those presented by Schön and Gambrill have not yet been developed in consultation training.

In truth, there has been little empirical work on either the nature of professional expertise or how to enhance its development. Nor has there been much research on how professional expertise is related to the personal characteristics of effective consultants that have emerged in the literature (for example, Alpert, Ballantyne, & Griffiths, 1981; Weissenburger, Fine, & Poggio, 1982). Yet educators must still "define expertise, define the relationships between codified knowledge and experiences in the formation of expertise, and determine the appropriate type and scope of transitional experiences" (Kennedy, 1987, p. 160).

Consultation Training Research

A number of studies have indicated the limited opportunities for structured training in consultation at either the preservice or the in-service level (Hughes, 1992; Meyers, Wurtz, & Flanagan, 1981; Ott, 1991; Stewart, 1985). The need to attend to training in consultation is evident from Stewart's survey (1985) of both training programs and practitioners in school psychology. She found that while 97 percent of doctoral-level practitioners and 99 percent of nondoctoral practitioners reported engaging in consultation, only 66 percent of doctoral and 39 percent of nondoctoral practitioners acknowledged receiving any formal training in consultation as part of their preservice professional training. Further, nearly half of those who had received training rated it as poor. A more recent study of school psychologists, school social workers, and educational consultants indicated that structured opportunities for consultation training continue to be rare (Hughes, 1992). According to this study, approximately 40 percent of the sample of psychologists and educational specialists and only 30 percent of the social workers responded that they had completed a required course in consultation at the preservice level; even a lower percentage indicated that they had received supervised consultation training at the practicum or internship level. The most frequently indicated means of acquiring consultation knowledge was through professional articles and work experiences, representing sporadic and loosely structured training.

Reviews of the research on training consultants reveal few studies directly investigating the effectiveness of training modalities for the acquisition of skills and the subsequent effect of such skills on consultation effectiveness (Brown, Spano, & Schulte, 1988; Knoff, 1985; Medway & Updyke, 1985). Behavioral consultants have been most prevalent in directly researching training issues (see, for example, Anderson, Kratochwill, & Bergan, 1986; Bergan & Tombari, 1975, 1976; Curtis & Zins, 1988; Kratochwill, VanSomeren, & Sheridan, 1989), especially training centered around developing communication skills (Safran, 1991). These studies have investigated the impact of various training modalities on acquisition of particular interviewing skills. For example, Goodwin, Garvey, and Barclay (1971) studied microconsultation as part of an eight-week in-service program emphasizing competency-based training and found increases in specific interviewing skills. McDougall, Reschly, and Corkey (1988) extended that research and investigated the effectiveness of one-day in-service programs in increasing problem-identification interview skills.

Other researchers, particularly those involved in behavioral consultation, have filled in the training picture with a variety of competencies and specific procedures for training them (Conoley, 1981; Froehle, 1978; Bergan

& Kratochwill, 1990; Bergan, Kratochwill, & Luiten, 1980; Kratochwill et al., 1989; Stum, 1982; West, Idol, & Cannon, 1989). For example, Kratochwill et al. (1989) were able to evaluate the utility of different training procedures, including a structured manual and videotapes, to develop interviewing skills. Although the generalizability of the research was limited in many respects, it provides an example of how the behavioral model lends itself to·training evaluation. As more consultation competencies are described in observable terms, this type of microanalysis of specific skills may provide some guidance as to the most effective ways to teach individual skills.

Research from behavioral trainers has also attempted to link training modality to skill acquisition and ultimately to outcome measures, including changes in client behavior (Kratochwill et al., 1989). The work of the behavioral consultation researchers has provided initial guidance for studying the technical training of consultants. While it is difficult to conduct rigorous consultation research (French & Anderson, 1983), it is imperative that trainers investigate training practices so that consultation training can develop an empirical base.

Consultation Competencies

For trainers of consultants, defining consultation and establishing good training procedures may not be as difficult as deciding which competencies to train. Given the limited training time devoted to consultation, trainers must often make a choice between depth and breadth of knowledge, skills, and competencies. Moreover, trainers are increasingly held responsible for ensuring that consultants have met minimum standards of training, including consultation-related experiences, as part of their formal training (Robinson & Gross, 1985).

A review of the literature yields a representative listing of competencies that "experts" consider essential for training consultants. Most theoretical models of consultation propose and use either stage-based problem solving or phases in describing the process of consultation (Goldenberg, 1983; Idol et al., 1986; Kratochwill & Bergan, 1978; Parsons & Meyers, 1984; Rosenfield, 1987; Sandoval & Davis, 1984; West & Cannon, 1988). Because of the similarities among the stages of consultation suggested, the stages provide a useful structure by which skills and competencies can be organized. Table 19.1 presents such a conceptual framework.

However, the search for basic competencies is complex, as would be predicted by Kennedy's (1987) review of the problems with technical-skills definitions of expertise. The literature abounds with recommendations of necessary and essential skills and competencies, although in many instances, such competencies are difficult to operationalize (for example, entry skills, relation-

Table 19.1. Skills and Competencies Indicated Across Models.

	Mental health	Behavioral	Collaborative/educational	Organizational
Entry and contracting	Gallessich (1974): knowledge of environmental forces, skills in professional collaboration, self assessment and understanding Gallessich, McDermott-Long, & Jennings (1986); entry skills; contracting Conoley (1981): listening and feedback skills Parsons & Meyers (1984): communication skills; conflict resolution; counseling skills; applied affective responding Brown (1985): entry; relationship building; contract setting		Idol & West (1987), Idol-Maestas & Ritter (1985): interactive communication (paraphrasing, reflection, clarification, summarizing, feedback, managing conflict) Idol, Paolucci-Whitcomb, & Nevin (1986): communication skills; active listening	
Problem identification	Caplan (1970): questioning Parsons & Meyers (1984): interview and informal observations; formal observations; interpretation of self-reports and standardized tests Sandoval & Davis (1984): summarizing; tentative responding Gallessich (1974): expertise in diagnosis and problem solving Conoley (1981): diagnosis and assessment	Kractochwill & Bergan (1978): behavioral assessment techniques; problem-identification interviewing; direct observation skills	West & Cannon (1988), Idol & West (1987): interviewing; data collection; observation Idol, Paolucci-Whitcomb, & Nevin (1986): curriculum-based assessment; observations; data collection and measurement; interview skills	Maher & Illback (1982): structured interviews; organizational assessment; survey methodology; observation

Problem analysis	Parsons & Meyers (1984): diagnostic assessment; task analysis Sandoval & Davis (1984): questioning; dealing with resistance; organization of data Gallessich, McDermott-Long & Jennings (1986): organizational diagnosis	Kratochwhill & Bergan (1978): problem-analysis interviewing skills; applied behavioral analysis; observation; identifying variables; data-based management; data collection; effective communication (clear, objective, complete definitions); teaching skills; knowledge and use of reliability	Idol, Paolucci-Whitcomb, & Nevin (1986): applied behavioral analysis; knowledge of antecedents and consequences	
Intervention development and evaluation	Gallessich (1974): conceptual framework for evaluating helping strategies Sandoval & Davis (1984): goal setting; "experimental attitude" Conoley (1981): design and implementation skills; evaluation skills	Kratochwill & Bergan (1978): skill in single-subject design; principles of behavioral psychology	West & Cannon (1988), Idol & West (1987): feedback skills; brainstorming strategies; data-based evaluation	Maher & Illback (1982): synthesis of data; evaluation skills; skills in selection of criteria for evaluation

ship-building skills) for purposes of training. But there are frequently few indicators of at which phase or stage of consultation such skills would be especially beneficial or how they differently affect the various stages, as predicted by critics of technical-skills approaches to training. In presenting the competencies depicted in Table 19.1, we tried to link recommended competencies to a particular stage of consultation whenever possible. It is likely that once acquired, a majority of the competencies would be beneficial throughout the process of consultation.

A synthesis of the literature suggests a number of skills that appear to transcend specific models or theoretical perspectives of consultation. These are the ability to:

- Understand and integrate information about the context or culture in which the consultation is to occur
- Use effective interpersonal and communication skills, including paraphrasing, active listening, questioning, reflecting feelings, providing feedback, summarizing, interviewing, negotiating, and contracting
- Understand and effectively implement problem-solving stages
- Develop and evaluate interventions such as single-subject research, goal setting, brainstorming, data-based evaluation, and selection and monitoring of criteria
- Apply the skills and relationship factors in complex practice situations including multicultural and interdisciplinary settings
- Reflect on the practice situation and evaluate one's own skills
- Understand how ethical codes apply to consultation practice and apply principles of ethics appropriately

These skills represent a basis for training within any theoretical model.

Values and Self-Knowledge in Training

Skill development and competencies are only part of what must be addressed in training consultants. The reality is that, like most aspects of mental health services, skills and competencies are attached to a person. Trainers of consultants must consider the total person being trained—including that person's values and beliefs. The trainee brings certain values and beliefs that directly affect the consultative relationship and ultimately the effectiveness of consultation (Zins & Ponti, 1990). Specifically, the values, beliefs, and attitudes of the consultant largely determine how consultation is conceptualized, how problems are defined, and how the process is conducted. For example, trainees' beliefs about the competence of certain teachers or whether students with handicaps should be integrated into mainstream settings, will affect the type of consultation that will occur. If consultants do not believe a teacher to be competent, they are more likely to assume an expert position, to provide information, and to fail to acknowledge a teacher's contributions.

It is impossible to deny the importance of the values and belief systems of students in training. It is equally clear that consultants must have an understanding of themselves—their own attitudes, values, needs, beliefs, skills, knowledge, and limitations (Kurpius & Lewis, 1988). Trainees should be provided the opportunity within the training experience to explore their own beliefs and values.

One set of values that should be considered is those pertaining to the ethical aspects of consultation practice. A number of specific issues, including confidentiality, client welfare, and practice in institutional contexts, have been delineated for consultants (see, for example, Davis & Sandoval, 1982; Gross & Robinson, 1985). Discussion of these issues in consultation training is essential.

Multicultural Knowledge, Skills, and Attitudes

Both exploration of attitudes and skill development are especially important as consultants work with diverse populations. Practice requires increased sensitivity to cultural, racial, ethnic, and gender differences and issues and, on a cognitive level, sensitivity to philosophical differences, all of which are an undeniable part of the interpersonal nature of consultation. Conoley and Henning-Stout (1990, p. 24) express their concern for "how training programs prepare psychologists to deal with women (and know themselves as men and women in an oppressive culture)" along with the competing concern "that we prepare students to deal with minority children, poverty cultures, and institutional discrimination of all varieties."

There is a small literature indicating the importance of these issues for consultation and their implications for consultation training. For example, Henning-Stout and Conoley (1992), after reviewing the ways that gender-linked expectations and cultural conventions might affect the delivery of psychological services in the school setting, make a number of suggestions relevant to consultation in the schools. Most basically, their recommendations imply that gender issues should be explicitly considered rather than gender stereotypes being allowed to guide the behavior of consultants and others in the school culture. However, another arena in which gender issues play a part is the gender of the consultant and consultee. In establishing a working consultation relationship between a male consultant and female consultee or vice versa, consultants may need to consider gender influences on communication style (see, for example, Tannen, 1990), expert versus collaborative styles, and sexual interest (although all of these influences may, of course, affect a same-sex consultation relationship).

Multicultural issues related to racial, ethnic, and linguistic differences are also essential to consider in developing training programs. Although there has been some attention to the content aspects of the consultation process—Heron and Harris (1987), for example, examine multicultural considerations in educational programming for educational consultants—there has been less attention to multicultural issues in the consultation process itself. However, there are some interesting directions emerging. Pinto (1981) focuses on the perspective of the consultant in the cross-cultural interaction, emphasizing awareness of personal values, cultural empathy, and flexibility in meeting the consultee's needs. Wyner (1991) provides a case study, focused on bilingual and English as a second language programs, on understanding multicultural issues in developing an understanding of school culture. In an analogue study using videotaped vignettes, Wiese (1991) reports that a group of white preservice teachers rated consultants who seemed responsive to cultural issues and concerns during problem identification as more competent and trustworthy than those whose behavior seemed culturally blind. Gibbs (1980) has also addressed the effect of the ethnicity of the consultee, proposing a model in which black consultees focus on the interpersonal relationship with the consultant, whereas white consultees are more likely to approach the consultation from an instrumental perspective, evaluating the effectiveness with which the task is accomplished. Issues relating to black consultants and white consultees also need to be considered within a multicultural framework. One black school psychology student, working with a white teacher on the classroom problems of a black child, found that the teacher was concerned that the psychologist would be more empathetic with the child's mother than with the teacher's concerns.

At this time, the knowledge base in multicultural consultation is slim and should provide research opportunities for students and faculty alike. There is not much of an empirical base for training skilled multicultural consultants. Much of the current theory is drawn from the area of multicultural counseling, which has developed considerably over the past decade. However, consultants in training can be made aware of the perspective and given the opportunity to explore their personal values and attitudes in the consultation context.

Issues in Consultation Training

Selection of training content—the competencies and skills to include in training—has been our major focus thus far. However, educating consultants also requires an understanding of how best to impart such knowledge and skills.

Whether training occurs within the structure of a preservice academic program or through on-site in-service training, trainers must consider the issues that will have an impact on the effectiveness of training outcomes. These issues include developing appropriate conceptual approaches to training and ensuring that training procedures produce appropriate skill usage. This section addresses some critical issues that are encountered in either in-service or preservice training.

Training Formats

There have been several attempts to develop conceptual approaches to the training of consultants. Gallessich (1974, 1980) has attempted to provide a broad framework for the preservice training process, raising the major issues in terms of sequence of training and evaluation of student progress. She suggests four training modes: didactic, laboratory, field placement, and supervision. This sequence provides a structure for moving from knowledge about consultation to active practice on a continuum from more to less restrictive settings—from classroom as laboratory to field-based practicum sites to internships and practice settings with supervision.

At the in-service level, a useful training model for developing professional expertise has been conceptualized by Joyce and Showers (1980). They suggest four levels of training: awareness of an area of practice or knowledge; knowledge of theory and principles; basic skill acquisition; and application of these skills in practice. Training components to develop these different levels have also been identified, moving from lectures and workshop presentations at the awareness and knowledge levels to coaching for application of skills in the practice context. (See the related discussion in Chapter Eighteen.)

At each level of training, one of the most critical questions in the development of consultation expertise is the optimal way to facilitate the transition from knowledge to practice (Kennedy, 1987). In reality, there is often a blurring between the knowledge- and skill-development stage and the use of skills in practice settings. Students frequently enter their fieldwork placement before completing the didactic segment of their courses. Moreover, instructors often struggle with whether the best way to use class time is discussion of fieldwork experiences or preplanned didactic activities. There continue to be questions about how and when practicum experiences should be initiated and about the evaluation of the fieldwork component for students in training.

In-service training provides a different challenge for developing new skills. Professionals receiving in-service training often express concerns about learning on the job, feeling vulnerable as they practice newly developing skills in their work settings (Rosenfield & Feuerberg, 1987; Gravois, Rosenfield, &

Greenberg, 1991). They feel uncomfortable as novice consultants in the face of the expectations of their colleagues for competent professional performance. Further, if consultation represents a significant role change for them, anxiety or fear about change needs to be addressed as well as issues related to learning and practicing new consultation skills.

Supervision Issues

Major training issues revolve around the supervision of consultation practice. Using a training procedure based on the Gallessich (1974) model of mental health consultation training, Conoley (1981) provides a comprehensive view of concerns about supervisory issues at the different modes of experiential training, from both the trainee's and the instructor's perspectives. There may be issues of multiple supervisors as students move from laboratory to real-world settings. Other important issues include pressures on students and supervisors for direct service to clients rather than consultation in agency and school settings, and the limited consultation knowledge and experience of many field supervisors. Whenever practical, trainers may find it necessary to carefully select sites and investigate field supervision options, take time to inform field supervisors as to what the experience should entail for students, and negotiate evaluation procedures.

From the supervisor's perspective, Conoley (1981) raises the question of how trainers can model consultation skills while meeting the demands of the supervisory role. She provides a number of examples of problems that arise from a failure to carefully delineate the distinction between the two roles and suggests that the supervisor develop comfort with the role of supervision and acceptance of its necessity. Instructors often try to model consultation in their interactions with students, and students sometimes become confused about the boundaries between the supervisory and consultation roles of the course instructor. Therefore, being clear about the distinction is critical. For example, grading criteria should be very explicit, particularly criteria for interpersonal skills and practicum activities.

For supervisees, the ability to hear negative feedback is an important skill, and it is necessary to define criteria for demonstrating this ability. While students "need not accept the feedback as being relevant or accurate, . . . they must examine it carefully, consider what important information it might contain, and make plans to change behavior *if* that seems appropriate" (Conoley, 1981, p. 254). Conoley's advice to supervisors is to remain as "open and nondefensive as possible" (p. 261), to actively invite feedback, and to model positive acceptance of feedback.

Because of the strongly interpersonal nature of the supervisory process, some problems with student-instructor relationships may be unavoidable. These may be a function more of student issues than of the consultation course itself. Students can be "didactically warned," according to Conoley (1981), about the development of these issues. As these issues arise, it would be helpful for consultation supervisors to have a peer network for support and feedback.

Field Concerns of Students

Related to the supervisory issues of the instructor are the concerns that consultation trainees feel (and express in numerous though not always direct ways) when they are placed in fieldwork settings to do consultation. At the preservice level, many courses require the student to spend one-half day to two days per week, for a semester or a year, in the school or agency setting. For professionals learning consultation on the job, the situation may be even more sensitive, because they are expected to have moved beyond the entry level of performance. In these real-world settings, the novice consultant struggles with developing and projecting a professional image.

According to Light (1979), there is considerable uncertainty for professionals in training, whether in-service or preservice. Consultants in training confront whether they have actually mastered the available knowledge and skills, as well as whether their own field (consultation, counseling, school psychology, and so on) has adequate knowledge in a given problem area. In the practice setting, the novice professional asks, "Do I know enough to treat this case?" and "Does the field know enough to act effectively?" (Light, 1979, p. 311). The more consensus knowledge a field achieves, the easier it is for students to evaluate their progress and the less need there is for developing strategies to control the uncertainty. Given the early stage of the consultation knowledge base and many interventions, students will need support from faculty and peers to address and control their sense of uncertainty. There is the danger here that faculty may find it easier to focus on technical skills, which seem more easily teachable, and be less open to assisting students with the problem of developing expertise in reflecting on these types of issues.

From a review of supervisory records, Conoley (1981) has identified several specific concerns from the student consultant's perspective. First, students express concern about entering the system. While one can acknowledge that some anxiety is present for even experienced consultants because of the complexity of this process, the plight of the student entering as student deserves consideration. Conoley (1981) found that "Students reported embarrassment at entering staff lounges uninvited, insecurity about which people to contact upon entering a new building, fears about being overwhelmed with difficult cases, and/or having no cases at all. They were reluctant to plan a presentation at a faculty meeting as a way to explain their services and, in fact, felt ambivalent about how consultation would be received and perceived by their consultee, and they felt unsure about explaining their own role" (pp. 228–229).

Conoley suggests that these entry issues arise again when students begin to expand their role in the applied setting, such as moving from one individual teacher to a systems orientation in a school. Instructors unaware of these sources of anxiety can often find themselves confronting hostile students in class, particularly if entry into placements does not develop smoothly (as it often does not). Students often need reassurance that the normal problems of entry and contracting, as well as moving through the other stages of consultation, in real-world settings will not have a negative impact on their evaluation but in fact are opportunities for learning more about consultation. For example, acknowledging potential problems through discussion and role playing before the entry phase begins have been helpful, if not fully reassuring to the students. Difficulties in the actual entry process need to be given the same supervisory attention as those in the consultant-consultee relationship, and strategies for effective entry need to be developed to meet the situation. One student developed a written format to express her understanding of consultation and found that a helpful strategy in the entry phase. It forced her to clarify the nature of the services that she was offering and decreased the ambiguity of her message with those she contacted.

A second issue for student consultants is lack of knowledge in specialized areas (Conoley, 1981, p. 229). This issue has also been raised from the perspective of training models in terms of when the consultation sequence should be placed in the training program (Meyers, Alpert, & Fleisher, 1983). Determining what content prerequisites need to be in place before the course in consultation remains a continuing dilemma: "If field training opportunities occurred in work settings after graduate academic course work has been completed ... the trainee would begin practice with a strongly developed knowledge base; s/he might begin training experiences with increased credibility with regard to consultees and clients, as compared with graduate students who are often saddled with the 'stigma' of studenthood" (Meyers et al., 1983, p. 14). Of course, such a model would require both that agencies had the capacity to train consultants and that consultants were provided the opportunity to practice skills. The latter may be most difficult to achieve, especially in the arena where the press for direct service is strongest.

On the other hand, it certainly seems reasonable to provide students with support for perceived and often real gaps in their knowledge base and for them to know some content that would enable them to feel able to consult. For example, some programs require a course in applied behavior analysis prior to or concurrent with the consultation course work. In collaborative consultation models, it may be an advantage in some respects to be aware of the limitations of one's own knowledge base. Rosenfield (1987) cites the example of a student consultant with limited information about kindergarten curriculum. The student's openness about this lack of information stimulated a clarifying question in which she asked the teacher for additional information. The request brought out information about this particular teacher's orientation that might not have surfaced if the consultant had assumed that she had a strong knowledge base about kindergarten curriculum in general. While ignorance is not a desirable state in general, the student consultant might be more invested in collaborative, mutual problem solving and openness to exploring information than the expert. As with many other training issues, empirical research needs to demonstrate the effect of the training sequence on outcomes.

Once the student consultant is in a fieldwork setting, there are a number of issues related to professional norms that need to be addressed. Conoley (1981) reminds us of the ambivalence that even consultation-oriented practitioners often feel in the applied setting. If consultation is seen as impractical, if consultant and supervisor alike experience discomfort with developing interventions without extensive direct assessment of the client, and if consultants worry about being perceived as less competent if they allow consultees to participate in the recommendation and implementation process, practitioners will neither develop nor persevere in the use of their skills in consultation. While there is no research base to guide our training practice here, awareness of these issues is necessary to provide students with an experience that will stimulate their confidence and continued interest in developing consultation expertise.

In-service Training

In-service training in consultation is increasing. Given the trend toward alternative service delivery models in the schools, consultation is taking on a new role as the foundation on which these alternative systems are based (Curtis & Meyers, 1988). However, since most personnel working with children and schools have not received strong training in consultation skills, according to our best available evidence (Curtis & Meyers, 1988; Stewart, 1985), much consultation training needs to be done in an in-service format.

While a number of in-service programs have been developed to train personnel in the schools in using consultation and problem-solving skills (see, for example, Chalfant, Pysh, & Moultrie, 1979; West et al., 1989), there remain some generic problems that are recurrent in field-based in-service programs. Trainers find it easiest to provide awareness and basic knowledge through workshop presentations. However, even at this level, it is sometimes hard to provide the depth of knowledge about principles and theory that is facilitated in university courses through assigned readings. Although bibliographies are frequently provided during in-service presentations (and usually requested by participants), it is often difficult for professionals in the field to obtain the materials and to find the time (and motivation) for study.

If enough training time is provided, it is possible to begin developing skills in workshops and in-service training. Modeling through films and videotapes or with live clients can be provided, and simulated training experiences through activities can be constructed. However, it is in the later stages of skill development and application of skills that in-service training presents its greatest challenges. Opportunities for practitioners to receive feedback and coaching on their skills as they apply them in real situations are difficult to structure, and training for on-site supervisors or facilitators for this purpose is usually not a high priority for agencies or school districts. However, without these resources, consultants often do not reach high skill levels in practice. Their lack of comfort with the consultation process undermines the institutionalization of consultation practice.

Future Directions

Much additional work needs to be done. West (1988) suggests that the various fields of consultation should attempt to define successful consultation and then investigate which knowledge, skills, attitudes, and personality characteristics are common to successful consultants. Such investigations can extend the attempt here (Table 19.1) to establish basic competencies determined by experts in the field. Verification of competencies in this manner would lead naturally to research on appropriate and effective training methods necessary to instill such competencies. The questions would then be: What are the necessary skills of consultants? How and when are such skills best trained; that is, what teaching and supervisory activities are most effective for the different types of knowledge, attitudes, and skills? Is the acquisition of specific attitudes and skills related to successful consultation outcomes? Hardest to address, however, would continue to be questions about the best process for training consultants for the application of consultation skills in complex practice settings. It is these issues that require not only empirical verification but also further theoretical and conceptual development regarding training professional practitioners.

In sum, consultation needs to be taught as a process. Psychotherapy and counseling training could not focus on such problems as depression or anxiety without also educating students in the processes of therapeutic interactions. Similarly, consultation instruction must focus on the consultation process as well as the specific problems that impel the consultee to seek assistance. This chapter has attempted to highlight the current state of the art of consultation training and to alert the reader to some of the major instructional issues. Without attention to these issues in consultation training, the practice of consultation will not achieve its potential for serving the needs of consultees and clients.

References

Alpert, J. L., Ballantyne, D., & Griffiths, D. (1981). Characteristics of consultants and consultees and success in mental health consultation. *Journal of School Psychology, 19,* 312–322.

Alpert, J. L., & Associates (1982). *Psychological consultation in educational settings: A casebook for working with administrators, teachers, students, and community.* San Francisco: Jossey-Bass.

Anderson, T. K., Kratochwill, T. R., & Bergan, J. R. (1986). Training teachers in behavioral consultation and therapy: An analysis of verbal behaviors. *Journal of School Psychology, 24,* 229–241.

Bergan, J. R., & Kratochwill, T. R. (1990). *Behavioral consultation and therapy.* New York: Plenum Press.

Bergan, J. R., Kratochwill, T. R., & Luiten, J. (1980). Competency based training in behavioral consultation. *Journal of School Psychology, 18,* 91–97.

Bergan, J. R., & Tombari, M. L. (1975). The analysis of verbal interactions occurring during consultation. *Journal of School Psychology, 13,* 209–226.

Bergan, J. R., & Tombari, M. L. (1976). Consultant skill and efficiency and the implementation and outcomes of consultation. *Journal of School Psychology, 14,* 3–14.

Brown, D. (1985). The preservice training and supervision of consultants. *The Counseling Psychologist, 13,* 410–425.

Brown, D., Spano, D. B., & Schulte, A. C. (1988). Consultation training in master's level counselor education programs. *Counselor Education and Supervision, 27,* 323–330.

Caplan, G. (1970). *The theory and practice of mental health consultation.* New York: Basic Books.

Carter, J. (1989). The fact and fiction of consultation. *Academic Therapy, 25,* 231–241.

Chalfant, J., Pysh, M., & Moultrie, R. (1979). Teacher assistance teams: A model for within building problem solving. *Learning Disabilities Quarterly, 2,* 85–96.

Conoley, J. C. (1981). Emerging training issues in consultation. In J. C. Conoley

(Ed.), *Consultation in schools: Theory, research, procedures* (pp. 223–263). San Diego, CA: Academic Press.

Conoley, J. C., & Henning-Stout, M. (1990). Gender issues and school psychology. In T. R. Kratochwill (Ed.), *Advances in school psychology* (Vol. 7, pp. 7–31). Hillsdale, NJ: Erlbaum.

Curtis, M. J., & Meyers, J. (1988). Consultation: A foundation for alternative services in schools. In J. Graden, J. Zins, & M. Curtis (Eds.). *Alternative educational delivery systems* (pp. 35–48). Silver Spring, MD: National Association of School Psychologists.

Curtis, M. J., & Zins, J. E. (1988). Effects of training in consultation and instructor feedback on acquisition of consultation skills. *Journal of School Psychology, 26,* 185–190.

Davis, J. M., & Sandoval, J. (1982). Applied ethics for school-based consultants. *Professional Psychology, 13,* 543–551.

Dougherty, A. M. (1990). *Consultation: Practice and perspectives.* Pacific Grove, CA: Brooks/Coles.

French, D. C., & Anderson, G. (1983). Consultation in schools: Helping educators meet students' needs. *Contemporary Education Review, 2,* 225–229.

Froehle, T. C. (1978). Systematic training for consultants through competency based education. *Personnel and Guidance Journal, 56,* 436–441.

Gallessich, J. (1974). Training the school psychologist for consultation. *Journal of School Psychology, 12,* 138–149.

Gallessich, J. (1980, August). *Training psychologists for consultation with organizations.* Paper presented at First National Conference on Consultation Training, Montreal, Canada.

Gallessich, J. (1985). Toward a meta-theory of consultation. *The Counseling Psychologist, 13,* 336–354.

Gallessich, J., McDermott-Long, K., & Jennings, S. (1986). Training of mental health consultants. In F. V. Mannino, E. J. Trickett, M. F. Shore, M. G. Kidder, & G. Levin (Eds.), *Handbook of mental health consultation* (DHHS Publication No. ADM 86-1446, (pp. 279–317). Washington, DC: U.S. Government Printing Office.

Gambrill, E. (1990). *Critical thinking in clinical practice: Improving the accuracy of judgments and decisions about clients.* San Francisco: Jossey-Bass.

Gibbs, J. T. (1980). The interpersonal orientation in mental health consultation: Toward a model of ethnic variations in consultation. *Journal of Community Psychology, 8,* 195–207.

Goldenberg, I. (1983). Synthesis on values and advocacy in consultation. In J. L. Alpert & J. Meyers (Eds.), *Training in consultation: Perspectives from mental health, behavioral and organizational consultation* (pp. 213–220). Springfield, IL: Thomas.

Goodwin, D. L., Garvey, W. P., & Barclay, J. R. (1971). Microconsultation and behavior analysis. A method of training psychologists as behavioral consultants. *Journal of Consulting and Clinical Psychology, 37,* 355–363.

Gravois, T., Rosenfield, S., & Greenberg, B. (1991). *An analysis of implementation concerns of school support teams.* Unpublished manuscript.

Gross, D. R., & Robinson, S. E. (1985). Ethics: The neglected issue in consultation. *Journal of Counseling and Development, 64,* 38–41.

Gutkin, T. B., & Curtis, M. J. (1990). School-based consultation: Theory, techniques, and research. In T. B. Gutkin & C. R. Reynolds (Eds.), *Handbook of school psychology: Theory, techniques, and research* (2nd ed., pp. 557–611). New York: Wiley.

Henning-Stout, M., & Conoley, J. C. (in press). Gender: A subtle influence in the culture of the school. In F. J. Medway & T. P. Cafferty (Eds.), *School psychology: A social-psychological perspective* (pp. 113–135). Hillsdale, NJ: Erlbaum.

Heron, T. E., & Harris, K. C. (1987). *The educational consultant* (2nd ed.). Austin, TX: PRO-ED.

Hughes, C. A. (1992). *A knowledge utilization investigation of the adoption and implementation of a consultation-based indirect service delivery model by multidisciplinary teams.* Unpublished doctoral dissertation, Fordham University, New York.

Idol, L., Paolucci-Whitcomb, P., & Nevin, A. (1986). *Collaborative consultation.* Rockville, MD: Aspen.

Idol, L., & West, J. F. (1987). Consultation in special education: Training and practice. *Journal of Learning Disabilities, 20,* 474–494.

Idol-Maestas, L., & Ritter, S. (1985). A follow-up study of resource/consulting teachers: Factors that facilitate and inhibit teacher consultation. *Teacher Education and Special Education, 8,* 121–131.

Joyce, B. R., & Showers, B. (1980). Improving inservice training: The message of research. *Educational Leadership, 37*(5), 379–385.

Kennedy, M. (1987). Inexact sciences: Professional education and the development of expertise. *Review of Educational Research, 14,* 133–167.

Knoff, H. (1985). Assessing the development of professional consultation skills: An evaluation procedure for training and supervision. *Journal for Remedial Education & Counseling, 1,* 192–198.

Kratochwill, T. R., & Bergan, J. R. (1978). Training school psychologists: Some perspectives on a competency-based consultation model. *Professional Psychology, 9,* 71–82.

Kratochwill, T. R., & VanSomeren, K. R. (1985). Barriers to treatment success in behavioral consultation: Current limitations and future directions. *Journal of School Psychology, 23,* 225–239.

Kratochwill, T. R., VanSomeren, K. R., & Sheridan, S. M. (1989). Training behavioral consultants: A competency-based model to teach interview skills. *Professional School Psychology, 4,* 41–58.

Kurpius, D. J., & Lewis, J. E. (1988). Assumptions and operating principles for preparing professionals to function as consultants. In J. F. West (Ed.), *School consultation: Interdisciplinary perspectives on theory, research, training, and practice* (pp. 143–154). Austin, TX: Association of Educational and Psychological Consultants.

Light, D., Jr. (1979). Uncertainty and control in professional training. *Journal of Health and Social Behavior, 20,* 310–322.

Maher, C. A., & Illback, R. J. (1982). Organizational school psychology: Issues and considerations. *Journal of School Psychology, 20,* 244–253.

McDougall, L. M., Reschly, D. J., & Corkery, J. M. (1988). Changes in referral interviews with teachers after behavioral consultation training. *Journal of School Psychology, 26,* 225–232.

Medway, F. J., & Updyke, J. F. (1985). Meta-analysis of consultation outcome studies. *American Journal of Community Psychology, 13,* 489–505.

Meyers, J. (1981). Mental health consultation. In J. C. Conoley (Ed.), *Consultation in schools: Theory, research, procedures* (pp. 35–58). San Diego, CA: Academic Press.

Meyers, J., Alpert, J. L., & Fleisher, B. (1983). Models of consultation. In J. Alpert & J. Meyers (Eds.), *Training in consultation: Perspectives from mental health, behavioral and organizational consultation* (pp. 5–16). Springfield, IL: Thomas.

Meyers, J., Wurtz, R., & Flanagan, D. (1981). A national survey investigating consultation training occurring in school psychology programs. *Psychology in the Schools, 18,* 297–302.

Ott, C. A. 91991). *Prereferral intervention teams in a small rural state: An overview of team practices and effectiveness.* Unpublished manuscript.

Parsons, R. D., & Meyers, J. (1984). *Developing consultation skills: A guide to training, development, and assessment for human services professionals.* San Francisco: Jossey-Bass.

Pinto, R. F. (1981). Consultant orientations and client system perception: Styles of cross-cultural consultation. In R. Lippitt and G. Lippitt (Eds.), *Systems thinking: A resource for organization diagnosis and intervention* (pp. 57–74). Washington, DC: International Consultants Foundation.

Pryzwansky, W. B. (1977). Collaboration or consultation: Is there a difference? *Journal of Special Education, 11,* 179–182.

Robinson, S. E., & Gross, D. R. (1985). Ethics in consultation: The Canterville Ghost revisited. *The Counseling Psychologist, 13,* 444–465.

Rosenfield, S. (1987). *Instructional consultation.* Hillsdale, NJ: Erlbaum.

Rosenfield, S., & Feuerberg, M. (1987, August). *Supporting child study team change to alternative delivery systems.* Paper presented at the annual meeting of the American Psychological Association, New York.

Sandoval, J., & Davis, J. M. (1984). A school-based mental health consultation curriculum. *Journal of School Psychology, 22,* 31–43.

Safran, S. (1991). The communication process and school-based consultation: What does the research say? *Journal of Educational and Psychological Consultation, 2,* 343–370.

Schön, D. A. 91987). *Educating the reflective practitioner: Toward a new design for teaching and learning in the professions.* San Francisco: Jossey-Bass.

Stewart, K. J. (1985, August). *Academic consultation: Differences in doctoral and nondoctoral training and practice.* Paper presented at the annual meeting of the American Psychological Association, Los Angeles.

Stum, D. L. (1982). Direct: A consultation skills training model. *Personnel and Guidance Journal, 60,* 296–301.

Tannen, D. (1990). *You just don't understand: Women and men in conversation.* New York: Ballantine Books.

Tharp, R. G., & Note, M. (1988). The triadic model of consultation: New developments. In J. F. West (Ed.), *School consultation: Interdisciplinary perspectives on theory, research, training, and practice* (pp. 35–51). Austin, TX: Association of Educational and Psychological Consultants.

Weissenburger, J. W., Fine, M. J., & Poggio, J. P. (1982). The relationship of selected consultant/teacher characteristics to consultation outcomes. *Journal of School Psychology, 20,* 263–270.

West, J. F. (Ed.) (1988). *School consultation: Interdisciplinary perspectives on theory, research, training, and practice.* Austin, TX: Association of Educational and Psychological Consultants.

West, J. F., & Cannon, G. S. (1988). Essential collaborative consultation competencies for regular and special educators. *Journal of Learning Disabilities, 21,* 56–63.

West, J. F., Idol, L., & Cannon, G. (1989). *Collaboration in the schools: An inservice and preservice curriculum for teachers, support staff, and administrators.* Austin, TX: PRO-ED.

Wiese, M. R. (1991, August). *The effects of culture-sensitive behavior in school based consultation.* Paper presented at the annual meeting of the American Psychological Association, San Francisco.

Wyner, N. B. (1991). Unlocking cultures of teaching: Working with diversity. In N. B. Wyner (Ed.), *Current perspectives on the culture of schools* (pp. 95–107). Boston: Brookline Books.

Zins, J. E., & Ponti, C. R. (1990). Best practices in school-based consultation. In A. Thomas & J. Grimes (Eds.), *Best practices in school psychology* (2nd ed., pp. 673–693). Silver Spring, MD: National Association of School Psychologists.

20

A Review of
Continuing Education Programs

Daniel J. Reschly

Continuing education for current practitioners in consultation is essential to the delivery of effective services for a variety of professions. This chapter first focuses on the need for consultation continuing education and reviews published programs. It then provides an extensive review of a statewide continuing education program for support services personnel, followed by a discussion of the factors that should be considered in the design, implementation, and evaluation of consultation continuing education.

Importance of Continuing Education

Greater emphasis on consultation as well as diminished emphasis on certain other roles was prominent in the 1980s literature of several human service professions, including counseling psychology (see Brown & Kurpius, 1985); special education (see Friend, 1988; Idol & West, 1987; West & Cannon, 1988) and counselor education (Brown, Kurpius, & Morris, 1988; Brown, Spano, & Schulte, 1988; Kurpius & Brown, 1988). The importance of consultation has been especially prominent in the school psychology literature for more than thirty-five years. The Thayer Conference Report (Cutts, 1955, p. 174) noted the need for consultation services to "assist school personnel to enrich the experiences and growth of all children." This theme was repeated in the early conceptions of school psychology (Bardon & Bennett, 1974; Gray, 1963; Magary, 1967; Reger, 1965; White & Harris, 1961) and continues to be emphasized in all the basic textbooks (Bergan, 1985; Gutkin & Reynolds, 1990; Hynd, 1983; Phye & Reschly, 1979; Reynolds & Gutkin, 1982; Reynolds, Gutkin, Elliott, &

Witt, 1984; Ysseldyke, 1984). Consultation is an essential role of school psychologists and increasingly prominent in the recent role statements of other professions.

Many of the same goals for increased consultation are emphasized across the human service professions cited above (also see Chapter One). Consultation is viewed as a means to improve the effectiveness of services through, for example, developing interventions rather than diagnosing possible internal attribute deficits; to positively influence greater numbers of students; to improve the functioning of organizations and systems, such as schools and families; to broaden the impact of services beyond schools to families and other social systems; and to improve the range of intervention options for students with learning and behavioral problems, beyond or in place of special education placement, for example (Graden, Zins, Curtis, & Cobb, 1988; Curtis & Meyers, 1988; Reschly, 1976).

The consultation training needs of psychologists and other professionals have been discussed in many sources (see Chapter Nineteen), but nearly all statements address graduate programs; that is, the preservice level. Professional association standards also identify consultation as an essential component of graduate programs (for example, see Standard 3.4 in National Association of School Psychologists, 1984). In recent years, programs without clearly defined consultation components have been denied approval by the National Association of School Psychologists through the folio review process. Currently, about half the programs appear to have appropriate consultation components (Reschly, 1992).

Despite the prominence of consultation in school psychology for more than three decades, the many articles on training issues, and the requirements of professional standards, studies of graduate training programs strongly suggest that consultation is not adequately incorporated into the preservice preparation of school psychologists. Studies of graduate programs have yielded consistent results (Brown & Minke, 1986; Meyers, Wurtz, & Flanagan, 1981; Reschly & McMaster-Beyer, 1991). Consultation graduate education was more likely to be provided in doctoral than nondoctoral school psychology programs, many programs apparently did not have consultation courses, and other areas, such as assessment, received considerably greater emphasis.

A further concern about consultation training was expressed by the authors of these studies: the nature of "consultation" was often unclear, with conceptions within programs varying from formal delineation of and systematic instruction in two or more consultation models to the beliefs that everything that school psychologists do (including testing children for special education eligibility) is consultation. The actual amount and quality of preservice consultation training are likely even poorer than indicated by the graduate program surveys.

Although consultation training in doctoral programs may be quite good in many instances, the vast majority of school psychology practitioners have not completed doctoral programs. All studies through 1991 indicate that only 20 to 25 percent of practitioners have completed doctoral programs (Graden & Curtis, 1991; Reschly & Wilson, 1992). These results suggest that the consultation competencies of current practitioners are not sufficiently well developed for them to meet their responsibilities in the provision of a broad range of psychological services and to contribute to the development of alternative delivery systems (Graden et al., 1988; Curtis & Meyers, 1988; Reschly, 1988).

Consultation continuing education for current practitioners is imperative if the goals for psychological services endorsed for more than thirty years are to be met. Changes in the regular and special education delivery system also depend on the development of consultative problem-solving skills. Convincing evidence from multiple studies suggests that most current practitioners have not completed graduate programs with strong consultation components. The degree to which effective consultation continuing education is provided will markedly influence the course of delivery system reform and the overall development of school psychological services.

Programs in Consultation Continuing Education

A limited number of consultation continuing education programs have appeared in the literature over the past twenty years. The defining features of the programs reviewed here are training sequence beginning with elementary knowledge and proceeding through the development of service delivery competencies; clearly delineated consultation components and skills; use of written and other media as part of the consultation training; and evidence that the program has been used with one or more groups as part of continuing education.

Programs meeting these criteria have been developed for school psychologists and special educators. These programs vary significantly on the features of consultation model and the degree to which the success of training was evaluated. Generally, behaviorally oriented consultation training programs have been evaluated more rigorously, an observation made previously in reviews of consultation outcome research (Alpert & Yammer, 1983; Gresham & Kendell, 1987; Medway & Updyke, 1985).

Microconsultation and Behavior Analysis

The training technique of microconsultation, patterned after microteaching, was used by Goodwin, Garvey, and Barclay (1971) to train school psychologists as behavioral consultants. Microconsultation training consists of dividing the overall consultation competencies into smaller skill sequences developed through identification of behavior analysis principles and interviewing skills; observations of models exhibiting those principles and skills in interviews with teachers; and trainees' videotaped interview practice sessions followed by feedback from workshop instructors and other participants. The training procedures make explicit use of the principles of modeling, shaping, and practice with feedback.

The consultation sequence used in this training involved a cluster of interview skills designed to assist a consultee in *selecting target behaviors,* including defining the behaviors to be eliminated or decreased, an appropriate behavior to be increased, and the development of an observation procedure to determine the rates of the acceleration and deceleration target behaviors; *identifying the environmental events maintaining the target behaviors,* including an analysis of antecedent, consequent, and reinforcing events; *developing a strategy for change,* including developing explicit changes in the events antecedent and consequent to the target behaviors; and *evaluating the plan,* including observing the rates of target behaviors, seeking the judgments of parents and teachers regarding the success of the plan, and interviewing the consultee to determine whether additional target behaviors need to be identified and changed.

The microconsultation and behavior analysis training occurred in half-day sessions over an eight-week period during the summer (apparently in 1967 or 1968) at California State University, Hayward. The participants were ninety experienced school psychologists divided into three groups of equal size. Group 1 received microconsultation and behavior analysis training over eight weeks; group 2 received a one-day workshop on consultation and behavior analysis featuring videotape and discussion; and group 3 was a no-treatment control.

The effects of the training were rigorously evaluated through analysis of interviews, characteristics of intervention plans, and changes in services provided by psychologists. Statistically significant differences were identified on a variety of measures in the direction of microconsultation means exceeding those of both control groups. These differences persisted through the two-month follow-up conducted at the psychologists' employment setting. No evaluation of effects was conducted beyond two months, leaving unanswered questions regarding the long-term persistence of training and the possible erosion of skills from system influences that may not have supported a consultation role.

The Goodwin et al. (1971) consultation training appears to be one of the strongest programs to appear in the literature. For unknown reasons, this program has not received the attention it deserves. The training sequence implemented well-researched behavioral change principles such as modeling and practice with feedback. The training procedures and consultation components were carefully defined and systematically taught through multiple methods, and acquisition of skills was rigorously evaluated. The use of a highly effective training methodology (microconsultation) was especially noteworthy.

The traditional cardinal features of consultation were, however, only partially embedded in the training. The *indirect* feature of consultation was clearly implemented in that the goal of the training was to assist psychologists in developing competencies "to help the teacher, parent, or others to perform their function fully and effectively" (p. 355). Although the importance of establishing and maintaining rapport was emphasized and participants' interviews were evaluated on this dimension, the voluntary, collegial, and egalitarian dimensions of the consultation relationship were not clearly incorporated into the training materials and procedures. It should be noted that these defining features of the consultant-consultee relationship have been incorporated into later behavioral consultation training programs.

The Tucson Early Education Psychological Services Program

The Tucson Early Education Psychological Services Program (TEEPS) (Bergan et al., 1973) was a continuing education program for psychologists serving Follow Through program students in ten communities throughout the United States. (Follow Through was a federally funded program to improve the academic, social, and affective performance of economically disadvantaged students in kindergarten through third grade. Several different model programs were designed and implemented in selected communities throughout the United States [Stallings, 1975]). TEEPS was the basis for the now well-known and widely cited "Bergan model" of consultation (Bergan, 1977; Bergan & Kratochwill, 1990; Kratochwill & Bergan, 1990). The critical features of this four-stage consultative problem-solving model are well known and will not be discussed here.

The continuing education of psychologists in the model (Bergan et al., 1973) and subsequent evaluation of implementation of the model (Bergan & Tombari, 1975, 1976) were undertaken between 1971 and 1974. In summer 1971, an intensive four-week workshop was conducted for eleven experienced school psychologists from ten communities that had adopted the Tucson Early Education Model as the basis for their Follow Through programs and TEEPS as the basis for the psychological services component.

The content of the summer workshop included "a) methods for defining child behavior and the procedures used to change it into observable terms; b) research and theory dealing with psychological processes, particularly thinking and learning processes; and c) training in the consultation process" (Bergan et al., 1973, p. 8). Training procedures included lecture and discussion, viewing videotapes, role playing with feedback, and supervised practice during the workshop and at the psychologists' employment setting during the next year.

The TEEPS training placed more emphasis on psychological principles for addressing learning problems and teaching intellectual skills than other consultation models. Participants were required to master knowledge pertaining to an impressive list of learning and behavioral change concepts and principles. The foundation for consultation training was the now familiar four-stage problem-solving process (problem identification, problem analysis, plan implementation, and plan evaluation), use of appropriate interviewing skills (Bergan & Tombari, 1975, 1976), and accomplishment of explicit objectives in each stage of consultation (Bergan, 1977; Bergan & Kratochwill, 1990). Extensive interview outlines, similar to those that appear in Bergan and Kratochwill (1990) and Kratochwill and Bergan (1990), were provided to participants.

Rigorous evaluation of training was conducted during the summer institute and throughout the next academic year. Extensive pre- and posttests of content knowledge taught during the summer reflected changes in knowledge mastery means from 10 to 95 percent (Bergan et al., 1973). The Consultation Analysis Record (CAR) (Bergan & Tombari, 1975), a means for coding verbal discourse during consultation, was developed and validated as part of the extended training of participating psychologists during 1971–72. The CAR was the primary basis for a study in the Follow Through communities of the influence of consultant skill and efficiency in implementing consultation problem solving, accomplishing the objectives associated with each stage, and producing successful interventions for children.

The impressive results of the TEEPS consultation continuing education are abundantly apparent in the original technical report and subsequent journal articles (Bergan & Tombari, 1975, 1976). The TEEPS continuing education model, materials, and training procedures formed the basis for the Bergan model and are clearly reflected in current behavioral consultation textbooks and training manuals (Bergan & Kratochwill, 1990; Kratochwill & Bergan, 1990). One of the most important contributions of Bergan, Kratochwill, and their collaborators has been numerous continuing education studies over the past twenty years that were stimulated by this early work. Behavioral consultation following the Bergan model has set a standard for training and research that all consultation models would do well to emulate.

Collaborative Consultation in Special Education

The term *collaborative* is now used in several conceptions of consultation processes and procedures (see, for example, Gutkin & Curtis, 1990). Although there are some significant differences among the various consultation programs that authors call collaborative, a common characteristic among them is the emphasis on the relationship between the consultant and the consultee. Collaborative models emphasize the voluntary, egalitarian, and collegial nature of the consultant-consultee relationship; typically with less emphasis on the consultant's knowledge base and the content of consultative episodes.

A continuing education program in collaborative consultation was designed for special educators in the early 1980s and has since been widely used in workshops (Idol-Maestas, Nevin, & Paolucci-Whitcomb, 1984; Idol, Paolucci-Whitcomb, & Nevin, 1986; West, Idol, & Cannon, 1988, 1989). The materials and workshop procedures have gradually evolved; the current materials are structured into forty-seven areas reflecting essential consultation skills established through the deliberations of a national panel of experts. The published materials include an instructor's manual, learner's manual, and videotape (West et al., 1988, 1989). The length of the continuing education program apparently is variable, with references in materials and articles to training sequences of from two and a half to five days.

This form of collaborative consultation uses the Tharpe (1975) triadic model, which defines separate roles for the consultant (for example, consulting teacher or psychologist), the mediator or consultee (for example, teacher or parent) and the target learner, or client (for example, a student exhibiting a learning or behavioral problem) (Idol-Maestas et al., 1984). The Bergan behavioral consultation model uses virtually identical conceptions of these roles (Bergan, 1977; Bergan & Kratochwill, 1990). The consultant and the consultee are seen as having different responsibilities, which are implemented primarily through interviews in which the consultant's relationship skills, interactive communications, attitudes, and other personal characteristics are essential to successful collaborative consultation.

The strong emphasis on the consultant's affective domain competencies is clear in the training documents and activities (West, Idol, & Cannon, 1988; 1989). Of the forty-seven modules, twenty-two (47 percent) appear to be devoted to relationship skills such as "ability to be caring, respectful, empathic, congruent, and open"; establishing and maintaining rapport, positive self-concept, and enthusiastic attitude; willingness to learn from others; being flexible and resilient; active listening and responding skills; "ability to grasp and validate overt/covert meaning and affect in communications"; ability to "interpret nonverbal communications of self and others"; ability to handle conflict and confrontation appropriately while maintaining collaborative relationships; and use of positive reinforcement to maintain collegial relationships.

The collaborative problem solving is organized into six stages, which have been described in recent publications (West & Idol, 1987, 1990). Stage 1, goal and entry; involves gaining mutual acceptance, explaining the consultative process, building the relationship, and initiating consultation. Stage 2, problem identification, involves establishing a clear definition and assessment of the presenting problem. Potential interventions are then considered, prioritized, and selected in stage 3, intervention recommendations. During stage 4, implementation of recommendations, the exact intervention procedures are described, along with time lines and consultant and consultee responsibilities. In stage 5, evaluation, the success of the interventions is evaluated at the child, consultant and consultee, and systems change levels. Finally, the intervention is continued, redesigned, and discontinued on the basis of the evaluation information in stage 6, redesign.

Little information is available concerning the evaluation of the effects of collaborative consultation continuing education. The training program has been used widely as the basis for continuing education for more than 5,000 professionals in local, intermediate, and state educational agencies in twenty-four states and provinces (West & Idol, 1990, p. 27). In another source, the training modules are described as having been field-tested by forty-five school-based teams, as well as staff teams from intermediate and state educational agencies in in-service training sites in seven states and Canada (West, Idol, & Cannon, 1989, p. iii). Although popularity is a kind of evaluation, I could not locate any published data concerning the success of the continuing education program in changing the consultative skills of participants or any research on the student outcomes associated with the implementation of the model by participants. Information of this sort would significantly enhance our knowledge of the usefulness of collaborative consultation continuing education. Careful assessment of changes in relationship skills, although difficult, would be especially interesting to the scholarly and professional practice communities in the several disciplines interested in greater emphasis on consultation services.

A recent article (Fuchs & Fuchs, 1992) highlights a major concern with collaborative consultation models: the relative emphasis on the adult-to-adult interactions versus the effective implementation of interventions that lead to changes in students' patterns of achievement and behavior (Gresham & Kendell, 1987). As Fuchs and Fuchs (1992, p. 95) note, "The tendency to view interpersonal skills as most salient and to believe that collegiality is an appropriate bottom line for school consultation encourages an adult orientation, rather than a student orientation, and an interest in style over substance."

Although a positive consultant-consultee relationship may be necessary, it is not sufficient to ensure positive consultation outcomes. Consultation effectiveness rests on changing something that leads to enhanced learning or behavioral competencies, an issue that collaborative models must address.

The collaborative consultation continuing education program developed by the team of Lorna Idol, J. Frederick West, and Glenna Cannon provides an exemplary array of materials that are clearly designed to produce changes in consultative competencies. The materials are attractive and engaging. Especially laudatory is the effort to explicitly train participants in relationship skills, an area emphasized in the several versions of collaborative consultation but rarely taught through a carefully designed combination of self-assessment, modeling, and role-play activities.

The Counseling Professions

Earlier in this chapter, I cited references documenting the increasing emphasis on consultation in counselor education and counseling psychology. This increasing emphasis has not, to date, produced descriptions in the literature of continuing education materials and programs. My impression is that the development of consultation preservice and continuing education training documents in the counseling professions is occurring about ten to fifteen years later than similar developments in school psychology and special education.

Two consultation handbooks have been developed under the auspices of the Association for Counselor Education and Supervision (Brown, Kurpius, & Morris, 1988; Kurpius & Brown, 1988). The first addresses consultation processes and methods with individuals and small groups, while the second focuses on advocacy consultation. Both conceptualize consultation within traditional counseling skills and counselor roles. In Brown et al. (1988), the relationship issues in consultation are interpreted within the framework of Carkhuff's core conditions of empathy, respect, genuineness, and concreteness (1983). These handbooks place primary emphasis on the nature of the consultation relationship, with somewhat less stress on consultation content, goals, procedures, and evaluation. Both handbooks present perspectives that should be of interest to professionals in other disciplines, and both could be expanded to provide the basis for continuing education.

Summary

A small number of consultation continuing education programs have been described in the literature or through published programs. These programs vary widely on critical dimensions such as intended audience (for example, psychologists, special educators, or counselors); model of consultation, relative emphasis on consultation processes (for example, relationship factors) versus consultation procedures (for example, specification of interview content and problem-solving steps); assumptions about the necessary background of participants, such as knowledge of behavioral principles; training intensity (for example, length of program); training techniques (for example, demonstration of skills to participants versus participants' direct involvement in cases with detailed feedback on skill acquisition); sophistication of the materials and media; the number of participants and replications; and evaluation of changes in participants as a result of the continuing education.

Although these continuing education programs varied on many dimensions, they shared a common core of characteristics that match the defining features of consultation. Consultation was viewed in all programs as a problem-solving technique; an indirect service involving three parties—consultant, consultee, and client; utilizing a collegial relationship among consultant and consultee; directed toward the primary goal of producing desirable changes in client behavior; and a means to create greater problem-solving and intervention skills among consultees.

Two intense training programs implemented more than twenty years ago used highly effective training techniques (Bergan et al., 1973; Goodwin et al., 1971). No consultation continuing education programs over the past twenty years have matched these programs on the dimensions of intensity, quality of training techniques, and rigor of evaluation procedures. Both programs were, however, restricted to a small number of participants, and neither has been replicated in original form. The following section is devoted to a discussion of the development, implementation, and evaluation of a statewide consultation continuing education program for support services personnel involving a large number of participants, varied training techniques, and multiple evaluation criteria.

A Statewide Consultation Continuing Education Program

The Relevant Educational Assessment and Intervention Model (RE-AIM) was a federally funded continuing education program that provided training in consultation and curriculum-based assessment to support services personnel (psychologists, social workers, and special education consultants) throughout the state of Iowa (Grimes & Reschly, 1986; Reschly & Grimes, 1991). The RE-AIM project was designed to prepare professionals directly involved in the traditional determination of eligibility and placement of students in special education for the provision of services in alternative delivery systems (National Association of School Psychologists, 1985; Cobb, 1990; Graden et al., 1988; Heller, Holtzman, & Messick, 1982; Reschly, 1988; Wang, Reynolds, & Walberg,

1990; Will, 1988; Ysseldyke, 1984; Ysseldyke, Reynolds, & Weinberg, 1984). Consultation-based interventions in regular and special education were viewed as a key component of system reform in all of these statements. The RE-AIM continuing education provided the foundation for the large-scale system reform plan currently being implemented in Iowa.

The RE-AIM continuing education project involved the cooperative efforts of the Iowa Department of Education (principal leadership by Jeffrey P. Grimes), Iowa State University (principal leadership by Daniel J. Reschly), the fifteen Area Education Agencies (AEAs) (the employer of all Iowa support services personnel), and state professional associations. Three modules constituted the continuing education program: behavioral consultation (Bergan, 1977; Bergan & Kratochwill, 1990; Kratochwill & Bergan, 1990; Reschly & Casey, 1987); referral question consultative decision making (Batsche, 1985; Batsche & Ulman, 1986; Knoff & Batsche, 1991); and curriculum-based assessment (Shapiro, 1989; Shapiro & Lentz, 1985).

The training procedures were designed to teach skills and provide opportunities for supervised practice (Reschly & Grimes, 1991). The content of each module was taught in two-day workshops at ten sites (behavioral consultation by Daniel Reschly and Ann Casey, referral question consultative decision making by George Batsche and Joseph Ulman, and curriculum-based assessment by Edward Shapiro and Francis E. Lentz). Each workshop used a printed manual, lecture-discussion, modeling of skills, role playing, and small-group problem solving. Extensive follow-up training activities and support provided over a four-month period included telenet phone conversations with module developers, question-and-answer printed documents, video- and audiotapes providing further demonstration of skills, and participants' completion of two case studies with feedback from module developers.

Behavioral Consultation Training

The behavioral consultation module relied heavily on the Bergan model of behavioral consultation, a prepublication version of a training manual graciously shared with us by the authors (Kratochwill & Bergan, 1990), and research on behavioral consultation training (Anderson, Kratochwill, & Bergan, 1986; Bergan & Neumann, 1980; Brown, Kratochwill, & Bergan, 1982; Carlson & Tombari, 1986; Curtis & Zins, 1988; Kratochwill & Bergan, 1978; Kratochwill & VanSomeren, 1984; Kratochwill, VanSomeren, & Sheridan, 1989; McDougall, Reschly, & Corkery, 1988). Our interpretation of this research led to a heavy emphasis on interviewing skills, particularly the appropriate use of questions and summary statements regarding behavior, data collection, conditions, interventions, and evaluation and the appropriate content for each stage (for example, in problem analysis, the interviews were to focus on functional analysis of behavior, plan strategies, plan tactics, precise specifications of plan characteristics, and provision of training and support for the consultee).

We placed less emphasis on use of the Consultation Analysis Record (CAR) (Bergan & Tombari, 1975) because of time considerations and our prior research indicating that achievement of the objectives of the problem-identification stage was a much better discriminator than CAR categories among interviews before and after behavioral consultation training (McDougall et al., 1988). Our training also placed more emphasis on the voluntary, collegial, and egalitarian nature of the consultant-consultee relationship than the original (Bergan, 1977) or recent (Bergan & Kratochwill, 1990) conceptions of behavioral consultation. Participants were encouraged to use existing relationship skills, such as active listening, in interactions with consultees.

The effects of the behavioral consultation training were evaluated at three levels: changes in participants' knowledge and skills; student outcomes in the cases completed subsequent to the workshops; and consultee satisfaction with consultative problem solving. The overall RE-AIM evaluation also examined the effects of the other modules and changes at the systems level (Reschly, Wilson, & Pierce, 1992).

Evaluation of Participants' Knowledge and Skills

Two studies were conducted to assess knowledge and skills. In the first, an eleven-item objective test was administered to participants before and after completion of the behavioral consultation workshop. The pretest and posttest means of 3.07 and 7.93 for 304 participants were different at a statistically significant level ($p < .001$). Clearly, knowledge of consultation changed as a result of the training.

Changes in consultant skills in guiding interviews with consultees toward the accomplishment of objectives for the various problem-solving stages are a more substantive criterion for the success of behavioral consultation training. Samples of audiotapes of 57 preworkshop and 165 postworkshop initial problem-solving interviews were examined for the accomplishment of eight objectives generally associated with the problem-identification stage: behavioral definition; estimate of strength; tentative examination of antecedent, situational, and consequent conditions; use of summary statements; development of a tentative goal for behavioral change; and specification of a data-collection procedure.

Statistically significant changes occurred for seven of the eight objectives (the exception was use of summary statements). Substantial improvement with clear practical significance was apparent in the most important problem-identification objectives: achieving a behavioral definition of the problem, estimating the strength of the behavior, and developing a method to collect data. These results provide strong support for the assertion that participants' knowledge and consultative interviewing skills changed significantly as a result of behavioral consultation continuing education.

Success of Consultative Problem Solving

The most important criterion for the success of any continuing education program is the degree to which participants can successfully use the skills in their work setting. Participants were expected to complete at least one and preferably two consultative problem-solving cases during the extended four-month training period after the workshop was completed. During this phase, we observed the powerful impact of system influences on the professional services of school psychologists and other support service professionals.

Participation in RE-AIM continuing education workshops and completion of case studies varied from being entirely voluntary to being part of the expectations established by the employer and supervisor. In the latter circumstances, Area Education Agency supervisors established participation in RE-AIM workshops and completion of at least one of the case studies as a part of the annual personnel evaluation system. In these agencies, a modest amount of time released from current responsibilities (for example, reassignment or postponement of eligibility evaluations) was provided for case completion. This moderate level of system support had a dramatic effect on the completion of case studies. In supportive agencies, 75 percent of the participants completed at least one behavioral consultation case study; absence of such support yielded completion rates of less than 10 percent. Participants in nonsupportive agencies frequently complained that case study completion was a bothersome add-on that was very difficult to accommodate within already demanding schedules.

A total of 211 behavioral consultation cases were completed by participants (101 psychologists, 58 special education consultants, and 52 social workers). An eight-page summary form with portions completed separately by the consultant and consultee (97 percent teachers), revised from Bergan et al. (1973), was submitted for each case along with copies of the data-collection forms or graphs (for example, time series analysis graphs or tables of pre- and postintervention rates of behavior). Two criteria were used to determine case success: the consultee's judgment of the degree to which the goals of consultation were achieved and the consultee's judgment combined with examination of the tables or graphs submitted for the case (see Table 20.1).

Application of the first criterion (consultee judgment) to these data pro-

Table 20.1. Outcomes of Behavioral Consultation Interventions from RE-AIM Continuing Education.

Goal status	Consultee judgment[a]		Consultee judgment confirmed by records or graphs[b]	
	N	*Percentage*	*N*	*Percentage*
Goals met	112	53	94	45
Goals largely met	27	13	24	11
Goals partially met	53	25	34	16
Goals not met	19	9	59	28
	211	100	211	100

[a] Based on consultees' conclusions regarding attainment.

[b] Based on consultees' conclusions *and* the submission of graphs or other records confirming the degree of goal attainment. Forty cases were recoded as not met because verification of consultees' judgment was not provided.

duced a success rate of 66 percent for the goals of consultation being met or largely met and 91 percent for the goals being at least partially met. These success rates declined when we applied the more rigorous second criterion and recoded cases as "goals not met" when documents were not submitted with the case showing actual changes in the student's behavior. For example, cases in which the teacher indicated that goals were met but no tables or graphs were submitted verifying goal attainment were recoded as "goals not met." Even with this very stringent criterion, at least partial satisfaction of the goals of consultation was achieved in 72 percent of the cases.

These results have significance for the continuing education programs that are needed to accomplish the system-reform objectives described by numerous authors. Through continuing education, practitioners with limited consultation training in graduate programs and poorly developed problem-solving interviewing skills can learn behavioral consultation competencies and successfully apply them to the resolution of educational problems. The critical link for current practitioners and many of the system reform goals appears to be effective consultation continuing education.

Consumer Satisfaction

A follow-up study was conducted three to four months after case completion with the teachers who served as the consultees (Pierce, 1987; Pierce, Casey & Reschly, 1992). A substantial proportion of these teachers (43 percent) indicated that they had had no previous experience with consultative problem solving. The overall reactions of the consultees were very positive on statements scaled in a Likert format where 1 = strongly agree and 5 = strongly

pertaining to overall effectiveness in resolving problems, intent to use consultation services in the future, and preference for consultative problem solving
rather than special eligibility determination. A significant proportion (more
than half) indicated that they had acquired skills that would be useful in intervening with similar problems in the future.

In a regression analysis using an item on overall satisfaction as the
dependent variable, three items out of a total of twenty-two added significantly
to the amount of variance accounted for by consultee perceptions. The compo-
sition of these items was extremely interesting. The strongest relationships
occurred with the consultee's perception of the consultant's empathy and understanding ($r = .75$), the degree to which the problem was successfully
resolved ($r = .61$), and whether the consultee thought that skills had been
acquired that would be useful in the future. The multiple r for the three items
was an impressive .83.

The consumer satisfaction results have vast implications for consultation
continuing education programs. First, these results suggest that consultees
accustomed to traditional classification and placement services are willing to
engage in alternatives such as consultative problem solving. The reactions of
one of our major consumer groups (teachers) may be more positive than
initially anticipated. Second, satisfaction with consultation appears to be determined by multiple factors, including the consultant's relationship skills and
technical knowledge of interventions and consultative problem-solving stages.
These competencies are used to guide the problem-solving process through
stages that result in accomplishment of the consultee's goals and promote the
consultee's acquisition of skills that can be used in the future. Although the
correlational nature of these findings needs to be acknowledged, tentative
application to consultation continuing education seems to be appropriate.
Consultation continuing education programs should emphasize both relationship skills and the acquisition of the technical knowledge base that guides the
problem-solving process and the development of interventions.

Summary

The RE-AIM consultation continuing education was highly successful on broad
criteria reflecting participants' knowledge and skills, student outcomes, and
consumer satisfaction. This success can be attributed to the use of the well-
developed materials and well-researched training procedures that have appeared in the literature, primarily as the result of work done by Bergan, Kratochwill, and their students. The training model incorporated both intensive
workshop experiences and extensive follow-up training and support. The submission of case studies on which participants received feedback from training

staff appears to be one of the strongest features of this program. This feature permitted the training to continue in the natural setting beyond the workshop and ensured that skill development moved beyond the cognitive knowledge level to actual practice.

The RE-AIM continuing education was not, however, sufficient to substantially change roles of support services professionals who were then operating in a traditional delivery system. We sought substantial changes in the overall approaches of support services personnel to referral problems. Specifically, we anticipated that the initial question would be changed from "Is this student eligible for special education?" to "What interventions can be established in regular education to change learning or behavior?" Changing the initial question was expected to increase the use and quality of prereferral interventions and perhaps reduce the proportions of students classified as handicapped and placed in special education. None of the changes on variables related to these broader system changes was statistically significant at the conclusion of the project.

The RE-AIM results led to further recognition of system influences on priorities for time allocations and roles and the importance of system support for implementation of alternative services such as consultation. Reforms in funding mechanisms and the classification criteria are necessary prerequisites to changing roles. Both individual practitioner and system changes are needed. RE-AIM successfully addressed at least some of the individual practitioner needs, creating readiness for broader system change.

Current efforts in Iowa focus on implementation of the Renewed Services Delivery System (RSDS), a large-scale system reform program for which the skills from the RE-AIM modules provide an essential foundation (Reschly et al., 1992). The RSDS involves efforts to change from eligibility determination to a consultative problem-solving model with all referrals, use noncategorical classification criteria, use functional assessment procedures, and establish alternative funding mechanisms. Rigorous evaluation procedures are being implemented to determine the degree to which these changes are occurring in a phased implementation plan, to assess systems-level changes, and to monitor individual child effects. The RSDS program along with additional continuing education provisions will provide a test of our conviction that changes will occur in the services provided to students with learning and behavioral problems through a combination of continuing education and system reform.

Designing Consultation Continuing Education

Decisions concerning the design of consultation continuing education need to be based on careful consideration of consultation models, content versus process dimensions, participants' knowledge base, effectiveness of different training procedures, system support, and evaluation of effects. The decisions made in each of these areas will markedly influence the nature, delivery, implementation, and success of consultation continuing education.

Consultation Models

It is now trite to point out that there are vast differences among consultation models (Reschly, 1976; West & Idol, 1987). Consultation continuing education needs to be designed around one or, at most, two of the models in order for the training staff and participants to use the literature and training research associated with several of the models. Furthermore, the selection of a model should be based on participants' roles and the anticipated applications of consultation. Training in organizational change consultation, for example, is likely to have little practical application for most special education resource teachers, while ample opportunities probably exist for most of them to use behavioral or collaborative consultation on a daily basis.

Content Versus Process

Continuing education decisions need to be made regarding the relative emphases on consultation process (for example, relationship skills, consultant-consultee shared responsibilities, building trust, ensuring collaboration) and consultation content (for example, interview skills to accomplish objectives for well-defined stages, knowledge of instructional design and principles of behavioral change, and methods to collect data on problems in natural settings). My impression is that content-process decisions are made when a model is selected without careful consideration of the participants' continuing education needs or existing knowledge and skills. It seems rather inappropriate to emphasize relationship skills with participants who already have excellent competencies in that domain and to ignore knowledge deficits in instructional design or behavioral change principles. Consultation continuing education obviously needs to be individualized, with the relative emphases on content and process determined by the current competencies of participants.

Participants' Knowledge Base

Implicit assumptions are made about the requisite knowledge base by proponents of different consultation models. These assumptions are more likely to be explicitly acknowledged in the behavioral model. Specification of the required or assumed knowledge base and assessment of participants' mastery become important to developing efficient and effective consultation continuing education that meets needs and avoids boring participants.

Most consultation continuing education programs, including Iowa RE-AIM, did relatively little to assess prior knowledge. The Bergan et al. (1973) and Goodwin et al. (1971) programs were exemplary in specifying and assessing participants' knowledge base. This area seems to be less developed in the collaborative consultation models, where additional efforts regarding specification of knowledge base are needed to improve their continuing education.

Training Procedures and Follow-Up

Most continuing education reflects a "train-and-hope" strategy, often due to necessity. The obvious general training principles are that training should be sufficiently intense to ensure mastery of knowledge and skills; effective methods should be used, such as expert and colleague modeling, shaping skills through a sequence, and practice with feedback in the context of real cases; and training should include supervised practice with feedback in the professional's work environment. Given the findings in the literature discussed in this chapter and our experience with statewide continuing education, it is impossible to overemphasize the importance of application in the individual's actual work setting with follow-up opportunities for feedback and continued training. A number of follow-up and continuing training methods are available; for example, shadowing an experienced practitioner of the approach, mentoring by previously trained and successful colleagues, and peer support groups. The essential feature of these approaches is the continued training in the actual work environment.

I believe that the training principles just described are well known and widely endorsed; unfortunately, they are equally widely ignored. Leadership personnel responsible for continuing education might well reconsider the current train-and-hope strategies in favor of developing fewer but more intense continuing education offerings that use effective training strategies and follow-up procedures. Training procedures and follow-up do make a significant difference in the success of continuing education.

System Support

System support is crucial to the acquisition of consultation competencies and to their use in practitioners' services. The Iowa RE-AIM project demonstrated the impact of a moderate level of system support for participants. Establishing system support and expectations *prior* to selection of participants and scheduling of offerings will have an enormous influence on the degree to which participants attempt to apply skills during training and whether the skills are incorporated into their usual services. System support must extend to accommodating and supporting effective follow-up training and to establishing demands that the new competencies be incorporated into the usual services provided to students.

Evaluation

Ongoing evaluation during consultation continuing education is essential to ensuring that changes are produced in participants' skills. As noted earlier, behavioral consultation continuing education typically has incorporated a strong evaluation component (for a recent example, see Kratochwill, Sheridan, Rotto, & Salmon, 1991). Continuing education programs using nonbehavioral models have placed less emphasis on the essential component of evaluation.

The evaluation must be based on clearly formulated goals that are incorporated into pretests, assessments of skill acquisition, and follow-up measures of the application of consultation in the work setting. The information from the evaluation must be used to individualize the training experiences and to assess the short- and long-term success of the continuing education. Multiple criteria should be used, including measures of initial skill acquisition, skill application after training, outcomes of cases in which skills were implemented, consumer satisfaction, and system effects. Consultation continuing education without appropriate evaluation components becomes a haphazard exercise that is likely to fall short of everyone's expectations.

Conclusions

Although much remains to be done in the development and implementation of continuing education, there are some well-developed and carefully evaluated programs that can serve as models for efforts to improve practitioner consultation capabilities. Successful programs are structured around clearly formulated goals, use intensive training and effective training methodologies as a means to produce changes in participants' consultative problem solving, employ follow-up to ensure successful implementation in the work setting, and conduct rigorous evaluation. These programs provide useful models for the development of continuing education in various consultation approaches. The use of these models and the delivery of effective continuing education will have a large impact on the degree to which current practitioners acquire the consultation competencies that are crucial to the provision of a broad range of services and the successful implementation of system reforms.

References

Alpert, J. L., & Yammer, M. D. (1983). Research in school consultation: A content analysis of selected journals. *Professional Psychology: Research and Practice, 14,* 601–612.

Anderson, T. K., Kratochwill, T. R., & Bergan, J. R. (1986). Training teachers in behavioral consultation and therapy: An analysis of verbal behaviors. *Journal of School Psychology, 24,* 229–241.

Bardon, J. L., & Bennett, V. C. (1974). *School psychology.* Englewood Cliffs, NJ: Prentice-Hall.

Batsche, G. M. (1985). *Referral oriented consultative approach to assessment and decision making.* Des Moines: Iowa Department of Education, Bureau of Special Education.

Batsche, G. M., & Ulman, J. L. (1986). *Referral question consultative decision making.* Des Moines: Iowa Department of Education, Bureau of Special Education.

Bergan, J. R. (1977). *Behavioral consultation.* Columbus, OH: Merrill.

Bergan, J. R. (Ed.) (1985). *School psychology in contemporary society: An introduction.* Columbus, OH: Merrill.

Bergan, J. R., Curry, D. R., Currin, S., Haberman, K., Nicholson, E., & Ronstadt, M. (1973). *Tucson early education psychological services.* Tucson: University of Arizona, College of Education, Arizona Center for Educational Research and Development.

Bergan, J. R., & Kratochwill, T. R. (1990). *Behavioral consultation and therapy.* New York: Plenum Press.

Bergan, J. R., & Neumann, A. J., III. (1980). The identification of resources and constraints influencing plan design in consultation. *Journal of School Psychology, 18,* 317–323.

Bergan, J. R., & Tombari, M. L. (1975). The analysis of verbal interactions occurring during consultation. *Journal of School Psychology, 13*(3), 209–226.

Bergan, J. R., & Tombari, M. L. (1976). Consultant skill and efficiency and the implementation and outcomes of consultation. *Journal of School Psychology, 14,* 3–14.

Brown, D. K., Kratochwill, T. R., & Bergan, J. R. (1982). Teaching interview skills for problem identification: An analogue study. *Behavioral Assessment, 4,* 63–73.

Brown, D., & Kurpius, D. J. (Eds.). (1985). Special issue on consultation. *Journal of Counseling Psychology, 13*(3).

Brown, D., Kurpius, D. J., & Morris, J. R. (1988). *Handbook of consultation with individuals and small groups.* Alexandria, VA: American Association for Counseling and Personal Development.

Brown, D., Spano, D. B., & Schulte, A. C. (1988). Consultation training in master's level counselor education programs. *Counselor Education and Supervision, 27,* 323–330.

Brown, D. T., & Minke, K. M. (1986). School psychology graduate training: A comprehensive analysis. *American Psychologist, 41,* 1328–1338.

Carkhuff, R. R. (1983). *The art of helping* (5th ed.). Amherst, MA: Human Resource Development Press.

Carlson, C. I., & Tombari, M. L. (1986). Multilevel school consultation training: Preliminary program evaluation. *Professional School Psychology, 1*(2), 89–104.

Cobb, C. T. (1990). School psychology in the 1980s and 1990s: A context for change and definition. In T. B. Gutkin & C. R. Reynolds (Eds.), *Handbook of school psychology* (2nd ed., pp. 21–31). New York: Wiley.

Curtis, M. J., & Meyers, J. (1988). Consultation: A foundation for alternative services in the schools. In J. L. Graden, J. E. Zins, & M. J. Curtis (Eds), *Alternative educational delivery systems: Enhancing instructional options for all students* (pp. 35–48). Silver Spring, MD: National Association of School Psychologists.

Curtis, M. J., & Zins, J. E. (1988). Effects of training in consultation and instructor feedback on acquisition of consultation skills. *Journal of School Psychology, 26,* 185–190.

Cutts, N. E. (1955). *School psychology at mid-century.* Washington DC: American Psychological Association.

Friend, M. (Ed.) (1988). Special issue: Dimensions of school consultation practice. *Remedial and Special Education, 9*(6).

Fuchs, D., & Fuchs, L. S. (1992). Limitation of a feel-good approach to consultation. *Journal of Educational and Psychological Consultation, 3,* 93–97.

Goodwin, D. L., Garvey, W. P., & Barclay, J. R. (1971). Microconsultation and behavior analysis. A method of training psychologists as behavioral consultants. *Journal of Consulting and Clinical Psychology, 37,* 335–363.

Graden, J. L., & Curtis, M. J. (1991). *A demographic profile of school psychology: A report to the NASP Delegate Assembly.* Silver Spring, MD: National Association of School Psychologists.

Graden, J. L., Zins, J. L. Curtis, M. J., & Cobb, C. T. (1988). The need for alternatives in educational services. In J. L. Graden, J. E. Zins, M. J. Curtis (Eds.), *Alternative educational delivery systems; Enhancing instructional options for all students* (pp. 3–15). Silver Spring, MD: National Association of School Psychologists.

Gray, S. W. (1963). *The psychologist in the schools.* New York: Holt, Rinehart & Winston.

Gresham, F. M., & Kendell, G. K. (1987). School consultation research: Methodological critique and future research directions. *School Psychology Review, 16,* 306–316.

Grimes, J. P., & Reschly, D. J. (1986). *Relevant educational assessment and intervention model.* Des Moines: Iowa Department of Education, Bureau of Special Education.

Gutkin, T. B., & Curtis, M. J. (1990). School-based consultation: Theory, techniques, and research. In T. B. Gutkin & C. R. Reynolds (Eds.), *The handbook of school psychology* (2nd ed., pp. 577–611). New York: Wiley.

Gutkin, T. B., & Reynolds, C. R. (Eds.). (1990). *The handbook of school psychology* (2nd ed.). New York: Wiley.

Heller, K., Holtzman, W., & Messick, S. (1982). *Placing children in special education: A strategy for equity.* Washington DC: National Academy Press.

Hynd, G. W. (Ed.). (1983). *The school psychologist: An introduction.* Syracuse, NY: Syracuse University Press.

Idol, L., Paolucci-Whitcomb, P., & Nevin, A. (1986). *Collaborative consultation.* Rockville, MD: Aspen.

Idol, L., & West, J. F. (1987). Consultation in special education (part II): Training and practice. *Journal of Learning Disabilities, 20,* 474–494.

Idol-Maestas, L., Nevin, A., & Paolucci-Whitcomb, P. (1984). *Facilitator's manual for collaborative consultation: Principles and techniques.* Reston, VA: Council for Exceptional Children.

Knoff, H. M., & Batsche, G. M. (1991). Integrating school and educational psychology to meet the educational and mental health needs of all children. *Educational Psychologist, 26,* 167–183.

Kratochwill, T. R., & Bergan, J. R. (1978). Training school psychologists: Some perspectives on competency-based behavioral consultation models. *Professional Psychology, 9,* 71–82.

Kratochwill, T. R., & Bergan, J. R. (1990). *Behavioral consultation in applied settings: An individual guide.* New York: Plenum Press.

Kratochwill, T. R., Sheridan, S. M., Rotto, P. C., & Salmon, D. (1991). Preparation of school psychologists to serve as consultants for teachers of emotionally disturbed children. *School Psychology Review, 20,* 530–550.

Kratochwill, T. R., & VanSomeren, K. R. (1984). Training behavioral consultants: Issues and directions. *The Behavior Therapist, 7*(2), 19–22.

Kratochwill, T. R., VanSomeren, K. R., & Sheridan, S. M. (1989). Training behavioral consultants: A competency-based model to teach interview skills. *Professional School Psychology, 4,* 41–58.

Kurpius, D. J., & Brown, D. (Eds.). (1988). *Handbook of consultation: An intervention for advocacy and outreach.* Alexandria, VA: Association for Counselor Education and Supervision.

Magary, J. F. (Ed.). (1967). *School psychological services in theory and practice: A handbook.* Englewood Cliffs, NJ: Prentice-Hall.

McDougall, L. M., Reschly, D. J., & Corkery, J. M. (1988). Changes in referral interviews with teachers after behavioral consultation training. *Journal of School Psychology, 26,* 225–232.

Medway, F. J., & Updyke, J. F. (1985). Meta-analysis of consultation outcome studies. *American Journal of Community Psychology, 13,* 489–505.

Meyers, J., Wurtz, R., & Flanagan, D. (1981). A national survey investigating consultation training occurring in school psychology programs. *Psychology in the Schools, 18,* 297–302.

National Association of School Psychologists. (1984). *Standards for training and field placement programs in school psychology.* Silver Spring, MD: Author.

National Association of School Psychologists. (1985). *Advocacy for appropriate educational services for all children.* Silver Spring, MD: Author.

Phye, G., & Reschly, D. (Eds.). (1979). *School psychology: Perspectives and issues.* San Diego, CA: Academic Press.

Pierce, K. D. (1987). *Variables related to teacher attitudes toward and satisfaction with consultation.* Unpublished specialist degree thesis, Iowa State University, Department of Psychology, Ames.

Pierce, K. D., Casey, A. M., & Reschly, D. J. (1992). *Teacher satisfaction with behavioral consultation: Relationship factors, problem resolution, and improved consultee skills.* Manuscript submitted for publication.

Reger, R. (1965). *School psychology.* Springfield, IL: Thomas.

Reschly, D. (1976). School psychology consultation: "Frenzied, faddish or fundamental?" *Journal of School Psychology, 14,* 105–113.

Reschly, D. J. (1988). Special education reform: School psychology revolution. *School Psychology Review, 17,* 459–475.

Reschly, D. J. (1992). *NASP program approval: Characteristics of successful and unsuccessful programs.* Unpublished manuscript.

Reschly, D. J., & Casey, A. M. (1987). *Consultation techniques for collaborative problem solving.* Ames: Iowa State University, Department of Psychology.

Reschly, D. J., Flugum, K. R., Atkinson, P. J., Golbert, K., Johnson, T., Jordison, T. D., McMaster, M., Starkweather, A. R., Ward, S., & Yoo, T-Y. (1992). *Special education and related services: Characteristics of current programs and implications for system reform* (Iowa Renewed Services Delivery System Research Report No. 4). Des Moines: Iowa Department of Education, Bureau of Special Education.

Reschly, D. J., & Grimes, J. P. (1991). State department and university cooperation: Evaluation of continuing education in consultation and curriculum based assessment. *School Psychology Review, 20,* 519–526.

Reschly, D. J., & McMaster-Beyer, M. (1991). Influences of degree level, institutional orientation, college affiliation, and accreditation status on school psychology graduate education. *Professional Psychology: Research and Practice, 22,* 368–374.

Reschly, D. J., & Wilson, M. S. (1992). *School psychology faculty and practitioners: 1986 to 1991 trends in demographic characteristics, roles, satisfaction, and system reform.* Manuscript submitted for publication.

Reschly, D. J., Wilson, M. S., & Pierce, K. D. (1992). *Continuing education in consultation and curriculum based assessment: Changes in practitioners' skills, consumer satisfaction, student outcomes, and system effects.* Manuscript submitted for publication.

Reynolds, C. R., & Gutkin, T. B. (1982). *The handbook of school psychology.* New York: Wiley.

Reynolds, C. R., Gutkin, T. B., Elliott, S. N., & Witt, J. C. (1984). *School psychology: Essentials of theory and practice.* New York: Wiley.

Shapiro, E. S. (Ed.). (1989). *Academic skills problems: Direct assessment and intervention.* New York: Guilford Press.

Shapiro, E. S., & Lentz, F. E. (1985). Assessing academic behavior: A behavioral approach. *School Psychology Review, 14,* 325–338.

Stallings, J. (1975). Implementation and child effects of teaching practices in Follow Through classrooms. *Monographs of the Society for Research in Child Development, 40* (7 & 8).

Tharpe, R. G. (1975). The triadic model of consultation: Current considerations. In C. A. Parker (Ed.), *Psychological consultation: Helping teachers meet special needs.* Reston, VA: Council for Exceptional Children.

Wang, M. C., Reynolds, M. C., & Walberg, H. J. (Eds.). (1990). *Special education research and practice: Synthesis of findings.* Oxford, England: Pergamon Press.

West, J. F., & Cannon, G. S. (1988). Essential collaborative consultation competencies for regular and special educators. *Journal of Learning Disabilities, 21,* 56–63.

West, J. F., & Idol, L. (1987). School consultation (part I): An interdisciplinary perspective on theory, models, and research. *Journal of Learning Disabilities, 20,* 388–408.

West, J. F., & Idol, L. (1990). Collaborative consultation in the education of mildly handicapped and at-risk students. *Remedial and Special Education, 11,* 22–31.

West, J. F., Idol, L., & Cannon, G. (1988). *Collaboration in the schools: Communicating, interacting, and problem solving.* Austin, TX: PRO-ED.

West, J. F., Idol, L., & Cannon, G. (1989). *Collaboration in the schools: An inservice and preservice curriculum for teachers, support staff, and administrators: Learner's booklet.* Austin, TX: PRO-ED.

Will, M. (1988). Educating children with learning problems and the changing roles of school psychologists. *School Psychology Review, 17,* 476–478.

White, M. A., & Harris, M. W. (1961). *The school psychologist.* New York: Harper-Collins.

Ysseldyke, J. E. (Ed.). (1984). *School psychology: The state of the art.* Minneapolis: University of Minnesota, National School Psychology Inservice Training Network.

Ysseldyke, J. E., Reynolds, M. C., & Weinberg, R. A. (1984). *School psychology: A blueprint for training and practice.* Minneapolis: University of Minnesota, National School Psychology Inservice Training Network.

Appendix A

Books on Human Service Consultation

1967

Newman, R. G. *Psychological consultation in the schools.* New York: Basic Books.

1969

Beckhard, R. *Organization development: Strategies and models.* Reading, MA: Addison-Wesley.

Bennis, W. G. *Organization development: Its nature, origin, and prospects.* Reading, MA: Addison-Wesley.

Schein, E. H. *Process consultation: Its role in organization development.* Reading, MA: Addison-Wesley.

Tharp, R. G., & Wetzel, R. J. *Behavior modification in the natural environment.* San Diego, CA: Academic Press.

1970

Caplan, G. *The theory and practice of mental health consultation.* New York: Basic Books.

1971

Schmuck, R. A., & Miles, M. B. (Eds.). *Organization development in schools.* LaJolla, CA: University Associates.

1972

Zusman, J., & Davidson, D. L. (Eds.). *Practical aspects of mental health consultation.* Springfield, IL: Thomas.

419

1973

Dinkmeyer, D., & Carlson, J. *Consulting: Facilitating human potential and change processes*. Columbus, OH: Merrill.

Havelock, R. G., & Havelock, M. C. *Training for change agents: A guide to the design of training programs in education and other fields*. Ann Arbor: University of Michigan, Institute for Social Research.

Steele, F. *Consulting for organizational change*. Amherst: University of Massachusetts Press.

1975

Berkowitz, M. I. *A primer on school mental health consultation*. Springfield, IL: Thomas.

Dinkmeyer, D., & Carlson, J. (Eds.). *Consultation: A book of readings*. New York: Wiley.

Mannino, F. V., MacLennan, B. W., & Shore, M. F. (Eds.). *The practice of mental health consultation*. Washington, DC: U.S. Government Printing Office.

Parker, C. A. (Ed.). *Psychological consultation: Helping teachers meet special needs*. Reston, VA: Council for Exceptional Children.

1976

Blake, R. R., & Mouton, J. S. *Consultation*. Reading, MA: Addison-Wesley.

1977

Bergan, J. R. *Behavioral consultation*. Columbus, OH: Merrill.

Kadushin, A. *Consultation in social work*. New York: Columbia University Press.

Meyers, J., Martin, R. P., & Hyman, I. (Eds.). *School consultation*. Springfield, IL: Thomas.

Plog, S. C., & Ahmed, P. I. (Eds.). *Principles and techniques of mental health consultation*. New York: Plenum Press.

1978

French, W., & Bell, C. H. *Organization development* (2nd ed.). Englewood Cliffs, NJ: Prentice-Hall.

Goodstein, L. D. *Consulting with human service systems*. Reading, MA: Addison-Wesley.

Katz, D., & Kahn, R. *The social psychology of organizations* (2nd ed.). New York: Wiley.

1979

Brown, D., Wyne, M. D., Blackburn, J. E., & Powell, W. C. *Consultation: Strategy for improving education*. Needham Heights, MA: Allyn & Bacon.

Hamilton, M. K., & Meade, C. J. (Eds.). Consulting on campus. *New Directions for Student Services, 5.* San Francisco: Jossey-Bass.

Meyers, J., Parson, R. S., & Martin, R. P. *Mental health consultation in the schools: A comprehensive guide for psychologists, social workers, psychiatrists, counselors, educators, and other human service professionals.* San Francisco: Jossey-Bass.

Platt, J. J., & Wicks, R. J. (Eds.). *The psychological consultant.* New York: Grune & Stratton.

Rogawski, A. S. (Ed.). Mental health consultations in community settings. *New Directions for Mental Health Services, 3.* San Francisco: Jossey-Bass.

1980

Beer, M. *Organizational change and development: A systems view.* Santa Monica, CA: Goodyear.

Cummings, T. G. *Systems theory for organization development.* New York: Wiley.

Huse, E. F. *Organization development and change.* New York: West.

1981

Block, P. *Flawless consulting: A guide to getting your expertise used.* San Diego, CA: University Associates.

Conoley, J. C. (Ed.). *Consultation in schools.* San Diego, CA: Academic Press.

Curtis, M. J., & Zins, J. E. (Eds.). *The theory and practice of school consultation.* Springfield, IL: Thomas.

Ketterer, R. F. *Consultation and education in mental health.* Newbury Park, CA: Sage.

1982

Alpert, J. L., and Associates. *Psychological consultation in educational settings: A casebook for working with administrators, teachers, students, and community.* San Francisco: Jossey-Bass.

Burke, W. W. *Organization development.* Boston: Little Brown.

Conoley, J. C., & Conoley, C. W. *School consultation: A guide to practice and training.* Elmsford, NY: Pergamon Press.

Gallessich, J. *The profession and practice of consultation: A handbook for consultants, trainers of consultants, and consumers of consultation services.* San Francisco: Jossey-Bass.

Heron, T. E., & Harris, K. C. *The educational consultant: Helping professionals, parents, and mainstreamed students.* Needham Heights, MA: Allyn & Bacon.

O'Neill, P., & Trickett, E. J. *Community consultation.* San Francisco: Jossey-Bass.

Ritter, D. (Ed.). *Consultation, education, and prevention in community mental health.* Springfield, IL: Thomas.

1983

Alpert, J. L., & Meyers, J. (Eds.). *Training in consultation: Perspectives from mental health, behavioral and organizational consultation.* Springfield, IL: Thomas.

Cooper, S., & Hodges, W. F. (Eds.). *The mental health consultation field.* New York: Human Sciences.

Idol-Maestas, L. *Special educator's consultation handbook.* Rockville, MD: Aspen.

1984

Maher, C. A., Illback, R. J., & Zins, J. E. (Eds.). *Organizational psychology in the schools: A handbook for professionals.* Springfield, IL: Thomas.

Parsons, R. D., & Meyers, J. *Developing consultation skills: A guide to training, development, and assessment for human services professionals.* San Francisco: Jossey-Bass.

1985

Kirby, J. *Consultation: Practice and practitioner.* Muncie, IN: Accelerated Development.

Lippitt, G. L., Langseth, P., & Mossop, J. *Implementing organizational change: A practical guide to managing change efforts.* San Francisco: Jossey-Bass.

Randolph, D. L. *Micro consulting: Basic psychological consultation skills for helping professionals.* Johnson City, TN: Institute of Social Sciences and Art.

1986

Idol, L., Paolucci-Whitcomb, P., & Nevin, A. *Collaborative consultation.* Rockville, MD: Aspen.

Lippitt, G., & Lippitt, R. *The consulting process in action* (2nd ed.). San Diego, CA: University Associates.

Mannino, F. V., Trickett, E. J., Shore, M. F., Kidder, M. G., & Levin, G. (Eds.). *Handbook of mental health consultation.* (DHHS Publication No. ADM 86-1446). Washington, DC: U. S. Government Printing Office.

Plas, J. *Systems psychology in the schools.* Elmsford, NY: Pergamon Press.

1987

Brown, D., Pryzwansky, W. P., & Schulte, A. C. *Psychological consultation: An introduction to theory and practice.* Needham Heights, MA: Allyn & Bacon.

Heron, T. E., & Harris, K. C. *The educational consultant* (2nd ed.). Austin, TX: PRO-ED.

Hord, S. M., Rutherford, W. L., Huling-Austin, L., & Hall, G. *Taking charge of change*. Alexandria, VA: Association for Supervision and Curriculum Development.

Rosenfield, S. A. *Instructional consultation*. Hillsdale, NJ: Erlbaum.

Schein, E. H. *Process consultation: Lessons of managers and consultants* (Vol. 2). Reading, MA: Addison-Wesley.

1988

Brown, D., Kurpius, D. J., & Morris, J. R. *Handbook of consultation with individuals and small groups*. Alexandria, VA: Association for Counselor Education and Supervision.

Kurpius, D. J., & Brown, D. (Eds.). *Handbook of consultation: An intervention for advocacy and outreach*. Alexandria, VA: Association for Counselor Education and Supervision.

Schmuck, R. A., & Runkel, P. J. *The handbook of organization development in schools* (3rd ed.). Prospect Heights, IL: Waveland Press.

West, J. F. (Ed.). *School consultation: Interdisciplinary perspectives on theory, research, training, and practice*. Austin, TX: Association of Educational and Psychological Consultants.

Zins, J. E., Curtis, M. J., Graden, J. L., & Ponti, C. R. *Helping students succeed in the regular classroom: A guide for developing intervention assistance programs*. San Francisco: Jossey-Bass.

1989

West, J. F., Idol, L., & Cannon, G. *Collaboration in the schools: An inservice and preservice curriculum for teachers, support staff, and administrators*. Austin, TX: PRO-ED.

1990

Bergan, J. R., & Kratochwill, T. R. *Behavioral consultation and therapy*. New York: Plenum Press.

Cole, E., & Siegel, J. A. (Eds.). *Effective consultation in school psychology*. Toronto: Hogrefe & Huber.

Dougherty, A. M. *Consultation: Practice and perspectives*. Pacific Grove, CA: Brooks/Cole.

Hansen, J. C., Himes, B. S., & Meier, J. *Consultation: Concepts and practices*. Englewood Cliffs, NJ: Prentice-Hall.

Kratochwill, T. R., & Bergan, J. R. *Behavioral consultation in applied settings: An individual guide*. New York: Plenum Press.

1991

Brown, D., Pryzwansky, W. B., & Schulte, A. C. *Psychological consultation: Introduction to theory and practice.* (2nd ed.). Needham Heights, MA: Allyn & Bacon.

Morsink, C. V., Thomas, C. C., & Correa, V. I. *Interactive teaming: Consultation and collaboration in special programs.* Columbus, OH: Merrill.

1992

Conoley, J. C., & Conoley, W. C. *School consultation: A guide to practice and training* (2nd ed.). New York: Macmillan.

Conyne, R. K., & O'Neil, J. (Eds.). *Organizational consultation: A casebook.* Newbury Park, CA: Sage.

Friend, M., & Cook, L. *Interactions: Collaboration skills for school professionals.* White Plains, NY: Longman.

1993

Caplan, G., & Caplan, R. B. *Mental health consultation and collaboration.* San Francisco: Jossey-Bass.

Dettmer, P., Thurston, L. P., & Dyck, N. *Consultation, collaboration and teamwork for students with special needs.* Needham Heights, MA: Allyn & Bacon.

Erchul, W. P. (Ed.). *Consultation in community, school, and organizational practices: Gerald Caplan's contributions to professional psychology.* Bristol, PA: Taylor and Francis.

Heron, T. E., & Harris, K. C. *The educational consultant* (3rd ed.). Austin, TX: PRO-ED.

Idol, L. *Special educator's consultation handbook* (2nd ed.). Austin, TX: PRO-ED.

Idol, L., Paolucci-Whitcomb, P., & Nevin, A. *Collaborative consultation* (2nd ed.). Austin, TX: PRO-ED.

Sugai, G. M., & Tindall, G. A. *Effective school consultation: An interactive approach.* Pacific Grove, CA: Brooks/Cole.

Zins, J. E., Kratochwill, T. R., & Elliott, S. N. (Eds.). *Handbook of consultation services for children: Applications in educational and clinical settings.* San Francisco: Jossey-Bass.

In press

Pugach, M. C., & Johnson, L. J. *Collaborative practitioners: Collaborative schools.* Denver, CO: Love.

Appendix B

Examples of Special Issues of Journals Devoted to Human Service Consultation

Gallessich, J. (Ed.). (1976). Conceptual bases of school consultation models (symposium). *Professional Psychology, 7*(4).

Kurpius, D. J. (Ed.). (1978). Consultation I: Definition, models, programs. *Personnel and Guidance Journal, 56*(6).

Kurpius, D. J. (Ed.). (1978). Consultation II: Dimensions, training, bibliography. *Personnel and Guidance Journal, 56*(7).

Kupisch, S. (Ed.). (1978). Consultation: A necessary alternative in the provision of psychological services. *School Psychology Digest, 7*(3).

Kurpius, D. J. (Ed.). (1979). Theory and practice for instructional developer consultants. *National Society for Performance and Instruction, 8*(4).

Brown, D., & Kurpius, D. J. (Eds.). (1985). Consultation. *The Counseling Psychologist, 13*(3).

Conoley, J. C. (Ed.). (1986). Indirect service delivery. Miniseries of *School Psychology Review, 15*(4).

Friend, M. (Ed.). (1988). Dimensions of school consultation practice. *Remedial and Special Education, 10*(6).

Kurpius, D. J., & Fuqua, D. R. (Eds.). (1993). Consultation I. *Journal of Counseling and Development, 71*(6).

Coufal, K. (Ed.). (1993). Collaborative consultation: Implications for the language impaired. *Topics in Language Disorders, 14*(1).

Kurpius, D. J., & Fuqua, D. R. (Eds.). (1994). Consultation II. *Journal of Counseling and Development, 72*(2).

Note: Issues of journals devoted solely to consultation (for example, *Consultation: An International Journal, Consulting Psychology Journal,* and *Journal of Educational and Psychological Consultation*) are not included.

Name Index _____

Subject Index _____